The Enemy in Your Hands

The Enemy in Your Hands

A True Story
of
Radical Forgiveness

~

Tina Genaro

For information contact;

tinajgenaro@gmail.com

Book and Cover design by Francajoes's Gigs

Childhood photo held by Andy Genaro

ISBN-13: 978-1516900053

ISBN-10: 1516900057

First Edition: August 2015

10 9 8 7 6 5 4 3 2 1

Table of Contents

PROLOGUE

"**S**IX MINUTES!"

He yells above the roar of the rushing wind. My heart jumps into my throat as my mind tries to wrap itself around the gravity of the situation.

"STAND UP!"

My legs move in obedience and lift my body to the standing position. I turn to my right, grasp my webbed seat, pull it up out of the way and hook it closed.

"HOOK UP!"

I grip my static line with my left hand and unclasp it from my harness. Holding it tight in my sweaty hand I reach above my head, hooking it to the metal jump line running along the middle of the aisle. I loop the static line in my left hand and hold the loop above my head.

"CHECK STATIC LINE!"

"Check static line!" I yell. My right hand reaches up and slides down the yellow static line tracing it over my left shoulder.

"CHECK EQUIPMENT!"

"Check equipment!" I yell back.

My right hand runs across my reserve as my eyes scan the pack of the man in front of me searching for twisted lines. I tap him on the shoulder and give him the thumbs up. My heart is racing in my chest, my breathing is shallow, and I'm having a hard time swallowing as fear grips my entire body.

"THREE MINUTES!"

As I stare at the Kevlar of the soldier in front of me, I utter a small prayer. *Please God...I think I want to live.*

"ONE MINUTE!" the Jumpmaster yells.

We shuffle closer together heading towards the gaping hole in the C-130.

"GREEN LIGHT! GO, GO, GO!"

My heart pounds loudly in my chest. Despite my fear, I shuffle quickly towards the door. I thrust my static line at the Jumpmaster; I let go, turn to my right, do a little hop, grip my reserve with both hands, tuck my chin into my chest and start my count. The sound of the engine is deafening as the fierce wind grabs hold of my body and I'm yanked horizontally from the plane. My body clears the plane and the shock of the static line yanking my canopy jerks me violently...I forget to be afraid. Within seconds, I'm swinging from side to side and my hands reach up to grab my risers. The hot sun is blinding and my eyes focus. I am floating in the air and for the first time in my life I feel completely free...and alive...

INTRODUCTION

This book chronicles my search for an identity; one founded on love. I had to fight for it. I was born and raised in fear and rejection, so for a long time, my true identity was hidden under the cover of bitterness, hurt, pain, suffering and un-forgiveness. I sought out my true identity and fought for it through the power of forgiveness and I discovered that love wins out in the end. And let me tell you, it is worth the fight. I pray that through my testimony you will find the courage to fight for your true identity too.

Love. Family. Relationships. We are all shaped by the people closest to us. Their identities and values influence us and who we are and what we believe to be true. And so it was with me and my family. I love being around people and I think that came from the love and bond I had with each of my six siblings.

My oldest sister Marie was born six years before me and she was a dreamer and a romantic. My love for horses comes from her. She owned a horse for a few years, named Smokey. He lived in the shed in our back yard for about two years when I was nine, until the township forced her to find him a new home.

Marie loved people, music and conversation. Mom called her "Mouth." I'm not so sure Mom meant it in a nice way but Marie sure loved to talk! She had an infectious smile and a heart for children and people who were "lost" in life. She introduced me to The Beach Boys, The Rolling Stones, Elvis, Buddy Holly, and Chuck Berry. Marie loved to dance and she loved to laugh. She had a wonderful ability to point out the positives in people and genuinely cared about people others were quick to overlook. My family and I still repeat a dinner grace she taught me years ago:

"Thank you for this food.

Thank you for each other.

Help us be good people and love one another. Amen"

Lee is the second oldest and always had a "get 'er done" attitude. She seemed to have an endless energy and was always cleaning something when I was growing up. I could usually find her with a broom in her hand. She had a wonderful work ethic even when we were kids. She was like a little mommy. If I were dreading a chore I had to do she'd come in and encourage me and tell me it wouldn't take very long. "Just do it," she would say. Lee also has a servant's heart, she loves children and she's an amazing cook. If you ever have the honor of meeting my beautiful sister Lee, ask her to make some apple bars or Finnish meat pasties (past-eeze) for you. They are awesome!

My sister Lynn has an amazing spirit and never backs down from a fight. She always stood up for me when I was being picked on as a kid. I'll never forget late one school year on a warm afternoon Lynn stepped off the bus and turned to challenge Randy, a guy who'd been picking on me, to a fight. She was about his size with her shoulder-length brown hair and her brown eyes blazing mad. I can still picture his blonde shaggy hair blowing in the breeze; he has a little bit more meat on his bones but is obviously a little nervous. They face off, circling each other to see who will throw the first blow. I am standing off to the side with a mixture of pride and fear in my heart. Lynn, tired of waiting—stops. She stretches out her left foot and draws a line in the sand.

"You cross this line and I'm gonna punch you out."

Randy looks down at her foot…looks at the line in the sand…clenches his fists and…

Punches her in the nose!

Randy takes off like a shot running down the road.

Lynn, blood gushing out of her nose, hurtles after him with me hot on her heels. She chases him all the way to his house and up the sidewalk where he makes it into his front porch and locks the door. She beats on the door, blood pouring out onto her clothes, trying to get at him.

His mom eventually came out and sent us home.

I really admire Lynn and I want to be like her. A fighter. Someone who stands up and fights for other people. I never question her love for me. I look the most like her and want to be like her. Fearless.

Penny is closest to me in age and she was always my playmate. I think it was partly because she had to, but I didn't care. I loved being with her. I'd do just about anything as long as she was with me. Penny is courageous and she fought for me too. She loves children and animals and has a wonderful, loving heart, like my sister Marie. Penny is an amazing, intelligent woman. She's also talented and resourceful. I always call her if I have a question about a car, any car, my Jeep...even my RV. If she doesn't know the answer, she finds out for me. She is awesome.

My younger brother Jimmy is amazing. I was six when he was born and it was my "job" to take care of him when he was younger. I have always admired his intellect and search for knowledge. As a youth he read stuff like "The Guinness Book of World Records." Jimmy always questions things and is never satisfied with pat answers. I love the way he analyzes facts and has a different perspective. Jimmy is quick to point out fallacies of arguments and circular reasoning does not satisfy his desire for truth. He seeks knowledge and is almost always reading something. If I ever have a computer question, he is the one I call. Jimmy is very handsome with blonde hair, blue eyes and wonderful dimples. My favorite thing about my brother Jimmy is his laugh. I love to hear him laugh.

My youngest brother Derik is my heart. I was almost twelve when he was born and I toted him around on my hip when I was younger. Everyone thought he was my child because we looked so much alike. With his brown hair, beautiful dimples and huge heart he was a constant playmate with all his cousins. He was loving and fiercely devoted to Mom, family and friends. He loved music and the outdoors and he had a wonderful sense of adventure. He loved to love.

My mom, Karen, was one of the hardest working women I have ever known. An awesome cook, she loved family gatherings and knew how to transform almost any ingredient into something that tasted good and would feed everyone. Mom was creative and extremely resourceful, and by watching her I learned how to cook, make cedar wreathes from coat hangers and candles from crayons.

Mom had the wonderful gift of hospitality and loved Christmas time so she could give gifts. She started in December right after Christmas and purchased gifts for people throughout the year, so by the time Christmas came the next year, she had something for everyone. Over the years, Mom became a Santa Claus to everyone! She genuinely loved to give.

Mom's dad died when she was just sixteen years old. Soon after his death she became pregnant with Marie so she dropped out of high school. Eventually she enrolled in night classes. Four children and six years later she received her GED, a month before I was born. That was 1969, the same year her husband, my biological father, left her to raise five young girls on her own. When I was three years old, Mom met and married my stepfather, James, a US Marine Vietnam veteran. My mom's brother died a little over a year later at the age of 18. By then heartache, tragedy, and hardship had become a way of life for our family. It was a legacy I inherited.

*   *   *

It's a desire in every person's heart to know where they came from and learn about who they are. Children love to hear their stories, look at baby pictures and ask questions about the events surrounding their births. They inquire about a time that exists in their lives which their brains don't have access to, a precious time only others can reveal to them. What was it like? Who was there? What time was I born? What did Mom crave when she was pregnant with me?

Dad, what was I like as a baby? Mom, when did I talk? What was my first word? Questions answered again and again, the parents reminiscing and laughing about stresses and details and aspects of their lives. Through their memories, a past is created for the child to imagine and rooting the child in their identity—an identity sprung from celebration of a new life brought into the world. The pain of childbirth forgotten, cancelled out by the pure joy of counting fingers and toes, and the parents looking in love upon the wonder of what God created.

But that's not how my story went. Whenever I asked Mom, just like any normal child wanting to know my birth story, she would sigh. "You were born in the summer of 1969," she'd say. "When I was pregnant with you, I found out your father was engaged to another woman. We were still married, but I saw an invitation in the college newspaper announcing his upcoming wedding. When it was time to give birth to you I rode my bicycle to the hospital and checked myself in. You were two days old when he decided to show up at the hospital to see if you looked like your sisters. I guess you did."

Not quite the loving, magical nativity story I'd hoped for, but it is what it is. I don't remember if I sat down and asked Mom to tell me about my father, or if I just pieced it together over the years. Regardless of how I came to know this information, that's the story of my birth. Those are the words I grew up believing about how I was brought into the world and about my biological father. It shaped my belief system and influenced my choices. It's the beginning of my life story, a story of rejection and abandonment from my father. The story of my birth obviously caused Mom pain whenever we discussed it, so eventually I learned not to ask.

*   *   *

I'm sure it took courage to "step into" the role of father and be financially responsible for five children, especially in 1972. But James brought his own demons from the past, and he dealt with them through drinking. His strong voice soon became the dominant one in our home.

Our small four-bedroom house was located on the outskirts of a small mining town way up north in Michigan where it seemed like it was always cold, wet and snowing. A place so bitterly cold that, when the thermometer plummeted in the middle of winter, I stepped outside and the snot froze in my nose. Sometimes the snow banks were so high they could be buildings themselves. The winters seemed like they lasted all year long because the summers were so short. Did I mention it was cold?

I grew up in a culture centered on drinking, hunting, fishing, drinking some more, and guns. Going "out camp fer huntin seazin" usually meant the men left the women and children and went drinking for weeks at a time in a cabin way out in the woods, hopefully to return home in one piece, bringing enough deer meat to last through the winter. Both men and women spent nights and weekends at the bars drinking, dancing and shooting pool. The bars sponsored athletic teams as well as pool, horseshoe and cribbage leagues— all to entice people into the bars on different days, nights and weekends—to drink.

James received his technical certification in construction, but was employed as a prison guard for a long time until he was fired for hitting a prisoner. After that, he was usually either unemployed or self-employed as a handy-man, mechanic, electrician, in the bars drinking, or out at camp getting drunk. There wasn't anything he couldn't fix or remodel, drunk or sober. James remodeled our house over and over throughout the years and it always seemed to have some sort of construction project going on. Our house was usually cold and drafty and had an open wiring box in the kitchen, pink insulation in the walls, and exposed nails. The walls in our upstairs bedrooms were unfinished dry wall. As children we were always trading rooms and juggling space trying to find a place to call our own. We would fight about changing rooms and whose side was whose. Between James's moods and projects, our house—and our lives—were in constant flux and disarray.

There was always some drama going on in our home with people yelling and arguing. The place was cluttered with things, but also with people and emotions. It was hardly ever quiet and empty. But regardless of what kind of chaos was going on, one thing was constant. James was either drinking, drunk or hung over. And if he was home it meant I was in danger of being hit, beaten or ridiculed in some way for something I did, planned to do, was thinking of doing or was going to do some time in the future. If he wasn't home, I had to be careful not to commit a crime that would get me punished when he did get home.

The long winter months meant all the windows were covered in thick plastic to keep out the cold wind. We had a wood stove that blasted heat in the entry way but it never seemed to reach the corners of the house. During the winter months, the nights and weekends usually meant cards and drinking at our house or someone else's, or time spent in the bars. James sometimes brought us kids to the bars with him and I learned real early how to drive home when he was too drunk. So, I spent much of my childhood hanging out in local bars waiting to go home. I was also bored a lot as I spent many hours in bed reading books because that's where I was sent for lengthy periods of punishment for "being in the way." James and my mom both chain smoked so our house smelled like an ashtray. In winter I felt especially trapped because I couldn't see out and it was always smoky and cold.

The ongoing chaos, drama and constant tension made me feel like I'd been birthed during a war and lived in a battle zone as a prisoner of war (P.O.W.), living my life in fear of being hurt, ridiculed or abused. My captor was my stepfather and our family was "The Enemy in His Hands."

Note: Everything written in this book really did happen to me, but in some cases I edited conversations for chronology and changed the names and descriptions of clients and family members to honor and respect the privacy of people involved.

{ 1 }

ESCAPING CAPTIVITY

"**W**ell, your ASVAB scores came back and they're not too good." Tossing the papers on his desk the Army recruiter levels his eyes at me. The news doesn't surprise me but it does scare me.

"What does that mean...can I still join?" fear creeping into my voice.

I face the man who holds my future in his hands and I feel tears stinging my eyes. Joining the U.S. Army is my only escape plan, my only hope of freedom, my only option. I'm almost eighteen, I live in an isolated town in Northern Michigan, I have no money and I'm a female. I don't have any other skills, goals or plans for the future. This is it. If I can't join the military, I don't know what I'll do.

"Yeah, you can join, but your options are limited."

Relief floods my body and I take a deep breath as my tears dry up. As long as I can go, that's all that matters.

"You'll hafta go in as an E-1 and the best MOS I can get you is 76 Victor—which is supply. That's the only way you can get the GI Bill. If you want the college fund too, you hafta go Airborne."

"I really need both. I'll do whatever," I reply, not knowing what Airborne is. I don't know anyone who was ever in the Army, much less Airborne, but...how bad could it be?

"Sign me up."

*   *   *

I'd never been on a plane before and had to board one to fly to Milwaukee, Wisconsin, for my physical. I'm afraid of heights, a fear I never really thought about until that moment. I eye the small plane as I walk across the pavement and climb the six steps to the small door. I board the little plane, hunching over to get to my seat on the left side and plop into it. I am finally taking a positive step in my life and escaping my past, but in a good way. Trying to drink my memories away only seemed to make them float to the top. I look through the little square window and can almost see Mom's head watching the plane. It is hard to tell, since the plane is so far from the building. I realize that this is the first time I'd ever been "allowed to leave." As my mind clears from my weeks of partying, my memories drift back to my first escape attempts.

* * *

I was about five years old the first time Penny and I tried to escape to Gram's house. To get to her house we had to travel four and a half miles one way, up and down hills, in the dark, through the woods and past the town dump. I remember when Penny asked if I'd go with her that first time. We took my tricycle and fled in the middle of the night. Gram turned us in the next morning and we were sent back home.

This time though—we are going out on foot. We pull on every sock we own to keep our feet warm and sneak out into the blackness, hope lighting our way, our hearts and minds filled with plans of our new life together, just the two of us at Grams.

Escaping to live at Gram's means homemade blueberry pie, 7-up and weekly "baths in da sowna." Gram doesn't have an indoor bathtub or shower so she "fires up da sowna" and takes a "bath" every week. We hope Gram is strong enough to save us this time cause Gram is a Fin lander through and through. She built her house alongside her husband before he died and she never shied away from chopping wood, carrying water, or climbing on the roof to shovel off snow. She is tough and strong, not a huggy-feely woman, but she never yelled, lectured or turned us away when we woke her up in the middle of the night. Gram's is the only place we ever really feel safe—and tonight we need a savior.

* * *

"COME ON!" Penny screams, dirty blonde stringy hair blowing in the spring breeze. I stare out the window in disbelief at my sister as she backs away from the car on the deserted road. Tears streaming down my face, I silently shake my head "no." Our "savior" didn't save us; she just called Mom and turned us over to be taken back home. We were told to wait in the car while Mom talked to Gram...alone.

"Come ON!" Penny yells again, a little less hopeful, waving her arm urging me to follow. "Now's our chance...I don't wanna go home!" I see the pain and fear on her tear-stained face but I'm too afraid to go with her this time.

I watch sniffling as Penny realizes her time is short; she panics, turns, and sprints around the bend in the road. She knows if she doesn't run now, she's going to "get it" when we go home. We aren't sure what "get it" means this time but I know she is scared. Penny is almost two years older than me and she knows she'll get the blame for us leaving home in the middle of the night...again. Our attempt at running away to Gram's and the dreams of a different life are abruptly coming to an end.

I look up and see Mom, pregnant, tired and struggling down the steep hill, making her way towards the car. Her blue eyes glaring at me in the backseat, she asks through the open window, "Where is she?"

I sink lower, shaggy brown bangs covering my eyes. She climbs in the rusty, beat up black station wagon and slams the door.

Sniffling, I stare down at the floor.

Silence.

Mom sighs in frustration, "I don't know what I'm going to do with you two."

Jamming the car in reverse she glances down the road. There are only two ways to go on this gravel road. One look and Mom knows the answer. She knows Penny won't run towards home so it isn't too hard to figure out. A few minutes later Penny is sitting next to me sobbing, shaking and firing angry glances at me. I feel bad for her...and for me.

We had sought refuge from the abuse at home only to be returned the next day to added punishment and cruelty. We are like dogs on choker chains—hoping to run free—but going through obedience training. We keep straining to escape and run away only to find out, the more we struggle and pull, the tighter the chain digs into our necks—cutting off our breath. If we just stopped trying to escape and learned to obey, maybe we could breathe.

*　　*　　*

"Make sure you can breathe through your mask before helping your child," the stewardess interrupts my thoughts. I glance around the seat in front of me to watch as she demonstrates the safety procedures. "We'll be taking off in a few minutes. Please remain seated throughout the flight with your seatbelt securely fastened."

I look back out the window trying to make out Derik's little brown head next to Mom's blonde hair. He's really grown these last few months I think to myself.

The plane lurches forward and my belly flip-flops reminding me of my fear of flying. "I can do this; I have to do this. I don't have a choice. I'm already on the plane," I whisper. Fear grips my body as the plane picks up speed and the noise grows louder and louder. I wonder if the noise is supposed to be this loud. I squeeze the little plastic armrest leaving my fingernail marks as evidence of my escape. I feel the plane slowly rising then it dips and drops my stomach on the runway before it starts to lift off. I let the air out of my lungs and realize that I cannot hear.

*　　*　　*

"Did you hear me? Why are you so stupid?" he asks, flicking me in the head with his finger as if I am an unwanted bug. James was waiting for us when we got home. "What are ya, retarded or somethin?" Alcohol and stale smoke linger on his breath.

At six years old, I've already been trained not to answer, or even look up, so I stare at the floor watching the puddle of tears begin to spread at my feet. He towers above me as I stand trembling—waiting for my punishment. He is a thick burly man weighing at least 180 lbs. I'm about thirty pounds soaking wet. He seems like a mean scary giant to me.

He raps the top of my head like he's knocking on a door, "Don't ya have any brains in there?" Flinching in pain, I remain silent, tears and snot streaming down my face. I wait for my punishment, wondering what it might be this time. I really don't have any answers. I don't know if I have brains; maybe I don't. I thought I did, doesn't everyone? Am I stupid? What is wrong with me?

I don't remember the punishment I received but the words stuck. It wasn't the first time I'd heard them and it wouldn't be the last. I started to believe I was stupid. There are only so many times someone has to "hit you over the head" with words until they start to sink in.

I thought running away to Gram's would be my escape. I thought that when I told her how bad it was, maybe she would love me enough to step in and say, "Okay, enough! Come and live with me." I'd hoped the scales of justice would tip in my favor.

It never happened. Each time I thought it might be different...but it wasn't. Gram never stood up to James and I realized she was tough, but not tough enough for this. She just called Mom and sent me home again. Eventually I gave in. I am stupid, maybe even retarded, and escaping to Gram's house wasn't working. So I stopped running...to Gram.

* * *

It's been about thirteen years since my first escape attempt and I have finally chosen an escape route that should work: The U.S. Army. I am no stranger to fear as I face that familiar enemy again when the plane lands in Milwaukee. Emerging from the plane victorious and alive, I begin to feel a bit more confident of my choice to join the Army and start a new life— an Army life.

{ 2 }

FREEDOM'S FRONT DOOR

The motto over the door to the Military Entrance Processing Station, or MEPS as it is called in Milwaukee, states "Freedom's Front Door" and this is where my journey begins. If they only knew! This new life will provide a freedom I have been yearning for as long as I can remember. I hope my choices from the past five years don't interfere with my future. As the litany of thoughts about my recent drinking and partying flow into my mind, they rekindle my fear of being sent home. A knot of anxiety and fear takes up residence in my stomach, waiting to be discovered as I face the long day of medical exams and completing forms.

Answering questions requires a clear mind, and as the alcohol saturated neurons in my brain detox with each line on the form, it reveals my lack of knowledge concerning my medical and personal history. Some questions are easy. Sex? Yes. Oops...I mean female. Then come the tough ones. Pregnant? I better not be. List father's middle name. I guess people normally know that but I wrack my brain. I don't know the answer so I leave it blank. Father's birth date? What? Am I *really* supposed to know that? I wonder. I glance around the room; no one else seems to be struggling with this simple form. I skip that one too.

* * *

During my medical exam the doctor inquires about the six-inch-long surgery scar on my back. I sigh and explain that it's not a surgery scar but from a fall I had as a child. The painful memory comes flooding back of when my sister Penny and I were jumping on the bed. She pushed me off and I fell on a metal drawer we kept our clothes in.

When I went screaming, bleeding and crying to my mother all she said was, "You'll live." I screamed again when Mom

21

sprayed my bleeding gash with first aid spray and told me to go play. Over the weeks following the injury every time the huge scab from the gash cracked open and began to bleed, the painful scene was repeated. But Mom was right, "I lived."

I reconsidered the motto above the door. I thought freedom meant I didn't have to think about the bad stuff anymore. I guess it depends on which way you're going through the door. Can't I just walk through the door, close it and not have to go back through it again?

*   *   *

My time at the MEPS ends with an oath. As I lift my right hand, relief floods my body as the anxiety and fear of being sent home melts away. I pledge to "support and defend the Constitution of the United States against all enemies, foreign and domestic; I will bear true faith and allegiance to the same; and I will obey the orders of the President of the United States and the orders of the officers appointed over me, according to regulations and the Uniform Code of Military Justice. So help me God."

So help me God. Why do I need God's help? I did this. "I've lived." I've survived. God never helped me before. So help me God. What does that mean? Was it like when Mom used to say "I'm gonna smack you…so help me God!" Help me what? Smack you?

{ 3 }

CENTRAL PROCESSING

It was an extremely cold day in February 1988 when my mother drove me to the airport. My mom, my brothers Derik and Jimmy, and my best friend 'Chelle saw me off. I was in a relationship at the time but the guy never showed up to say good-bye. I waited until the very last minute to board the plane hoping he would come—but he never did. Typical.

Mom sold my car to some guy while I was at the MEPS station. Why a grown man would pay a hundred bucks for a spray painted black '68 Plymouth Satellite with orange and yellow flames, the word "Submission" painted on the hood, that wouldn't even go in reverse, is beyond me. The money was nice, but I loved that car. It was the ultimate party car. I'd done so much partying and drinking in my adolescent years Mom had to clean out the trunk full of liquor bottles before she sold it. Apparently drinking and driving was okay but littering was not.

I was wearing my favorite white thigh-length sweatshirt with the huge Pepsi logo on it and black leggings the day I left for Basic Training. My long hair was poofed up and sprayed for the trip. I only brought one pair of jeans to change into and one other sweatshirt. It was freezing but I gave Mom my winter jacket before I boarded the plane because I knew I wouldn't need it where I was headed. Fort Jackson, South Carolina, was my first duty station where I was to report for central processing.

With my small bag of possessions, I boarded a puddle jumper plane that seated about ten people. I escaped my cold hometown in the middle of winter and flew off to my new life. My life of freedom.

* * *

At the processing center I was assigned a bunk and the week began with formations, paperwork, drills and fundamental marching practice. I was issued uniforms, boots, gray shorts for physical education (PE), brown shirts, green socks, hats, and all the personal equipment I needed for basic training. I filled out endless forms and decided to get my hair cut short. We exercised every morning to prepare us to pass the required PE test before we could transfer out of the central processing unit into basic training. I realized very quickly that the amount of partying I'd done to celebrate my escape seriously outweighed the little bit of exercise I'd done to prepare. I did not pass the initial PE test and was left behind for the weekend to try again the following week.

Not feeling very proud of myself, I line up on Friday afternoon with the small group of soldiers who would remain throughout the weekend. The drill sergeant in charge of our time in the processing center carries around a whip-like switch, one like I'd seen used on horses. When it hits his leg, it makes a SMACK sound.

"Tomorrow at ten hundred hours there will be a church bus in front of the barracks," he announces.

SMACK. He hits his leg with the switch.

"That bus will take you to a church where they will feed you and return you at sixteen hundred hours."

SMACK.

"Sound off with a 'Yes Drill Sergeant' if you want to go."

SMACK.

That sound...SMACK. My mind flashes back to one of the many times I was placed in formation with my sisters. I am seven years old.

"I'm gonna ask you dummies one more time!" James staggers in front of us.

Lynn is standing to my left and Penny is on my right. We are crying, sniffling and hurting. My flesh is burning from the welts on my thighs. I hate this part—the tormenting. I tremble in fear.

"Who tookkk da pencil outta my den?"

We already got one whippin with his belt. If I admit to it now, even though I didn't do it, I get as many hits as Penny and Lynn got put together...that's three hits. But if I don't admit to it, I get hit just one more time, with the hope of someone else admitting to it after the next round of beatings. I struggle in my head as to what to do. Either way I'm gonna get hit.

I hope someone else admits to it. I try to look at Penny out of the corner of my eyes and she doesn't seem to be ready to talk. I cut my eyes to the left and Lynn's fists are bunched up, she won't say she did it. I really hate standing here watching my sisters get hit. I could stop it. My thoughts are interrupted by James grabbing Lynn by her shirt and yanking her out of the line-up.

"I guess you guyz are too stupid to admit it, eh?" Forcing her down across his knees.

Too late.

SMACK.

I'm next.

Lynn is screaming.

SMACK.

"PRIVATE! I'M TALKIN TO YOU!" My mind snaps to attention and refocuses on the Drill Sergeant standing in front of me.

"Yes sir," I respond quickly agreeing to the church outing.

"DON'T YOU SIR ME PRIVATE, I WORK FOR A LIVIN!"

SMACK.

"Yes Drill Sergeant!"

*　*　*

That night, as I'm lying in my bunk, my mind wanders back to the time when I thought I outsmarted the system. I came up with a plan for getting fewer beatings. I knew I would get beaten if I was guilty and beaten even if I wasn't. If I lied and admitted to committing crimes early on, then I'd get fewer beatings and I wouldn't have to watch my sisters get beaten as well. It was a win-win situation in my head.

My plan worked...for a little while. My sisters caught on real quick and began to bribe me into admitting to "crimes" in exchange for favors and small toys. I didn't care because it was worth it to me. The beatings were less as was the drama of having to watch other people be beaten. I felt smug because I had taken the power out of the threat of being beaten. I willingly admitted to "crimes" even if I had no clue as to what they were—until the day Mom became a detective.

"Who left this sandwich crust by the couch?" Mom asks.

"Oh, that was me," I respond quickly, glancing up from my book.

"Really?" narrowing her eyes at me. "If it was you, then what kind of jelly is on it?" Mom responds, challenging me from across the room. Surprised by the question, I look up and try to see the sandwich from where I'm sitting.

"Um...grape?"

"No" she snaps. "Why are you lying to me?"

After Mom found out, the punishments increased. Apparently James did *not* like to be lied to. I still had to be in the line-up, but even if I did do something—and admitted to it—no one believed me and we all ended up being beaten anyway. And, I earned a new label...liar. Every time something was missing I was first to be blamed...and beaten.

*   *   *

Trying to forget the past, I turn over in my bunk. My fingers grasp my dog tags and I look down at my new identity. "I'm not that little kid anymore," I whisper. "This is who I am." My dog tags say Lutheran. I was baptized Lutheran when I was nine years old and it's one of the best labels I've ever been given. I worked for it and was awarded it after confirmation class. They even gave me a Bible and a certificate that said so.

I entertained the idea throughout my youth that God would show up and save me. He might send Jesus to help me. But God never showed up and neither did Jesus. So help me God...so help me God. God sure wasn't around when I needed him the most, but I did like the Lutheran label. I think I'll keep it.

My dog tags also list my blood type...B positive. I didn't know there was such a blood type until I joined the Army.

Actually, I didn't know there were different kinds of blood types period. But, when they handed me my dog tags and it had B positive listed on it, it made me happy. It confirmed a decision I'd made about my identity when I was about ten or eleven years old. I'd made a conscious choice to be positive. I remember the day I made that choice years ago...

I was sitting on the edge of my bed with a big brown photo album in my lap. I wrote my name and date of birth inside the front cover. We didn't own a family Bible to record important names and dates but I must have seen one somewhere, so I was making my own record. I wanted my life to matter...for someone to remember I lived. I wanted someone, somewhere to care. I wrote date of death, and pondered the thought. The ultimate escape. I'd considered it several times before. What would it be like to not feel anymore? No more sorrow, no more pain? Would I go to hell? But...what if hell is worse than my life here? Would hell be painful? What about my brother Jimmy? Who would take care of him? What about Penny? Who would she play with? I could never think of a painless way to kill myself and more pain was not what I wanted...I'd probably mess it up anyway.

So... I made a profound decision that impacted the rest of my life. I purposed in my heart that when I **did** die the one thing people would be able to say about me was that I was a positive person. I could do that. I remember sitting on my bed for a long time before I crossed out "date of death" and then I closed the book.

Now the Army tags confirm it. I am a "B positive" person, it's in my blood. God actually made me that way! Owning a dog tag proves there is something good in me, despite my past, all the stuff I've done and all the dirtiness I feel inside. I have proof that my life matters. *And* I'm a Lutheran. My real dog tags are so much better than the imaginary choker chain I felt around my neck as a kid.

Eventually my mind stops wandering around in my past and allows me to rest. I really am looking forward to the church outing tomorrow. It sounds like fun.

* * *

O-nine forty-five on Saturday morning, I realize I don't have anything appropriate to wear. The air outside is already sticky and warm and I don't own a pair of shorts. I don't know if I'm allowed to wear my PE shorts and I don't want to wear them with my brown, Army-issued shirt. I pull on my black leggings and my Pepsi sweatshirt. I feel very self-conscious as I stand with all the other females in their shorts and T-shirts. I really don't want to go now, but I made a commitment.

At ten hundred hours the bus arrives and I climb on with the others.

"Hi! Welcome!" greets a perky blonde lady about thirty years old. She is wearing a T-shirt and shorts. Great.

A short ride takes us to a large brick church surrounded by a sprawling compound of buildings, athletic fields and picnic areas. Despite my outfit, I join in the volleyball game, eat the best chicken I've ever tasted and actually have a wonderful time. I'm sitting on a bench watching another game of volleyball when the lady from the bus plops down near me.

"It's Tina, right?" the blonde perky lady asks, looking at me.

"Yes."

"May I talk with you for a minnut?"

"Sure," I respond, marveling at her Southern accent.

"Do you know Jesus?"

"Um...yeah... I guess."

"I mean, do you reeaallly know Jesus... as your personal savior?" she scoots closer to me on the bench.

"Um...well, I'm Lutheran."

"That's nice dear and are you saved?"

"I guess I am." Her questions are confusing me. She scoots closer to me like she wants to be my very good friend.

"Do you want to go to heaven?"

"Yes."

"Did you know you're a sinner and you need Jesus?"

"Yes."

"Would you like to be baptized today and accept Jesus as your savior?" she asks, excitement creeping into her voice.

"No."

"No?" her eyes widen.

"I told you. I'm Lutheran. I've already been baptized."

"Oh," she taps my hand, "okay dear."

A half hour later I find myself in a pew sitting with the blonde perky lady who has yet to tell me her name. We were asked to come in for the message and to witness the baptism of the people who wanted to accept Jesus as their Lord and Savior. There are about thirty people in the congregation including people from our group.

The lady is sitting close to me and has placed her arm around my shoulder in a very maternal way that touches my heart. I begin to feel like she might care about me. I half listen to the message about how Jesus died for us but my thoughts are really focused on the charming, motherly lady actually caring about me and how nice it feels. I re-focus as the preacher directs our attention to the baptismal tank.

"Every one of our guests today has made a commitment to accept Jesus Christ as their personal savior and be baptized." The preacher announces.

I clap my hands in applause, rejoicing with the small congregation.

"Except Tina," he says, pointing at me. Heads turn in my direction. "She said she's on her period."

What? I never...my face burns with shame and embarrassment as the blonde perky lady tightens her grip around my shoulders like she is hugging me.

No more church outings for me.

{ 4 }

BASIC TRAINING

"FACE FRONT PRIVATE!"

The voice startles me and immediately tears start to flow from my eyes. Oh no, I think…not now. I struggle to control the flow before she sees them.

"WHAT'S THE MATTER WITH YOU PRIVATE? YOU CRYIN?"

"No Drill Sergeant."

"I THINK YOU'RE CRYIN AGAIN AREN'T YOU PRIVATE?"

I sniff really hard and finally manage to pause the flow from my eyes. If she just quit looking at me—I could stop for good.

Drill Sergeant Smith is a beautiful strong black woman. She is momentarily distracted by another recruit and forgets about my tears. I mentally kick myself for not paying attention. I should have been standing at parade rest with eyes front but I'd allowed my thoughts to drift back to the many other times, the many days I'd spent standing perfectly still in fear of getting caught if I moved.

* * *

"FACE THE WALL!" booms the voice as he saunters into the kitchen. I jump at the sound of his voice as fear courses through my six-year-old body and tears rush out of my eyes.

Trembling, I turn my watering eyes back to the wall. I can usually hear James coming—but not this time. I'd been caught stealing a glance at the clock, trying to count the hours I'd been standing in the corner.

I try shifting my weight onto my other leg, hoping to relieve the pressure on my tummy and the pain in my feet. I hear the familiar zip of the keys snapping back to his side as he unlocks the padlock hooked to the chain on the refrigerator door.

"Can I go pee?" I squeak out feebly through my tears. Staring at the dead space between the cabinet and the wall, I can feel the heat of his eyes boring into the back of my head. I hold my breath and wait in silence.

The clock ticks. I try to remain motionless. I hear the familiar crack of the aluminum can as he opens his Pabst Blue Ribbon beer and takes his first gulp.

Silence.

I hear the clock tick.

I listen as he swallows.

"Hold it," he sneers, brushing past me.

My heart plummets.

As he passes, he stirs up the stale stuffy air and the pungent smell of urine reaches my nose. My hope plunges into my chest and tears continue their course down my cheeks. I try to re-focus and search the ugly brown paneling for the familiar rings surrounding the knothole. I distract my mind away from the pressure I feel in my belly by recounting the rings. Immediately bored, my mind grasps for a tiny ray of hope. Maybe Mom will let me go pee when she comes in to cook supper. Two hours. I hope I can "hold it."

The smell of urine lingers in the air and my eyes sneak over to Penny on the other side of the cabinet facing another corner. Penny is standing perfectly still, struggling to take shallow breaths. Out of the corner of my eye I see her shift her weight, too, as silent tears spill over the urine-soaked bed sheets wrapped loosely around her mouth and nose.

One of the many punishments for the prisoners in our house is to stand us in a corner facing the wall for hours at a time, sometimes for days. Leaving us to count the seconds, minutes, and hours until we are allowed to sit down to eat or go to bed for the night, all the while dreading the next morning when we'd get up and be sent back to our corners. The "crimes" can be eating something outside of meal times, for "stealing" a pencil from James's desk, looking at him wrong, not doing a chore correctly, or just because he feels like it. The accusations are many as are the variety of punishments. Penny's crime is wetting the bed, but...how do you stop something when you're asleep? It doesn't seem right. It doesn't seem fair. My heart aches for her.

She is being taught how to "hold it."

* * *

"WHY YOU CRYIN AGIN PRIVATE? YOU MISS YER MOMMA?"

"No Drill Sergeant," urging my words to sound confident. I wish she'd just stop focusing on me. I'd be okay if she'd just ignore me. I'm standing in formation and every time she gets in front of me and looks at me...I cry.

"YOU JUST A LITTLE BABY AIN'T YA?"

"No Drill Sergeant," trying to stifle my flowing tears. I can't control them. I wish I could. The other soldiers make fun of me because I cry so much. I try to control my thoughts and force them to remain in formation and not wander off into my past...to other attention...unwanted attention.

* * *

"It wasn't me; I didn't eat it!" I protest through my sobs, quivering in front of him. I'm ten years old and I don't know what's about to happen. James came home and Mom told him she thought I ate peanut butter out of the jar. But it wasn't me.

"Pick up the books...one in each hand," he orders as he cracks his beer. I struggle to wrap my small hands around the binding of the large books and hold one in each hand. The books are "A" and "T" from the "World Book Encyclopedia." He must have brought them in from the living room—remnants of one of his short-lived, failed sales jobs.

Blowing smoke in my face, James straddles the orange paisley kitchen chair. He's twirling a screwdriver in his right hand. He has decided on a new form of punishment and seems to be enjoying himself. He orders me to stand with my arms outstretched to each side. My mind is reeling. What's he going to do with the screwdriver? These books are heavy; how long will I have to hold them up? My arms aren't very strong. What if I said I ate the peanut butter? Maybe he'll let me go with just a beating if I said I did. I don't know. My thoughts search frantically to grasp at something...anything to help me in this situation.

He sits smirking at me, sipping his beer calmly as if he is watching an interesting TV show. "I don't believe you." Whack! James hits the bottom of my left arm with the handle of the screwdriver. I cry out in pain as the use of the screwdriver becomes abundantly clear and my thin arms struggle to keep the heavy books up. Tears run in turrets down my face joined by the snot now gushing from my nose into my mouth.

"Get yer arm up," he sneers, twirling the screwdriver again. "And stop cryin or I'll give you something to really cry about."

Whack!

Right arm this time. The sound of the hard plastic on my flesh echoes in my ears. I totally abandon trying to control my tears.

"I don't care if ya did it or ya didn't...you probly did somethin else that I don't know about."

Are you there God? Are you listening? God...this hurts. God, I'm in terrible pain...do you see me? Now would be a really good time to send Jesus. God...do you care? Mom how can you just let this happen? I didn't eat it. Mom...why did you tell him? Mom?

No...I don't think I "miss my Momma."

* * *

"Why you always cryin, Ace?" Purty asks me.

Our platoon name is The Mighty Aces and Purty is one of the older soldiers in my squad. She pauses at my bunk on her way back from the latrine. "What's wrong with you?" Her questions make me want to cry. No one's ever really cared if I cried.

"I don't know," I lie. "I just wish everyone would leave me alone about it. I'd be okay if they'd just leave me alone."

"I don't think Sarge is gonna leave ya alone...ya just gotta stop cryin all the time," Purty says, turning away.

I flop over in my bunk and the harsh fibers of my green Army blanket rub my already raw cheeks. I face the wall and let the tears flow freely. Purty's tough, but she's nice too. She's kind of like a platoon mom. I know she cares and maybe that's the problem. I'm not used to anyone being concerned about me, especially someone like a mom. It'd be easier if everyone just left me alone. I quietly repeat our motto to encourage myself to be strong, "we are the Aces, mighty, mighty Aces."

Later, I search for positive memories and I find them at camp. Camp was wonderful. It was where we went as a family during the summer months and the one place where the kids were left alone to run around in freedom. The key to survival was to remain invisible while the adults played cards, threw horse shoes and drank.

I knew we were at camp when we passed by a huge chain-link fenced-in area the size of a small house filled with nothing but empty beer cans—a monumental tribute to the alcohol consumed on the property over the years. A concrete path lined with pine trees led to the back door. Inside a screened in back porch off to the left was an old, flat-looking, flowery davenport with doilies over the arms and chairs situated around an old kitchen table tucked in the corner.

The area off to the right, near the screen door was a concrete area large enough for various wooden Adirondack chairs, small tables, a large brick grill and a large porch swing. The three-person wooden swing was hung at the edge of the concrete patio from a fat iron bar perched between two trees. Beyond the edge of the patio were the horseshoe pits, more seating and across a short field were the single seat swings made from carved up pieces of rubber tires.

I loved being outdoors. I loved swinging on the swings, wind blowing in my hair. I loved fresh air…the sweet smell of the pine needles baking in the rare sunlight of summer, fresh mowed grass and wild blueberries hidden underneath the ferns growing near the hand-made swings. I can still hear the clink of the horse shoes being knocked together between throws and the deep earthy thuds as they land near the post. I think of the sweet smell of toasted marshmallows and sizzling hotdogs cooked one at a time stuck on the end of a switch, no…on a stick…over the camp fire. A switch…what a weird word that is…a switch. Sometimes we'd have to go and pick out our own switch for our beatings. What's better, a thin one or a thick one? A long one or a short one? A switch. Okay back to positive memories, I loved the swings. I loved the feeling of pumping my legs, moving back and forth, higher and higher to freedom. I wondered what it would feel like to fly and be free. Not have to come down…ever. Not have to return to the pain.

Oh, the pain. My mind conjures up one hot August day. The smell of pine trees, dust and aged wood fill my nostrils. I'm ten years old and I'm playing with my cousins Shelly and Bucky on the big swing, pushing them from behind. As I push them higher, they laugh with delight. I can hear the joy in their laughter as my mind switches gears. I decide to get down on the pavement and roll underneath to surprise them on the other side.

WHACK!

The sound of the heavy swing hitting me squarely on the right shoulder takes me by surprise. Immediately pain shoots down my arm and I scream in agony and fall back onto the pavement bumping my head. Lying there bawling, holding my arm, I try to remain motionless as the swing slows to a stop.

Trying not to kick me Shelly peeks over the edge. "Are you okay?" her young eyes filled with concern.

Unable to respond, I sob in pain. Every breath sparks shock waves of pain throughout my body as I scrape and struggle out from under the swing and make it to my feet. No one dares to follow as I turn and head slowly to the screen door leading into camp. I know the rule about having to stay outside, but I hope I won't get in trouble. Tears streaming down my face, I spot Mom through the thick cigarette smoke and head in her direction. I'm hurt and I need my mommy. A thought crosses my mind. Maybe it's bad enough this time she'll love me and take care of me.

Through my tears I relay the story to her. "I…" sniff… "I was pushin 'em" … sniff… on da swing" …sob… "and it hit me."

Mom glances up from her card game, cigarette dangling from the side of her mouth, smoke circling her head.

"Are you bleeding?" she squints at me, annoyance creeping into her voice.

"No…but it hurts."

She pauses to discard. "Go get a cold dishrag and get back outside."

"But it hurts *real bad*," I respond, trying to convince her quietly so I don't attract James's attention.

"I SAID…get outside!" she repeats louder.

I steal a glance at James and he is glaring at me. Dropping my head, I obediently turn and slowly walk to the kitchen to retrieve a dish rag. With every step new pains shoot down my arm and up to my neck. My mind races as the rejection from my mother sinks in. How do I tell her that this is the worst pain I've ever felt in my life? How can I make her hear me? I struggle to take shallow breaths. She doesn't care about me; nobody cares about me. I dutifully grab a dishrag with my left hand and rinse it under cold water. I struggle to open the screen door with my left hand and I retreat to the deserted, screened in porch, holding my arm as still as possible.

I will myself to stop crying because every deep breath I take causes more pain. As I struggle to suppress my cries, to maintain my shallow breathing, my eyes search the walls around me trying to find something to focus on to keep me from thinking about the excruciating pain in my body that matches the ache in my heart.

I'm alone.

I spot the clock and start counting the time. "Five, ten, fifteen, twenty." I whisper the seconds out loud to distract my mind. Ten minutes turns into twenty and then thirty. God, please help me, this hurts.

I sit by myself on the davenport completely still and my mind starts gaining control of my emotions. I realize my dishrag, no longer cold, isn't helping and the pain is not going away. I peek under the rag to see if I'm bleeding yet. Between my neck and shoulder something's poking up that wasn't there before.

"Uh oh," I whisper. "I've gotta go back in there. Maybe it's been long enough. I hope I won't get a spankin."

I carefully ease off the couch and new pains shoot through my body as a fresh wave of sobs wrack my thin frame. As the pain threatens to overwhelm me, I stifle my sobs and purpose in my heart to be strong. Crying like a baby didn't help me last time, but I know I have to do something. The pain is just too much to bear.

Mom glares at me the second I enter the room. "What is it now?"

Tears streaming silently down my face I lift the wash cloth and show her the thing poking up half way between my shoulder and my neck.

"Is it spose ta look like that?" I whisper softly through my tears.

"Mm...hhhmm," she responds, letting out a big sigh and cusses under her breath. "Go wait in the car, I guess I hafta take you in."

The ride to the emergency room is excruciating. The bumpy gravel road from camp seems like it goes on forever and the long, curvy road into town seems like it takes hours. I grit my teeth as Mom drives around each bend so as to not scream out in pain. Mom's already mad and I don't want to make it worse.

My collar bone is broken. There's no cuddling, no apologies, just complaints about how she's going to have another bill to pay. I feel like a burden. She doesn't care about me...I must be really bad. What did I do? Why does she hate me? God...am I unlovable? I learned the "Jesus Loves Me" song in Sunday school...but...is it true? How can He love me if he doesn't know me? I've never met Him. How can He love me if my own mother doesn't? What can I do to make my mom love me? How do I make her care? Mom, why don't you love me?

*   *   *

I loved mail call in the Army. Derik drew me pictures, Jimmy wrote to me, Mom even signed her letters "Love, Mom." I'd never seen that before and it surprised me when I saw the words for the first time. I wept as I ran my fingers over the words. Does she love me? I also enjoyed letters from Gram with her really small tight handwriting. She wrote like she talked. It was like Gram was right there "talkin' up a storm." My sisters wrote to me too. Everyone said they were proud of me, except for Mom. She wrote stuff about what was happening, usually with my sisters, or work, but she always signed them "Love, Mom."

Still…I kept crying. But why, I wondered? I'd escaped my prison; why did I cry like I was still there? The mail I received proved that my family loved me. I just needed to stop crying and be positive like it said on my dog tags. But…how?

* * *

"Come in here Private," Drill Sergeant Smith says, pointing to her small office.

Uh-oh. My mind reels, did I do something wrong? What does she want? Am I in trouble?

I obediently march into her office and stand at attention in front of her desk. I don't know why I'm here, but I feel the familiar sting in my eyes and I will them not to water.

"At ease Private." She says as she walks around me and sits down behind her desk. The deep brown chair creaks as she leans back a little bit looking up at my face. I assume parade rest and stare straight ahead, focusing on the wall above her head trying to will my emotions to go back down into the recesses of my body where they belong.

"Private, I'm concerned about you." She starts off almost nice like. "Anything you need to tell me?"

"No Drill Sergeant." I feel the heat as blood rises up my neck and starts to creep across my face.

"Are you sure?" she asks, watching my face flush in embarrassment.

"I'll try to do better Drill Sergeant."

Silence.

She sighs. I feel my cheeks and neck burning as I use sheer willpower to keep the tears from breaking the barrier and slipping down over the edge of my eyes.

"You sure you don't wanna talk to me?" she tries again. My brain is confused. Do I say yes, I'm sure I don't, or no, I'm sure that I don't. I don't know. The confusion causes me to lose the battle with my tears and a tear escapes over the edge. I immediately regret the distraction.

"Um…no?"

She sighs again.

"Okay, you can go."

I snap to attention, perform a perfect right face, and almost double-time from her office.

How do I tell her that every time she focuses on me, it brings up memories I try to forget? It's like my eyes betray me and leak every time any kind of attention is placed on me. I can't control it. No one is hitting me from behind, no one is slapping me in the head, no one is intimidating me, but I can't control my tears! I try to harden my heart and not let anything bother me. I don't understand it; I'm supposed to be free from my past. Isn't that what the sign over the MEPS door said? "Door to Freedom?" I thought I was free to leave. Instead I feel like I brought James to Basic Training with me! I am no longer "The Enemy in His Hands." He can't hurt me anymore. I escaped from my captor...from my old life. So, why do I still feel like I am bound in captivity? This does **not** feel like freedom to me...it feels like torture.

* * *

I finally completed Basic Training and retreated home for a week before starting Advanced Individual Training (AIT). I scheduled my return flight to Fort Lee, VA from Chicago as it was much cheaper and Mom agreed to drive back and forth despite the eight hours each way. I read my flight information wrong and we arrived a day too early, but Mom had to return home. I was stranded in Chicago and needed transportation to the airport for the next morning. For the first time in my life my mom called my dad—my biological father, Larry—for help.

Larry came and met us in a motel room when I was eighteen years old. I don't remember being introduced or even much about the interaction, I just know it happened. Mom arranged the transportation as I stood in silence: a mute witness to the uncomfortable exchange of information.

Larry arrived the next day and drove me to the airport. All I remember from the ride was almost hugging the passenger side door yearning to escape from his presence. I vividly remember that the inside of the car door was reddish brown and the crank for the window was pointed towards the dash.

The dash. That's what I did…I dashed from the car. A dash—that's what the memory is like—a dash. Larry is a dash. My biological father is a —.

* * *

When I report to Fort Lee for AIT, my mind is filled with new reminders of rejection and abandonment from a father I never knew…the man who dashed from my life before I was even born. I didn't even ask Larry about his middle name. I bet *his* children knew it. Larry has five kids with his wife Janet; they even have a girl almost the same age as me. I wonder why he chose a life with them rather than with me and my sisters.

Oh well…it's in the past. Move on. Face forward private. I try to purpose in my heart to face forward. I adjust to the long days of training, classes, and PE. And, during the evening free-time, I learn that people in the military enjoy my favorite hobby—drinking.

Soldiers met down at the little snack bar on base for drinking and dancing in the evening. But I learned very quickly that drinking, fighting, chaos, and lack of integrity did not blend well with military life. I soon found myself face to face with my First Sergeant who bore an uncanny resemblance to my mother with her blonde curly hair and Coke bottle glasses.

It was in her office—in no uncertain terms—the Uniform Code of Military Justice (UCMJ) was explained clearly and concisely. I was informed that no amount of "blubberin and bawlin" would prevent me from being discharged and sent "home to Momma." I heard those words and sheer panic seized my heart.

I escaped her office that day with a summarized Article 15 and a renewed motivation to remain abstinent and focused on becoming more like a soldier in the United States Army rather than a "blubberin" baby "bawling" about my past. I was extremely grateful for the second chance and completed my AIT with high scores and set my sights on Airborne School. I made a firm decision to let go of my past, focus on my future and quit being pitiful.

* * *

I pry my eyes open at o-four hundred hours and stare at the ceiling above my bunk in Fort Benning, Georgia. The words I spoke to my recruiter drift into my mind. "I'll do whatever." Airborne... "how bad could it be?" What was I thinking? I'm still afraid of heights! Just climbing up the 34-foot tower is scary. Sheer obedience propels my body upward one boot at a time, footsteps echoing throughout the tower. Not to mention that my body is so sore from repeated parachute landing falls (PLF's), sit ups, push-ups, double-timing, and flutter kicks...I can't even lift my head off my pillow. I have to literally roll my body out of my bunk.

My mind shifts gears and I refuse to focus on my aches, pains, and sore joints. Suck it up, Airborne, you've been through worse! At least they don't hit me, I reason. What's the worst they can do? Make me join the Army? My close call in AIT had filled me with new resolve to be motivated, dedicated, and disciplined. If it doesn't kill me it makes me stronger, I chuckle, sarcasm replacing my weepy emotions. I've even stopped crying when my drill sergeant focuses on me. In Airborne School they are called Black Hats and all the instructors are men. A smirk spreads across my face as I roll from my bunk to prepare for another long hot day of training. It's halfway through Tower Week and almost all the females have dropped out. I won't quit, I'm not giving up, and I'm not giving in no matter what. I'm a fighter like my sister Lynn!

*   *   *

My sister Penny is a fighter too—she fought for me when she was almost fourteen. I was upstairs nursing my wounds the night she held a knife to James's throat. "You touch Tina again," she said through gritted teeth, "you won't wake up cause I'll f---n' kill ya."

Mom stood in silence behind her and watched.

*   *   *

"It's not the jump that'll kill ya," the Black Hat instructor jokes, "it's the sudden stop!"

We are training, preparing our bodies for the "sudden stop" in hopes of preventing serious injuries or death. Repeatedly practicing our PLF's by jumping off concrete walls into sawdust filled pits.

A proper five point PLF is landing with my feet and knees together, knees slightly bent, chin tucked in and my arms curled up protecting my head and neck. The "sudden stop" should be absorbed through my five points of impact: balls of feet, side of calf, the side of my thigh, hip and then my shoulder. Usually though, my landings end up being three points: feet, butt, head. It takes a lot of practice and I line back up on the three-foot wall. It was repetitive mindless training and sometimes my mind wandered back to the past. "Hit it!" the Black Hat yells and I jump down and perform my PLF again and again and then I get back up...back up.

My thoughts drift to when I thought I'd had a back-up...

* * *

It was the July I turned twelve. I'd been grounded to my bed for the entire summer. I'd read all the books I could escape into, but when my parents hosted one of their many card parties, I really wanted to play with the other kids. I watched and listened through the window crack to the laughter and games the other kids played outside.

After dark, all the kids gathered upstairs in the next bedroom to tell stories. So, I made a "pillow Tina" in my bed and snuck into the next room to listen to the stories and be around my siblings and the other kids. That was my back-up. I thought maybe James would be too drunk or distracted to remember my punishment. I was wrong.

I wrapped myself in blankets on the top bunk to hide as a back-up plan in case anyone came upstairs to glance in to check on us. We never had doors on our bedrooms growing up so I thought I could sneak over to my bedroom if I needed to. As I hid up on the bunk, my back was up against the wall—another back-up.

* * *

"Get in line!" the Black Hat shouts at us to line up for our time in the mock parachute harness. We take turns being strapped into the harness suspended by ropes and springs, holding onto my risers and responding when the instructor yells "Hit it!" Then I get back up and get in line.

*   *   *

He must have crept silently up the stairs, carefully stepping over the very creaky third step from the top. When he passed the doorway into my room and discovered "pillow Tina" panic seized my heart, my muscles wouldn't move and I knew beyond a shadow of a doubt my back-up failed and I had crossed the line.

He ordered everyone downstairs. Penny disobeyed and stayed around the corner to listen. When James dragged me screaming from the top bunk by my hair, the sheets wrapped tightly around me, restricting my ability to fight back. I felt like I was bound in a harness and when he hit me in the face—I collapsed on the wooden floor.

When he picked me up and threw me across the room…I must have fallen correctly. Maybe my body already knew how to absorb the impact of the "sudden stop." I crumpled to the floor against the wall. I survived the interaction without any broken bones. I wonder if I did a proper landing fall.

*   *   *

"Good job, Airborne!" the Black Hat says to me, as I double-time back up onto the wall. It is a very rare encouragement. I get back in line.

*   *   *

"Do you wanna come downstairs for ice cream?" she asks, sitting on the edge of my bed. Mom offers me ice cream as a consolation for surviving the beating. Hair is missing from my scalp, my twelve-year-old face is swelling and my body hurts from being battered and bruised. I decline her offer.

Mom didn't fight for me, but Penny sure did. "You touch Tina again; you won't wake up 'cause I'll f---n' kill ya."

After she threatened James with a knife, Penny stopped coming home from school. Eventually Social Services took her away and placed her in a group home. I ran away too—only to be returned by a social worker. I guess it's my turn to fight.

I could never do less b/c then I would have nothing.

* * *

Well... I fought my fear of heights, I didn't quit, I didn't give up and I didn't give in. As I suit up for my first jump a knot of fear and anxiety form in my gut. I suppress the useless emotions and force myself to obediently follow orders. "This is what I trained for," I reason in my mind; if I live, then I did well. If I don't, then at least Mom will receive a little bit of money from the Army.

I wasn't worried too much about dying because I'd never really felt alive. I was almost positive I wouldn't go to hell because I'd tried to be a nice person. Either way, it really didn't matter much to me. *I always did the best I knew how.*

As I wait to board the C-130 airplane, my mind flashes back to another time, long ago, when I tried to face my fears head on, a day I'd tried to forget. It was my turn to fight.

* * *

In January of 1983, we moved from Michigan all the way down south to Lake Worth, Florida. James had too many drunk driving arrests and the judge threatened him with prison if he saw him again. Rather than not drink, he relocated what was left of his prisoners—our family—to Florida.

Our new place was a hot, humid dingy place with windows shaped like sideways shutters and opened by using a little crank. The small three-bedroom duplex sat among large fern like plants, mounds of biting red fire ants and patches of brown grass on a dead-end dirt road.

The move was quick, and with Penny gone, I suddenly became the oldest child, taking on the role of protector, babysitter, and defender. All of my sisters had escaped one way or another by then and I couldn't just blend into the chaos. I had to be responsible for Jimmy and Derik. James had already started following Jimmy around, calling him names. The intimidation was so bad that Jimmy woke Mom up at five a.m. one day to ask her to drive him to school so he could escape; he was only seven years old. She told him to go back to bed.

It was during that time, of increased intimidation and abuse, that James began middle of the night visits to my room. It became way too much for me. Finally, at thirteen years old, I remember very vividly the moment I challenged James to a fight.

I had grown taller and could almost look James in the eyes. I was a skinny wraith of a kid and he'd been yelling at me for something I'd done or thought I'd done. Mom is sitting at the kitchen table off to my right drinking her Coke-a-Cola and smoking a cigarette. I am waiting for my punishment with my head down when the thought crosses my mind, "He wouldn't dare hurt me...not with Mom right here."

I don't know where the thought came from, or what sparked it. Maybe it was birthed from the new identity of being the eldest, caretaker and protector of Jimmy and Derik. Wherever it came from...I didn't analyze it, I just reacted.

I look up and meet his glare for the first time in my life and I feel angry. I'm tired of being hit, ridiculed, pushed, ignored, slapped, beat, molested and abused. I'm tired of the humiliation, intimidation, pain and suffering. I have my brothers to protect and I'm tired of this drunk hurting me. I clench my fists preparing myself to fight and the look of defiance registers in my eyes.

James doesn't flinch for a second and, before I know it, his hand shoots out at my face and locks onto my nose in a vise-like grip. He begins twisting my nose like he is tightening a loose bolt.

I immediately drop to my knees in excruciating pain and surprise. He keeps twisting my nose until I'm in the fetal position on the floor amongst a puddle of tears, snot and blood.

Leaning over me with his hand still gripping my nose, his hot smelly breath on my cheek, "You think you're tough do ya? Well...YOU'RE NOT, you're just retarded!"

Squeezing even tighter he leans in for a final push, "STUPID KID."

He finally releases my nose and walks away, leaving me curled up on the floor weeping and crying, utterly defeated, humiliated and betrayed.

"Stupid Fin landers," he sneers in my mother's direction as he leaves the room.

My mom never responds. No shouts…no arguments…no please stops…no…nothing.

She drinks her pop and smokes her cigarette in silence.

I drag myself to the bathroom on my hands and knees. She never moved, never even said a word… she never did.

Resentments towards Mom grew daily in my hardening heart. My anger was compounded by the betrayal of being hurt right in front of her and her refusal to help. I couldn't believe she just sat there and allowed him to hurt me like that. I vowed in my heart that when I grew up—I'd fight for the people I love. I wouldn't let people around me get hurt if I could help it. I would fight. I would speak up. I would not be silent. I was angry with her and I continued to add her name to the stone wall that I was constructing around my heart.

After that day, the torture and intimidation grew worse and James continued his nightly visits to my room. For the first time in my life I actually had a bedroom door but it didn't have a lock on it and my hope began to dwindle as there was nowhere I could run—no chance of escape. I felt like Mom either couldn't or wouldn't protect me and she really didn't seem to care. She and James had many fights of their own.

In the past, every time I'd tried to escape, or tell an adult of the physical abuse, it had been met with heart ache, agony and an increase in abuse. I felt trapped. I didn't even have any friends I could trust to share my secrets with.

God didn't really seem to care either, so I stopped asking him for help too. The questions I had when I was younger about why a loving God allowed people to be treated so badly were replaced with strategies on how to survive each day without being hurt or molested.

Mom worked at a gas station down on the corner and I was helping her at work one day when I finally gathered up my courage to tell her about the night time abuse. I didn't really think that she would or could do anything about it, but I didn't have any one else to tell. She asked me a couple of questions and then told me she'd have Derik sleep in my room. During the conversation Mom told me that James was using drugs and that's why everything was so bad. That was it. No anger, no coddling just, "I'll take care of it." It was about what I'd expected.

Derik started sleeping in my room, but it didn't help. James would use Derik falling asleep on the couch as an excuse to come into my room. God...where are you? Why do you allow this? God, did I do something to make you hate me too? Am I being punished because Eve at that apple? What did I do that was so bad that I deserve this? Mom...? This is **not** helping.

A couple months later, Mom finally decided she had had enough and in the middle of the night woke us up, shoved us in the car, threw in some clothes and drove off into the darkness. All the way back to Michigan it was my job to watch for cars that might be following us. It was stressful, but I was happy. Mom had finally stepped in... Escape... Freedom... No more fear!

The night we escaped from our prison in Florida was the very first time I saw Mom afraid of James; it would not be the last.

* * *

"Are you afraid?" Diggs asks me as we pull on our jump boots. Her broad shoulders and muscled arms are larger than mine and I'm kind of surprised by her question.

"No, not really," I respond thoughtfully lacing up my shiny boots.

I pause.

We are preparing for our graduation ceremony from Airborne School and are discussing Blood Wings. Receiving Blood Wings is a rite of passage and I want them because I earned them. During our graduation ceremony my Parachutist badge will be pinned on my uniform by a Black Hat and he will present me with a choice. Responding with a "yes" means the badge is punched into my flesh and depending on how hard he punches, will determine how much I bleed. It's just pain...nothing to be afraid of.

"It's just pain," I continue as she studies my face, "it'll go away."

"I think I'll say no," she looks at me sideways to gauge my reaction and I detect fear in her voice.

I don't like fear...it's overrated.

* * *

No more fear. I faced my fear of heights and survived all five of my jumps. I accepted my Blood Wings with bravery and honor. I was promptly shipped to Fort Bragg, North Carolina, and there, I became a proud member of the 82nd Airborne Division.

I loved wearing my uniform with my maroon beret. I felt confident and sure of my identity for the first time in my life. I felt proud of something I'd done. I experienced a sense of value in belonging to a greater good, something with a purpose. A glimmer of hope sparked in me that maybe, despite my past, I had some worth in this world.

The endless drills, guard duty, and trainings I'd endured through Basic, AIT and Airborne School had been a welcome atmosphere of structure compared to the chaos and unpredictability of living with alcoholism and abuse. I knew how to be obedient, follow commands without question and perform quickly. James had trained me well. I didn't mind being yelled at, or forced to exercise as punishment for someone in my squad making mistakes, because I was used to receiving consequences for the behaviors of others.

The United States Army freed me from my small town, drinking and drug use, failed relationships, chaos of family life, and even poverty. At eighteen I'd lived a lifetime of betrayal and abandonment as well as physical, emotional, psychological and sexual abuse from family, acquaintances and friends. The Army freed me to build a life worth living.

I settled down into my new life as a soldier with a "B positive" attitude, a growing love for the military, pride in my uniform, and of being a soldier. I felt like I'd accomplished something worthwhile. My heart was filled with hope, and I felt confident and prepared to live in a new world. I felt a little bit lonely and hollow inside, like I was missing something, but I thought it would be resolved when I found the right person and fell in love for real.

Not that I needed some guy to rescue me, and I certainly didn't need God or Jesus. I'd proved I was strong enough and could do it myself. I'd endured and finally escaped...or so I thought.

*   *   *

When it came to being challenged on road marches, physical training or volunteering for jumps, I rose to the occasion, but my regular life in the military was mundane and repetitive. I worked in a repair parts warehouse and spent endless days identifying and sorting truck parts by their stock numbers, looking them up on micro fiche, categorizing, counting inventory, moving pallets, unloading and loading trucks in an old drafty, dusty dirty warehouse. Day in and day out the work was the same broken up only by twelve-mile road marches, training exercises and monthly jumps. I'd been challenged during my training, but as a regular soldier...I was bored. As a result, I ended up spending more and more of my time drinking, dancing and partying.

When I wasn't out drinking or being challenged, my mind drifted back to the life I'd left behind. Without the alcohol I was forced to experience emotions that kept re-surfacing from my past that spilled over into my life as sarcasm and bitterness—directly contradicting my pledge to be positive.

In my growing anger and resentment, I decided to write James a letter confronting him about the years of abuse he'd put me through. I described a family I'd seen depicted on TV and expressed confusion because there wasn't any drinking, fighting, beatings or yelling. There wasn't any night time molestation, or intimidation. I wrote that he'd been wrong about me. I wasn't stupid or retarded and I was a good person. And despite everything he'd done to me, I turned out okay, no thanks to him. It was kind of an "in your face" letter.

He never responded and never wrote back. The only acknowledgement I ever heard he even received the letter was through Mom. He'd told her, "I got a letter from Tina the other day."

But, other than that...nothing.

No response. No repenting. No apology...nothing.

Silence.

I didn't know what else to do, so I just tried to forget it. I returned to drinking, partying and filling my time with the social aspects of military life, but the consequences of my actions resulted in missed formations, poor performance evaluations, and lower PE scores.

*　*　*

Following some strong urgings from my squad leader, platoon Sgt. and my 1st Sgt. to make better choices... "or else." I chose to focus my attention on building a life around the core values of being in the U.S. Army and attempted to limit my drinking to weekends. I challenged myself to study and I trained for the Soldier of the Month competition for my company and then went on to earn it for the 782nd Maintenance Battalion as well.

I wanted to live my life based on loyalty, respect and honor. Concepts I was never taught at home. I began to value duty, selfless service and integrity. I'd faced and overcome fear in jump school and was not afraid to die for my country. The problem was—I didn't know how to do any of those things except follow orders and commands. Rules and regulations were great for structure, training, studying and winning competitions, but bad for actually feeling loved. I didn't know how to live or relate to other people.

This I had @ home

I began to think more like a soldier, act like a soldier and take pride in being a soldier at all times. The Army didn't allow women in Ranger School or Special Forces so I set my sights on training to become a Drill Sergeant. I'd thought many times about my Drill Sergeant in Basic Training and how she seemed to care about me. I wish I could have told her what was going on with me. But, too little too late, just forget about it. The past is behind me. Face forward...eyes front...look ahead...

{ 5 }

LOVE IN A WAR ZONE

Being in the military and living on base provided numerous opportunities for relationships, especially since the ratio of men to women in the 82nd Airborne Division was definitely in my favor. I craved love and a real relationship and the man I picked appeared to be a very rational choice.

Payne, a tall blonde, blue-eyed young soldier was smart and friendly. He had a wonderful, loving family and Christian parents. He appeared to be perfect. I believed I'd found an answer, believing that if someone was raised in a loving environment then they must know how to treat the other person to ensure a long loving relationship.

Because of my intent on marriage I dismissed the problems we had during our short-term courting as issues that would magically be resolved just by the pure act of marrying. I "fell in love" with his family and with the idea of being married. My plans in life were to become a Drill Sergeant, get married, have kids and live happily ever after...simple.

Payne proposed and we were planning our beautiful southern wedding when he received orders for a hardship tour in Korea. A hardship tour meant a soldier could not bring a non-military spouse, much less a fiancé. We made a decision to marry quickly so I could also be assigned to Korea and we planned to have a "real" wedding upon our return.

I was nineteen years old when we drove down to Dillon, South Carolina—the "Marriage Capital of the East" —and married in May of '89. Payne and I celebrated our wedding with a cake at Pizza Hut and a weekend in Myrtle Beach. We spent a couple short months living together before he was shipped overseas and I followed my new husband approximately one month later.

Korea was exciting, new and different than anything I'd ever experienced. It was the first time I'd been in another country. Payne and I had an opportunity to live in off-base housing in the town near the Army base and we were really fortunate to experience the culture in a unique way. While living in Korea, I noticed the honor the people used in their speech and the respect they displayed towards elders as well as in family relations. Koreans chose their words very carefully. I learned what honor actually looked like when it was carried out daily and living in that culture had a profound impact on me.

However, mine and Payne's "honeymoon period" was short lived, and the problems began almost immediately. We were newlyweds in a foreign country and just getting to know each other. I quickly became aware that neither of us knew how to have a healthy relationship. The only models I'd had in my life were mired in negativity, drinking, and arguments. I tried to use what I'd learned from my in-laws as a model, but we had such limited contact with them in our first year. So, I resorted to what I knew. We were surrounded by single lonely people separated from relationships, spouses, and family. A majority of the soldiers filled the void through daily drinking and partying. Beer was even sold in vending machines in the barracks.

I became a part of the problem by pointing out the negative things that I thought were wrong. I had a desire for our relationship to work, but didn't realize I lacked basic communication skills. I had an expectation that love came with marriage vows. Allegations of infidelity, jealousy, lack of trust, inability to communicate, and different priorities, all contributed to our deepening marital problems.

I never talked to Payne about the abuse and abandonment feelings I'd endured as a child because I wanted to forget about them. When I began to have medical issues related to endometriosis and experienced severe monthly cramping, it became such an issue, that my doctor scheduled me for exploratory surgery. Payne traveled to Seoul with me for the surgery, but left me alone to face it by myself. I felt abandoned, alone and unloved…again. I was in a foreign country at twenty years old facing surgery for the first time in my life and my husband left me to face it alone. Following the surgery—still recovering from the pain—I traveled the six-hour train ride back to Camp Carroll by myself. Trusting him with my heart became even more difficult after that.

* * *

Despite our marriage being an emotional war zone, Payne and I remained together and, following our one-year anniversary, we learned that we were expecting a child. We weren't trying to have a baby, but we weren't trying not to either. Around that time, Payne was offered a scholarship to become an officer and I had to make a decision between my dream of becoming a Drill Sergeant or having a family. We could not be a "dual service" family which meant an officer could not be married to an enlisted person as a stipulation of acceptance. I gave up the Army and chose love and family instead.

* * *

When we learned of the pregnancy, we called Payne's mom on the phone from Korea and put it on speaker. I was excited to hear what she would say about being a grandmother for the first time. I looked up to her and valued her opinion of me. I admired her relationship with her husband as it was the only healthy model of marriage I'd seen in my entire life.

We huddle together in the small office near the phone so we can both hear her response. She answers the phone and Payne says, "Tina's pregnant."

Not knowing I can hear her, she doesn't miss a beat, "Are you sure it's yours?"

My heart is crushed.

In that moment I realize what his mother really thinks of me.

Payne glances at me as tears fill my eyes and the horror registers on my face.

"Um…yeah," Payne responds.

She didn't know I heard her. Her response stirred up the rejection, betrayal and hurt I'd experienced from my own mother. As a result, I was plagued with nightmares throughout my pregnancy as the fear I experienced as a child resurfaced in my dreams. I dreamt of giving birth to alien babies, Korean ones and African American babies too. Yet, through it all, I never spoke a word to anyone about my fears.

Despite her rejection, and my fears, the news of my pregnancy completely altered my perspective of life. I realized how unprepared I was to be entirely responsible for raising another human being. A child totally dependent on me for their needs, their wants, their future; shaping their beliefs and their very world view was to be—my job. Questions and doubts began to rise. What do I want my child growing up to believe? What do I believe? I began thinking about my future and my life in a totally different way.

I knew I didn't want to raise my child the same way I'd been raised, but I didn't have a frame of reference as to how to "do it." I returned to the one thing that had never let me down: reading books. I researched how to be a parent and assigned readings to Payne. When we returned to the States I even tried to read my Bible and we attended church with Payne's parents, who were Baptist. I still cared deeply what they thought of me.

* * *

One look at our beautiful brand new baby girl totally changed my life. I was very grateful Jordan looked like her dad and her Nana and *not* like me, thus immediately removing any paternity concerns. She was blonde, blue-eyed and gorgeous. I felt an immense love, a love I didn't even feel for my husband. In the first days of her life I wouldn't even let the nurses take her from me at night. I knew, that I knew, that I knew, that no matter what, I would always love her and I would fight for her. I was deeply aware that what I taught her and how I demonstrated my love for her would affect her for her entire life. I wanted to be a great parent. No, I wanted to be the perfect parent.

So, I purposed in my heart to make some changes. We dedicated Jordan in the Baptist church and I started to believe God might actually care about me. I also decided to make an attempt to have a relationship with my biological father. I'd only seen Larry that one time when he took me to the airport. He never attempted to contact me, ever. With high expectations I sent him a birth announcement, but never received a response.

Nothing.

I was hurt.

I dealt with the rejection by rationalizing that he probably didn't have time for me. I tried to forget and put it behind me and not allow it to deter me from making personal changes. I began working on my self-esteem. I'd witnessed the damage that low self-esteem had on my sister Marie's relationships and didn't want Jordan growing up to believe negative things about herself.

I began to repeat positive affirmations that I learned from watching Stewart Smalley on "Saturday Night Live." I started by telling myself I was smart and I kept repeating it despite my unbelief. I kept repeating my positive affirmations until they actually worked. Positive thoughts began to replace the negative identity that had been beaten into me my entire life. Positive thinking helped me to have the confidence to enroll in a community college English class. The "A" I earned in class boosted my self-esteem immensely and I began to consider that I just might be smart enough for college.

Despite the work I was doing on my self-esteem and education, my marriage was not healthy and we fought almost daily. I never felt like I was good enough for Payne or his family and I didn't know how to fix it. I also felt like I was more invested in change than he was. I kept trying different things with minimal or short-lived results. I so wanted a happily-ever-after once-in-a-lifetime relationship, but it just wasn't working out. And my biggest fear was that Jordan would grow up feeling rejected, criticized and unloved like I did.

* * *

I can't make Payne love me and I don't know how. The moment of clarity punches me in the chest and I can barely breathe. I can't force his heart to feel something it doesn't.

It's spring of '93, I'm sitting in a deserted supermarket parking lot in the middle of the night in Dunn, NC with hot tears streaming down my face. I am alone in the car after being ridiculed and rejected—again—by my husband of almost three years. My heart breaks as the revelation of the truth of my failing marriage filters into my awareness, forcing me to make a choice. I listen to the painful lyrics of a love song on the radio and the answer is clear...I'll give up this fight.

I'm not winning and it's killing me inside. I can't take it anymore. The lies, criticism and rejections are too much to bear. At just two years old, the arguing is already causing damage to Jordan as she is unhappy and cries a lot.

I'm in Dunn, NC, and I feel totally "done."

I kept trying, but when our relationship became violent, we both decided it needed to end. Payne willingly gave me sole custody and I made sure that Payne knew he could request extra visitation at any time so that what happened to me at fourteen would never happen to Jordan.

*　*　*

I was babysitting my brothers the night James found us. I heard the knocking and peered out the window. He saw me looking out through the curtains and immediately started threatening me through the closed window telling me to open the door. Mom was out shooting pool with her team in a bar located about half an hour from the house. I ran to the phone and called her at the bar.

"DO NOT LET HIM IN," Mom yells. "Hang up and call the police!" She orders.

As I hang up, I threaten James through the window, "I'm calling the police...you better leave!"

"I just want my kids!" he begins cussing and banging on the door. "IF YOU DON'T OPEN THIS DOOR I'M GONNA KILL YOU!" he yells, as his pounding grows louder and more insistent. Frantically I dial 9-1-1 on the tan rotary phone. The dispatcher tells me that she'll send a car, but it will take fifteen minutes to reach me.

As I dial the bar again, I yell at James for the first time in my life, "I CALLED THE POLICE YOU BETTER LEAVE!"

Derik is crying.

When the police arrive twenty minutes later, James had already given up and left. Shaking and crying—with Derik on my hip, clinging to my shoulder—I give my statement. The policemen say they'll remain in the area for a while and I should call 9-1-1 if James returns. I contact Mom at the bar and she tells me that she is almost finished with her game and will be home in an hour. If James comes back, I'd better not let him in or I'll be in big trouble.

About half an hour later, I watch out the window as my sister Lee drives up in her car and James pulls in right behind her. They both race to the back door and reach it about the same time. Lee has her one-year-old son on her hip.

"Open this door bitch or I'm gonna kill you!" James threatens. I can tell he's drunk.

"Open the door Tina! He just wants the boys!" Lee yells.

"MOM TOLD ME NOT TO!" I scream back at her.

Derik is screaming in the living room as Jimmy tries to comfort him.

Terror grips my entire body as I dial 9-1-1 again and pray that someone—anyone—will save me. I'll even take Jesus if He feels like showing up. I hang up and shakily dial the number for Mom at the bar and she begins yelling her own threats through the phone. "YOU BETTER NOT LET HIM IN!" she screams.

Bam…Bam…Bam… James is kicking at the door. I hear myself screaming.

CRACK…CRACK…

The moments that follow are a blur of activity…a combination of fight and flight. Lee, with her child still on her hip, somehow gets between James and me, his intended target, and trips him.

I throw the phone at James and flee. Flying objects, flurry of activity, and screams. At some point, Jimmy escapes from the house out the front door and I run around the other way and escape out the door that James had just kicked open.

Trembling and scared, Jimmy and I hide when James comes out the front door to call for Jimmy who is hiding behind a tree. I see James through the living room window as he picks up Derik and tries to comfort his sobbing, terrified two-year-old son.

The police arrive minutes later. I emerge from the shadows to tell them what happened and inform them that James is in the house. Jimmy comes out of hiding, and we stand together trembling and watching through the window as James hands a still sobbing Derik over to Lee.

I feel a bit more confident and bolder as the police escort James out of the house and handcuff him up against the police car. Jimmy, who had never seen his favorite TV show "Dukes of Hazzard" play out in real life, looks at me with confusion in his eight-year-old eyes and asks, "What are they doing?"

"They're cuffin 'im and stuffin 'im." I respond as relief floods my body. James had crossed the line and the police were taking over. Finally, someone had stepped in and saved us. I felt much safer knowing the police had taken him away. I thought the drama was over...I was wrong.

*　*　*

Mom arrives home soon after the police leave and takes charge. She makes several phone calls and I hear her tell the police that when James left the house the first time he'd found her at the bar where Mom was shooting pool, pinned her to the floor and threatened her. He told Mom he was going to take Jimmy and Derik away and she'd never see them again.

Within the hour, Mom threw some clothes in a bag, packs the three of us into the car, and speeds off into the darkness. She frantically drives the twenty miles to the bus station. It is another flurry of activity as we race to get to the ticket office before it closes at midnight and the last bus leaves. We arrive with six minutes to spare only to find out that we don't have enough cash for the tickets. Crying and trembling, mom sends me outside with a bag of coins as she pleads with the clerk to give us a few more minutes while we count to see if we have enough change.

Under a street lamp at midnight, we group nickels and dimes and count out the pennies placing them in piles on the hood of the car. Once Mom realizes we have enough money for the tickets, she rattles off instructions to me about taking care of the boys.

Derik, still in diapers, is learning how to use the bathroom, "there will be a bathroom on the bus, but don't let him go alone." Weeping, Mom tells me she is sending us to my sister Marie's house in Arlington Heights, Illinois and it will be at least a 15-hour trip. She repeatedly tells me to "watch the boys" closely when we stop at different stations and not to talk to strangers. Mom only has a little bit of money left for food, "only use it when you really need to…for the boys." I try to reassure her I can handle it, but I am scared. I've never been on a bus. I don't know what to expect. I'm afraid.

It's a long bus ride and people stare at us. I use the leftover nickels and dimes to feed the boys crackers from vending machines, but it's not enough. Some people try to talk to me about my children, but we huddle together and I pretend to be strong and in control. Jimmy never talks much, but I can tell he's scared too. Derik is a handful and no matter how much I rock him he keeps waking up. Some people give me dirty looks when he cries. We finally make it to Marie's and she meets us at the bus station.

*   *   *

It was nice to be reunited with my sister and be treated as the adult I already felt like I was. Marie was married and had a beautiful little girl the same age as Derik. Marie welcomed us into her small family with open arms and I enjoyed being a part of her life. Despite Marie's hospitality and love, she was experiencing her own marital problems and had already started trying to drown them in alcohol. She had no problem with me drinking so, at age fourteen, I began to drink with her when her husband was at work.

Our time with Marie passed quickly and after two weeks, Mom arrived to take us back home. James had his day in court. A restraining order was issued and an emergency custody hearing granted Mom sole custody of the boys. I overheard Mom tell Marie that she had spent those weeks sleeping with a shotgun under her bed terrified James would return.

We returned to our home and school life, but things had changed for me. Mom tried to reclaim a life focused on bettering herself and raising the last of her children. For me, it was too little too late. I was empowered and transformed by the police stepping in to save me, but my heart remained hardened. I was bitter and angry and fought Mom and almost anyone that treated me poorly, or even looked at me wrong. In my adolescent years I modeled the behaviors James taught me my entire life. I wreaked havoc, spewed negativity, drank, fought and rebelled. I despised my own behaviors, but the battle was raging within me and I lacked the knowledge, skills and abilities to do anything different. I was no longer "The Enemy in His Hands," but I was acting exactly like the enemy I'd been trying to escape from. As a result, I created many enemies of my own.

* * *

When Payne and I separated, I remained in the same area for Jordan's sake—I did not want her to grow up without a father like I did. However, Payne and I continued to fight and argue through our friends. The constant reminders of rejection along with my need for space created a hostile home environment and made it difficult to stay close. I wanted Jordan to be with both her parents, but eventually I reluctantly retreated north to the land I had tried so hard to escape.

I thought leaving Michigan and joining the Army would solve my problems. I thought escaping to live a new life would work, that marriage would work. I'd chosen someone who made sense. I'd chosen someone from a good Christian family.

How could it not work? It must be me. What is wrong with me? Am I unlovable? Do I not love right? Love failed. I tried to be good and go to church, but turning to God didn't help…again.

Belief in God's love didn't help my marriage, never answered my questions, never soothed my broken heart, or protected me from rejection. My belief and hope turned to bitterness as I added more marks to my tally sheet of God's wrongs against me. No way would a loving God allow all the stuff I'd been through to happen just because some guy somewhere ate some stupid fruit.

I officially abandoned my Lutheran faith, and when people asked, I simply stated "I'm agnostic" and refused to go any further. I pitied people who were foolish enough to believe in such a powerless religion. I promised myself I would guard my heart from future hurts and not be vulnerable again.

It worked. I remained strong…until death came knocking on my door.

{ 6 }

CASUALTY OF WAR

"**H**e's dead...Derik's dead!"

Lee ran to meet me as I enter the lobby of the emergency room.

"WHAT? NO! WHAT? HOW?"

My mind reels as I try to piece together the stream of words coming out of her mouth, something about a snowmobile and a truck. Lee keeps talking, tears streaming down her face.

"Oh my God! Where's Mom?"

Frantically trying to gain control of my mind and emotions...this can't be happening...

* * *

I'd retreated home to Michigan to start a new life as a single parent at age 25. With the money the Army provided, I became a full-time college student and worked as a bartender on weekends. I lived with Mom and Derik for a while until I rented a place of my own. College was where I was re-united with my old friend that had never let me down, that had been with me my entire life providing answers, direction and insight, allowing me to experience a vicarious life—books.

Books had allowed me to escape into their pages and helped me survive my childhood. Books taught me about childbirth and parenting, and now challenged me to learn and grow in a whole new way. I fell in love with learning and chose psychology as a major. I stopped trying to drown my past and became engrossed in learning about human behavior, applying everything I was learning about communication, parenting and relationships to my life. I joined the Army Reserves, enrolled Jordan in Head Start and began to feel like I was "getting it" for the first time in my life. I volunteered in her classroom, spent time with family and friends and was really learning how to live a life based on love—not fear.

Funny thing though, there are no classes about love and how to love. It's the most important thing in the world and yet there are no classes offered on it. There are many poems, songs and stories written about love, but no classes. Perhaps it's because love must be experienced in order to fully understand it.

Like the love I have for my brother Derik, no poem, song or story about love can help me in this moment...the moment I learn that my brother, the one I carried around on my hip for years, the one who looks like me, the one who always tells me he loves me, the one who wants to be like me, the one I was supposed to protect and love...and fight for... is...dead.

*   *   *

I have to see his body. I feel like I can't breathe, but I have to see him with my own eyes. I just can't believe it. What do I do? I don't want to believe it. I'd just seen him two days ago. How can he be dead? God...how can he be dead? God...no...

Crying and numb I enter the stark cold room. The first thing I notice is the antiseptic smell mixed with something wet. Like the smell of wet clothing. He's lying on a table and his body is covered with a sheet up to his chest. I look at his pale puffy face tilted towards me. His brown hair is plastered to his head and his eyes are sewn shut with black thread. Someone sat there and sewed his eyes shut before I came in here. He is dead. His eyes are sewn shut...with black thread.

My brother Jimmy, the strong football player, is standing to my right and I see tears rolling down his face. I've never seen him cry before and the whole scene is so completely unreal to me.

"You're crying," I say to Jimmy.

Shocked and confused by my words, Jimmy nods his head towards Derik's dead body like he has to validate his right to have emotions in this situation.

Derik is dead and lying on the table, and Jimmy, the stoic, unshakeable, analytical one, is weeping. We hug. We cry together. In the cold stark room...through our loss...we weep and we experience love.

* * *

My youngest brother Derik was fourteen when he was hit by a truck in January of 1996. He was driving a friend's snowmobile with the owner riding on the back, crossing a snow-covered road. The police told Mom that the only thing that saved the other young boy, was that Derik turned at the last moment. Derik turned towards the truck and bore the brunt of the collision head on. It was an act of self-sacrifice that sealed his fate.

Later that night, Jordan wept in my arms when I told her that Derik would not be back from heaven in time for her birthday party in two weeks. We rocked and cried together as we experienced love and loss for my brother, her uncle, her playmate, her friend.

* * *

Right before the funeral, I saw James for the first time since he'd kicked in our door and tried to kill me when I was fourteen. Apparently the local police granted him permission to return to the state to attend the funeral. I no longer feared him and actually felt sorry for him as the years of alcoholism were evident on his blotchy wrinkled face. He didn't seem as large and menacing as I'd remembered him to be from my youth. After the funeral he disappeared.

* * *

The days and nights following the accident were a blur of activity, full of tears and faces of young boys and girls searching for comfort. They visited in packs and pairs at first, not knowing what to say, but just needing to come. We welcomed them—but they didn't stay long. There wasn't much to say as the disbelief and grief hung in the air. Several of Derik's closest friends kept coming and we cried together. I listened and we comforted and fed them. The ones that seemed to adjust the best were the ones who were Christians and professed their faith in God. Their grief was no less, but there seemed to be a sense of strength inside of them that wasn't immediately evident in some of his other friends.

Derik was enrolled in a Lutheran confirmation class at the time of his death. The Pastor shared during the funeral service that Derik was the only teen he ever knew that invited his friends to the class. In Derik's Bible the only highlighted verses were the ones that spoke of love. We engraved them on his headstone. "Love one another as I have loved you." Derik knew love. I don't know if he realized what he was doing, but his last act of love saved his friend's life. Derik acted in love and he was love.

* * *

The first time I ever heard anyone in my family talk about forgiveness was my mother. She spoke forgiveness for the man driving the truck. She didn't blame him and didn't want him to feel bad. Mom even modeled forgiveness by asking me to write a letter telling him that our family was not angry and did not blame him for Derik's death.

On the other hand, she blamed God, which I had no problem with because I had my own tally sheet of wrongs committed against me by so-called God. If there was a God, He had a lot to answer for. How could I protect my brother, to fight for his life, if I wasn't even invited to the battle? My job as his older sister was to protect and defend him. I had made a vow to protect him and to fight for him. But…how could I fight death?

{ 7 }

TRAINING TO LIVE

Following Derik's death, I moved back in with Mom. While trying to finish college, I tried to help her through her grief while I struggled with my own. I had my sights on graduate school but I had a lot going on. My unresolved bitterness about my marriage influenced some unhealthy relationship choices that were impacting Jordan and I also began to have more medical problems. I was dealing with low thyroid, endometriosis, and irritated bowel syndrome, along with repeated cases of bronchitis from working as a bartender and living in Mom's smoky house. Being in her home was starting to feel more and more like the prison I had grown up in. It was exactly what I did **not** want for my child.

* * *

Many of Derik's friends had stopped coming to visit, but there were a few, the ones who had no one else to talk to, who kept coming back. It reminded me of my years of searching for an adult willing to listen, someone who cared. I wanted to be the one adult willing to care for adolescents, the one person who would listen. My heart grieved for Derik's young friends, especially the ones that appeared to be lost or alone. I altered my career goals and decided to become a counselor for adolescents.

I knew my emotions surrounding my brother's death were too raw to begin working with adolescents immediately. So, for an internship placement, I chose an outpatient substance abuse program for adults instead. I thought, if there was anything I knew about, it was the effects of alcoholism and addictions on a family. It was during my internship I first encountered the twelve-step recovery model.

The twelve steps of Alcoholics Anonymous (AA) appeared to be a wonderful model to follow. During my internship, I met people who were really working on bettering themselves through the use of an organized skill set. I experienced empathy for the day-to-day fight many clients dealt with just trying to refrain from taking one sip, one toke, or one hit that, if they failed, usually led to catastrophic consequences.

I listened to their stories, I felt their pain, and I re-lived and worked through a lot of my past by counseling them in their struggles. Working with and learning about alcoholism and addiction also helped me to understand my sister Marie, who was also struggling. I started to think about addiction from a medical standpoint rather than just a moral choice. I co-facilitated a women's group that met weekly to discuss how to practice the steps daily and I learned a new way to live, a model I could follow. A new way to communicate, relate and interact with people. While there, I participated in retreats and personal counseling, and had wonderful supervision and support from the staff.

Several of the twelve steps of AA address forgiveness and encourage people to make amends. "Made a list of all persons we have harmed and became willing to make amends to them all. Make direct amends to such people wherever possible, except when to do so would injure them or others. Continue to take personal inventory, and when we were wrong, promptly admit it." The clients I worked with all seemed to struggle with making amends and what that actually meant. Does it mean pay them back? Say you're sorry? Ask for forgiveness? How many times do you ask?

Many of the women in the group I was involved in had different opinions and they never seemed to be clear about the answers. Making amends seemed to vary depending on the situation. No one clearly defined it and it seemed to be a life-time process. How many times do you say I'm sorry? Where is the cut-off? Some women felt like someone needed to make amends to them before they could ever forgive. The whole issue seemed vague and convoluted and even though it was a great motto, I rarely witnessed it being really productive, or clearly demonstrated in their lives. Pain and fear seemed to be active and alive and love seemed to be an elusive concept as well.

Living up north again provided me with an opportunity to talk to some of the people I'd fought with and hurt during my adolescent years, and make amends by apologizing. Asking for forgiveness from them did feel really good...but how could I find everyone? I'm sure I even hurt people I wasn't aware of. It seemed like the more I learned...the more I learned that I didn't know the answers.

I discovered during my internship placement that my supervisor and one of my co-workers identified themselves as Wiccan. They talked about gods and goddesses as well as warlocks. I'd given up on believing in any kind of caring God. I believed I'd already answered that question. If there was a God, He was an angry God like James and punished you if you were good or bad. Jesus might have loved someone somewhere at some time, but it sure wasn't me, because believing in Him never helped. I walked in one day when my colleagues were discussing how they felt a "disturbance in the force." I mocked their spiritual realm talk and told them it sounded like they were living in "Star Wars." I was pretty sure there weren't any gods or goddesses and the "spirit realm" was all in their heads.

Ultimately, I learned a lot from my internship, my wonderful supervisor, the recovery community and the twelve steps, but I skipped over the higher power and the spiritual stuff. I also wasn't willing to take on the identity of an alcoholic myself. I'd worked too hard to build my self-esteem up and it seemed like accepting a label of an alcoholic would move me backwards, not forwards. Besides, I reasoned, I'd already made lifestyle choices such as being a parent and an aspiring professional in the counseling field, so the label no longer applied to me anyway. And I wasn't quite sure how following the twelve steps would take away my anger unless James joined AA and made amends to me. Maybe all the people who had hurt me would try to make amends with me. It seemed highly unlikely.

↳ Am I waiting for/wanting this too?

didn't belong

*   *   *

It was during my undergraduate years that I was introduced to Maslow's Hierarchy of Needs. I examined my past from that psychological theory. I realized that during my childhood, I was deprived of many of my basic needs: safety, food, water, clean air, stability, and warmth to mention a few. Thinking about my past I was reminded of the chain on the refrigerator door, the food restrictions and the constant atmosphere of fear. But the basic fundamental need that was not fulfilled was a sense of being loved and feeling like I belonged somewhere. So, while I gained a lot of insight about my past and was able to identify my issues, the theory itself didn't tell me how to solve anything. I was left with vague answers about "working through" my issues. What I wanted was concrete answers and "how to" build a life based on love and not fear.

didn't know this for a long time

Meanwhile, living with Mom was becoming extremely difficult. I fought with her about how she punished Jordan by pulling her hair and Jordan was beginning to fear my mother, her grandmother. I also had to live with Mom's negativity and cussing and it reminded me of her neglect and apparent dislike for me when I was a child.

Living with Mom allowed me to witness her devastation and pain of losing Derik and provided many glimpses into her own prisoner of war experiences. It was during this time that I questioned her about the abuse she allowed to occur when I was younger. To my amazement Mom genuinely appeared to be surprised by the events I described. Really? How could she have not seen it? What about the blood, scars, and the screams of her children? Her lack of awareness confused me and it made me angry. I tried to balance my empathy for her pain and my growing anger. It was like she didn't even care enough to notice the abuse? How could she not notice? It happened right in front of her! Then she told me that the reason we fled Florida was because James threatened to take the boys away from her. Not a word about the fact that he was molesting me. Wow. I felt betrayed again.

How do I forgive someone who doesn't even acknowledge the abuse occurred? Mom appeared oblivious…was she in denial? I didn't have an answer, so I didn't even try. I graduated with my BS in psychology in '97 and Jordan and I moved south to live in Virginia. I packed up my anger, renewed feelings of betrayal and bitterness and I shoved them all into boxes, loaded them on a U-Haul truck and fled. Escape once again.

*   *   *

My first year of graduate school in Radford, Virginia, was one of the happiest times that Jordan and I enjoyed together. We had a pool in our complex and Jordan swam while I studied in the sunshine. She loved the water and—with swim lessons—became like a "little fish." I enrolled Jordan in ballet classes and she learned to dance. She had developed a love for sledding up north so when it snowed in Virginia, I made a sled out of cardboard and duct tape and we spent our snow days off from school traipsing up and down a large hill in the area. We lived closer to Payne's parents in NC (her Nana and Papa) and she was able to spend long weekends and more time with them. Our home was filled with love, laughter and tickle fights.

Even though it was difficult being a graduate student, a single mother, and an employee, I continued to work on my personal issues. I loved learning and growing in my knowledge of counseling and self-examination. Along with several of my grad school classmates, we utilized a Claudia Black book called "Repeat After Me" to help us work through issues that could potentially inhibit us from being effective counselors. The more therapy and healing modalities I was exposed to, the more I realized I still had a lot of work to do to heal from my past. Still, I remained motivated, positive I'd finally found the answers I was searching for all of my life. And yet in graduate school there were no classes offered on how to love, just theories, research and techniques. Even in graduate school, love would have to be an independent study.

*   *   *

"Do you see that?" I ask Jordan, pointing at the pair of Jehovah's witnesses knocking on our neighbor's door. Her curly blonde hair bobs up and down as she looks at me inquisitively from the back seat. I continue, quite indignantly, "I don't care what you grow up to believe. But whatever you do, don't go pushing your beliefs off on other people!"

As I continue driving away from our duplex in Radford, she is quiet for a few moments. Her soft voice breaks the silence, "I know you don't believe in God the way my Nana does...but I do." She pauses. "I'll believe for you until you believe."

Her words pierce my heart and I marvel at the sweetness. I am grateful she has her Nana's faith and influence in her life. The only religious education she gets from me is when I sing "Amazing Grace" to her before bed. I know that I am angry and bitter, but I see my emotions as only affecting my relationship with God. I began to see that despite my efforts at concealing my pain, Jordan notices it too, and I worry that I am becoming negative and cynical like my mother.

*   *   *

Jordan was in first grade when I met Brad in graduate school. He seemed safe because he was married and I didn't view him as a potential partner. I had sworn off men for a while, vowing that the next one who entered my life would be the one I'd marry. Someone who would love Jordan as his own, and wouldn't have problems with alcohol like some of the failed relationships I'd had.

Brad and I worked on a research project together and he spent a lot of time in our home. I knew Brad was unhappy in his marriage, but he surprised me when he suddenly chose to leave his wife and move into our duplex right next door. Almost immediately we began a relationship and Brad even asked Jordan if she wanted him to be her dad. Jordan and I both loved him very much and we were excited about our future with Brad in our family. He brought us home to meet his parents and Jordan immediately fell in love with them and was excited. We loved having Brad living right next door. He appeared to be perfect for us, as he said and did all the right things, and he was smart, fun and handsome.

Our relationship lasted only a couple of months before he hooked up with one of my classmates and dumped me. I didn't know what to tell Jordan... love hurts? He had said he wanted to be her dad and now he no longer wanted her around. How do you explain *that* to a seven-year-old? That love means being rejected? Her heart was so pure and loving; I didn't want this experience to harden her heart toward love.

As I dealt with my own pain and anger, I felt like Jordan was torn again between needing me and desiring a father and a family. I couldn't believe I'd made another huge mistake in judging character. I wanted to protect her and be a perfect parent, but I kept messing up and hurting her more. I had to get Jordan out of the situation. Payne and his new wife were living in Texas at the time so I made the extremely difficult decision to allow Jordan to go and live with him for one year while I finished graduate school. At least she would have structure and consistency. So, I drafted an agreement that Payne would return her to me upon my graduation...and I let her go.

* * *

I drove Jordan to Texas by myself. I said good-bye and cried for almost a thousand miles on my way home to Virginia. I experienced love for my child in a whole new way, through self-sacrifice. I renewed my promise to guard my heart from future hurts. The experience with Brad reminded me that love had failed me...again. And it had hurt my child.

Upon my return to Radford, I moved out of the duplex and re-focused my life on being the best student and counselor I could be. I had one year to figure my life out, create structure for my child and become the perfect parent I had purposed in my heart to be. Somewhere—through psychology—there had to be an answer...I was determined to find it.

{ 8 }

NEW FAMILY

It was a hot humid day in late August of 1998. I eyed the squat gray building with a mixture of doubt and anxiety. There were no signs advertising what type of business it was, no flashy motto above the door, and nothing remarkable about it at all. The building was located on a corner in a poor section of town. I'd run out of options and hoped this building would provide me with the placement I needed for my graduate internship.

Upon my return from Texas, I had to change my graduate internship at the last minute. Brad worked at the counseling center I was scheduled to intern for and it was no longer an appropriate option. A lot of the other placements had been taken by my fellow classmates by then and this was what was left.

I took a deep breath, walked up to the building, reached for the handle, swung open the door and stepped over the threshold totally unaware that I had just passed through "Freedom's Front Door."

* * *

The agency accepted walk-in clients off the streets, from the jails, courts, psychiatric hospitals, homeless shelters, and from other agencies as well. It was a triage of sorts and appeared to be the "front lines" for the mental health and substance abuse field. It was a detoxification center (detox) and a thirty-day residential substance abuse facility for adults and it was there that I met my family of professional battle buddies.

* * *

On the day of my interview, within the first fifteen minutes, in that un-remarkable building I met three remarkable people who would become very important in my life. Darlene, the secretary, was the first person I met. A beautiful African-American woman with long manicured fingernails and tight curls around her oval face; directed me to have a seat in the lobby. I sat down on a small orange-cushioned vinyl seat with wooden arms and looked around the plain, slightly run-down but spotless open waiting area.

That's where I encountered Karen for the first time. Otherwise known as "Mama Bear" to those privileged to know her personally, who had long, salt-and-pepper hair, rosy cheeks and a hearty laugh.

"Now, who might you be?" she asks, scanning me up and down.

"Hello," I stand to introduce myself. Karen was the nurse in charge of the detox program and she worked alongside Jon, the man I was scheduled to meet.

Jon was the director of the "down-stairs" residential portion of the program. He turned out to be a wise, but eccentric man, who resembled a bear with his long, curly brown locks and round belly. I was accepted and welcomed as a graduate intern that day and Jon became my supervisor.

* * *

"I have a new client for you," Jon says with a smirk and a twinkle in his eyes. He hands me a file. I am sitting in his office next to a huge mound of papers trying to suppress my urge to organize. Jon's office looks like a Xerox machine malfunctioned and vomited out random files, memos, notes and folders that have piled up into a thick forest of paper bushes and trees that make Jon look even more burly and bearish.

"Oh-kaaay." I eye him suspiciously as I reach for the thick brown file. I am very familiar with Jon's motto of "baptism by fire" which means he gives me challenging clients and watches me as I struggle and squirm. Or, he informs me during the morning staff meeting that I'll be teaching an education group, ten minutes prior to the start time. Another common saying that applies to staff as well as clients is, "If you're not squirmin', you're not growin'."

Jon continues with his instructions, "Her name is Cindy, she's in detox and ready to transfer down. Go get her."

I go.

When I went to "get her" she is standing on the detox balcony repeatedly banging her head against the cinder block wall because her psychiatrist discontinued one of her favorite medications. I speak to her four times before she turns around to acknowledge me.

After several days of reviewing her chart and examining her past, I make a decision to educate her on what I believe she needs to do next...

"You want me to forgive?" Cindy's blue eyes darken and her head rears back. "NO!"

"Let go, and let God," I respond confidently.

"You've got to be kidding me." Curses and spit spray from her mouth. Her intensity surprises me and I recoil in my chair.

"You don't know what I've been through, you don't know my pain! You can't imagine what it's like living with my pain every day! How can you suggest I forgive him for what he did to me? F--- this I'm outta here."

Before I can form a word in response, Cindy springs up, sprints out of my office and slams my door violently as she leaves. The slamming assaults my ears and embarrassment sinks in as I listen to her tirade in the common area about her counselor being "frickin crazy."

Apparently this teaching does not apply to her situation. I feel hypocritical telling her to "let go and let God" since I don't even believe in God. It is just a motto.

Twenty-eight-year old Cindy, with her mullet-style haircut, and short, thin frame is a well-known "frequent flyer" in the residential substance abuse program. She had numerous other treatments and psychiatric hospitalizations. I am four months into my graduate intern placement. Her chart is a long list of diagnoses, labels and assessments: addictions to alcohol, marijuana, benzodiazepines and tobacco, cocaine, Bipolar Disorder, Borderline Personality Disorder (BPD) as well as numerous medical conditions, economic problems and lack of social skills and support. Due to her various labels, diagnoses and medical issues she ingests over thirty prescribed medications every day. Her file is as thick as her battle scars.

She is one of those clients counselors tended to shy away from due to her repeated hospitalizations, incarcerations, potentially explosive personality, extensive history, and long list of diagnoses. Some day she will more than likely succeed in killing herself or someone else. Many people think she is one of the hopeless cases. My co-worker Brett calls her a "tootsie pop." He said she has a tough exterior, but is all chewy in the middle. I "squirm" through my own growth process in working with her and I stick with her and am blessed to get to know her heart and enjoy her "chewy middle." She too, is trying to escape from an enemy camp.

*   *   *

My internship was supposed to be for two semesters, but half way through, a paid position became available and the staff encouraged me to apply. I was hired and became a full-time employee five months before I graduated with my Master's Degree in Counseling Psychology.

I can't say enough about the many amazing people I had the honor of working with during this time, truly some of the best. My co-workers became my family. Aside from Darlene and Karen, there were nurses, counselors, case managers, aides, and supervisors all fighting together for our clients. We battled for each other in our personal lives as well, going through each other's marriages, divorces, illnesses, deaths, and trials; we also celebrated births, triumphs, and accomplishments together as well.

My time working in residential treatment was a magnificent time of learning and growing personally and professionally. I learned not only from the clients I had the privilege of serving, but the men and women I had the honor of serving alongside of on a daily basis. They poured their hearts and souls into their work and demonstrated it by their sacrifices, struggles, and choices. I gleaned so much wisdom from each of them, warriors willing not only to encourage me, but to challenge and confront me as well.

*   *   *

"Tina," Mary Lynn starts off slowly, smiling and looking at me intently. "You need to learn to confront." Mary Lynn is one of my favorite battle buddies. Leaning back in her well-worn office chair, she provides evidence to support her assertion. I love Mary Lynn and admire her amazing ability to tell people in a loving way what they need to hear, and do, in order to change and grow.

I stare down at the files in my lap as her words of wisdom resonate in my heart. I know she is speaking truth and I know exactly where my fear is coming from. What if they hurt me? I think to myself. Worse yet, what if I cry in front of them? I know I have to be strong. How can I ever encourage my clients to face their fears if I am unwilling to face my own? How can I lead if I'm being pitiful and afraid? I have a choice. I choose to fight my fears.

Mary Lynn and I discussed ways to appropriately confront and set boundaries with clients. Then I went out and practiced in public. First I confronted a drive-thru lady I thought was being rude to me; then I challenged two nurse practitioners I thought were being unethical discussing a client in an elevator. Eventually, I gained mastery in being able to lovingly highlight and confront inappropriate behaviors without disparaging the person. I learned to demonstrate care and concern for people despite their behaviors.

I learned a new way to fight: with love and honor, and without fear. I learned to confront so well I earned the nickname "Stone Cold" and built a reputation for rigorously holding clients accountable for their behaviors. Many of the clients who initially feared me would later thank me for the care and concern I demonstrated to them by consistently holding them accountable.

Through many more loving confrontations, encouragement, and challenges put forth by so many of my family of co-workers, I continued to learn and grow. I am eternally grateful for having served with and fought alongside each and every one of my battle buddies.

* * *

While working in residential, I began to alter my perspective of my childhood and began to view it in a more positive light. I was no stranger to pain and I could relate better to my clients as a result. I witnessed first-hand the power of forgiveness and how making amends could restore relationships, transform lives and free people from hurts and pains. As a result, I genuinely encouraged my clients to forgive others based on my experience rather than it simply being a technique or motto that I used in counseling.

"Why should I forgive him?" Cindy asks glaring at me. "He's not worth it."

"It's not for him, it's for you."

"I can't, I don't feel like it."

"What about writing him a letter?" I ask, thinking of how this kind of helped me when I was in the Army. It felt good just writing the letter to James.

"I don't know where he is."

"You don't have to send it; you could just tear it up or burn it."

"What good would that do?"

"It would help you get free from him and what he did to you. Cindy," I sigh. "You carry him around with you everywhere you go."

"What?"

"It's affecting every relationship you have. He shows up every time you get close to someone. It's like you're expecting everyone to treat you like he did, so you're guarding your heart…you need to let it go…let him go if you ever want to be happy."

"I can't. I don't want to."

"Okay…now you're just being willful."

"I don't want to."

"Okay…Let's start out smaller. How about trying to forgive someone a smaller thing first? Like your niece. You can practice forgiving in the small things and then maybe it will get easier to forgive the bigger things."

"What if they don't deserve it? What if they tried to hurt me?"

"It doesn't matter. This is not for them. This is for you," I say, feeling a tad frustrated. "Besides, it's good for relationships.

If you start by forgiving the little things, it will help you build better relationships."

"What if they don't ask for forgiveness?"

"Cindy, you can't wait for everyone else to get healthy before you take action. If I waited for everyone else that hurt me to get healthy and ask for forgiveness, then I'd be waiting forever! This is not for them, it's for you!"

* * *

If clients were tough, unwanted, or challenging for others, I wanted them. I rose to Jon's challenges and I "squirmed" my way through learning and growing. As a result, I worked with many clients diagnosed with personality disorders, usually Borderline Personality Disorder (BPD).

Cindy was labeled as such and usually exhibited the typical BPD behavior pattern that included extreme emotional reactions, fear of abandonment, unstable moods, impulsivity, and her relationships were very chaotic. Counseling someone labeled like Cindy was similar to trying to establish a relationship with a six-month-old puppy that's been beaten, malnourished, abused and then abandoned. She was unpredictable, hyper-vigilant and sensitive to my every move. Sometimes she 'bit' me if I 'touched' her the wrong way, or raised my voice. Other times she barked a lot or panicked and 'peed' on the carpet. But mostly, she sat in my office, shook, and broke my heart.

Cindy—like many of my other clients—struggled with spiritual questions and beliefs. I tried to counsel them in relation to what they were experiencing, but it was difficult. I could only help them as far as I was willing to go myself. Working with the most challenging clients forced me to not only examine my own behavior and relationships, but to question my personal beliefs regarding spirituality.

* * *

I understood facing my fears, being tough and fighting, but loving and accepting love, remained an issue for me. I questioned a loving creator, or 'being' that existed outside of me. The twelve steps called it a "Higher Power," but what does that mean? It kept coming up. I looked to nature for answers.

Someone told me to sit next to an ocean, ponder the world, and imagine a loving creator of the universe, a supernatural being greater than myself. Instead of an ocean I found a pond with a fountain and thought about gods and goddesses. I pondered the Lutheran faith in which I was confirmed as an adolescent and I realized I didn't know enough about faith and spirituality to make an informed decision.

Many times in counseling, I felt like a fellow prisoner of war trying to lead prisoners out of captivity only to realize that our escape route ended up right back to the place we were trying to escape from. I couldn't find the exit.

Despite my frustrations, I decided I didn't have time to delve into any kind of religious study as I was preparing to graduate. I had orals to prepare for, classes to complete and exams to pass. Spirituality and higher power questions were important for my clients, but I had 'actual' work to do. I stuffed my questions into the recesses of my mind and continued learning, studying and applying myself to the world around me.

* * *

The agency was expanding, growing and began admitting clients from local emergency rooms on Temporary Detention Orders (TDO). The staff assessed the TDOs and facilitated civil commitment court proceedings on the premises. Our facility became host to the doctors, lawyers and judges involved in the hearings.

When a person presented to the emergency room during a crisis, demonstrating suicidal or homicidal ideations, appearing delusional, or in a substance-induced state, threatening their ability to function appropriately in society, they were admitted temporarily on a TDO. During the hearing, they were released, admitted voluntarily for treatment, or involuntarily committed against their will, possibly for up to 180 days. Over time, I was assigned more responsibilities related to assessing clients, as well as facilitating the commitment proceedings.

Despite the challenges confronting me at work, I still struggled with anger and emotional pain in my personal life. It took a lot of time and effort to learn the rules and regulations of the residential program, facilitate groups, manage my caseload, learn the TDO regulations, and complete my final year in graduate school. On top of all that, I was dealing with my own sadness concerning my separation from Jordan. It was the longest I'd ever been without her and I missed hugging her, loving her, and being her mommy on a daily basis. Although we spoke weekly, exchanged mail, and learned how to hug long-distance, it was one of the loneliest times I'd ever experienced in my life.

I used some of that time to reconnect with my siblings and discuss their perceptions of our childhood. They shared information about Mom's past that helped me to view her more as a fellow prisoner of war rather than my enemy. When I connected more with my siblings and shared our common experiences, I felt more cared for and loved by them. I discovered that, although we all grew up in the same home, we each had our own prisoner-of-war experiences. We bore our own battle scars and some were a lot more traumatic than mine. Despite deepening my relationships with family and co-workers, I still felt lonely, depressed, and angry when I was by myself.

Alone at night, my thoughts often turned to my past. I was still angry with God about my abuse, my failed marriage and my brother's death. I used God's name in counseling because that's what my clients believed. In spite of all my self-help stuff and professional training, <u>nothing ever seemed to reach the root issue: I don't feel loved.</u>

How can I go back and get that love? I can't re-live my life the way I want it to be…a loving beginning with loving parents. I yearn to feel that I am loved, to have that knowing deep down inside of me that I am wanted. Instead, I just feel angry. Really angry.

*   *   *

"Why do people believe in God? Because it FEEELLS good?" I yell out bitter, angry, and sarcastic…to…no one in my car. "That's just stupid! Why do people believe in God? Because it feels better thinking about Derik as an angel rather than thinking about him rotting in the ground somewhere?" I rant on. "Is that all there is?" Driving to the Army Reserve

Center for my last drill weekend, hot tears course down my face as I question my spiritual beliefs with a vengeance. "I'll believe for both of us until you believe." Jordan's words resonate in my head. But none of it makes sense to me. My thoughts gravitate to the sick, diseased and dying. What's the use?

It's January of '99, the three-year anniversary of Derik's death, an event that forever changed my life. He was so loving and kind. If there was a God, why didn't he stop it? Why didn't God keep my brother alive? Was my brother not good enough? He was so sweet and kind, if there was anyone deserving to live, it was him. What did he do wrong? As I drive the hour and a half to the center, my anger and emotions escalate as I recall the long list of my own pain and suffering.

I've had enough of God talk. The psychological band-aide I've placed over the gaping wounds of my youth rips off as my mind flashes back to all the suffering and heart ache I've endured. Where was Jesus then? God didn't seem to care during my fear-filled years of intimidation and abuse. Or even later when I brought by sister Marie clean clothes to replace her blood stained ones following yet another beating from her boyfriend, and God sure as hell didn't seem to be around when Derik was killed. I didn't have much use for a seemingly angry, invisible, uncaring God. There is enough of that in the real world. I don't know why people believe in God anyways. What's the use?

I kept my intellectual shotgun loaded with all the abuse, fear, hurt, rejection, pain, and bitterness that had festered in my heart over the years and I leveled my weapon at anyone who got in my way. No "Jesus Loves Me" song would soothe me and no pat answers would satisfy me.

That day, I showed up at the reserve center primed for a verbal fight with anyone willing to respond. Not exactly an easy 'sale' to be had for the kingdom of God. I managed to keep my thoughts, feelings and questions at bay throughout the morning, but when I sat down to eat and started a lunchtime conversation, it all came flooding back. I cocked my weapon and challenged the blonde haired, blue-eyed, young man sitting across from me.

"Why do you believe in God?" I ask Paul, my tone loaded with sarcasm and judgment.

"Well...my father is a pastor..."

"Oh, so you believe because your parents believe?" I interrupt.

"No, I believe because Jesus loves me and died for my sins so I can go to heaven when I die," Paul continues confidently.

"What? Paul you are one of the sweetest people I know...are you telling me that you're a sinner?"

"All have sinned and fallen short of the glory of God." He recites quickly.

"So, let me get this straight," I say, "you're telling me that I have to believe I'm bad, which I refuse to believe, accept Jesus, who makes me good, just so I can go to heaven when I die?"

"Um...kind of, yeah...I guess."

"What about the people who don't have Jesus in their lives? I know a lot of really nice people who don't believe in God. Do I have to go around and convince them they are bad so they'll accept Jesus and become good in order to be loved by God? Does that make any sense to you?"

"Um...yes...I mean...no..." he trails off.

Peter, another young soldier, chimes in from across the table, "I love God because God first loved me."

"How do you know that? Did you ever see God? Did Jesus ever show up and say He loves you?" I retort.

"Um, no," Peter responds, "but I believe He does."

"Why?" I ask.

"It says so in the Bible." Peter states matter-of-factly.

"Oooooh the Jesus loves me song. Not a good place to go. That's like telling an addict to just say no to drugs because they're bad for 'em. Yeah...that's *soooo* **not** working for me."

Silence.

Even in the face of my intensity both young men gaze at me with kind eyes.

"Hey, let's go talk to John," Peter suggests. "He's a Sunday school teacher."

We enter John's office and Peter and Paul update him about our conversation. John knows about Jordan as he has children of his own and we have shared parenting stories in the past. John is older than the other two men and, as he listens, John reaches into his desk and pulls out a "Creation vs. Evolution" booklet. John starts talking about how I need to teach my daughter about the amazing love of God as I glance through the booklet with the pitiful 80's graphics.

"I am raising my daughter to believe what she wants," I retort, tossing the booklet back at him.

"Fine," he replies, matching my intensity. "What happens when she grows up and decides to worship Satan?"

I stop cold.

What? I'd never thought of that. Is that possible? Could my unbelief hurt her faith? How long will she believe for me? My mouth opens to respond, but I freeze as something inside me finds it revolting that my beautiful seven-year-old daughter could someday worship the devil.

Why am I having such an emotional reaction? If I don't believe in a God, how can I believe in Satan? How can I believe in one and not the other? How can I believe in the evil and not believe in the good? Just because of what I see?

More questions surface. I can't see the devil, but I believe in evil. All the evils my clients described to me as they shared their traumas of gang rapes, beatings, fights, tragedies, drug-filled lifestyles of abuse and death. One look at the news, our culture, or even my past and a certainty takes root in my heart that evil does exist in the world. My arrogance starts to melt away carrying my bitterness and sarcasm along with it.

I sit down and John squats down next to my chair.

"If you don't teach your daughter the right way…how will she know to stay away from the wrong way?" he inquires a little more gently. "If you don't teach her how much God loves her then she will look to the world for love and acceptance."

My shoulders slump as I realize I am out of intellectual ammo.

"But, what if I don't believe it?" I ask.

"Then change your mind." John states matter-of-factly.

I sit in silence pondering the simplicity of his statement.

Just change my mind. Can it be that easy?

Change my mind. His words resonate inside of me. "Change your mind."

* * *

I left that weekend with the silly booklet and headed back to my life. Intellectually I had sparred for two days and the score seemed pretty even. But deeper questions stirred in my heart...why did I have such a problem with Satan worship if I didn't believe in God? Could it be that easy...just change my mind? Would changing my mind help me to feel loved? It didn't make any sense to me.

I drove back to Radford in silence, pondering all the conversations and arguments. I examined the pros and cons of making a choice to believe in God and Jesus and what that would mean for my life. I still hadn't made a decision, but was looking forward to discussing my questions with my Christian friend Sandy, a strong believer. I loved Sandy's genuine bubbly personality and her love for life. Many times Sandy had openly shared about her experiences as a Southern Baptist and a Christian athlete.

Later that evening, Sandy listened to my story and marveled at the names of the men who had spoken into my life over the weekend. She chuckled at my surprise when I learned they were all names of mighty men in the Bible. (Their names really were Peter, Paul and John.)

Acknowledging my desire for truth, Sandy talked about how Jesus died for love. A kind of love I'd never experienced before. The kind of love I felt for my child. The love I had for Jordan began to fill my heart. I started to imagine what it was like for God to see His Son die on a cross for sins He did not commit. I would die for Jordan, but I would never ask her to die for me. I still didn't understand why a loving God would, or could, allow His own Son to die. Why didn't He stop it? It still didn't make any sense to me. The more I learned, the more I questioned. It bothered me when Sandy responded with answers that seemed like circular reasoning to me. I tried to patiently listen, but the reasons weren't adding up.

But, out of all this came the question that really made me think. Why did it make me feel better to think God loved me?

Was I *that* desperate for someone to love me that I had to imagine an invisible creator that loved me? What difference would it make? Somewhere deep in my heart, I knew it did make a difference. A loving creator, a higher power, a possible purpose for my life, a hope that maybe I was loveable, despite my mistakes. But...I still had questions.

That night a conversation with Jordan would alter my understanding of God forever.

* * *

Jordan was still living with Payne in Texas and I called her every Sunday so she could read to me and tell me about her week. I called Jordan that evening to explain to her I was at Sandy's and couldn't talk long because it was long distance.

Jordan begged me, "Please, please let me read this book to you, I've been savin' it all week."

Still trying to process all the stuff that happened over the weekend, I resist and try to bargain with her and promise to call her again tomorrow.

"Plleeeeaassseeee, I've been savin' it just for you. It's not a long book."

"Okay Punkin, go ahead," I relent, "I'm listening." I settle deeper into my chair, close my eyes and focus on her sweet young voice.

"The book is called "God Knows How You Feel," she starts out joyfully, and reads a short story about how God knows my heartache, my pains, and all of my fears. He knows my doubts and He loves me anyway. The words wash over me. I feel vulnerable and exposed. Tears stream down my cheeks and I feel overwhelmed. For the very first time in my life, I feel loved by God. It reaches deep inside of me and melts my heart.

Okay God...you got me... I think to myself.

Jordan finishes the story as I weep quietly.

"Thank you, thank you, thank you Punkin!" I say through my tears. "That's exactly what I needed to hear."

"You're welcome. Did you like it?"

"Yes, yes I did. In fact, I LOVED it! Thank you so much for reading to me Jordan, it touched my heart." I wipe my tears on my sleeve. "I'll call you tomorrow when you get home from school, okay?"

We exchange our usual way of saying good-bye. "Okay Mommy, I love you ten tousand times I tell ya, I tell ya!" We wrap our arms around ourselves and squeeze at the same time for our long-distance hugs and say our good-byes.

I grab a box of tissues and briefly share the story with Sandy before saying good night.

*　*　*

As I close the door to the small stuffy bedroom I feel the onrush of emotions welling up inside of me. I fall to my knees on the carpet beside the bed and my hands grasp the plaid blanket as my body starts to shake and quiver. All the burdens I've been carrying around, trying to be strong, doing everything myself, feeling so alone, being afraid inside, feeling rejected by the world, feeling not good enough, all surface and I release my heart onto the twin bed. I weep long and hard, crying from somewhere deep within. I bow my head and ask Jesus into my heart. "Please forgive me God for being so angry with you. Sweet Jesus, please forgive me, forgive me, forgive me," I cry and cry. I weep for myself for the first time in a very long time. As my tears soak the blanket, my heart softens and I feel the stone wall built around it come crumbling down.

Eventually, my tears subside and I work my way up off the carpet. As I lay on the bed staring up at the ceiling, I feel accepted for the first time in my life. I don't have to be perfect. It's not about how I look, what I own, how smart I am, or anything I do…it's just…love. I feel loved just for being me. Just…because.

In those moments, I don't get all of my questions answered, but they don't seem to matter so much anymore. I feel loved. Even there by myself, all alone, I feel loved for the first time in my life. It's not about a man, or a job, or even having my child's love. I feel amazingly loved by a God that I don't know a lot about. The next morning, I feel light-hearted for the first time in my life. I feel free from my burdens and can genuinely smile and feel it all the way to my eyes. I left Sandy's with a renewed hope for my future.

When I called Jordan, I told her how much the book had really helped me and that I had given my heart to Jesus. I told her that when she came home, we would go to church together and I promised to start searching immediately. Jordan was excited and I was reminded again of her sweet words, "I'll believe for both of us until you believe." I felt so grateful...thank you God for her enduring faith!

{9}

LOVING FROM A SOURCE OF PEACE

I changed my mind and turned my life over to God. I remained true to my word and started searching for a church home. I picked random churches close to the house I was renting and attended weekly Sunday services. Craving acceptance and answers, I listened intently to the sermons. Many years had passed since I'd been involved in church and every one I attended seemed strangely hollow compared to the love I'd experienced in Sandy's guest bedroom.

Even in church people didn't talk much about why bad things happen. They seemed to struggle just as hard as my clients and I did. I shared my observations and frustrations during supervision with my boss, Jon. He told me that he met more sick and mentally ill people in church than he did at work. It was a profound statement that confused me, but stuck with me.

I experienced God's love when I made a choice to believe in Jesus, but I had to learn to act different. God loved me despite my past, but experiencing that love didn't answer all my questions or solve all my problems, so I continued to seek truthful answers to help myself, and my clients, make sense of our struggles, pain, and abuse.

Many of my battle buddies at work were Christians. I gained so much from their prayers, wisdom, and ongoing personal growth and support I experienced by working with them. I began to apply some Biblical truths in my classes and counseling sessions, using scriptures and words of wisdom I learned to help keep my clients sober, alive, and out of hospitals, or jail. I enjoyed the battle a little bit more now that I believed Jesus was with me, but I continued to have trouble identifying God as a loving Father since I'd never had one in my life. The only father I'd ever known was James and he still felt like my enemy. It was kind of easy to believe that Jesus loved me, but I still wasn't too sure about a loving God as a Father. I also continued to struggle in my relationship with my mom.

* * *

I graduated with honors when I completed my Master of Science degree in Counseling Psychology in May of '99. Mom drove to Virginia to celebrate my graduation from graduate school. I was the first of her seven children to graduate from college and then with a master's degree. I desired an acknowledgment of some sort from her. I wanted her to express pride in my accomplishments.

On the day of my graduation, because of all my hard work and diligence, I expected I would somehow feel smarter, more intelligent, or maybe a little bit wiser. I finally proved I have a brain and that I'm smart. However, despite my expectations, the skies did *not* open up the day of my graduation and shine a light of wisdom down upon me and Mom never said she was proud of me.

Silence.

The world kept turning and the battle around me kept raging. The battleground was the same, as was the fight. The only noticeable difference was the M.S. now following my name. Okay, that was anticlimactic...now what? Family?

* * *

I'd sworn off men until I worked on myself. I had learned not to expect a relationship to complete me and hadn't been on a date for about eight months. Not since Craig. Craig was tall, handsome, smart, funny, and showed up for our date wearing a black cowboy hat. My head and heart were still reeling from the wonderful evening of dinner and dancing we had shared when he was admitted to detox on a TDO two nights following our first date.

I was mortified when I walked into work and saw Craig, minus his cowboy hat, wearing the standard detox scrubs clients were required to wear. Despite my protests of conflict of interest, embarrassment, and shame; Jon smiled, and forced me to assess Craig anyway. I squirmed and grew through the assessment interview, the commitment hearing, his discharge, and then never saw Craig again. With that, I swore off relationships. However, God had other plans for me.

* * *

"I know a guy that is perfect for you," says T.J., one of my co-workers. T.J. promises that Ben is different than all the men I've met and dated. Ben is a pharmacist and T.J. describes him as intelligent, psychologically healthy, good-looking and talented. For three months I refused to go on a blind date with a long haired man who played in a band. My brother Jimmy asked me one day, "What do you have to lose? It's just a date."

What did I have to lose? I relented and finally allowed T.J. to give his friend my phone number. Ben and I played phone tag over answering machines and he asked me to come watch him perform in a local park. I arrived early, blended into the crowd, and sat down on the grass to watch Ben play guitar.

As I examined him from a distance, I was struck by his handsome dark eyes, olive skin and long black hair pulled back in a pony-tail. My heart stirred in my chest when I watched him humbly acknowledge the applause from the crowd with a genuine nod of gratitude. I loved how he closed his eyes when he played; genuinely focusing on the music he was creating and not on the dancing girls in front of the stage.

Following the short performance, I approached him as he stepped down from the stage.

"Hi!" I say, extending my hand in greeting, "I'm Tina."

"Wow, what a beautiful dress." he responds enthusiastically as his warm hand grasps mine.

"Thank you…you are Ben, right?" His band had introduced him as "Ben Jammin" and I want to confirm his identity.

"Yes, nice to meet you! I wasn't sure you were coming." He nods towards his equipment still on stage. "Could you give me a minute?"

"Sure. I'll be over there." I point to a bench.

As I head towards the bench, I realize my heart is beating faster, not in fear of rejection, but with excitement. Moments later, Ben joins me on the bench. We smile at each other and, very easily, delve into a conversation. Gazing into his deep brown eyes I feel like the world melts away. He seems so gentle and kind.

I tell him about seeking a church home and he said he recently realized his own need of returning to his spiritual roots as he was raised Catholic and then Lutheran. We agree to continue our date with dinner and as I walk away from the bench, I feel like I have just been reunited with my best friend after years of separation. So, in my head I began listing things I needed to "update" Ben on. It was the weirdest most exciting interaction I had ever experienced.

About an hour later, Ben drove his little red Honda into the driveway of my small rented house. My heart leapt in my chest when I saw that he had changed into dress clothes and was wearing a tie. We agreed on Italian for dinner and spent the evening discussing our lives and the expectations we each had in a potential mate.

In my head I evaluated Ben's psychological and emotional stability, conducted a mental status exam, and evaluated his pros and cons. I had developed a list of requirements for what I desired in a mate and Ben, not only met, but exceeded them all. It was one of the most honest conversations I had ever had on a date. I even told him I was a good liar…how is that for blatant honesty? I was tired of wearing masks and pretending I had it all together. Jordan was expected home after she completed her school year and I wasn't going to waste my time dating anyone who didn't have the requisite qualities of honesty and integrity.

Within weeks of our first date I knew with deep certainty that Ben was the man I wanted to marry and spend the rest of my life with…as soon as he cut his hair. That ponytail had to go. He felt the same way I did, even about his hair.

* * *

When Jordan finally came home from Texas I slowly introduced her to Ben. It was really rough at first as she expected it to be just the two of us when she returned. Eventually he earned her trust and Jordan came to love Ben as well. We continued visiting a variety of churches, but felt most at home and welcomed in a local Lutheran church led by a wonderful Pastor named Rod. I attended Sunday school with Jordan because I wanted to learn as much as I could and I also wanted to know what she was being taught.

All three of us became involved in our church through various activities, groups, trips, studies, classes and meetings. We loved the amazing people we encountered and Jordan had many wonderful experiences and eventually she found her three best friends in the church youth group. I took my faith very seriously and began studying and learning as much as possible.

On a very chilly Easter Sunday, when Jordan was nine years old, she was baptized in the Lutheran church: a choice she made on her own to demonstrate her faith and love for God, like her Nana had taught her. Before Ben asked me to marry him, he consulted with Jordan for permission and they picked out my ring together. Through God's grace and forgiveness, Ben and I would be able to provide a stable family for Jordan. A family based on love birthed from forgiveness.

All appeared right. I believed in Jesus, engaged to Ben who had Jesus in his heart, and reunited with Jordan who had Jesus in her life. But I still had a lot to learn about my identity and who God said that I am. I'd received forgiveness, but had not yet learned how to forgive freely. I appeared healthy on the outside, but I still suffered from internal injuries; scars from my past. As a result, I became a "walking wounded."

{ 10 }

WALKING WOUNDED

My mom has free long distance on the weekends and calls me every Sunday afternoon. One day she says nonchalantly, "James asked for your phone number the other day. He wanted me to ask you if it was okay for him to call you."

James always called Mom on their anniversary and her birthday every year. I don't know when he started this, but my brother Jimmy told me that James never seemed to remember his or Derik's birthdays, but consistently called Mom on hers, no matter where he was.

"WHAT?" I repute back to my mom, incredulously. "Are you kidding me? No! Absolutely not! I do **not** want to talk to him!"

"Okay," Mom responds, "I'll tell him." She quickly changes topics and we discuss her work week instead.

* * *

After their divorce in October of 1984, James moved back to Michigan. He moved in with another woman and they had a very tumultuous relationship. We heard stories of knife fights, stabbings, and domestic violence over the years. Eventually I guess he left the state again. That was many years ago and I couldn't understand why James wanted to talk to me now. I thought I'd dealt with my pain very effectively by writing him that letter so long ago. I held tight to the belief I could just "let go and let God." I'd confronted him in my own way and didn't want anything more to do with him. Besides, my life is going great! I do **not** need to dig up the past.

Mom didn't press me and we never spoke of it again.

* * *

It started insidiously. When my eyes opened at two o'clock in the morning, I didn't think much about it, just thought I wasn't tired. I used the wee hours to start reading a popular book called "Left Behind." It's the first book of a Christian series based on what the authors believe the end times will be like based on the book of Revelation. The book describes "the rapture" as occurring when all the Christians who believe in Jesus suddenly disappear, which marks the beginning of a period of fighting and was known as the tribulation. In the book, some people who said they believed in Jesus were not raptured and were, in fact... "left behind."

The book causes me to question if I believe "enough" to disappear with the rest of the Christians in the rapture. How much "faith" do I need? Is it based on my knowledge of the Bible? I've never heard of such a thing. I don't know the Bible well enough to have confidence in my faith. Pastor Rod recently taught our Sunday school class a song about the difference between goats and sheep. A song based on the end times, which separates those that truly believe, sheep, and those that don't, are goats.

"I just want to be a sheep, bah, bah, bah, bah." Jesus says He is a good shepherd and His sheep know His voice. "I don't want to be a goat, no, no, no, no!"

I am thirty years old, have an M.S. in Counseling Psychology, have jumped out of planes, and jumped off a cliff, but reading the "Left Behind" book scares me so much that when I finally go back to bed that night, I rock myself to sleep crying and singing, "I just want to be a sheep, bah, bah, bah, bah!"

The next night I woke up again around two a.m. and decided to continue reading. I didn't want to be deceived, so I read the book of Revelation and compared it with the book in the series. After reading Revelation I decided that I didn't want to be "taken up" in the rapture anyway; I want to stay and fight.

So, when I woke up at two a.m. the next night, and the next, and even the next night—I kept reading. But, it wasn't long before my two a.m. reading sessions started to interfere with my life and cause problems for me.

I was working full time at the residential substance abuse facility and had ongoing supervision from peers as well as supervisors. I loved my job, which consisted of counseling, facilitating both process and educational groups, and assessing clients for civil commitment hearings. I was striving for excellence through training, supervision, and case managing.

But, as time wore on, the nightly awakenings began to interfere with my ability to function. I started to experience emotional instability and had a hard time focusing at work. I became an expert in dealing with insomnia, applying the same skills I taught my clients: evening routines, preparing my body for sleep, refraining from reading or watching TV in bed, deep breathing exercises, diet, exercise, decrease caffeine, progressive relaxation and so forth. Nothing worked. My skills worked to get me to sleep, but they did not help when I woke up in the middle of the night. I began to monitor my sleep cycle and discovered my eyes would pop open at exactly two a.m. and I'd be awake for about two and a half hours before finally getting back to sleep around four thirty a.m., sometimes later.

My fiancé, Ben the pharmacist, encouraged the use of natural remedies like valerian root, melatonin and other over-the-counter sleep medicines. I tried several with a variety of success. The medicines would knock me out, but would leave me with a drug hangover so it became a balancing act of trying to find the right dosage to keep me asleep for the entire night without the annoying side effects the next day.

I didn't want to become addicted to anything, so I monitored my usage and stopped after a few nights of rest. My weekends became "sleep ends" where I took naps trying to rest enough to maintain my focus and energy throughout the week. I became sad and depressed and after a couple months of online research, consultation with peers, supervisors and friends, and experimenting with a variety of behavioral methods, I decided to go to the doctor and request an anti-depressant with a side effect of sleep. I discussed various options with my doctor who knew me well enough to know that I was not depressed. He refused to prescribe an antidepressant, but instead prescribed a short-term anxiolytic (anxiety medication to help me to relax) but he was not entirely convinced it would work for my situation.

Several months went by and my focus became singular in nature. All I wanted in life was to have uninterrupted, un-medicated, eight hours of sleep without having to work at it.

One day my awesome co-worker and friend, who likes the easy, shortened version of her name "Q", looked me straight in the eyes and told me my emotions were interfering with my work and I needed to go for counseling. In the counseling field it's wise to have a trusted counselor who "counsels the counselor," to help maintain accountability as an ethical professional. For me, it had been about eight months and many life events since I'd scheduled a "maintenance" session, so I followed her advice, and scheduled an appointment. That may seem like a 'no brainer', but it sure hadn't occurred to me!

*   *   *

It's four o'clock in the afternoon and I feel the warm sun shining on my back through the big bay window behind me. I'm sitting comfortably on the tan sofa cushions in Dr. Charlie's office with my hot cup of decaf tea on the wooden table to my left. Dr. Charlie studies my chart and re-familiarizes himself with my past and previous sessions we've had over the years. We chat about my upcoming wedding as he evaluates my mental status and records details in my chart.

"Tina, what brings you here today?" his warm brown eyes stare at me intently under his furrowed brow. "Your life seems to be going really well."

His fatherly concern touches my heart and tears sting my eyes. I breathe deeply, trying to control my emotions, and begin sharing all the struggles I've been having with insomnia and its side effects. Pure desperation creeps into my voice as I give him an overview of the methods I've tried and the situation that is threatening to overwhelm me.

As I finish my shortened version of the past few months, he taps his pencil to his lips and glances up at the ceiling. I can tell he is processing all that I'd shared, so I take a deep breath and relax my body. After a couple of seconds, he looks at me calmly and asks, "What happened three months ago when the insomnia began?"

Startled at the simplicity of the question I search my internal calendar of events. I calculate time frames and my focus narrows in on one afternoon, one phone call, one question, one person. James. The correlation dawns on me. Two a.m. was the time when he came into my bedroom in Florida to molest me.

Mom had said he wanted my phone number to call and talk to me. Wow! How could a simple request wield that much power over my life? I hadn't even thought about our conversation or my past since her phone call. How did James creep into my wonderful life without my awareness? It was like he'd skipped the third creaky stair from the top and passed right into my room. I felt violated again. How could I have allowed him to wreak such havoc? It's been almost twenty years since he molested me. I'm a professional counselor…how could this happen to me?

I processed the questions, feelings and events with Dr. Charlie. I left with an appointment for the next week, but I already felt lighter. I arrived home with a joy and a hopefulness I had not felt in months. Ben and I prayed that evening before bed and I slept an entire nine hours of glorious, drug-free sleep!

In psychology, what I experienced is called a conversion disorder, which is when a psychological event triggers a physical manifestation. Identifying the root cause usually takes care of the symptoms. It taught me a very important lesson. If I am experiencing any kind of physical or psychological problem: search my internal calendar and go back to where I lost my peace. Shine a light on it, pray about it and see if I notice a difference. Whatever is brought to my awareness take care of it right then. I didn't want to go back to being one of the "walking wounded."

I had shined a light on where I lost my peace, but instead of speaking out forgiveness, I became angry that James still had control over me. It didn't dawn on me to forgive him. I did **not** do what I had been counseling people to do for years. So, it was not long before I began experiencing an increase in cramping associated with endometriosis, symptoms consistent with low thyroid, and I began sleeping too much. And yet, every time I went to the doctor for help, I was told my lab reports didn't reflect a need for an increase in medications. At the time, I did **not** correlate my physical problems with the lesson I had just learned about James and my psychological insomnia because I was able to identify a root medical cause. I knew that I'd had problems with low thyroid in the past and thus, I kept my anger, my medical concerns, my resentments and…life moved on.

* * *

Ben and I were married in a beautiful church ceremony in June of 2001 and we finally became an official family of three. Jordan participated in the ceremony as we included her in reciting our vows. This time, I was surrounded by family and friends rejoicing in the mutual love, honor, and integrity our relationship was founded upon.

On our one-year anniversary Ben and I brought home my second child, Derik. Jordan adored him and had named him prior to his birth. To our delight he bore an amazing resemblance to my brother Derik with his beautiful brown eyes, matching hair and chubby little cheeks. Derik was welcomed home with love by Ben's parents, my mom, Penny, Jimmy and his fiancé who all visited for a few days to celebrate his arrival. Our home was filled with laughter and joy.

I chose not to send Larry a birth announcement as I didn't see the need, considering his previous lack of response. Ben couldn't understand my decision about not having an ongoing relationship with my own father based on the close relationship he had with his Pop. Still, I remained firm. I had learned to choose my battles and this one didn't seem to be worth the fight. I had other issues more pressing…

{ 11 }

THE FIGHT OF FAITH

Cindy had a gun. Throughout her frequent treatments she became one of my regular long term clients. I tried several times to persuade Cindy to get rid of the gun, but she would only place it in a lock box. She claimed she needed it for protection. She used to threaten me that if I called the police to do a wellness check on her, she would shoot at them and let them kill her. I rose to her challenge, giving her permission to kill herself, but then asked her why she would make someone else live with the pain of ending her life. I made it personal and told her to imagine the person who was called to the scene. It might be someone with children. I challenged her to think about what it would do to the children whose father had to deal with the pain of killing her. I had to get her to think about the impact of her actions on others more so than on herself. When that stopped working, I asked her who would be responsible for cleaning up her blood. What kind of trauma would that cause?

I knew Cindy and I knew her heart. The desire in her heart was to live, but that meant living with emotional suffering she did not know how to handle and was not willing, or able, to let go of. She ultimately viewed holding onto her pain as somehow hurting the other person. She defended her 'right' to be angry.

She was tormented by the demons of her past and they kept trying to get her to end her life. She also lacked interpersonal skills, so any time she experienced a new hurt, it would be added on top of all the other emotional pain and unforgiveness she was dealing with.

However, she did not want to be the cause of anyone else's trauma. Many times, that was the leverage I needed to keep her alive until her next session, or her next skills class. The goal was to keep her alive until she built a life worth living. I was shameless in the fight and she challenged me every step of the way. I used our relationship, her dog, her sister, her niece, her mom, anyone that I knew she cared about, as leverage to keep her alive until she accessed her own will to live. I did this by teaching her skills along the way and loving her as she was. I encouraged her by 'calling out her greatness' and I was not afraid to face the darkness because I had a big old spotlight I would shine on it. The darkness would flee long enough for her to learn a new skill to use for when it returned.

Over time, we developed a relationship and her trust for me increased. We began to dissect her trauma bit by bit, separating it into smaller parts capable of being dealt with and she became more skillful and knowledgeable as we progressed. We called it cleaning out her fridge. She had many periods of sobriety between binges.

The recovery center program grew and expanded. My role in our agency changed as well. I became a better teacher and counselor because she and other clients challenged me every step of the way. She told me I ruined her high because every time she would light up she would see my face.

"Good, I'm glad," I'd respond, "Maybe I should give you a picture of me to put on your fridge."

As our relationship grew, she began to share more of her story. Every time I challenged her I had to be one or two steps ahead of her. I used my knowledge to try and help her to forgive. I learned that when she was a child, she'd been abused and rejected by her father and he forced her to sleep on a blanket in a corner. Growing up, she was a tomboy and really wanted to fit in with the boys. But they tied her to a steering wheel and took turns raping her instead.

When she cried I comforted her.

When she was tough I was tougher.

When she was loud I whispered.

When she was bold I encouraged her.

When she was pitiful I challenged her.

Cindy was a Christian so when she had a problem forgiving herself I asked her, "Who are you to place yourself above God? He said you are forgiven. Do you know more than God? If you don't believe you are forgiven, then why did you ask Jesus to forgive you?"

* * *

When I wanted to give up on clients, I thought of my sister Marie who was struggling with her own alcoholism and growing list of labels. I tried to treat every client like I wanted a counselor to treat my sister. I lived so far away from her, I couldn't help her so I tried to help the one in front of me. I could only "give away" what I had. So, I sought more and challenged myself to go farther than my clients because I had to be at least one step ahead of them. I couldn't lead them if I was behind.

I sought out treatments that were proven to work and discovered Dialectical Behavior Therapy (DBT). DBT is one of the most researched treatment programs proven to significantly reduce suicidal outcomes. The well-documented therapy program involves fundamental daily skill building that I utilized to help Cindy and many of my other clients stay alive to fight another day.

However, the time-intensive comprehensive structured treatment program, required hours of supervision, specific trainings and an entire treatment team of therapists in order to be effective. It consisted of specific skills addressing all areas of life.

I loved it. I utilized the skills, diary cards and behavioral modifications in my own life and I taught them to my clients. I believed I'd finally found a "how to" for relationships, stress, honoring other people, thinking clearly, and handling emotions. Learning DBT helped me to be a better parent, spouse, and therapist, as my own past kept resurfacing during counseling. I was learning how to act lovingly and accept love from family and friends, but I had a hard time helping other people understand love. I couldn't give it to them: they had to experience it for themselves.

Although love is mentioned as an emotion in DBT it skips over how to love. In fact, I was learning that actually caring about clients and expressing an ongoing concern was a delicate balance. I was challenged to accept them in their current state, encourage them to trust me to not hurt them, *and* tell them that their behaviors were not acceptable or not effective. I also had to be rigorously consistent over time to develop their trust.

*   *   *

The phone rings.

I glance at my caller ID and recognize it as one of my clients struggling with anxiety and constant fear, which often led to cutting behaviors. I am sitting on the back deck of our newly rented house enjoying a few minutes of peace before Ben and Jordan get home.

*   *   *

Another component of the DBT program is allowing a client access to the therapist's phone number—one of the main reasons why many professionals do not participate. Phone calls between sessions allow issues to be taken care of quickly. Clients receive coaching on how to use their skills in the moment, as well as share their successes. The phone calls are supposed to be brief and have many rules attached, but they do provide ongoing "air support."

*   *   *

I take a deep breath and enter into the fray.

"Hello, this is Tina."

"I can't do this, I just can't…it's too much for me," Dante says. Dante is in his early twenties, very intelligent and is familiar with his skills, but has been afraid I won't answer his calls, or will be angry with him when I do. Despite my reassurances, he has resisted calling in the past, usually ending up in an emergency room and then a psychiatric hospital.

"Okay, I hear what you're saying. First of all, I'm really glad you called, that's real progress for you. What's going on and what skills have you tried?" He was beginning to trust me.

"I tried to use my mindfulness skills, but I keep thinking that I'm going crazy, I really want to go and get my knife."

Ignoring the knife comment for the moment I focus on skills. "Can you identify what state of mind you *are* in?"

"Yeah…obviously emotion mind." Dante responds with a hint of sarcasm.

*   *   *

DBT's mindfulness skills include three states of mind: emotion, reasonable and wise. Dante identified that he's in "emotion mind" which is allowing emotions to dictate behaviors. The opposite extreme is reasonable mind which is allowing pure reasoning, thinking or rationale to determine behavioral choices. The goal of using the "wise mind" skill is to identify the current state of mind and help move Dante from the emotional extreme to a more balanced center as a way of accessing his wise mind, which is a gut feeling, an internal 'knowing' or a certainty within–based on a balance of emotions and reason. Guiding him in this process will help him to trust himself and his choices in the future.

*   *   *

Our conversation continues as Dante and I join together and develop a skillful way for him to handle his emotions and urges. "Okay, hold off on acting out for a few minutes. Can you do that?"

"I guess."

"Great! What about broken record, you could speak out your positive affirmations over and over."

Dante pauses. "I can't think of any good things right now."

I am very familiar with Dante's positive affirmations as we had developed them together. I remind him of one that is opposite to how he is feeling in this moment. "How about, I am a calm and peaceful person?"

"I don't believe that."

"It doesn't matter. That's the point. You don't have to believe it yet; you just have to say it. Keep speaking it until you believe it, not the other way around."

Silence.

"Try it. Tell yourself out loud. I am a calm and peaceful person, I can do this, I can do this, I can do this. And pretty soon…you can!" smiling I think back to Stewart Smalley from "Saturday Night Live." "It will help you change your mind."

"I guess…okay." He repeats out loud the affirmations and I immediately hear a shift in his voice from hopelessness to hopeful.

"Okay, that's great. What else can you do? Look at your skills list and tell me at least two other things you are willing to do in the next twenty minutes so you can call me back and let me know how well they worked."

"Well, I could try "half smiling" and "opposite to emotions.""

Wanting him to be more intentional about using his skills I challenge him. "Okay, that sounds great. Are you going to *try* them or are you going to *do* them?"

"Um...I will...smile and listen to my favorite happy song."

"Awesome! That's sounds like a great plan! Will you put off getting the knife until you do those skills and then call me back?"

"Yeah."

"Okay, great! I am so proud of you for calling before you cut. That is really great progress for you! When you call back in twenty minutes we'll re-evaluate then, okay?"

"Okay, thank you."

I take a breath and refocus on my life. I hear the front door close announcing the arrival of my family. I don't get paid for phone calls and sometimes it interferes with my personal life, but I know it made a difference to Dante.

* * *

Examining Cindy's diary card I notice a pattern of negativity related to what she is listening to and her cutting behaviors. "Guard your ear gates and listen to upbeat songs."

"I like country," she says.

"I know," I respond. "You can listen to country, but not the 'My doggee ate ma chickennnn and left me with no dinnnner—my wife...she stole ma truck and I just want to die... cause I'm allll aalllloooonnne' stuff."

Cindy laughs. "Oh my achin ass."

I smirk. "Listen to stuff that is opposite to your emotions. If you are feeling bad listen to uplifting happy music."

* * *

I saw a bumper sticker hanging on a co-worker's wall one day: "Don't believe everything you think." It struck me as odd and I pondered what it could mean. In skills class, I taught clients how to hold every thought captive and examine if it was helpful or hurtful, to accept it as truth, or reject it as a lie, but I never wondered where a thought actually came from. Where else could a thought come from, if it wasn't from me? What did it mean? It stuck with me.

*   *   *

"I'm stupid," Cindy announces one day in skills class.

"Is that a judgment?" I ask.

"It's a fact," she responds.

Immediately grabbing the teachable moment, I lift my leg and plant my foot firmly in the middle of the conference table.

THUMP! The sound echoes in the small group room. Startled and confused, all six women focus on my foot.

"I have big feet!" I announce to the class. "Is that a judgment or a fact?"

"Umm..." Cindy looks at me.

"The fact is, I have size nine feet. It becomes a judgment when I start to think of them as being too big for a woman, or if I think of them as being good or bad, or if I believe women *should* have smaller feet," I explain.

"Okay," she responds, "I'm stupid it's a fact, because it just is."

"All right class...is that a judgment or a fact?"

"Judgment," they respond.

"Everyone look at that painting," I point to a watercolor print hanging on the wall. "Describe it for me. Tell me the facts."

I hear a variety of responses describing the painting as blue, square, in a frame, green, and then someone in the class says that it is pretty.

"Okay, stop right there. What's the difference? You described the facts up until the word pretty. Then you compared it to something...you judged it based on what you think of as being pretty or ugly. It's our beliefs and thoughts that make it a judgment."

Sara, a woman in her late thirties raises her scarred, burned, and tattooed arm, "We all judge...you can't not judge. That's impossible."

"That's true," I respond, "but, we choose what we judge and how we judge it. There are people who are paid for their judgments, like grocers. They are paid to judge whether or not fruit is good enough to place out for sale in the grocery store. Saying that an apple is bad is a short-hand way of saying it is not good to eat and will not sell. Judging fruit is helpful, judging people is not."

Lisa, a new member of the group, looks at me quizzically. "How do I do that?"

"Well, we judge what comes out of people's mouths, **not** the person themselves. We don't say that a person is bad just because he says something mean." I glance around the room to make sure I'm connecting with each of my clients.

"We examine the words (or the fruit as it were) and say the words are not helpful, effective or appropriate in a particular situation." I pause for a moment to give them an opportunity to grasp this extremely important concept.

"The person is one of God's creations. He or she is **not** bad...or *stupid*," I say, my eyes zeroing in on Cindy, who rolls her eyes at me.

"Oh my achin' ass," she whispers.

* * *

I am paid to help my clients no matter what bad things they have done. It is my job to help them build a life worth living. To keep them alive for another day, another hour, another minute longer so that hopefully they can learn new skills to live. I walk a delicate line between validating their identity of being a person worthy of being loved, and helping them to grasp the depth of damage done in their lives without destroying them in the process. It's challenging and I love it. But, it becomes even more challenging when clients struggle with spiritual issues that I don't know how to answer.

"God hates me." Cindy cries.

"Why do you say that?"

"Cause I'm gay. The Bible says He hates me."

"God doesn't hate you, He loves you." I know this is a source of pain for her and this is not the first session we've had on the topic. Cindy made a vow of chastity in her attempts to please God months ago, but had recently begun to have feelings for another woman.

"If God don't hate me, why does the Bible say He does?"

I want to believe God loves her just like He loves me, but I'm not quite sure how to respond to her questions. What made her same sex attraction, or struggles, any different from mine or anyone else's? I've been unfaithful, who am I to judge? Doesn't the Bible say "sin is sin"? I wait in silence for her to continue.

"I'm trying to be good," she continues. "I just want God to love me."

"Cindy, God knows everything. He knows you're trying."

Cindy verbalizes questions I struggle to answer myself. Does God love everyone...even the ones that don't believe in Jesus? The Bible identifies the "chosen" or "predestined" ones that believe in Jesus. I don't know the criteria, or if Cindy is one, or if I'm even one. What about my non-believing clients...are they unloved by God? When does God's love for His "children" start or stop? When do we even become "children"? Did God love me before I gave my heart to Jesus? I think so...my mind flashes back to when Jordan read the book to me about God knowing how I felt. I hadn't given my heart to Jesus yet, and God loved me...why wouldn't He love Cindy when she is struggling?

I attempt to help her in her pain. "If you had a child and you knew it would take your child ten times to learn how to walk, would you get mad at them if they fell down on the seventh time?"

"No," she responds.

"Do you remember the class on judgment?" I ask.

"Yeah, kind of."

"Well, judgments apply to behaviors, too," I explain gently. "God doesn't say you are bad and unlovable just because you make mistakes."

With that statement, I begin to think of all the mistakes I've made and God still accepted me even before I asked for forgiveness.

Silence.

I watch as hot tears stream down Cindy's face as the truth of my words tries to seep through the stone wall she has built around her heart. My heart aches along with hers and I make a firm decision to believe that God loves everyone...we are ALL God's creations. I think the Bible says one "sin" is no greater or less than the other. I convey my belief to Cindy and as the truth takes root in my heart; my words become more powerful and firm.

"God **does** love you, I **know** He does."

Cindy hates to cry, she says it makes her feel weak, vulnerable and out of control. As she struggles to suppress her tears I glimpse a crumbling of some rocks...a melting, a softening, and I am grateful and hopeful for her.

*　*　*

I met Cindy at the beginning of my graduate internship and had the honor of working with her off and on for almost ten years as I held a variety of positions in the community. I grew to love her. Sadly, Cindy never learned to forgive herself or others. If Cindy were alive today I would send her this letter from God and tell her to read it every day.

Dear Beloved,

I love you. You are worthy of My love. You are important to Me, and your life matters. I loved you before you learned about Me and I will continue to love you forever. That will never change.

I formed you, fashioned you, and knit you together inside your mother's womb. I took the time to create you in such a way that you are different from every single person on the planet. Every cell, hair, and molecule of your body are unique and tailor made to you. There is no one like you and you **are** the best you there is. I love you.

You are My amazing awesome creation. Before I created you, I imagined what you would look like: the color of your eyes, the shade of your skin and the shape of your face. I placed every freckle on you, and molded the curve of your lips and the roundness of your cheeks. I counted every hair on your head, placed every eyelash on your eyelids and only I know how many cells there are in your body. I love you.

You are My masterpiece–My beloved. I am well pleased with you and I love you. I was there the day you were born. I protected you and breathed life into your body. As I gazed upon you, My amazing creation, I saw your little eyes, your ears, and your little nose. I noticed the roundness of your nose and the fullness of your cheeks. As I held you, I breathed in the smell of your skin and listened to the beat of your heart.

I am the Creator of the heavens and the earth, the stars, the moon, sun and the sky. I held you and breathed in the smell of your skin and listened to your heart. As I held you against me, I whispered in your ear. "I love you! .... I love YOU .... I Love YOU!" I was there the day you were born.

I like how I placed your eyebrows and the shape of your ears. You look just the way I imagined you to be! I see Me in you! You are amazing! You look like Me! I love you and the way you look. You are unique! No one else in the world has your finger-prints, DNA or even the smell of your skin. No one talks like you, thinks like you, or creates in the same way as you do; you are unique.

I know you inside and out. I love your voice and the sound of your laughter! The thoughts I have towards you are more than the grains of sand upon the earth...and they are all good! I love you!

I watched you grow and learn, and, as you took your first steps–My heart grieved when you fell. As you grew, I heard your thoughts, rejoiced when you were happy, and I wiped away your tears when you were sad. I love you! I was there when you were hurting. I took care of you in ways you will never know.

I am your Father and I love you. You are no accident and you are not a mistake. You are not a bore, a bother or a problem. You are My beloved. I love you, I love you, I love you.

*I created you with special talents and skills only you have and I placed passions in your heart only you can fulfill. You are the best you there is! I know your thoughts, desires, hopes and dreams. I have such wonderful plans for you. AND I want you to know that I love you **not** for what you will do for Me, but just for **who** you are. It has nothing to do with how you perform, but just about who you are...you don't have to earn my love or try to be perfect...you already are. You are worthy. You are important. I love you!*

My love for you is not dependent on your beliefs or choices. My enduring love will remain and I will continue to love and choose you every single moment. My love for you is greater than any choice or mistake you could ever make! I know them all...it does not change My love for you. No matter what you choose to believe–I believe in you. Your choices do not change, or alter, My everlasting, enduring, eternal love for you.

NOTHING can separate Me from the love I have for you, My beautiful wonderful creation! No height, depth, power, principality, angel, or demon can ever separate Me from the love I have for you!

Trust Me. I love you. I love you. I love you. You are precious to Me. That will never change.

Love God

God loved me when I believed that I was unlovable, unworthy, ugly, stupid and useless. He did not count my angry, rebellious, cynical and sarcastic words and behaviors against me. God was not afraid or offended when I doubted, questioned, screamed or was abrasive. God loved me through it all and He loves you too. God knows how you feel. Beloved, if you have never accepted the love of God through Jesus you have a choice available to you. Perfect love always offers a choice.

My brother Derik modeled self-sacrifice in love by laying down his life for his friend. My mom forgave and Jordan interceded for me. Their behaviors highlighted a path for me to follow. Jesus showed me the path to follow too. He says in Luke 23:34, "Forgive them Father for they know not what they do." Jesus already prayed and paid for our forgiveness, all we have to do is agree with Him. God loves us and that will never change. Jesus shined a light on the path leading to our identity, identities birthed through forgiveness and love. I am interceding for you and "I'll believe for you until you believe."

You don't have to have it all figured out, just choose to believe that Jesus died so your heart can be cleansed of this worldly sin, sickness, disease and death, so you can experience God the Father's love fully and in a more personal way. It is your identity and it is your birth rite that is rooted and grounded in genuine love. A genuine love that will never go away, never leave and never end. It's your choice. Perfect love always offers a choice. God's not threatening you, He's not mad at you and God will always, always, love you.

Think about it.

Remember–all you have to do is change your mind.

{ 12 }

GROWING UP IN LOVE

As I was learning and growing in my ability to love more fully, I transitioned to work in an outpatient counseling program. I needed and desired experience in a different setting as a requirement for licensing as a professional counselor so I chose a family service agency. I did not want to be in private practice to be able to help only the people who could afford counseling. I wanted to have access to people who were un-insured, the ones, I believed, needed the most help. It was while working in that agency that I met another amazing family of professional battle buddies.

I was honored to work with co-workers and supervisors who challenged me to adapt my skills to the outpatient setting. I had to learn to be a kinder, gentler counselor because if I was the "Stone Cold" counselor I had earned the reputation of being in the residential setting; my clients wouldn't come back for their second appointment. I had to learn how to build long lasting rapport, earn trust and be consistent prior to confronting my clients. I had to demonstrate care and concern for clients before they were willing to trust me to help them facilitate change in their lives.

Ben wanted me to quit work and stay home with the kids, like his mom did with him. I refused as I had no clue as to how to be a stay at home mom. The only reference I had was my own mother and I did **not** want to be like her. I also really loved counseling and ultimately I wanted to be a successful professional and viewed just staying home with my children as some sort of failure. I had studied, trained and fought so hard to learn, grow, and apply all the lessons I learned through helping others that I didn't know how to be any other way. Ben reluctantly honored my choices and supported my desire to help people.

With the help of my co-worker, Vinnie, we created, implemented and facilitated a multi-family skills group for suicidal and self-mutilating adolescents. The program involved a weekly skills group for clients, along with their parents or guardians, individual sessions for the adolescent, family counseling, along with phone access for the adults and adolescents to help facilitate significant change outside of the counseling environment.

Counseling adolescents just struggling with daily life in group settings requires a lot of skill. The adolescent multi-family skills program consisted of ongoing weekly skills classes comprised of self-mutilating, often suicidal, adolescents labeled with personality disorder diagnoses, along with their parents in the same group setting. At times it was chaotic, exciting and scary. It was awesome and we loved it! Vinnie and I, as well as several other counselors who joined us in battle, fought for the lives of young people that no one else was willing or able to help. My goal of working with and helping adolescents finally became a reality.

* * *

"I wasn't talking about you!" Jen bursts out to Bree during group. Jen, frustrated with the ongoing situation turns her head and rolls her eyes towards her mother seated to her right. Bree, the heavier of the two girls, is dressed in designer sweats, a T-shirt, and her make-up and dark brown flowing locks are flawless.

Both girls attend the same school and ride the same bus. They are both vulnerable, emotional, and are often suicidal.

"Yes, you were…I know you were," says Bree with tears in her eyes. She struggles to control her emotions and hide the hurt, but the relationship means more to her than to Jen.

"How do you know…were you listening?" retorts Jen.

"No, but I know that you were 'cause you looked at me." Bree responds crossing her arms.

"Okay, okay…enough girls." I interrupt. "What's one of the rules of group that could help in this situation?"

Silence.

The girls fire dirty looks at each other.

"First of all, let's talk about assuming. Assume the best about the other person and in all situations. Will that help?"

Silence.

"Okay...let's say they *are* talking about you and they *are* looking at you *and* pointing...you could think...Hey! They're saying how great I look today, how awesome I am or how beautiful I AM!"

They smirk at me and roll their eyes simultaneously.

Silence.

"I'm just saying...choose to assume the positive, not the negative."

"It's also helpful to maintain an attitude of gratitude," says Vinnie.

"Right," I say nodding at him. "Choose to be happy, grateful and challenge yourself to find the good. Choose your thoughts and change your mind."

*   *   *

Later in skills class the girls continue to struggle with their feelings, so I lead them in a hands-on demonstration about perspective.

"Hey, let's try something; I want you two to sit across from each other."

Both girls roll their eyes, but obediently turn their chairs and face each other.

I hold up a book between them so each girl can only see one side of the book. "Okay," I say, "tell me what you see."

Each girl—in turn—describes what they see on their side of the book which is a completely different view from the other girl. One sees a picture and the title and the other girl doesn't see the picture, but the back of the book and the description. "Okay...are you both looking at the same thing?"

"Yes," they respond together.

"Then why are you both saying something different?" I ask them.

Jen answers first, "Because we are looking at it from different sides."

"Yes, now, how do you find out what the other person sees?"

Jen reaches out and tries to take the book and turn it around, but I stop her. "Nope! It is more effective for you to communicate what you see through talking."

Vinnie takes over and leads the girls through an exercise in active listening.

As he leads the exercise, I feel convicted. My mind flashes back to the argument I had immediately before I left for work earlier in the day. I am reminded that I need the lesson as well. I've been caught up in my belief that my point of view as Mom, counselor, professional, college graduate, experienced, older and wiser person was *the* only point of view that mattered with my own daughter. I was having difficulty listening and seeing life from Jordan's perspective.

*   *   *

Jordan is struggling with managing school and relationships. She is developing into an amazing young lady and I don't know how to relate to her. I'm struggling with my medical concerns, parenting a teenager and a baby, work, and chaotic friendships…among other things. I want to be her friend, but she needs a mother and I don't know how to be a loving mother to a teenager. I don't really have a frame of reference except to judge, label and categorize her mistakes and her "sins." Many of my friends are having a hard time with their teenagers as well and I am doing what I believe to be right, but I'm still struggling.

I believe that Jordan needs to be more grateful and hold tight to my perspective without realizing that she is doing her best in some of her own extremely difficult situations. Instead of assuming the best in my own daughter's—I've been pointing out her negatives.

The simple exercise I'm using with my clients is convicting my heart. I humbly admit that, even though I am teaching the class, and trying to get them to see the book from the other person's point of view. I too need to relearn the lesson.

Parenting doesn't come with manuals, but there are millions of books with numerous opinions, techniques and suggestions. I'd read so many, but I kept making so many mistakes with my own daughter, sometimes I felt seriously unqualified to counsel other people and their children. I was able to see what other people were doing wrong or how I could help them, but my relationship with Jordan was strained.

*　*　*

I battled for many people throughout the years and the most heart-wrenching ones were the adolescents. It broke my heart to see so many young people cutting, burning, scraping, scarring, carving, and mutilating their bodies; usually due to anger, resentment, and self-hatred. The numerous suicide attempts, fights, mistakes, and situations were gut wrenchingly painful. I fought for them, cried for them, and prayed for them. I confronted them, I challenged them, and I loved them where they were at.

Many of my clients recovered successfully, others had repeated hospitalizations with little progress and some eventually succeeded in taking their own lives. Learning how to escape their pain was a difficult process for them. Every time I wanted to quit, I thought about my brother, Derik, and his friends. I was reminded that I had not been invited—or equipped—to battle for his life. So, I fought for the lives of the adolescents that were in front of me. I fought for them the best I could with what I knew.

A huge lesson I learned while working with adolescents and their families, was that almost every single person involved, had their own list of hurts, wrongs, pains, battle scars and prisoner of war stories. It seemed like everyone was trying to escape from, or fight against something, that had happened to them. There were many times I felt like a parent, not only for the adolescents, but for the adults as well. It was a lot harder than I thought it would be.

I learned that many of the parents struggled with their own demons, not realizing how much their issues were directly affecting their children. I was experiencing the same struggle. Jordan was about the age I was when the sexual abuse from James was at its worst. I couldn't see that I was harboring resentments which kept a low level of anger just beneath the surface that often boiled over into my relationship with her.

* * *

Learning and growing with the group challenged me to do better with my relationship with Jordan and respect her perspective. I tried to honor her, but I lacked consistency.

I was able to recognize the need for basic honor to be established in the families I served. I thought of the honor I witnessed while in Korea. The Korean people demonstrated honor to family members and elders. Honor means to value something or acknowledge the worth in someone else. Honor is much more than a feeling. In the military I was taught to honor an officer with a salute from six paces away. Six paces. I think that's a good practice because you can only see the uniform, you don't have time to judge the character, choices, or appearance at six paces, which is equivalent to about twelve feet.

I want to take this opportunity to honor my own father, step-father and mother from six paces away. Yes…honor them. I honor their sacrifices, their lives and their "uniforms," and their identities as my parents. Thank you Larry and Karen for being my parents and thank you James for stepping into the role of parent in the absence of my own father. Parenting is hard, thank you for feeding, sheltering and providing for me. I am grateful for my life.

Everyone makes mistakes, and hurting people hurt people. The Bible says to "honor your father and mother." It does not say to only honor them if they made the right choices, treated us lovingly or raised us correctly…the way *we* thought they should have. It says to honor them. Period.

If all the people in my life who hurt me knew the amazing love of God, they wouldn't have made the choices they did. No matter what my family did, or did not do, God loves them just like He loves me. It's a fundamental truth, the beginning of my story…my inheritance. So, I honor my father, my step-father, and my mother right now…six paces away…I honor their lives.

* * *

Although I knew intellectually God loved me, I struggled with feeling loved. I rationalized through honoring my family and examining life from their perspectives, and it helped me to be more empathic towards them and move forward in my life. However, there were still times that I felt like I was stuck in the past.

{ 13 }

GLIMPSES OF THE ENEMY

"**H**e's the tall blonde guy facing the wall at the end of the hall," replies Judith, the psychiatric nurse nodding her head in the direction of a small cluster of patients gathered at the end of the long corridor waiting for their civil commitment hearing. "He's kind of creepy," she adds.

"Creepy...hhhmmm...nope, don't think I've seen that diagnosis in the DSM-IV," I respond wryly.

"You know what I mean, Tina," she retorts, giving me a stern look. "He's one of those odd ones." Judith has short reddish hair and a spunky spirit that accurately matches her hair. She has been a psychiatric nurse for many years and her genuine love for people shines through in her sense of humor.

"Is that what you want me to tell the judge?" I smile at her and wink. She pretends she is going to hit me with a chart as I duck and scurry out of the nurse's station hugging Mr. Jones's chart.

*   *   *

When I became licensed as a professional counselor (LPC), I obtained a position with the Supreme Court of Virginia as an independent evaluator for civil commitment hearings. The position was similar to the one I performed while working in the residential treatment setting, but instead of helping to coordinate the civil commitment hearing process, I was paid to replace the medical doctor as the professional independent evaluator.

Prior to the hearings, I assess patients to professionally gauge their potential to harm themselves or others. I document delusional or psychotic behaviors as well as auditory, visual hallucinations and determine their ability to function effectively in society. I review charts, interview staff, and speak with the patients in an attempt to accurately understand their world view and the events leading to their temporary detainment. Patients have the option to volunteer, or be involuntarily committed, to receive treatment as a means of keeping society safe from those who are deemed as having a mental illness. If they exhibit an inability to care for self, the state steps in to provide the necessary care.

My position was very challenging and required me to stay up-to-date on psychiatric medications, laws and regulations along with current trends in alcohol and drug use while expanding my working relationships in the community. I enjoyed being an integral part of the civil commitment hearings. It was always interesting and challenging. However, Mr. Jones challenged me in a way in which I was not prepared.

*   *   *

Walking towards the end of the hall, I turn my attention to the chart in my hands. I notice the sparseness of nursing notes on Mr. Jones and the vague terminology like "aloof" and "odd in nature" used to describe his behaviors and the interactions he had with staff and peers. The diagnosis is vague–Psychotic Disorder not Otherwise Specified–which means that Mr. Jones meets some of the criteria, but not all, in the category of psychotic disorder. Upon further examination of his chart, I notice that he'd been prescribed a standard anti-psychotic with no significant change in behaviors.

"Excuse me, Mr. Jones, I'm the independent evaluator assigned to assess you for your hearing. May I speak with you for a moment?" Although his back is towards me, I know he hears me because I see his muscles tense through the flimsy hospital scrubs and his shoulders square as he turns to face me.

The first thing I notice is the color of his eyes, they seem almost black. As he faces me and looks into my eyes I feel a sudden drop in air temperature. Along with the sudden chill, I become immediately aware of an uneasiness in the pit of my stomach. Surprised by my feelings I falter with my introduction.

"Um…How are you today?"

Silence.

"What…um…brought you to the hospital?" I focus on his chart to collect my thoughts and regain my composure.

Silence.

I look up and his stare is unnerving. It's not just his stare, but the intensity, almost like he can snap at any moment. He retells a short version of the events leading to his hospitalization in a hollow monotone voice.

I glance back at his records to cover my increasing uneasiness.

I continue with the interview and Mr. Jones responds with short answers void of emotions. His black fingernails, dark eyes and intense stare continue to unnerve me. I gather enough information to make my recommendation and excuse myself from the assessment.

Walking away, I feel his eyes on my back and my mind flashes back to a time long ago when I felt something similar, but I can't put words on it or identify it. I ignore my feelings and objectively evaluate the psychiatric implications of his symptoms to formulate my recommendations.

* * *

Mr. Jones enters the room for the hearing and the coldness I felt in the hall sends a chill up my spine, and the uneasiness returns to my stomach. When he sits down across from me at the table, the intensity of his presence in the small room is unpleasant. As the judge reviews the paperwork, examines his chart, and conducts his own interview I feel an urge to recite The Lord's Prayer in my mind, but I can't remember the words. I can't get past, "My Father in heaven" so I repeat the phrase over and over in my head. I start to feel almost dirty sitting in his presence and I don't know why. I glance at the judge and he does not seem to be affected. I provide my recommendation for involuntary commitment and Mr. Jones doesn't even look in my direction.

The hearing ends, I gather my belongings and exit the building. Despite the warmth and bright sunshine, the disturbing nature of our interaction lingers. In my attempt to shake the feeling and clear my mind, I head to Starbucks for a strong dose of caffeine. As the caffeine kicks in and I start to feel more like myself, questions flood my mind.

How could his mental illness affect me like that? Why couldn't I remember The Lord's Prayer? I recite it in my mind just to make sure I remember it...yup, all there. But why did I even feel compelled to recite The Lord's Prayer? If psychiatric illness is a chemical imbalance, why was I affected to my core? It's not that I was fearful for my safety, but there was a feeling of intensity that I can't explain or diagnose. The judge didn't seem to be uncomfortable, why was I?

The strange feelings remained with me for hours. The questions from that interaction lingered even longer.

* * *

I began to notice more and more of my regular clients, as well as the people I assessed in the psychiatric hospitals, reported ongoing symptoms of unexplainable feelings, symptoms and experiences that psychiatric medications were not working to suppress, manage, or maintain. I also noticed that the most tormented, medicated clients were of the "religious" type. I assessed people who identified themselves as Moses, Mary—the mother of Jesus—and even Jesus himself. I also assessed more clients like Mr. Jones and began to question the validity and reliability of some of the psychiatric medications. I was very grateful to have my own pharmacist at home to ask questions about some of the meds.

"I met Jesus today." I tell Ben one day after an especially long day of hearings.

"Really?" Ben raises his eyebrows. "Interesting."

"Yes, and if you are looking for him he was involuntarily committed," I smirk. "Just sayin'."

"You committed Jesus?" Ben continues, "Did you get to talk to him?"

"He wasn't really Jesus, Ben!"

"I know, but I'd still like to talk to him."

"Well, he's probably doing the Thorazine shuffle by now, so it wouldn't be much of a conversation," I respond, a little more thoughtfully. The prevalent treatment for psychotic or delusional disorders is to tranquilize the person which ultimately interferes with their ability to communicate effectively as well as their motor functioning.

*   *   *

Another one of my clients struggles with disassociating and "losing time." Heather's entire life history had huge gaps to which her mind does not allow her access, and she struggles with her identity as a result. We have weekly individual sessions and she also participates in the weekly skills class. Heather is usually late or doesn't show up for our sessions, but today she is on time.

"I lost time again," Heather says dejectedly. She hands me her skills card and slumps into her chair.

"How much?" I ask gently.

"Two hours on Saturday…and I missed work." She begins to sob softly. "I didn't mean to."

Sometimes the time gaps last only a few minutes, other times it lasts for hours. When it's really bad she loses days. She genuinely tries to use her coping skills and is extremely motivated to do better. Heather shares that she made it to our session because she asked her case worker to pick her up an hour early and she sat in the lobby waiting for forty-five minutes so she wouldn't miss her appointment.

"I hear you, I know you didn't mean to. Let's look at your diary card. What were you doing right before you lost time?"

"I was getting ready to leave, I was dressed fifteen minutes early and I was excited. I sat down at the kitchen table to put my shoes on and the next thing I knew it was over." She sobs openly, "My boss is going to be so upset with me! I don't know what I'm going to do, I just want to die."

I ignore the die comment for now and return to the moment she sat down in her kitchen. I encourage her to identify the last sense she remembers. I prod her to practice recalling every "body memory" in hopes of teaching her how to ground herself in the moment. We spend time identifying the smells, sights, sounds and feel of my desk, her chair as well as the visual experience of the paint on the walls and the decorations in my small office. This is not our first session addressing this and the process is slow, tedious, and frustrating for her. We tried many strategies over the years and sometimes therapy worked, sometimes it didn't. But the psychiatric medications sure weren't working and alcohol made her suicidal.

"You did a really good job with identifying your senses. Let's move to repairing your relationship with your boss." We get out her list and review the skills. Noticing her abilities in some areas and her resistance in others, I lead her to an area where she has had difficulty in the past.

"How about asking for forgiveness?" I suggest.

"She's tired of me saying I'm sorry."

"Are you sorry?"

"Yes."

"There is a difference between being sorry and asking for forgiveness," I explain. "Saying 'I'm sorry' makes you sound apologetic for *who* you are rather than asking forgiveness for *what* you did."

I pause.

"Your identity, or who you are, is not made up of one behavior that you did." I continue with my short teachable moment. "You didn't intend to disappoint her, that wasn't your heart. You are not sorry...you are awesome."

"I'd rather just kill myself...that would be easier." Heather responds totally ignoring the teachable moment.

I rise to her verbal challenge and meet her there. "Okay, let's get out a sheet of paper and look at the pros and cons of killing yourself."

"Great...another AFGO," rolling her eyes.

"AFGO?"

"Another F'in Growth Opportunity," she smirks.

"Is that what you call your skills? That doesn't sound very positive. Can we change that?"

"No...I'm tired of trying stuff that doesn't work!"

"I hear you and I know you've struggled," I sigh. "However, there is the power of life and death in your tongue. Let's speak positive and speak life. How about we change it to Another Faith Growth Opportunity, okay?"

"No, I really like mine."

"Okay...AFGO it is...get your paper," I say. Reflecting silently—I choose my definition.

* * *

The more I worked with Heather, and my other clients, it became increasingly obvious there was something more going on beyond what I could counsel. And I had numerous clients in which no amount of psych meds would help. They spent their time trying one after the other. Sometimes the side effects were too much for them to handle and they had to change meds. It was an endless game of trying to balance the effectiveness of the medications versus the negative side effects.

Ben and I discussed medications on many different occasions and he confirmed that many doctors, psychiatrists and even pharmacists do not know why specific drugs work for certain disorders. Sometimes a drug is released for one reason only to find out it works for a different disorder instead.

Psychiatric medications are used to treat the symptoms of mental illness and to maintain public safety. People who admit to experiencing auditory and/or visual hallucinations, once diagnosed and labeled, face a life-long medication management issue.

* * *

John is the cutest little alcoholic paranoid schizophrenic man I've ever met. His scruffy little beard, piercing blue eyes, dirty fingernails, and frail frame mask his heart of service, gentle demeanor and sweet disposition. He is another client we endearingly term a "frequent flyer" in the residential program. John has a loving heart, but struggles with auditory and visual hallucinations. He's sitting quietly in my office as I observe him. He has a funny little smirk on his face as he sits gazing at his knees. I watch him for a while before I speak.

"John, what are you doing?"

Looking up, his blue eyes clear and he focuses on my face. "I'm watching the little green men."

"Little green men?"

"Yeah, I know they aren't real," he pauses, "but, they are fun to watch."

"What are they doing?"

"Tricks mostly." John pauses. "They go up and down my legs, kind of like a circus show."

"Okkaayy." I respond slowly as I scan his paperwork searching for his next psych appointment. "Do they talk to you?"

A pained look crosses his face. "I know they aren't real," he says quickly, "but every time I tell people about them, they up my meds. I don't like my meds. I'd rather drink."

My heart went out to him. He had a long history of being placed on Haldol, Thorazine, and other medications that basically turned him into a zombie. Sometimes when he came in he was battered and bruised from being beat up while living on the streets. When his treatment time ended—and John was released back into the community—he stopped taking his meds and drank instead. It was a vicious cycle for John; I didn't have much hope for his situation. It didn't stop me from loving his heart. I loved it when he came in and "dried out" and it broke my heart when he left. I couldn't help him.

*　*　*

I examine Missy's chart and note her long list of hospitalizations, psychiatric admissions, medications, and suicide attempts. The 14-year-old sits silently in her chair with her knees drawn up to her chest and her chin resting on her knees.

"Why do you think you can help me? No one else has been able to," she says dejectedly.

I hear the hopelessness in her voice and my heart aches in my chest. I notice her soft brown curls falling loosely around her heart-shaped face as I thoughtfully examine her arms where there are over one hundred different scars. Self-inflicted scars upon scars, burns from cigarettes, and even the words "bitch" and "slut" carved on her skin. My heart breaks as I think about the many more that I can't see on her legs and even her stomach. I want to weep for her, but I know it's not my pity she needs—it's my help.

Her parents are Christians. She'd been baptized as a child and raised in church. According to her chart, she'd tried to fit into youth groups, but never felt accepted at school, home or church. The only places where she felt accepted and treated as "normal" were institutions and hospitals. My job in this moment is to instill hope and confidence in her concerning my abilities and our program, but I find myself struggling to see hope for her. So I keep quiet and wait.

"I see things ya know," her eyes glaze over in her moment of vulnerability. "No matter what meds they put me on, I still see them. My mom and dad fight about what to do with me every time I come home."

Silence. I wait.

Missy is quiet for a few minutes before she continues; her voice even softer than before. "I can't tell them about the visions because, when I do, they send me away."

"I believe you." I respond quietly and thoughtfully.

I do believe her; I just don't know how to help her. Will her life be like John's? Will it be an endless battle between medications and managing the side effects, or will she choose to escape through alcohol and drug use? How do I instill hope when my own hope is dwindling?

*   *   *

While I've highlighted some of the most difficult cases I encountered, I loved helping people through counseling and there are many success stories. However, even the ones who used the skills and worked really hard tended to gravitate to a life of suffering and pain and sometimes gave up in the end. Giving up either meant a return to drug/alcohol use, or the more permanent escape of suicide.

The people I remember most vividly are the ones that I lost because I believe I failed them. Like Heather, who was no longer my client when she finally succeeded in ending her own life. We never did determine the reason why she "lost time." If she were alive today, I'd send her this book and ask her forgiveness for not having the answers to help her create a life worth living.

I sought out supervision and trainings and tried to live my professional and personal life with joy and thanksgiving. There were many times, even as a Christian, I struggled to adhere to the promise I'd made in my youth to be positive.

There were times, as a Christian, I felt even more judgmental and critical of others because I now had a Bible that, I believed, gave me the 'right' to judge, categorize, and assess people's choices, beliefs, and behaviors as being "sinful." It wasn't really a conscious choice that I made to be that way, but more of an insidious one that I learned over time.

Ben and I loved our church family and, over the years, served in our Lutheran church. Ben taught Sunday school and Bible study, was elected to council and headed up the Evangelism team. He also wrote articles for the monthly newsletter. I taught Sunday school for a while, drove the church bus, participated in mission trips, and formed and coordinated a care ministry consisting of volunteers willing to help each other with a variety of needs including grocery shopping, transportation, prayer, meal prep, home communion, lawn care, birth of children, even bereavement meals.

We were also active in the Walk to Emmaus community. The Emmaus Christian community encourages Christians, through sponsorship, to participate in a sequestered weekend retreat consisting of a series of fifteen talks. They call these retreat weekends 'Walks' and the participants 'Pilgrims.' During the long weekend, the Emmaus community demonstrates love to the pilgrims in a tangible way. One of the fifteen talks focuses on forgiveness and encourages the pilgrims to let go of past hurts. Pilgrims are encouraged to identify a past hurt and pair it with a small stone, choosing when to throw it away, or allow it to remain symbolically by carrying it in a pocket. Ben went on his Walk first and a year later I was blessed to go on my own Walk. We sponsored several people over the years and participated in other ways as well.

Jordan also participated in several retreats, attended her own Walk, went on mission trips and participated in youth groups and service projects. Our faith life was a family affair and we all really enjoyed it.

For several years I participated in a Saturday morning women's Bible study called Women In Need (WIN) along with events they sponsored. Once that ended, Ben and I held a weekly Bible/book study in our home for four years, with a focus on building relationships, supporting each other, and gaining confidence in our faith by praying out loud for each other. Ben and I partnered with Joyce Meyer, a Christian author and speaker, listened to her teachings and even participated in the Franklin Graham trainings with his crusade of volunteers. We had an amazing, wonderful group of friends and co-workers who encouraged us and supported us.

Even though it appeared that I had, in fact, created my own life worth living, I still struggled with an underlying anger and desire to control things, which would often show up in fights with Jordan. I felt like a hypocrite because I was teaching relationship skills to my adolescent clients, their parents, helping my friends and families, but couldn't get along with my own daughter. I knew better, but was having difficulty consistently applying it to my own life. I *knew* better, but couldn't *do* better.

*   *   *

As I tried to educate and teach my clients to listen to their own "wise mind" I examined my own and discovered sometimes that my "wise mind" would say things to me that I wasn't too sure about; things that sometimes didn't even seem like me. It was like God's still small voice as described in the Bible, but sometimes…it was a little louder.

{ 14 }

FOLLOWING ORDERS

It is a beautiful warm evening and I am nursing Derik in my favorite blue plaid overstuffed chair. The big house is quiet and I am thoroughly enjoying my life. My thoughts are focused on my beautiful son in my lap when I hear a very clear voice inside my head.

"Forgive your father."

What?

"Forgive your father." I knew it wasn't my suggestion or my thought.

Why?

"Forgive your father."

Is this God? I quickly assess my own psychiatric stability. Assuring myself that I'm psychologically stable, and decide that it must be God…I continue with the internal dialogue.

He doesn't care about me…why should I forgive him?

"Forgive your father."

He's never tried to contact me; why should I forgive him?

"Forgive your father."

What should I forgive him for? Not caring?

"Forgive your father."

My thoughts drift to the lessons I was teaching my clients and their families about honoring their parents. I rationalize forgiveness in my head and consider my options. I choose to be obedient, to lead by example…I acquiesce.

FINE! I forgive my father.

"Call him."

What? Really?

"Call him."

Ugh.

* * *

It was the summer of 2002. I'd written Larry off and had no intentions of reuniting with him much less forgiving him. I still couldn't believe he'd never responded to Jordan's birth announcement.

Penny, the only one of us five girls to maintain contact with him, talked about him occasionally. Over the years I'd gleaned through conversations with Penny that Larry was sick. I really didn't care. Why should I care about him being sick when he obviously didn't care what was going on in my life? He could've asked Penny for my number, I reasoned, so he could have easily contacted me. Why did I have to be the one to take the first step and forgive? I also didn't think I had much to forgive Larry for because I never had any contact with him. How could he hurt me if I didn't care about him? I'd had enough to forgive with my step-father. I didn't understand why I had to forgive Larry, too. I wanted to honor him from a distance...and stay at a distance...but...out of obedience... "ugh."

Reluctantly, I contacted Penny who was happy to provide Larry's phone number in Illinois. I decided to call before I changed my mind. I spoke first with Janet, Larry's wife—the same woman Larry abandoned his family of five for when I was a baby. She confirmed that he was very sick. Larry had been diagnosed with bone cancer several years prior to my call and wasn't expected to live long. Ben and I prayed about it, and in October of 2002, I made a decision to load up Jordan and four-month-old Derik to make the fourteen-hour car trip from Virginia to visit the man who had given me life. Although I had learned to appreciate my own life, I struggled with my perceptions, emotions and my own judgements of viewing him as not much more than a sperm donor.

The visit was quick and void of a lot of emotions. Janet turned out to be a genuinely sweet woman and his daughter, my half-sister, who was a year younger than me, was amazing and wonderful. We didn't talk much about the past, or why things happened. When Larry tried, I told him the past was between him and God and I forgave him, period. I wept several times during our long car ride home, but felt truly grateful that I'd chosen to be obedient.

Through honoring Larry as my father, I'd forgiven AND I even traveled to visit him to meet his family and spoke forgiveness in person. Ben and I returned to our lives and I felt released from my responsibility. I added them to the Christmas list as part of "our family" and kept in phone contact for a while. I was feeling pretty smug in my behaviors as an obedient, forgiving Christian...but the voice was not done issuing orders...

*   *   *

During one of our Friday night book studies we read "Divine and Human and Other Stories" by Leo Tolstoy. One week we read a short story called "Stones." The story compared two women who went to a saintly old man to learn from him. The first woman thought of herself as a great sinner, was constantly tortured by her guilt and even though she repented and was tearful, thought she could never be forgiven. The other woman lived all her life according to the law and had committed no serious sins. She never really examined herself and was pretty pleased with her life.

The saintly old man listened to them and told the first woman to go and pick up a large rock and the second to pick up a bag of small stones and return to him. They did as he asked and then he instructed them to take the rocks and put them back exactly where they'd found them.

The first lady did so easily and returned quickly, but the other lady couldn't remember where she had picked up each specific stone so she gave up and came back still holding the bag full of stones.

The man then addressed the women and told them it was the same with their sins. The first lady was humbled by her sin, knew exactly where she'd picked it up, and therefore, was able to lay it down and be forgiven. She had also lived a life humbled by her sin and therefore she was mindful to not increase her sin, or her load, by harming others.

The second lady was told she couldn't return the stones because she didn't remember where she found each small stone. He told her she had sinned in small ways so many times, she didn't really remember them, couldn't confess them and, as a result, had grown used to a life of sin. In addition, through condemning the sins of others she had sinned more and more.

The story resonated in my heart and convicted me as I examined my journey and the stones I had been dragging around throughout my life.

*   *   *

Penny contacted me when Larry's condition grew worse. Ben and I prayed about it again and felt like I needed to return. So, I made plane reservations for the beginning of April 2004. Penny called again two days later to tell me Larry had had a heart attack and told me that he might not live until April. So, in March, I drove up to meet her in Ohio and we traveled together to spend a few hours with him so I could say my final good-byes.

*   *   *

The few hours Penny and I spent with him that day were short and emotional. Larry had just received his last rites from the Catholic priest earlier that day and actually seemed almost joyous despite the situation. We bought lunch from a local restaurant and he ate solid food for the last time. We said our tearful good-byes and I told my father I loved him. I left feeling grateful I'd made the trip.

After returning home, I felt a gnawing in my stomach, a sense I hadn't done something I was supposed to do. During an afternoon nap, I tossed and turned and made a quick promise to God that I soon regretted. I hadn't cancelled my flight plans, so I promised God that, if Larry lived until my scheduled trip in April, I would return to visit him and do whatever God told me to do.

As the day approached, I found myself dreading my flight. I felt guilty that I was dreading the trip because the alternative was that he'd died. I didn't want to go and spend time with Larry by myself. It was easier visiting with my sister, or my husband. I had told Janet that I would stay with Larry during the day so she could work to help out with their finances and give her a break. Plus, I was going to sleep on the couch while I was there, so there was absolutely no privacy whatsoever! Old, painful thoughts resurfaced and threatened to harden my heart. But, I'd made a promise to God and I had no plans of going against my word. Out of pure obedience, I boarded a plane and flew back into my past to provide care for a man who had never ever taken care of me.

{ 15 }

LETTING GO

His shallow breaths stop. I look up from reading my Bible to watch his chest. I silently begin counting: one, two, three, four, five, six, seven, eight...his gasp breaks the silence. Sighing, I take a breath as well as I become aware my breathing had stopped along with his. I watch his chest rise and fall for a few minutes before turning my attention back to my Bible, open on my lap, but the words blur as the gravity of the situation grips my heart. I glance around the small room in an effort to control my emotions.

My biological father is lying on his back on a twin bed, his long, thin frame visible under a light blanket. I am sitting a few feet from him, cross-legged on another twin bed. My eyes are drawn back to study his face. My eyes trace the outline of his facial features in the afternoon sunlight shining through the small window. I look intently at the wrinkles, sunken cheeks and pale skin. As I examine the face of the man lying across from me I wonder what kind of father he was to his other children. They seem to love him very much. I begin to wonder what my life would have been like if he hadn't left, if he had stayed and been my dad.

His shallow breaths stop, demanding my attention, and I mentally tick off the seconds in my head. Ten seconds pass this time before his gasp breaks the silence.

Please Lord don't let me be here alone with him when he dies. I pray silently.

"Forgive him."

I have...what do you think I'm doing here?

"Forgive him."

Okay. I forgive him, I forgive...you...I forgive you...I forgive...

My internal dialogue with God is interrupted by a sudden stirring in the bed as my father's eyes flutter open. His eyes search the room and settle on my face. As recognition registers in his eyes a smile spreads broadly across his face.

"You do love me," he whispers quietly.

"Yeah Dad, I do, I do love you." Tears slip down my cheeks as I smile back at him. He closes his eyes, the smile still lingering on his face. "*And...I forgive you...*" I whisper.

* * *

The Lord answered my prayer. I was not present when my father passed from this world, but that earlier moment with him is forever etched in my memory. I felt like I had been obedient to what God asked me to do and been forever blessed because of it. I had peace when I boarded the plane taking me back to my life.

My father died on April 30, 2004, at the age of 67, knowing I'd forgiven him from my heart and that I loved him. I chose not to attend the funeral. I grieved at home, reliving those final moments and feeling grateful for the freedom that forgiving my dad and obeying God had given me. I had released my enemy through the power of forgiveness and God allowed me to help my Dad put back one of his "stones."

* * *

Sadly, this lesson came too late for me to have a more meaningful relationship with my mom. It was soon after my father died that she was diagnosed with lung cancer which had metastasized to her liver. I rushed to her side to be with her, but it was my sister Penny and my nephew Gregory who really were Jesus to her when she needed it the most. It wasn't me. I prayed for her recovery, but never thought to work on our relationship because I thought *she* was the one who needed to change.

I thought I'd forgiven my mom because I was able to have an ongoing relationship with her. When I'd participated in the forgiveness activity during my Walk to Emmaus weekend, I picked up one stone for my mother and carried it around all day until I decided to let it go and spoke out forgiveness. I thought that was all I needed to do. I never talked with her about it directly, and never did speak words of forgiveness to her. I had numerous opportunities to release us both but it never even crossed my mind.

For years, before her illness, she had free long distance on the weekends and consistently called every Sunday. The calls usually involved me listening to the long list of wrongs and injustices she experienced during her work week. Mom carried her past and her hurts with her, every new hurt adding to her pain. It didn't matter how I would try to steer the conversation to the positive, it invariably led to negative thoughts and words.

Mother's Day was always a difficult holiday for me. I dreaded the long aisle full of cards gushing and professing how awesome and wonderful relationships with Moms were and I felt sorry for myself. It was difficult to say any loving things toward my mother. I knew the reality of our relationship, I remembered the abuse and neglect, and I usually resorted to purchasing a sarcastic or humorous card.

I never realized that the difficulty was because I had un-forgiveness and bitterness in my heart. My sister Penny was actually more of a Christian than I was because she was able to move past Mom's rejection of her, and all that pain, and see the soft interior. My mom was just a "tootsie pop" who had been hurt many times and didn't know how much God loved her. And there I was with my "Christian badge" on, judging her and trying to get *her* to see *she* just needed Jesus. I was busy defending my position and didn't even bother trying to see hers—to understand her experience of rejection, hurt, and bitterness.

I could have been shining a loving light into her world and highlighting how much God loved her. Instead I missed out on having a more loving relationship with my mom because I was guarding my heart just like she was, and carrying around more than one stone. I had a bag full of stones and didn't even know where I had picked them up. "Please forgive me, forgive me, forgive me."

In my wisdom, I wanted my mother to have an "attitude of gratitude" and view her cancer as an opportunity to cherish the people around her. However, the times that I was able to be there for her, her negativity affected me and increased my frustrations. Right before she started her chemo therapy, I discovered I was pregnant with Carter, my third child. I hoped my pregnancy would help motivate my mom to fight for her life.

Mom didn't want to be a burden and didn't like to be sick. The cancer took her life just four months after my father died. I had not honored her, or truly forgiven her in my heart. I was so bitter that I wasn't able to see that she was a prisoner of war herself. She had been trying to escape her own pain and heartache. This time I was present for the fight for her life, but I treated her like my enemy.

During Mom's illness, I was being counseled by a lady Christian counselor and when my mother died, my counseling shifted to writing letters, expressing my hurts and speaking out forgiveness to…an empty chair. She died. I missed the opportunity to forgive my mom in person so I spoke it into the air instead. I found out where I had picked up some of my stones and released them through speaking out forgiveness.

"I forgive you, I forgive you Mom, I forgive you Mom. I love you, I love you, I love you. Please forgive me for not being a better daughter, loving you, and honoring you. Please forgive me for treating you like my enemy."

* * *

A few short months later, I was still pregnant with Carter when my sister Marie died. Another battle lost to alcohol and the demons of abuse, rejection, betrayal, and abandonment. At times I had judged her as being hopeless and not willing to change. I originally viewed alcoholism as a choice, a medical, moral condition, and as a hereditary condition, and ultimately a matter of being willing to change. I was never able to see it for what it really was…her escape route from the enemy camp she'd known since childhood.

Marie never found an escape plan that didn't cause her and her family more pain, she didn't know another way. I begged her several times to move down south with me so I could help her but she never wanted to move away from her children. She tried so hard to grasp the shreds of relationships she still had.

I harbored my own resentments for her past abuses, and, as a result, I don't think I ever encouraged Marie to forgive. I knew the reality of her past, her struggles, and the rocks that she carried. I never modeled the behaviors I was teaching others and ultimately failed in helping my own sister to release her enemies through the power of forgiveness. Her wonderful joyful love for life, children, animals, music and those less fortunate, all the qualities for which I looked up to her in my youth, were smeared with the blood she shed after every physical and psychological beating she endured.

I know she had asked Jesus into her heart, because we talked about faith almost every time she was hospitalized, or when she was in a recovery program to help her remain abstinent. I know I'll see her in heaven one day, but I wish I could have helped her more while she was here. I'd been invited to the battle, but didn't think to encourage her to forgive. I didn't know how to fight for someone who had given up trying to battle for a life worth living. Marie lost hope in the end and was tired of fighting for a life filled with regret and heartache. Marie's alcoholism blinded her and kept her from seeing that she had a life worth living and fighting for.

"I didn't know how to battle for you. Please forgive me for not modeling forgiveness, not helping you to learn a better way and for judging you, Marie...I love you. Please forgive me, forgive me, forgive me."

* * *

I recently re-visited the cemetery where the headstones are lined up in a row: my sister Marie, my brother Derik and my mom, Karen. I repented again, honored them, forgave and asked forgiveness. I thanked them for their presence and influence in my life, shaping my beliefs, and solidifying my identity. I'd done what I could with what I knew at the time. When I know better I do better. I put back some of my stones.

There are many stones I carried around because I didn't know where to return them and there are stones other people are carrying with my name on them. We all have some stones to let go of. I beg you now, in this moment, to allow the Holy Spirit to well up inside you and reveal to you anyone you may need to forgive, or ask forgiveness for. Please don't let a moment more go by. You don't have to wait to "feel" it in your heart, just speak out forgiveness; speak forgiveness out in obedience. The Holy Spirit will reveal it to you in a very gentle way. Release your enemy. You deserve to be free today and so do they.

If you have a hurt you believe you are just not ready to let go of yet, I challenge you to go outside and pick up a stone, put it in your pocket and carry it with you wherever you go.

Every time you think about it and make a decision to *not* let it go, go outside and pick up another stone, adding it to the one in your pocket. Every time you get angry or offended by someone, pick up another stone and put it in your pocket. Keep them with you every day as a tangible reminder of the burdens you choose to carry. How many stones are you carrying? Are they weighing you down? It is your choice how many you decide to carry and for how long. Let go and let God take it for you. Just change your mind…

*   *   *

Every night before bed, Ben or I, lead Derik and Carter in prayer. We ask them in obedience to ask forgiveness and speak out forgiveness.

"Forgive me, forgive me, forgive me, I forgive, I forgive, I forgive."

Many times, after we have them speak it first, they come up with events that occurred during the day when they judged, or hurt someone by their words or actions. We call it our nightly heart cleansing. It is much easier and more effective to clean our hearts daily than wait until we "feel like" forgiving someone. If we wait for a feeling it may come too late—like it did with my mom. We also encourage daily cleaning of our messes, like the mess I made with my sister Marie. I learned from my mistakes and we encourage each other to take responsibility for our own actions as an ongoing evaluation to keep from carrying a bag of stones that weighs us down. We don't like to wait until the weekend to clean our hearts. It takes a few minutes, so we choose to "get er done!"

*   *   *

Jesus says to forgive others as we have been forgiven. The Lord's Prayer states, "forgive us **as** we forgive others." It is not an option; it is a command. It is done in obedience. I was learning to follow orders out of obedience. But first I needed to learn who was talking to me.

{ 16 }

EARS TO HEAR

Growing up I was birthed and raised in an atmosphere of negativity. The words I heard were mainly focused on what was "wrong" with me. Despite my desire and promise to be a positive person, I was pessimistic and sarcastic during my adolescent years and joined in the atmosphere of negativity, speaking out what I thought to be "wrong" with other people. In the Army I was asked, "What's wrong?" In my marriage, Payne and I took turns identifying what was "wrong" with each other. In psychology, I was mainly taught to diagnose, label and treat or counsel what was... "wrong."

In Christianity, I was even trained to make people aware of their sins, or what was... "wrong," so as to accept Jesus and become "good enough" to go to heaven when they died. In church, I was taught that I'm a sinner saved by grace and about my "sinful" heart. I was encouraged to be mindful to not act upon the sinfulness of my "flesh," which there was always something continually... "wrong."

Professionally, I was paid to categorize, diagnose, treat, bill, and determine what was... "wrong." Personally, and as an independent evaluator and LPC, I included the medical aspect of what was... "wrong."

Wrong, wrong, wrong, wrong...

The overwhelming negativity of there is something "wrong" even led me to question my own ability to love Carter before he was born because I didn't believe I had the capacity to love one more child. The phenomenal love I experienced with Jordan and Derik seemed to stretch the limits of my heart. Fears surfaced and caused me to question my ability to love. What if I had reached my limit like my mom had with me? Were three children too many? I was fearful and focused on the negativity. What was "wrong" with me??

Thankfully, all my fears quickly dissipated the moment I laid eyes on my gorgeous blonde haired, blue-eyed son. His birth—being like neither of my children—quickly established his reputation of never being underestimated, ignored or categorized. I immediately fell in love with him, his presence, identity and his spirit. I had been focused on negativity and my fears and what I thought was "wrong" with me rather than the amazing gift of life.

I was well trained to focus on what was wrong...so when I started 'hearing' God I wondered...what was "wrong" with me?

* * *

I don't remember when I started hearing God's voice clearly, it usually sounded like my voice. Being a counselor I described it as my wise mind, a leading within me, or a gut feeling...eventually I called it what it was. God. Period. It was internal and usually said things I wouldn't normally think and sometimes things I didn't necessarily want to hear. Or, tell me to do things I wasn't so willing to do, like when God told me to forgive Larry. Forgiving my father was something I didn't think up on my own or even wanted to do. Things God directed me to do were never bad or hurtful, just uncomfortable acts I really didn't want to do because I thought they might cause me embarrassment, make me uncomfortable, or didn't seem very important to me at the time.

Please understand, with all my training and my career path, admitting I was hearing the voice of God was **not** something I wanted to share publicly. It was easier to call it an urging or a sensing. I shared my experiences with very few people.

* * *

When my mom passed away, all my siblings gathered to clean out her house. We had three days to do it as we all lived in different parts of the country and needed to get back to our lives. My mom had collected over two hundred sets of salt and pepper shakers, numerous books, and had check stubs dating back to the seventies. We were all doing our best to get through the process, placing things in boxes, quickly taping them up, and having them shipped to our homes.

I took on the job of cleaning out the bathroom. As I sifted through drawers, I tossed some special razors into a box, taped it up and set the box aside. Penny wandered into the bathroom about fifteen minutes later and asked if I'd seen the razors. In my busy-ness I said "no."

Simple thing…no big deal, I just didn't want to have to go back, unpack the box, get them out for her, and re-tape the box. I didn't have time. It was a little white lie. No one was hurt and besides, it was no big deal to her, she was just asking and we moved on. Little did I know this was to be a loonnnggg faith growth opportunity. (AFGO)

*   *   *

Razors! RAZORS! For goodness sakes! It started when I returned home. Almost every time I took a shower. I'd be planning my day in my head, minding my own business and a thought would enter my mind.

"You lied to Penny about those razors."

So.

"You lied to Penny about those razors."

I continue to rationalize in my head. Penny doesn't care about those razors. She probably doesn't even remember them.

"You lied to Penny about those razors."

I'd be embarrassed to have to tell her I lied. It was just a little lie. Who cares about silly razors? It's been so long.

"You lied to Penny about those razors."

Day after day, month after month, as time went on the voice became softer and less frequent, as I usually ignored it until it stopped. One year, Penny planned to travel to Virginia and spend Thanksgiving at our home. A couple weeks prior to her arrival the voice returned.

I was minding my own business…taking a shower…planning my day.

"You lied to Penny about those razors."

"OH MY GOODNESS!" I cry out loud, "They are razors for goodness sakes!"

"You lied to Penny about those razors."

I try the old rationalizations. It's been almost two years, God! She doesn't remember those razors!

"You lied to Penny about those razors."

Yes! I agree! Fine! I'll tell her that I lied about the razors!

"Buy her some."

What?

"Buy her some."

Why?

"Sometimes, it's not about you."

"Ugh," I sigh.

I went to Sam's Club and bought her a huge pack of razors.

*   *   *

"Here." I say, slapping the huge pack of razors on the dining room table. Penny jumps as she is startled by my intensity. She eyes the razors.

"What are these?"

"Razors!" I relay the story of when I lied, admit to her why I did it and ask for forgiveness.

"I don't want these…I don't even use these anymore."

Feeling shame and embarrassment for my behaviors my words are harsh and forceful. "I don't care! You take these razors! You are going to take them with you, I don't care what you do with them…give them away…whatever! But, you WILL take these razors out of this house with you! God will **not** leave me alone about the razors!"

Confused and probably thinking her sister is a little off of her rocker, Penny obeys and takes the razors with her.

*   *   *

Aaaahhh…no more voice. Peaceful showers.

God was teaching me the difference between having an internal dialogue with myself and actually hearing from God. I am reminded about the bumper sticker related to the origin of thoughts. "Don't believe everything you think."

I was learning how to discern between voices.

God was also working out in me to be a radical truth teller. While growing up in my house I'd become a very good liar. I was labeled as one and treated as such. Learning to lie was a matter of survival and sometimes it was easier to lie than risk being hurt. I was vulnerable with Ben on our first date and told the truth concerning my ability to be deceitful; tired of playing dating games and presenting just the good-side in order to "win" a man. I desired honesty in all my relationships. If I want to be used by God for good, He has to be able to trust me to be honest and truthful in **all** situations. I have to be a person of integrity and truth. If God can't trust me to speak truth in the simple little things, like razors…how will He be able to trust me with big things?

* * *

Another faith growth opportunity occurred when I participated in Walk to Emmaus. It was a little over a year after Mom's death and I was examining my future. When I went on my Walk I'd been working through Rick Warren's book "Purpose Driven Life" and I was stuck on the chapter related to surrender, or giving up control, as I called it. Releasing control, especially now that I felt like I had it in my life, was not something I was ready to hand over to just anyone, especially an unseen God I had yet to fully trust. Trust is a two-way street, so I decided to take the book with me on my 72-hour Walk to really seek what God wanted me to do with my life. And so, in my wisdom, I gave Him some options…you know…just in case He needed some help.

* * *

It's a time of reflection and prayer. The lights are low in the big hall. I am seated in a row of brown plastic stackable chairs in a large room which, doubles as the cafeteria, or large meeting area during the day, but is now set aside for seeking God's will. It is nearing the end of my Walk and I'm ready and willing to hear from God about where He wants me to go and what He wants me to do in the next stage of my life.

I glance around the room and see many women scattered around and some are weeping at the makeshift altar set up in the front of the room. I've just experienced an amazing outpouring of love from the community and I am feeling genuinely loved.

I bow my head and begin my prayer. "God, what do you want me to do?" I start out. "Do you want me to go back to school to get my Ph.D., become a licensed marriage and family therapist, or do you want me to start that adolescent multi-family skills group?"

I pause.

Silence.

"Oh…Amen."

Silence.

"Go up to the snack room and tell them you lied."

Huh?

"Go up to the snack room and tell them you lied."

Immediately, I feel convicted and remember *kind* of misrepresenting or misquoting something I'd said about Ben when I first arrived on my Walk. It was a comment I'd made to a group of women in the snack room. I remember that when I originally said it I'd felt convicted, but I ignored the feeling. After all…it wasn't *really* a lie…just kind of one.

Um…God… about my question…

Silence.

I waited.

Silence.

I opened my eyes and sat there.

Bummer…I knew what I had to do…I examined my white Reeboks.

I know the snack room is filled with my fellow Pilgrims having an ice cream party.

Bummer…I looked down at my shoes again.

"Ugh."

My friend Anne sits down next to me and quietly asks me if I need prayer. I sigh deeply and explain my situation.

She looks at me confused trying to discern if I am being serious. "Okkkaayy," she says slowly. "Do you want me to go with you?"

Sighing deeply, I realize I'm actually trying to avoid embarrassment by taking my time. Hoping to avoid the whole situation, but knowing I'll regret it if I do. "You can, if you want." I respond, realizing God must have sent her over to prod me along.

I stand and stretch. Then Anne and I make our way up the hill to the snack room.

"May I have your attention please?" Anne announces to the groups of women scattered around the room. Twenty or so women turn their heads to look at us. "Tina has something she would like to say."

"Um...the first day we were here...I lied. I made a statement..." I continue to relay what I'd said and correct it, so it is the actual truth. The women listen dutifully, but many look puzzled and some even raise an eyebrow or two. Immediately following my admission, they resume their conversations.

Anne hugs me. "You did a good job."

"Thanks."

A lady I do not recognize approaches us.

Anne steps back.

"Thank you for your words," her voice begins to tremble, tears glisten in her eyes. "I really needed to hear that. Thank you for being an example." We hug and she weeps on my shoulder for several minutes.

Sometimes, it's not about you.

It seemed like a little thing to me. From her perspective it was huge.

*   *   *

Sometimes, it's not about you. And then...sometimes it *is* about you. It was about me when Ben and I were attending our Lutheran church one Sunday and I heard a voice inside my head state very clearly, "You are going to die."

It sounded like me, but I knew it wasn't my thought. Of course I didn't want to think something like that! But, by that time in my life I had already received a couple of clear messages and I knew God spoke to me, so it must be God. Besides, I was a Christian participating in a church service when it happened...what else could it have been?

Later, with some hesitation, I told Ben what I'd heard. It was the first time I had ever seen Ben cry. We prayed together and we both felt like it was truth and it was from God. We dealt with our fears very systematically. We put our affairs in order and made sure our family would be taken care of, and I wrote letters to all three of my children. Carter was just a baby,

Derik was almost four and Jordan was fifteen. It was a difficult message to receive, but we viewed it as some sort of warning.

I was still struggling with my thyroid and some other minor medical issues, but I wasn't really "sick," so we assumed I might be involved in some sort of accident. We cherished every moment together and tried to spend as much time as a family as we could.

Ben and I discussed plans for Jordan and assumed she would want to live with her father. We seriously considered what it would be like for Ben to have to raise the boys alone and then…we waited.

Every time I left the house…I didn't expect to return.

And we waited…

And waited…

This was an especially difficult time for me and for Jordan for many different reasons. Jordan was a teenager, developing into a gorgeous young lady, and had her first boyfriend. Jordan's dad, Payne, was scheduled for an overseas tour in Iraq and Jordan's best friend's mother was terminally ill. As a result, Jordan's emotions were all over the place and it was hard to discern as to what was really triggering them. Ever since Jordan reached her teen years the molestation I endured at her age took up residence in the back of my mind and I evaluated every choice I made coupled with the possible "what if's…" related to Ben being her step-father.

During this time, Ben disclosed to me that he was struggling with an online pornography addiction and had been for some time. We set up parental controls on the computers and discussed self-help options and accountability groups, but I didn't share my biggest fears with Ben as I wasn't even aware that the fears, anxieties and "what ifs" were influencing my choices.

After a couple of months of waiting and defensive driving…we re-evaluated the situation and decided maybe it wasn't Gods voice I'd heard. We weren't quite sure.

I examined the difference between the clear messages I thought were from God and noticed that they were specific and to the point, but the other one was vague. In the example with the razors, God repeated the sentence. *"You lied to Penny about those razors."* I had lied, and God would **not** let me get away with it.

The other voice was vague, and taunted me with "You're going to die," and caused me to be anxious, fearful and uneasy. If God is love, and encourages me to be honest, honoring, good, kind and forgiving, then I deduced that the opposite negative one—speaking about death—must be Satan. The war is between love and fear. The Devil knows scripture a lot better than I do, has been around a lot longer than I have, and tries to twist things to make it sound like God. The bumper sticker was becoming clearer, "Don't believe everything you think."

One way I learned to determine if it is God's voice or not is to ask: Does this sound like something Jesus would say? Is it truth? Is it specific, and does it line up with scripture? If the answer is no to any of them, it probably isn't God. I knew it was God when He told me to go and be truthful to the ladies in the snack room. I could have avoided the whole thing if I'd listened to the still small voice of inner conviction when I first spoke the small lie about my husband, but I didn't. God followed it up with a very specific command to speak truth.

Another way to know for sure if God is speaking is to consult others. Ask others; does this sound like something God would say? When I heard "You are going to die" I consulted Ben, but we did not ask our pastor, or even talk about it with anyone else. I wasn't quite ready to share that I thought I was hearing from God. Since I was so active in church, Bible studies, being a spiritual mentor for friends, teaching the adolescent multi-family skills group, and being an independent evaluator; it almost seemed like a weakness to admit that I was struggling with "voices." Besides, I felt like I was handling it appropriately.

Something I learned through scripture is that God is present and future oriented. I love Jeremiah 29:11 where it states, "...for I know the plans I have for you...plans to prosper you, not to perish you...a future and a hope..." I memorized those lines and began to seriously question the source of my thoughts. If God is present and future oriented I deduced that Satan must be focused on my past, all my mistakes, and stuff I've done wrong. I learned **not** to believe everything I think and just because it may *sound* like my voice…not all my thoughts are my own!

But what happens when you start to see things? AFGO?

{ 17 }

EYES TO SEE

Ben and I were enjoying a dinner with several church couples in one of the parishioner's homes. Standing in the kitchen facing Gina, and listening to her, a horrific vision of her with half of her skull missing with her brain exposed flashed in my mind.

What was that? I thought to myself. Was I hallucinating? This happened three times during the evening. I didn't mention any of it, but I did take note of when the visions occurred. Every time I saw the image she was talking about her upcoming travel plans to DC. The trip was scheduled for the end of the next month and she was planning to travel with her mother for the first time by herself.

Later, while driving home, I told Ben about the visions.

"Cool," he responds, smiling at me.

"Cool?"

"Yeah. Sounds like God's tryin' to tell you somethin'," Ben says calmly.

"What are you, crazy? That's not cool! If you told me you'd just seen visions of our hostess with half her skull missing, we'd be on our way to the ER to have you committed! That is NOT normal."

"I'm not saying it's normal, I'm just saying it sounds like God is trying to tell you something. People in the Bible had visions," Ben argues.

"Yeah, well I'm not in the Bible, am I?"

"I'm just saying be open to it."

I tried to just let it go, but it kept coming to mind at the most inopportune times. I'd be in the shower thinking about my day and the image would pop into my mind, coupled with an urging inside of me to tell Gina about it. I had to warn her.

"Yeah right," I thought, realizing how crazy it sounded. I didn't know her that well, there was no way I was willing to divulge that I was experiencing visual hallucinations!

But, as the days became weeks and the trip got closer, the urging became more often and almost insistent. Ben and I discussed it on many occasions; I consulted a trusted church member and my long-time counseling friend, "Q."

All were encouraging and understood my heart's intent to heed what had been shown to me, but they cautioned me as well. Telling people you have visions isn't something you share with everyone, especially the kind of vision I had experienced. I really didn't want to tell her, but knew if something bad happened and I hadn't said anything, I wouldn't be able to live with myself.

Ben and I chose to tell Gina and her husband together. I needed Ben's support and encouragement as I felt very vulnerable in admitting to having the visions and not really knowing what to tell her about them. Ultimately the interaction went as well as could be expected, and they didn't call the police on me. I shared with her very matter-of-factly what I'd seen and admitted that the only "feeling" I had from the entire situation was that she needed to consult God in prayer as to the route and timing when she traveled to DC. I encouraged her to maintain contact with God in prayer.

She questioned my psychological stability and asked if I was an anxious person, if I hated DC, or was afraid of traveling in some way. Gina expressed openly some of the same questions and concerns I had struggled to answer. I calmly shared my heart and did the best I could to be as specific, yet as vague as possible. It wasn't easy—but I did it. Immediately following the interaction, I felt free. I really sensed I'd been obedient to a message from God and followed through with what I was supposed to do. Even better was the fact that I quickly forgot about the incident and continued on with my life.

I thought about it once in a while over the next couple of weeks, not with any urgency, and the vision never re-occurred. Ben and I greeted the couple several weeks later during a church service following her trip to DC and I was grateful to see her. I do have to say, they kept their distance from us and never invited us back to their home, which was an unfortunate price to pay for expressing what was in my heart.

It was soon after that incident, our lives radically changed and we received a whole different kind of message. It was like God changed the channel and placed a new call on our lives.

{ 18 }

UPROOTING FROM UR

We appeared to be "doing all the right things" as a good Christian family, but Ben and I felt a stirring within. We were enjoying our lives, but all around us, friends, family and clients struggled with mental and physical illness, death, divorce, disease, suicide and negativity. The issues were the same, only the faces changed. We were in search of answers.

*   *   *

I had always wanted Jordan to have a closer relationship with her father. But my heart lurched in my chest the day she announced, during an argument, that she was going to leave home and go live with Payne full time.

I didn't want Jordan to go; I didn't even think she would. I was angry when I first agreed to her leaving and thought she would change her mind. As the days and weeks went by, I learned Payne wasn't going to be stationed in North Carolina like I originally thought, but all the way up north in Michigan. He recently returned from serving in Iraq and I was surprised at how quick he agreed to the decision. I was also surprised that Jordan followed through; left school, friends and a job she loved and moved three states away.

My relationship with Jordan was strained as I struggled to assume the best about her and her choices. I still had not fully forgiven my own mother, had guilt related to her death and was seriously questioning my own mothering abilities. My fears, concerns and "what ifs" were still rattling around in my brain concerning potential molestation despite the trust I had in Ben. My fears and doubts coupled with the concern about his pornography addiction, the words spoken by the evil one about my impending death, my increased medical concerns, raw emotions surrounding the recent death of Jordan's best friend's mom all factored into my decision to allow her to leave so easily.

Payne and I had always been amicable. I had purposed in my heart to not be like my mom and speak badly about Jordan's father, or to allow any sort of violence—emotional or otherwise—to arise. I wanted to make sure Jordan never felt rejected or abandoned like I had as a child. I don't know how well I did, but I certainly tried. Despite my trust in Ben, I also thought she would be safer with her own father. So, I drove her to Michigan and cried all the way home. I loved her by letting her go.

After Jordan moved, I felt rejected and abandoned. Probably the same way she felt when I left her in Texas. Ben worked night shift and the time I used to spend with Jordan in the evenings, talking or watching TV, echoed with silence. That was when my thoughts were the worst. I experienced hopelessness and detachment, still believing in some sense I was going to die and that losing my daughter was part of my "death." Thoughts of suicide resurfaced from my youth, but I kept them to myself and never told Ben. I applied my DBT skills and talked with my counseling buddy Mary Lynn and prayed a lot to get through it.

One day, I read the passage in Matthew 4:1-6 where Jesus was tested by the devil. Satan was trying to coax Jesus into throwing himself down from a high place. I viewed this as suicidal thoughts originating from the devil and rationalized that there wasn't anything "wrong" with me. If Jesus could be tempted with suicide…what I was feeling was "normal."

Keep in mind I'd had suicidal thoughts when I was younger. Plus, I'd heard the voice in church saying I was going to die, and now this. I recognized that the evil one was trying to plant "seeds" or "thoughts" in my mind that I was going to die. According to the diagnostic statistical manual and all my professional training, the way I was feeling was consistent with current life events. So, I treated it as transient in nature, rationalizing and "skilling" my way through. It worked and the thoughts went away…for a while.

*   *   *

Two months after Jordan went to live with her father, God spoke to us, telling us to uproot and move to Pennsylvania to live near Ben's parents. The message we got was to leave our jobs and our church behind, along with bunches of friends and people we loved, counseled and ministered to for years—and go. We listened and started on the road of obedience to 'walk it out.'

We began our walk of obedience by making preparations to move within the year. It was August 2007. We thought the calling was so Ben could pursue a pastoral training of some sort through seminary, but we had no clue as to God's purpose. When people questioned us, we weren't quite sure how to answer.

Immediately we began to experience a great deal of resistance to leaving. I had been struggling with my thyroid problems for twelve years and the condition suddenly turned into tremors. The tremors felt like an invisible hand grabbed a hold of my backbone and repeatedly shook it back and forth. I became an expert on tremors and examined the effects of my caffeine intake, exercise and strong emotions and their correlation with the increased intensity of the tremors. The tremors were so violent they interfered with my entire life.

My medical problems triggered a gamut of neurological tests, biopsies, MRI, and physicals, all of which culminated in a four-month leave of absence from work. The neurologist prescribed a combination of barbiturates and a highly addictive sleep medication, but believed my thyroid was the issue. The endocrinologist referred me back to the neurologist. I discovered that the sulfates in red wine calmed the tremors long enough to get me to sleep, but wouldn't keep me asleep for the entire night because I would wake after only a couple hours of sleep when the alcohol wore off. My life became a balancing act of alcohol and drugs, this went on for months and I became desperate for relief.

Ben and I believed that everything stemmed from a problematic thyroid and, in my desperation, I demanded a thyroidectomy. In January 2008, I underwent surgery and my thyroid was completely removed. The Dr. prescribed external thyroid medication; which will be required for the rest of my life. The medications replace the thyroid in my body that regulates my metabolism and other body functions. Without external thyroid I will eventually slip into a coma and die.

During my surgical follow-up appointment, I learned that the pathologist discovered a cancerous tumor encased inside my thyroid that the biopsies had missed. That was the good news, as it had been removed. The bad news was that my surgeon had inadvertently removed two-and-a-half parathyroid glands during the surgery. The mistake caused a new complication, an inability to regulate calcium levels. I learned that if I don't take calcium regularly I could end up in a coma...and die.

Ugh.

I almost died as I was learning the seriousness of my situation.

Following my near death experience, I researched and discovered I have to closely monitor my calcium and vitamin D intake for the rest of my life. I learned that people in my condition usually end up being on some sort of disability because calcium levels drastically change with the seasons and the amount of sunlight absorbed.

Despite the bleak news, I felt grateful the cancerous thyroid was out of my body, my tremors slowly decreased, and my sleep cycle returned to normal. I no longer needed daily "doses" of alcohol, sleeping medications and barbiturates to function in life...I traded them for daily doses of thyroid medication, calcium, vitamin D and a constant monitoring of vitamins and hormones. The physical storm within my body was quelled...what about my home?

*   *   *

I was recovering from surgery in February 2008 when an extremely violent wind storm with wind gusts of 60 mph blew through our town uprooting a huge oak tree that fell on our large brick home and mini-van. The tree was so large that two grown people hugging the tree would only touch fingertips and the removal required a crane to lift the tree from the house. As a result of the damage—and lack of power to the house—we had to move into an apartment.

Ben and I were intent on being joyful and continued to praise God as we spread our testimony of what God was doing. Many of our friends and church family stepped in to help us during our transition.

"You guys are awful chipper," Patrick, observes as he helps clean out our refrigerator.

"I'm grateful that Derik and Carter are alive," I explain. "They were in their bedroom ten minutes before the tree fell." Six-year-old Derik and two-year-old Carter would have been killed if they had been in their room.

"Wow!" Patrick was incredulous, "Really?" He'd surveyed the devastation the tree branches had caused after it ripped through the roof, attic, and the ceiling of the top floor of our home: ceiling fan on the floor, roof shingles on the bunk beds, and random rays of bright sunshine filtered through the gaping hole in the roof.

"It could have been worse!"

* * *

Every time we witnessed a miracle, we added it to our testimony to God and kept moving forward. Another act of God was getting the insurance company to pay for tree removal, temporary housing and over $70,000 in housing repairs as well as the $9,000 in damage done to our van. The construction company we hired expressed their disbelief as to why the insurance company paid for the things it did, but we believed God used the tree falling to prepare our home for selling and blessed us with a rebuilt freshly painted garage, new garage doors, storm doors, patio door, cedar siding (not there before), nine rooms professionally patched and painted, new central air conditioner, and a new roof...the list goes on and on. So we were ready to move even though we continued to experience attacks in other areas.

Once we moved back into our "renewed" home, we had a huge "paint, pack, clean and move-stuff-to-storage" party. We celebrated how God had turned a potential set-back to a huge faith growing opportunity and rejoiced with our friends. We then loaded up our U-Haul, placed our home up for sale and moved to Pennsylvania in July of 2008. We answered the call despite the interference because we believed it was really God telling us to go. We really didn't know why; we just went out of obedience.

* * *

We moved into Mom-mom and Pop-pop's three-bedroom split-level home during this time of transition. Our house had not sold and we weren't entirely certain where God wanted us to go—or why He even told us to move. The boys adjusted well to being in a new place and enjoyed being around their grandparents. Pop-pop has a huge garden as well as a yard filled with beautiful flowers. Our family learned about gardening, the little bugs that go along with fresh vegetables, living a greener lifestyle and learning to survive with a lot less stuff.

The company Ben worked for was able to transfer him to PA so he continued to work as a pharmacist, as he didn't feel led to apply to seminary. I registered Derik in the same school his daddy attended as a child and enrolled Carter in a pre-school program two days a week.

It was a time of adjustment and continued self-examination. Along with Ben's parents, we attended the same Lutheran church Ben grew up in. Mom-mom invited us to join her in a weekly discussion group focused on Phillip Yancey's book "What's So Amazing About Grace?" The book is a compilation of personal testimonies, stories and excerpts. Through the compelling stories, it challenges readers to extend God's grace, mercy, and forgiveness in challenging and sometimes horrific situations.

The weekly chapter discussions challenged me to personally examine extending forgiveness in all relationships. I'd never asked Payne's forgiveness, or forgave things that had transpired in our marriage. I felt convicted for days…a kind of urging in my heart.

I phoned him one evening and asked for forgiveness, and forgave him for his mistakes. The brief phone call surprised him and there were some awkward silences. Payne has a wonderful heart and I truly believe, despite our differences, we both made many mistakes that contributed to the ending of our relationship. Many years and life events have passed and I am extremely grateful for my marriage to Payne because I have the honor of being Jordan's mom.

It was also during that time I contacted Jordan's Nana and honored her and her husband for the positive influence they'd had on mine and Jordan's lives. I also expressed my gratitude for the relationship we'd maintained throughout the years.

Forgiving Payne and honoring his parents allowed us all to join in prayer and problem solving as a team throughout Jordan's last couple years of high school. She struggled with emotional turmoil and consequences of changing schools, states and transitioning into a new family life style. The forgiveness allowed us to clear the air and join together in love in a common goal of loving Jordan on her journey.

*   *   *

During weekly reading assignments, I was led to the scripture in Mathew 6:14-16 where it states in no uncertain terms that if you forgive you are forgiven, but if you don't forgive then you aren't forgiven. I'd heard these scriptures in church, but when I read them this time I really started to consider what it meant. It kind of freaked me out. I began to think of God not forgiving me and what that would mean for my life. It was extremely important to me that God forgave me for being angry with Him as well as for all the bad stuff I'd done and the mistakes I've made.

The new information brought up questions I had not thought of in years, like if I believed "enough" to disappear with all the other Christians during the "rapture." Even though I had made a decision that I really wanted to stay and fight, I still didn't know what the "end times" had in store and I sure didn't want to be "left behind" for my lack of forgiveness. But I also wondered why forgiveness of other people was such a big deal to God. I knew it was important for people. I experienced the powerful effect it had in my life and witnessed the effect it had on people and their lives. But...why did God care about it so much? I wasn't sure.

*   *   *

Months passed and Ben continued working, as he still didn't feel led to seminary, and I didn't feel led to search for a position in counseling. Every time I picked up the paperwork to apply for my professional counseling license in Pennsylvania, I felt a resounding "no" inside, but I couldn't explain it. It was a time of confusion for me. My medical issues had stabilized somewhat, but my energy levels seemed to be declining. I started drinking more and more coffee to maintain energy throughout the day, but the increase in caffeine was causing more intestinal irritability. I also continued monitoring my calcium and vitamin intake. I sought God in prayer, but felt confused and lonely. I didn't feel any kind of urging, nudging, or leading, and when I prayed the response was…silence.

Ben's parents were healthy and didn't really need us, we rented out our house, as it had not sold, and continued to seek God in prayer. I started to consider that maybe we had been wrong. Did we miss something…had we been deceived? Had Ben? I didn't have an answer…so I waited.

*   *   *

There is a story in the Bible about a man named Abram and it starts in Genesis Chapter 12. God called Abram out when he was 75 years old and told him to leave his father's house, his family, his country, and go to a land that God would show him. Ben and I joked that we felt like Abram in the land of Ur (the name of the land he was called out of) or "you are" as we called it. God wanted a relationship with Abram, but he first had to get him out of what the world said he was and how the world defined him. Abram made a choice to turn away from Ur and follow God.

We kept seeking God through prayer, but began to feel like life in PA was just like what we left behind except we were away from all our friends, and now we lived with Ben's parents. We wanted more. We wanted to know the reason why we had to relocate. The "new land" was okay, but we loved our old land of "Ur" (you are) and missed our life there. Without direction or identity we missed what the world said "we are."

Prior to moving to PA, a wonderful lady named Lila from our church, gave us some teachings about supernatural healing by a man named Randy Clark. I wasn't quite sold on the idea and was extremely cautious. I didn't want to be involved in any cult-like (or occult for that matter) activities as there was some talk of raising people from the dead. Stephen King's "Pet Cemetery" came to mind, and I was leery of being involved in anything like that. We kept praying and searching and trying to be aware of any kind of leading or nudging in any way.

God "called" me a long time before I knew it was Him. He called Ben in much the same way. God nudged us both to "squirm," learn, grow, and stretch the box we'd placed God in over the years. Although I knew God "talked" to me, I didn't know the difference between God the Father, God the Son and God the Holy Spirit. I wanted to understand my faith.

*   *   *

In the following pages I share some amazing events that have occurred in our lives since leaving our land of Ur. I was not easily convinced and I did **not** go quietly, I challenged, questioned, read, researched, and fought my way through. I like to say that I went 'kicking and screaming' and that's pretty accurate. But I went. Not because I understood it, but because I kept losing battles with tools that were not working. I was tired of the pain, heartache, and battles I was fighting, my friends, family and clients were fighting—and all losing in some way. There had to be a better, more effective, consistent solution. I'd tried psychology, medicine, counseling, and religion as I knew it. What else was there? I didn't know, but I wanted to find out.

Many of our experiences are almost unbelievable. I challenge you to read them and be open to them anyway. They **are real** and they happened to me. I share them to demonstrate in a very real way why I believe so strongly in radical forgiveness. My goal is to explain our experiences as simply as possible. When we were struggling for understanding and wisdom, I kept looking for a simple "how-to" book with clear consistent definitions and I couldn't find one. I needed straightforward truths not masked in "Christianese." What you have in your hands is the result of my own desire for spiritual clarity, discernment, and understanding my identity.

As you look around our world, if you're able to agree there is a supernatural evil realm that exists, then maybe, just maybe, you can agree there is the possibility of a supernatural good realm, too. It's okay to doubt...I'll believe for you until you do.

{ 19 }

ROOTING AND GROUNDING

"Okay," I think to myself, these people seem nice. I look around at the gathering of mostly successful business professionals, a doctor, accountant, business owners and a financial advisor—along with their spouses. We are in a huge beautiful home. No apparent occult-like activity going on here. This appears fairly normal. Ben and I sit side by side on soft chairs on the outskirts of the spacious room. It's just "house church," whatever that means. The host starts off with a simple prayer and his wife inserts a worship CD and presses play. A beautiful song about praising Jesus fills the room.

I close my eyes and focus on the words.

"You are worthy."

What? That was not in the song. My eyes fly open and I look around to see if anyone else heard the voice. Everyone seems to be listening to the music. Some are smiling and swaying in their chairs. I glance at Ben, his eyes are closed and he is smiling.

"You are worthy."

This time my eyes are open. Now I know that was **not** in the song. It came from outside of me; I heard it with my ears. I feel a stirring deep inside. I scan the walls and table near me to look for hidden speakers.

"You are worthy."

What? I don't like this, my brain screams! Tears sting my eyes. I clamp them closed, willing them to stop watering. My eyes cut back to the right and I notice a huge grin on Ben's face—his eyes are still closed.

"You are worthy."

I really don't like this! My body begins to tremble. Tears slip from my eyes. I'm having auditory hallucinations! I bow my head trying to hide my tears behind my hair.

"You are worthy."

"Okay, let's be logical about this," I tell myself silently. It's a CD for goodness sakes! Tears continue to spill onto my cheeks. I grab for tissues trying hard to be discreet.

"You are worthy."

This makes no sense! I am crying and shaking in a room full of strangers and I can't control it. I'm a professional counselor. This is **not** happening to me.

"You are worthy."

Stop saying that! They are going to have me committed for sure!

"You are worthy."

What is going on? I look around. No one is staring at me and no one seems to be planning my commitment. I keep weeping softly, trying hard to fight the love and acceptance softening my heart. No one has ever said that to me, why am I worthy? What did I do? Worthy of what?

"You are worthy."

Why? I have two mounds of tissues in my hands and the music is ending.

"You are worthy."

*　　*　　*

I escaped that day with some decorum and restrained myself from getting down on my hands and knees to check under the table—to see if there were hidden speakers. God had spoken to me and told me I was worthy…worthy of love.

God had to use the audio version not because I am special or different, but because it took the audio version to drown out the negative audio version I had listened to my entire life. I had changed the negative self-statements to positive affirmations concerning my intellectual abilities, but kept a negative view about my appearance, and my identity. I believed that I was ugly, fat and unworthy of love. God spoke to me and told me I was worthy, worthy of His love.

Ben didn't hear the voice, but described an amazing joyful experience in which he was unable to stop smiling for a long time. We called it a "perma grin." That was the first time I truly heard the voice of God…out loud…separate from me…but it would not be the last.

*   *   *

God didn't want me to question my worthiness anymore. God "rooted out" those feelings of unworthiness that had been with me all my life. If the root is bad, or negative, then the fruit is bad. I desire good fruit and so does God. I want everything that I do to be rooted and grounded in the amazing love of God. This rooting and grounding in love and worth is what I needed.

what do I want?

God kept confirming—in a variety of ways—that I am worthy. I am worthy of His love, the love of others and worthy enough to love myself. Instead of a psychological exercise of stating my positive affirmations, God affirmed me in my identity of being loved by Him. I just had to keep agreeing with that love consistently.

I want you to know that you don't need to wait for the audio version like I did. God loves you just as much as He loves me. He sent you a book of love, the Bible. God also wrote you a letter of love, it's on page 110, which I encourage you to go back and read now. God wants you to know that you are worthy, and He loves you. If you don't believe it…just change your mind.

*   *   *

That was our first time attending any kind of house church. Over the next several months we were exposed to a variety of experiences. I started attending a weekly Bible study that included watching a DVD recording of classes taught at Bethel School of Supernatural Ministry in Redding, California. We listened to the Randy Clark teachings that Lila had given us and I signed Ben up for a conference called "Greater Glory." We read a variety of books that increased our awareness of the supernatural occurrences that have occurred, and were occurring in and around our nation—as well as overseas.

House church was confusing for me because the structure was so different from what I knew. Not only was it a lot freer in expression of faith, people used words that I was not familiar with. What does it mean to be "spirit filled"? Don't we all have a spirit? How do I get "re-born"? If I am talking to God...which one is it? Jesus? Holy Spirit? How do I tell the difference?

I asked questions, researched and studied. Ben and I were encouraged to be baptized in the Holy Spirit so we could "speak in tongues," which sounded weird and confusing to me since we were both Lutheran and had been baptized as children. I'd been in church for years and had been repeating the words "Holy Spirit," but had no concept of what I actually believed to be true.

The first time I'd heard anyone speak in tongues was Miss Sarah—back in VA—when I was participating in WIN. When I heard her the first time, I scurried home and searched "speaking in tongues" out in my Bible to make sure it wasn't something demonic. It isn't, but I never thought I would be encouraged to speak in tongues myself. Questions brought up more questions and many times the answers were different depending on who I talked to or what book I read.

The lady hosting the Bible study lent me a CD by Joyce Meyer, so Ben and I settled down to listen to it one evening in October of 2008, after putting the boys to bed. Ben and I were "baptized in the Holy Spirit" through listening to a CD in Mom and Pop's living room.

Basically, in Acts 2:4 it states, being "immersed in the power of the Holy Spirit gave them the ability to speak in other languages as the Spirit gave ability to speak." Now that sounds interesting and everything, but what does it really mean? It's basically asking God for the gift of the Holy Spirit who enables us to speak "in other languages." At the time, it brought up more questions than it did answers, and we did not experience any kind of magical power, nor did we even speak other languages. We described it as our personal prayer language which the Holy Spirit helped us to develop over several months. It's like giving over our vocal chords to the Holy Spirit to pray whatever God wanted to pray through us. It came out as a couple of syllables at first and sounded like gibberish, but we persisted and allowed the Holy Spirit to work through us.

Over time it became a natural part of our lives as well as a very powerful spiritual battle tool.

Talking with God and asking for the baptism (or gift) of the Holy Spirit is easy. If you have never done so, you can take the opportunity to pray for it anytime. John the Baptist spoke of it in John 1:33 and Jesus states in Acts 1:5 that God the Father promises to baptize us with the Holy Spirit. The book of Acts 2:4 states that "they were all filled with the Holy Spirit and spoke with other tongues as the Spirit gave them utterance." When Peter preached in Acts 10:44-46, "the Holy Spirit fell on the people" and they began to speak in tongues.

It may sound silly, but I was afraid to be baptized in the Holy Spirit. I'd read some pretty dramatic stories by that time and was concerned I might "lose it" or something weird would happen to me. I had some negative connotations about ghosts...even if it was a Holy Ghost. I heard and read stories about how powerful the Holy Spirit is, but many people were unclear as to how that power "worked" and how to access it. Eventually, I realized that if I wanted to learn and grow I had to be willing to try new and different things. I "squirmed and grew" through it, eventually let go of control, and allowed God to speak through me...privately of course.

While in the military, my old identity was exchanged for my U.S. Army one. I exchanged my old identity of rejection, unwanted, and uselessness for the Army core values and identity. Similarly, the Holy Spirit helped me to change my core feelings of unworthiness, negative self-image, and values with a stronger, more secure identity. An identity spiritually birthed from the power of love and validated that I'm worthy of love. When I accepted the gift of the Holy Spirit through baptism, I was spiritually "born again" and became a "spirit-filled" believer. The baptism of the Holy Spirit is nothing to be afraid of like I was; it's a wonderful, loving, spiritual gift from God. I encourage you to talk with God about it.

* * *

"I hear God saying that what started three years ago—begins today," the man says to us. Ben and I are holding hands facing the tall young speaker with our heads bowed and our eyes closed.

"You are going to be schooled in the Holy Ghost," he continues "Amen."

What? That's it?

"Um...thank you," I say. I guess I was expecting a little bit more. Ben and I glance at each other, turn away from the man and head towards the door of the church.

* * *

Ben and I were told that the young man was an anointed prophet who regularly sees angels. A prophet is someone who believes that they know, and are able to proclaim, God's will. We weren't really sure what to expect when we asked him to pray for us. We had just witnessed this same man speak a prophecy to a woman in the audience all the way across the room. The woman went into what Ben and I thought resembled an epileptic seizure. She almost violently convulsed out of her chair. Concerned, we looked at each other and wondered if anyone else thought about calling 9-1-1. No one else seemed to think it out of the ordinary, so we waited. Her jerking body stopped after a few minutes and she appeared to be okay.

A short time later, the same man invited people up for prayer. So, Ben and I, expecting something exciting, or extraordinary to happen to us, approached to request what we believed was going to be an amazing prophetic word—coupled with a shaking, or at least something a little bit more exciting than the short prayer. Okay...now what?

* * *

Ben and I discussed our "prophesy" and the shaking lady on the way home. We realized that the, "three years ago" that the man was referring to, was when God had started working on us about being people of radical integrity. Remember the razors? How about the snack room? We agreed with the prophecy, but had absolutely no idea what he meant about being "schooled in the Holy Ghost."

I was struggling with my negative connotations about Ghosts. Ghosts have always been scary to me. I heard people describe experiences, the identity of, and their perception of the Holy Spirit differently. I accepted that the Holy Spirit was powerful, but seeing how it affected that woman—I wasn't sure I wanted to be a part of it. It seemed so unpredictable.

How did that guy cause that reaction from across the room? Did he have some sort of power? He had been described to us as being anointed, but we weren't quite sure what that meant. Does that mean he is special? How does someone become anointed? We didn't know what to think about the lady either…it was kind of weird. How did he do that from so far away? Questions led to more questions.

*　*　*

Being involved in WIN, back in VA, also exposed us for the first time to someone being "slain in the spirit," which is a descriptive way of saying someone was so overtaken by the power of God, they lay down, or sometimes fell down when someone was praying for them. Now, what they did while down on the floor was totally new to me as well.

When WIN hosted Bishop Jeff Billingsly, to preach and pray for people, Ben and I kind of "laid down" when he was praying for us. I knew from watching others that there is a time period in which another person may come over and cover you with a cloth while your eyes are closed. I guess I expected some sort of supernatural thing to occur while I was "slain," but I felt…normal…nothing. In fact, I sneaked a peek at my watch to try and gauge how long I "should" be down there. When I thought it was appropriate, I just got up and returned to my seat. No one ever asked me what happened to me while I was on the floor, but Ben and I had many conversations about what "slain in the spirit" really meant, what happened to people while they were on the floor, and so on.

Ben and I were both interested—but a little afraid—of what God might want us to do. We'd been exposed to a variety of supernatural teachings, occurrences and testimonies. We heard, and read, miraculous things and a yearning began to grow inside of us for something amazing to happen, but we kind of had some stipulations…you know…some things we weren't willing to do. It was kind of like when I was on my Walk to

Emmaus and I gave God some options—in case He needed some ideas, or some parameters. Some safety guidelines of sorts to make sure we were still able to maintain some semblance of control over our lives.

We weren't keen on being martyrs, or anything, and really didn't want to let go of a life we loved. Our concept of dedicating our lives to God included a preconceived notion we would have to go and live in a hut somewhere in another country and be missionaries to some lost tribe somewhere. We really didn't want to do that either. For a couple who were "radically seeking God" we had a lot of terms and conditions—and fears.

*   *   *

On my birthday in July of 2009, Ben and I set our GPS for the Catskill Mountains of New York, to celebrate a Jewish wedding for one of Ben's childhood friends. During our five hour trip, God led us in an awesome time of revelation, prayer, and forgiveness—as we discussed every single relationship, interaction, and involvement we'd ever had. It was an amazing time of forgiveness and release. Earlier in the year we had read a book called "Final Quest" by Rick Joyner and had agreed that it was our desire to honor each other in our relationship by having nothing hidden.

We didn't plan our weekend to be a marathon counseling session with the Holy Spirit, but God helped us to let go of our small stones—as well as some big ones. God knew our relationship needed a firm rooting and grounding in love. We were seeking supernatural things to be manifest right in front of us, and God was teaching us through scriptures and experiences—over a period of time. We didn't understand a lot of it when we were going through it, and often we just had to go out of obedience. Only after speaking out forgiveness through obedience, were we able to examine the benefits, and the freedom we felt in our relationship to share more openly and honestly.

{ 20 }

POWER OF JESUS

I'd participated in church services, listened to sermons, participated in numerous Bible studies, church activities and read Christian literature over the years, yet, I never thought of Jesus as powerful. I always thought about God as being powerful and Jesus being like a lamb led to slaughter. Jesus was the One who willingly gave up his life...that didn't sound very powerful to me. So, when Ben and I decided to attend a "Power and Love" conference, I wasn't quite sure what to expect.

* * *

There are numerous testimonies in the Bible about Jesus' healing miracles and deliverances. Demons manifested around Him, yet, He calmly told them to go. His life was a demonstration of love, radical forgiveness and the healing power of God. Jesus was the first spiritual Son of God and–as a man filled with the Holy Spirit–Jesus conquered death, disease, and sin. He then gave believers the authority to do the same. Jesus gave his life so we could also be filled with the power of the Holy Spirit and have authority over all flesh. Jesus walked in His authority and identity as an example for us to follow.

* * *

We attended the "Power and Love" conference in West Chester, PA in December 2008. The leaders taught us how to operate in our authority by praying for people in public. We also learned about God's loving, healing heart for people.

During the conferences, people are taught about the amazing love of God and then practice praying for each other. Following the teachings, participants are released for lengthy breaks. This allows them time to venture out into the community to practice praying for healings. Following the breaks—when the participants return—they stand up and share testimonies as witness to God's healing power.

*   *   *

Ben and I, and our friend Bill, who drove up from VA, attended the conference together and we prayed for several people the first day. Bill said that the work and preaching he heard from the speakers at the "Power and Love" conference was "cutting edge," a sentiment that was shared—and confirmed—by others in attendance who said they felt like they had heard the Gospel for the first time.

During the evening break of the first day, Ben and I split up and I ventured out with a group of ladies. Two of the people we prayed for were healed. The first was a gentleman with an abscessed tooth and when he told me his pain was gone after my second prayer—I believe I was more surprised than he was. He actually had to convince me that his pain was gone. The second healing involved a woman driving a motorized shopping cart inside the grocery store. When she realized her chronic knee pain was gone, she began to shout out Jesus' praises right there in the middle of the grocery aisle—while her daughter stood behind her and wept.

As we walked out of the store, I immediately began to question their healings. A barrage of negativity spewed a litany of doubts into my ear. My doubts kept me from sharing the testimony that night at the conference, and later on, Ben and Bill confronted me about not releasing the "power of the testimony." I made a decision to share the testimony the next morning despite my concern that those who had been healed—were lying to me.

*   *   *

Four thirty the next morning, I am jolted awake by a very painful cramp in my foot. It really hurts. With the teachings from the prior day echoing in my head, I reach down, place my hand on my right foot and very sarcastically state out loud in my bed, "Okkkayyy Jesus, in Jesus name, pain be gone!"

Instantly the pain is gone.

What? No massage, no stretching, no...nothing. Startled, I notice a strange tingling sensation deep inside, almost like electricity…growing in intensity. Then I hear God say to me very clearly:

You can be pitiful or powerful but you CANNOT be both!

The feeling stirring deep within me changes and I feel very powerful as the electrical feeling spreads throughout my body. I begin to weep.

I make my choice.

I raise my hand straight up in the air and speak out loud in my bed.

"Okay God! I CHOOSE to be powerful!"

I place my hand on my throat. With authority and boldness in my heart I continue, "IN JESUS' NAME MY THYROID IS HEALED!"

God speaks to me again…

That is going to be your testimony.

* * *

Prior to the conference, I was struggling with my thyroid levels. I was sleeping ten to twelve hours a night, while at the same time, addicted to caffeine and napping in order to function. I was not expecting, nor searching for, a supernatural cure because—I didn't believe in them. Three days prior to the conference, my doctor had increased the dosage of my thyroid medication.

Although Ben and I had already been exposed to several testimonies of supernatural healings in house church, and through a variety of other teachings, I was very doubtful—cynical even. I knew in the "real world" I have to be on medications for the rest of my life because I do **not** have a thyroid in my body—it was surgically removed. So, even though I was okay with learning about healing for other people, it never even occurred to me to request one for myself.

* * *

But in that moment…I knew, that I knew, that I knew, that I was healed. It was like God engraved it on my heart. On December 3rd of 2008, I stopped taking my thyroid medication. God said it and I believed it. He settled it deep within me with such certainty that no one was able to convince me otherwise. I chose to be powerful.

During the morning session of the conference, I released the powerful testimony of my healing, and every person I prayed for that day—told me they were healed. I felt exhilarated and powerful. It was amazing and exciting! No one challenged or questioned my healing that day. I was bold and confident in my belief of what God had told me…but it definitely was not the end of the discussion.

*   *   *

One of the speakers at the conference was Todd White. Throughout the conference, he'd been challenging us to step out in boldness and expect the miraculous to happen. He shared testimonies of uneven legs growing out several inches, restoration of hearing, freedom from bipolar disorder, blind eyes opening, and other unbelievable occurrences. His testimonies were powerful—I wanted to be like him and see miracles with my own eyes. Despite what I'd experienced the day before, I still had reservations, not everyone was healed and I didn't understand why. If this was truth—why wasn't it happening for everyone? Someone said it was based on our expectations, so, I "changed my mind" and made a decision to expect miracles to happen.

I partnered up with a new lady named Beth and we set off to a local store, determined to step out in boldness expecting the miraculous. We prayed for several people and were getting excited about people's testimonies. One lady told us that she felt something like electricity when we prayed for her, but Beth and I wanted more. We wanted to see with our own eyes a miracle like a leg grow out supernaturally.

We spotted our prospect in the middle of the pharmacy aisle comparing feminine hygiene product prices. He was in his late twenties, dressed in jeans and a plain white T-shirt. He was limping and kind of dragging his left foot a little. Beth and I looked at each other and got excited...

Noticing his wedding ring, I approach the man and start off the conversation with a lie about how I can't get my husband to ever purchase anything like that for me. Mistake number one: I lie.

Beth enters the conversation and the man's wife approaches. With boldness in our hearts and seeking a testimony, we ask the man why he is limping. Mistake number two: seeking a testimony.

In a moment of vulnerability, he calls himself a "gimp" and begins to share with us that one of his legs is shorter than the other and we get excited again. We respond with enthusiasm to his disclosure of this very personal information. Mistake number three: we treat him like a project—not a person.

We ask if we can pray for him and he refuses. I didn't blame him, because our hearts are not in the right place. We are not honoring him, his struggles, or his identity, and he definitely does not feel love from us. Shortly after his refusal I feel remorse and try to approach the couple to apologize. I have to apologize from a distance, because—when they see me coming—they quickly begin retreating down the aisle. As I turn the corner, a manager intervenes and politely, but firmly, orders us to leave the store.

Wow! I stepped out in boldness and I hurt someone in the process. I am **not** feeling very good about myself or my intentions. I was not acting in love, honor, integrity or truth.

"Please forgive me God." I shared the testimony at the conference, as an example of what **not** to do. I tried to be a Todd White and not a Tina Genaro.

* * *

On Friday night of the conference, Todd shares about a very powerful experience he had when he was ministering to some youths. I am sitting in the front row, listening, taking notes, when I start to feel a little strange. I feel mild cramping in my stomach. As Todd continues talking, and his voice gets louder, my muscles seem to tighten even more—it is extremely distracting.

Tears start to leak out of my eyes against my will and the cramping intensifies. I feel like I need to kneel on the floor. I am trying to focus on Todd's words, but the feelings in my body are taking over, and I don't even know what he is saying any more.

I try to be as discreet as possible…in the front row. I slide off of my chair onto the floor. As soon as my knees hit the carpet, my cramping becomes almost unbearable and I begin rocking, holding my stomach, weeping and crying and hurting. I rock back and forth whispering…out loud, "but…I'm Lutheran, I'm Lutheran, I'm Lutheran."

Apparently trying to communicate to God that, although I desire for supernatural and amazing things to happen, I'm having a hard time wrapping my Lutheran mind around what is happening in my own body. I want to let God know that this is **not** an appropriate way for a Lutheran—a licensed professional counselor no less—to behave in public.

Now you're loving him.

God speaks to my heart, referring to the man in the store. I know He is talking about the man, but I don't understand how my current feelings and behaviors are related to the man and his pain and suffering.

Weeping and crying in utter conviction and repentance concerning my behaviors towards the man, I repent. "Please forgive me God for not loving one of your creations the way that I should have." Despite my repentance, the uncomfortable cramping and weeping continue and I begin to moan…out loud.

By this time though, most of the people in the conference are experiencing something louder than my moaning, so I do not attract too much attention. My friend Bill has slid off his own chair and is lying face down on the floor next to me. As I rock and moan, I feel my heart softening and I begin to feel more love towards the man in the store.

The desire in my heart is to love people, not to hurt them. I vow to myself to never treat anyone that way again.

* * *

The last day of the conference there is a question and answer period and I have a lot of questions about beliefs and God's will. In the midst of my questioning, Todd looks straight at me and asks, "Do you believe it's God's will to heal everyone?"

I don't know. I don't know what to believe. I remember questioning Ben about pre-destination over the years. What about Romans 8:29-30 or Ephesians 1:4-12? Those scriptures, as well as some others, state that only certain people are the elect and pre-destined to be saved. When I questioned Ben at that time, he had provided a confusing explanation.

How do I know if someone is "chosen" or not? Is it the same for healing? What about God loving them? Does He love some and not others? Is there a sign? What about my brother, Derik? My mom, Dad, Marie, Cindy or Heather—all the other friends, family members and clients I lost over the years—what about them? Were they predestined to be healed? Loved? Saved? Could I have prayed for them to be healed? Other questions arose as well. Why didn't I know about healings? Had I been like an ostrich? Where had I been when they handed out this memo? I began to think about all the people over the years that I could have helped had I known this information and I started to get angry. Why wasn't I taught this? It seemed pretty important!

Following the conference Ben and I became almost obsessed with praying for people. Our eyes were opened to supernatural healings. Remembering my promise to myself and God, I attempted to pray for people in honor and love—but I still wanted to see something spectacular happen with my own eyes.

*　*　*

We prayed for people all over the place no matter what we were doing or where we were going. Ben was praying for people at work as well as in public. The boys joined in and prayed for people in malls, on the street, and at the YMCA. If people were willing, we were praying. We thought we were "behind" and needed to catch up. Ben and I really thought that we had missed out on the supernatural memo that God healed today and no one had told us. We believed that we were years behind and had some "catching up" to do.

Ben and I prayed for people in person and over the phone. Many people were healed and some of the testimonies included hearing aids no longer needed; pain gone from an elderly man who fell from a ladder; symptoms completely gone from a 92-year-old stroke victim; use of an arm returned after seven years of not being able to use it; tremors gone; and on and on.

This continued for months and the testimonies added up, we recorded names and dates of powerful testimonies in journals. I experienced "words of knowledge" which is when God reveals private information about another person. The revelation can be used to free a person from an emotional or physical ailment. The "word of knowledge" is God's way of communicating His love and desire for healing people. I just had to be open to hearing what God was saying and step out in obedience—to pray for the person. We have journals full of testimonies, including our own kids' stories.

*   *   *

Despite the fact that we were witness to so many miracles, including my own healing, I had to deal with the reaction of friends and family. Many of my friends did not believe God healed me. Mom-mom and Pop-pop had their doubts as well. People either thought I was crazy, or was secretly taking my thyroid medicine and calling it God's healing. Although God had settled it in my heart, He left it to me to convince everyone else.

*   *   *

"Just take your medicine Mom!" Jordan states forcefully. We'd met at Penny's house in Ohio for a long weekend and she and Penny were struggling with accepting my healing testimony. "You can't heal people," she continued.

I struggle with their disbelief and weep from my own frustration at trying to convey my heart. I am trying to balance being obedient to what I know to be a supernatural healing from God and being accepted by my own family.

*   *   *

I also had to deal with the "wisdom of man." My doctor didn't believe that I was cured and—despite the lack of symptoms—she based her recommendations on my documented thyroidectomy, and the lab results indicating I lacked thyroid. She recommended I go back on my medicine. I refused. My doctor knew—based on my history and labs—that I would die, so she recorded in my chart, "patient claims God healed her."

* * *

I also endured unnecessary, but well-meaning concern from loved ones. Ben's parents knew I was not taking my medication and if they saw me taking a nap, or if I appeared to be struggling in any way, would immediately suggest I start taking my medicine.

* * *

What I observed was that most people chose to avoid me, or the topic. Others tried to persuade me to take my medication. I had a nurse friend call and tell me I was going to die if I didn't take my meds. If anyone knew the importance of taking that medication, it was me, but I was so clear God had removed that need. It was easy to argue and dispute these things, until I started to allow thoughts of doubt to invade my mind and heart. I didn't consciously make a choice to believe the thoughts, but I didn't get rid of them, or speak out against them either. Then the cramping started.

I woke up in the morning and couldn't unfold my hands, couldn't write, and had a problem brushing my teeth because I couldn't move my arm back and forth. There were times when my jaw locked up and I couldn't form words and had trouble swallowing.

I knew it was a spiritual battle because when I asked Ben to pray for me the symptoms would subside. It was as though the symptoms would actually melt away—just long enough for me to be able to get out of bed. I didn't even tell Ben exactly what was going on because I knew the "power of life and death" was in my tongue (Proverbs 18:21) and I refused to speak death. Sometimes it was because I couldn't form the words with the muscles in my mouth.

I had a choice to make, either go back on my medicine, or take God's medicine—His word. I chose God's Word. As a result, I searched my Bible, memorized healing scriptures, read Ken Hagin's books on healings, read sermons from John G. Lake and filled my head with healing scriptures and teachings. Then I started exercising. Even when I had trouble walking around the house, I pushed myself to go to the YMCA. I put on my headphones full of praise and worship, focused on God, and ran on the treadmill. People looked at me funny because I worked out with joy on my face and at times would burst into praise, because I was running and I was alive! I had to literally walk—and run—out my healing while I was renewing my mind. I fought for it, every day, for months, sometimes hourly and sometimes every second. I refused to give up or give in. I fought for it because I knew that if I didn't...I'd die. The cramping, muscle problems, and swallowing problems eventually went away and I gained victory over them. God taught me that I did **not** need medicine to live.

It was when I allowed thoughts of fear, and questioning, to creep in suggesting that something was still "wrong" with me, rather than focus on what God said (I am healed), that the physical manifestations showed up. "Don't believe everything you think." The thought came first. So be careful what you think. Not all your thoughts are your own, and sometimes they can be planted there by the good intentions of other people.

*   *   *

During this time of radical seeking of supernatural occurrences, Ben and I listened to amazing testimonies of other people being taken to heaven, seeing angels, feathers, gems, gold, limbs growing out, gold glitter appearing on people, dancing with Jesus, visions, water into wine, and the list goes on and on.

During women's Bible study I listened to a testimony from a lady who claimed to visit heaven regularly and professed an amazing relationship with Jesus. She then led my group through a guided meditation in which we were to focus on being with Jesus.

I listened to other women describe their relationship with Jesus. Some identified Jesus as their Lord and Savior. Some women described Jesus as their husband, lover, and best-friend...their...everything. I thought about when Todd White outright declared "I'm in love with a man!" and Pastor Dan (another leader of "Power and Love") told us to visualize him wearing a white wedding dress—while he swayed back and forth on stage—stating that he was going to marry Jesus.

During the guided meditation, I was only comfortable with Jesus sitting across from me on the ground Indian style. I was having trouble with him getting any closer than that. I began comparing my relationship with Jesus to other people's relationship and I began to wonder if something was "wrong" with me. How could I have any kind of relationship, if I can't even imagine Jesus getting any closer than sitting across from me? I kept trying, and soon, I was able to allow Jesus to walk with me in the visualization and have his arm around my shoulders. Listening to other people describe their relationship led me to believe that I was doing something "wrong." How long would this take I wondered.... people are sick and dying around me and I'm trying to figure out how to get Jesus to marry me in the spirit realm.... What??

My logic kicks in with more questions. If Jesus is God's Son and I am a child of God...doesn't that make Jesus my brother? Why would I marry my brother?

I believe Jesus loves me and I love Jesus for what He did for me. I am learning about how powerful His name is, so, I decide there is nothing "wrong" with me...I stop trying to get Jesus to marry me and accept there are some things I just don't understand.

* * *

I desired to witness supernatural occurrences, like legs or arms growing out, with my own eyes—but it wasn't happening. I continued to seek and pray. I had a lot more time, now that I was not sleeping so much, had stopped having medical problems, and no longer needed glasses. I was also blessed to be at Mom-mom and Pop-pop's, with Ben working, Carter in preschool a couple days a week, and Mom-mom and I splitting the chores of cooking and cleaning. I was free to seek God's will, attend meetings, read and study.

It was during a lengthy time of prayer when I hear, "You're pregnant."

Wow, really?

I hear it again, "You're pregnant."

Wow, I didn't expect to hear that. I search my internal clock and calculate dates and realize, it is quite possible, that I am about two months pregnant, as I had stopped taking all medicines when God healed my thyroid. It was part of my act of giving up control. I know the voice is God and immediately call Ben to tell him the good news and request he bring home a pregnancy test. Ben is excited and begins praying as well.

The next morning, I feel nauseated, but I take the pregnancy test and it is negative. We are a little confused, but figure that it is going to be some sort of supernatural occurrence so we keep praying. Ben tells me he thinks God gave him the date of birth.

For the next few days, I begin to experience increasing physical signs, and symptoms, that I am indeed–pregnant. It reminds me of when I was pregnant with Carter. I experience nausea, but goes away once I eat. I contact my OB-GYN for an appointment and they inform me I need a blood test confirming the pregnancy–which is what I want anyway.

Ben and I keep praying about it and, in the meantime, he purchases prenatal vitamins for me to take. I keep having morning sickness and begin sleeping more and more. I make the appointment for the blood test, wait all day for the results and finally at four p.m. the lab tech contacts me and tells me that I am indeed…**not** pregnant.

What?

Not pregnant…I felt deceived. Had I not discerned God's voice? Am I listening to the wrong voice? If I am wrong about this, then what else am I wrong about? I had been seeking God and praying fervently, I feel like God has misled me. My nausea dissipates and I am not as tired.

Several days later, I finally enter into prayer and confront God in tears.

"God, what happened? Did I not hear you accurately?" I ask weeping and rocking on the floor in my room.

You never asked me what you are pregnant with.

"What?" I say out loud in surprise.

You never asked me what you are pregnant with.

Oh...the realization sinks in and I realize there are many things someone can be "pregnant" with—besides a child. Like ideas, ministry, so on, and so forth.

Oops...I guess I could have asked what was meant by the word "pregnant."

You got pretty pitiful, didn't you?

"What?" I say out loud again in surprise.

You got pretty pitiful, didn't you?

"Oh...the nausea and the tiredness thing." I start to get what God is trying to teach me. First of all, I didn't question something I heard. It was indeed God telling me I was pregnant and I took that little bit of information and ran with it. I didn't stick around to have a conversation about it. God wanted a relationship with me...one that involved communication.

The second thing God was trying to teach me about was the danger of agreeing with sickness, and what *I thought* the symptoms of pregnancy were that went along with the label of being pregnant. Because of that *thought*, I made a choice to be pitiful and not powerful. It began with a thought. A very important point—and lesson—I really needed. I was acting pitiful and *not* powerful and I could **not** be both. I had made a choice...a choice to be pitiful.

{ 21 }

LOVE OF A FATHER

Ben and I kept seeking, reading, studying, attending conferences and seeking guidance from people we were introduced to through house church, prayer group and Bible studies. It was a time of confusion and excitement for us as we were becoming more aware of the spirit realm and how God communicates.

Ben and I decided to get baptized by full immersion because that's what Jesus did. So, on Palm Sunday in 2009, our "house pastors" baptized us at a local Charismatic church. It was all part of our desire to learn and grow in wisdom and experience.

I wept a lot.

I cried when I prayed, cried when I worshiped, and I cried any time I felt the presence of the Holy Spirit. Many times I cried and rocked and, when this happened, I saw visions of Jesus with outstretched arms, bleeding from self-inflicted wounds, burns and cuts, like my adolescent clients in Virginia. I wasn't crying for me per se, I was weeping for all the ones I lost, couldn't help, or tried to help, but my counseling made it more painful for them. I repented for all the times I judged, labeled, categorized and committed people. I wept for clients, friends, and family members.

* * *

Church leaders advised us to find "spiritual parents." We tried. We searched around in our faith community. But, it seemed like everyone we thought God presented to us, they didn't feel qualified, they demonstrated a lack of integrity, or they did things that were inappropriate. When things were working out, something happened that took the person out of our lives for a season. We kept praying and seeking, reading, listening and learning.

In March of 2009, I attended Randy Clark's Healing and Impartation conference with my friend Katrina. She had been experiencing a lot more supernatural events and occurrences than I was and we were both excited about attending the healing conference. Randy is a minister known for his powerful healing impartations. An impartation is when someone prays and God transfers or "imparts" that person's gifting or "power" to the receiver. The belief is that the person receives—in the spirit realm—the same gifting or power from the person doing the praying or "laying on of hands."

I was taught through books—and by other people—that certain people were anointed more than others and carried more power. Anointing means to smear or rub with oil. Usually people are anointed for a certain position, like king. Jesus was anointed by God with the Holy Spirit to set the captives free. I wanted to receive a healing impartation that would give me more power to witness more lives transformed through healing. I wanted something amazing and powerful to happen to me, so that when I prayed for people—they would feel the power, or the fire, of the Holy Spirit.

*　*　*

Prior to the impartations, during his teaching, Randy called attendees up from the audience and prayed for them to demonstrate what the Holy Spirit power looked like when it was "on someone." He brought up people who appeared to be sweating, moaning or shaking (sometimes violently), or their eyes were fluttering. It was all very confusing and exciting at the same time.

I'd read so much by that time that I desired something…anything supernatural, to happen to me. Ben and I had talked about it several times and even though we had witnessed a great deal, we had not yet experienced the "fire of God" and we desired this manifestation for ourselves.

The second day of the conference, Randy announced he would be praying an impartation before lunch. During the morning break I called Ben and excitedly told him the news of the unscheduled impartation.

"Now honey, don't be upset if Randy doesn't pray for you," Ben says.

"Oh, I won't." I assure him.

Well…the time for impartation arrives.

Randy prays a general prayer over everyone and then asks people who are feeling the Holy Spirit "on them" to come up front. I have my eyes closed and am waiting for something to happen to me.

I wait…

Nothing.

Hhmmmph…

I open an eye and peek around. Katrina is gone as is half the row of people in front, and behind me. In fact—there are a whole bunch of people up front.

I still hadn't felt the Holy Spirit "working on me," but I almost run to the front. I jostle my way between people with their eyes closed and…Randy passes right by me. He doesn't pray for me.

I stand there with my eyes closed waiting with my arms outstretched like I am waiting for a gift…or a hug.

And I stand…

Eventually, one of Randy's ministry school students approaches me to pray for me. The man doesn't impart anything; he just places his hands in mine and asks me if I know a Jason, or a Jeremy, or someone. It's a weird prayer. Then it's over. Randy leaves for lunch.

I look around me and see people littered all over the floor in a variety of postures, weeping, crying, shaking, looking half-dead, some smiling, some laughing, and some leaving. Katrina is somewhere off to my right looking like she is doing a little rocking herself. And then there is me—standing there. I step out into the hall so I do not disturb what is going on while the Holy Spirit is "working on people."

I call Ben in tears.

"Randy didn't pray for me."

"I told you honey," Ben gently reminds me.

"I know, I just really wanted him to," I say, pouting. I am feeling a little pitiful and sorry for myself. "Katrina and I are going to lunch, I'll call you later."

I head to the bathroom.

I am in the bathroom stall when God yells at me.

WHO DO YOU THINK GAVE HIM THAT?

I know immediately what God is referring to…Randy's "power."

Within seconds I am a puddle of tears, snot, and repentance. "I'm so sorry God, please forgive me, forgive me, forgive me, forgive me, I'm so sorry." I don't even know what else I said, but I am crying−out loud. I am hugging the side of the bathroom stall in utter guilt, reverential fear, and repentance−clinging to the toilet paper roll like it is an altar. Weeping and begging forgiveness with my face plastered against the side of the stall.

I realize−even though my desire is to help people−I am seeking man's power, power like Randy's. I want an "anointing" of some sort. But, it is not God's power I am seeking. I feel remorseful and experience a reverential fear and awe like never before.

I wait a while, and compose myself, before emerging from my stall. I want to make sure that the ladies who probably overheard my very loud repentance, bawling, and commotion have left the bathroom. When I finally venture out from my stall I almost walk into a woman in a wheelchair.

We start talking and I ask her kindly why she is in a wheelchair.

"Oh, I'm in constant pain. I have bone on bone in both my knees and severe back pain," she says.

"Do you mind if I pray for you?" I ask.

"Sure."

Within seconds she is up out of her wheelchair praising God, doing back stretches and bending her knees with absolutely no pain in her body. I praise God. She praises God! The women in the bathroom are praising God. We rejoice! She is healed! Thank you Jesus!

And then…she sits back down in her wheelchair.

"What...what are you doing?" I ask, astounded by her behavior. "God just healed you!"

"Oh...someone told me that Randy is going to pray for me after lunch."

And she leaves.

* * *

Even after the admonishment in the bathroom, I continued trying to access God through other "anointed" leaders and healers including Heidi Baker, David Hogan, Curry Blake and several others. Finally, God got through to me. God wants me to listen to Him first and not seek "spiritual fathers or mothers." Jesus said it in Matthew 23:9. God said it is healing in Jesus's name, not in Randy's name, David's, Curry's or Heidi's, but healing in Jesus's name. I was lifting up the man instead of being in relationship with God. I looked around and noticed that I was not the only one seeking after an "anointed" person.

When believers gather together, and cry out, seeking God and yearning for His presence, they become open to the spirit realm. When they experience a healing at a conference, or in a service, they usually attribute it to the "anointing" of the person on stage rather than identifying themselves as loved by God, worthy of Jesus' blood, and recognizing that they are powerful and have authority. God didn't want me going to anyone else, but Him. I was learning about my identity and who God said that I am.

* * *

Randy did pray for me during the conference—and imparted several times. I did experience a supernatural loss of control that felt like I was giving birth. Very similar to what I felt at the "Power and Love" conference. That "birthing" experience I discovered much later is called "travailing in the spirit," and it occurs when God wants to "birth" something through me. Travailing brought up many questions for Ben and me that people couldn't answer clearly. And, after all, I found that the impartations from Randy, paled severely in comparison to the supernatural encounter I had with God in the bathroom.

When I changed my mind, chose to believe in the spiritual realm, and agreed with my identity as being a beloved daughter of God; supernatural things started happening to me. People told me they felt fire or heat coming from my hands when I prayed for them, a white feather fell from the ceiling and landed at my feet, I experienced prophetic dreams, and I knew things before they happened. It was exciting and confusing.

The more I learned, the more I questioned. The more I questioned, the more I realized I didn't know. I also noticed that many of the people around me didn't know either. Despite the excitement I kept seeking answers. The same questions kept coming up for me, like…why doesn't everyone get healed? Why do people still believe they are sinners? Why do Christians struggle with basics like forgiveness? People I thought should "know" provided me with vague answers and were sometimes even defensive when I asked questions. And, I still hadn't received the answer to my question about why forgiveness is so important to God?

{ 22 }

ENEMY REVEALED

"**T**here is a thirty-foot angel right over there," announces the speaker, pointing to the side aisle off to my left at Christ Community Church in Harrisburg. I look at the blank space where he is pointing and I don't see anything. The women attending the "Beautiful One" conference in August of 2009 are excited and I hear the chatter begin around me.

The handsome young man on stage, Brandon Hess, is claiming that he is able to see angels. He seems like a pretty normal kid, but I don't believe that people can see angels. All the people I've met over the years who admit to seeing things were usually sitting across from me in my office requesting psychiatric help...privately...not up on stage happily announcing to the world that they are experiencing visual hallucinations.

Even though I've read books about spiritual manifestations and angels, I am still questioning—and critical—of supernatural experiences and hold all new things suspect. Brandon instructs the large audience to line up and walk under the angel's arm.

Okay, I reason, I'll play the little game of getting up and walking through, but questions start to form in my head. Am I supposed to be reverent or something? What is the purpose of this? Are all these women this gullible?

As I scan the faces of the line of women, I see some people very excited, some praying, some almost giddy, some even weeping, as they wait their turn.

"I wish I could be a seer," the lady behind me comments to her friend.

"Me too! His life must be so amazing," her friend responds.

"Isn't this exciting?" a lady in front of me asks. I nod and smile politely. I think back to my clients who "saw things" and were labeled, medicated and involuntarily committed. They didn't identify themselves as "seers" they were labeled psychotic. Yeah…exciting. I guess it depends on what side of the "book" you're looking at.

I watch the audience's reactions to walking under the "arm." Some people are slain in the spirit (they cannot stand and usually fall down), some women are rolling on the floor laughing (being "drunk" in the spirit), and some are somber and just walk through. Some people are weeping. It really is a sight to see. It reminds me of the aftermath in a war zone, with the women lying in various positions on the floor of the church. It is very similar to what I witnessed at the healing conference after Randy Clark prayed. I watch the activities with some amusement and laugh to myself about how gullible the women are, and how easily they seem to be taken with the silly exercise.

I've attended numerous psychology conferences, conducted hundreds of group activities and have worked and been trained in sales. I know how to "work a crowd" and manipulate people to help them become more involved. I am stoic as I stand in line and refuse to be "taken" with the whole process. I've read about angels, demons and the spirit realm, but haven't witnessed anything myself and I am becoming immune to any kind of event happening to me. As I stand in line watching all the activities, I make notes in my head and purpose in my heart that I will **not** be one of those people. I dutifully proceed forward with doubt, cynicism and judgment.

Okkayy…maybe just a little bit of hope that something really cool will happen.

As I step up, Brandon grabs my arm to support me—just in case I fall—I pass through the angelic archway and feel…

Nothing.

No different. No electric shock. No wave of emotions. Nothing.

"Well…that was anti-climactic," I mutter under my breath.

I pick my way through the carnage of women in various postures. I could really make a case to commit some of these people, I think to myself. I pick up my bag and turn towards the entrance of the auditorium with lunch plans on my mind. I had already dismissed the entire event as mass hysteria, a kind of shared delusional event, and my focus is now on my stomach and what I will fill it with.

I take two steps when I feel the trembling in my legs.

"Uh oh," something is wrong. It starts in my thighs. My knees quiver and I feel weak. It just feels…weird. Determined not to fall down, I sit down in the nearest pew…hard. As I sit down, I notice a deep quivering somewhere in my middle. It is almost like an invisible hand is on my belly, shaking it back and forth. It's similar to the tremors I struggled with related to my thyroid problems years ago—it feels weird and uncomfortable. I take a deep breath and focus on my body—trying to relax my muscles in an attempt to stop the quivering.

"Uh, oh." It's not working. In fact, as I relax my body, the shaking intensifies. I can't walk without concern of falling. My mind is trying to logically make sense of this situation and I am running out of options.

"Okay…I'll just lie down in this pew," I whisper. No one is paying any attention to me. I lean over in the pew and rest my head on the cushioned seat. I close my eyes…

Immediately I flash back to my bedroom in Florida. I am thirteen and James is standing naked next to my bed. But, we are not alone in the room. An angel is with me on the bed with his arm around me and he is holding back a demon with the other. Wrapped in the arms of the angel, I look up from the bed, I see a demon standing behind James but kind of in him. It's like the lines between where James ends and the demon begins is blurred and the demon is moving him like a puppet. It is as though James is wearing the demon like an exoskeleton and the demon is controlling James's body. I look at James's pained face and I see his vacant glassy eyes. The demon's eyes are right above James's. They are black and are filled with pure hate.

Suddenly, I'm not afraid any more. Within seconds I experience a profound certainty. I realize an angel was with me all that time, protecting me. Even though it was molestation, it could have been a lot worse. God really had sent an angel to protect me.

In the vision, God gave me eyes to see into the spirit realm. My heart softens and I actually start to feel sorry for James. A new feeling of kindness and forgiveness begins to form in my heart. James had been controlled by a demon he couldn't even see. The demon used James to molest me. I have a very convincing glimpse of who my real enemy is. For the first time in my life I have a more accurate view of the situation.

I weep and cry silently in the pew. "I forgive," I whisper softly, "I forgive, I forgive."

God softens my heart by showing me what was really happening in the spirit realm when my abuse was at its worst. When I had felt the most alone, lost and helpless, God the Father had sent an angel. I was not alone. I was not alone. God had heard my cries and answered my prayers for help. God had not abandoned me. God loves me. I was not alone. As I embrace a deeper revelation of being loved...I am able to forgive again from a new softer heart. "I forgive, I forgive, I forgive."

When I sit up, I am physically exhausted. I feel like I've just been through a marathon counseling session where I'd forgiven James for the awful things he'd done to me. It is as though; I'd done it in person. I definitely hadn't been prepared for **that** session. It was like I showed up for counseling and my therapist surprised me with the presence of my perpetrator—and told me to forgive.

Despite my emotional exhaustion, I feel free from the prisoner of war identity that I identified with for my entire life. I finally found freedom. I am no longer a P.O.W.—"The Enemy in His Hands." I was released and I am free to go.

I glance at my phone and realize I've only been lying down in the pew for about ten minutes. In ten minutes God freed me from the emotional pain I carried with me for over thirty years. I am free. My fight is not against flesh and blood. It is against unseen forces and my enemy is not James. He was being controlled by a demon. I realize it wasn't James abusing me. I'd seen his eyes and his tormented face. He was not aware. It was like he wasn't even there. I looked into the eyes of my real enemy, the eyes of a demon, and I saw the hatred, anger, and evil for myself. "I forgive you, James."

I now believe in angels and I believe in demons. I finally experienced it for myself. I saw my enemy and it is NOT my step-father. It is Satan. Just as John 10:10 states, "It is the thief that comes to steal, kill and destroy…"

*   *   *

Seeing into the spirit realm for those brief moments was an amazing gift God gave me, but I left that conference with something even greater. I went there in search of techniques to help people obtain freedom from their hurts, pains and suffering, and I returned home with a Heavenly Father, a Father who really cares about me. I feel love from my Creator, my Dad in heaven. It was then that I began to identify God as being more of a Father than just an unseen higher power that was giving me orders from somewhere out there. It was through forgiving James, my step-father, that softened my heart and I was free to accept God as my loving Father.

I started noticing in scripture where Jesus says that God wants to come and live inside each person and communicate with us by speaking into our hearts. God the Father showed me that He didn't leave me alone to fight by myself. I was never alone and neither are you. I firmly began to believe that God is not outside of me trying to get in—He is living inside of me. It is the evil one that is on the outside trying to get in. The more I forgave, the closer I felt to God, my Father. I realized the importance of forgiveness. Forgiveness is the basis, the foundation, of my loving relationship with my Father.

{ 23 }

GROWING IN WISDOM

"I'm excited," my friend Lin says, glancing at me. Lin is an amazing woman of faith and spends almost every waking moment of her life seeking God's will. Her long auburn hair and rosy cheeks are a blessing to behold. She identifies God as "Papa" and exudes the love of Jesus wherever she goes. She is a blessing to me and my family.

I smile, grateful to be in her presence.

Knowing God as my Father felt amazing. I was no longer afraid of God's will for my life. I trust my Father. I feel grateful and excited. I am learning how much God loves everyone.

Lin and I are waiting to hear a doctor speak about experiencing miraculous manifestations of supernatural healings that have been occurring regularly throughout his ministry. We are seated in The Apostolic Resource Center in Mechanicsburg, PA, waiting for the speaker to start. Lin describes the speaker as prophetic, says he works with an angel, and reports witnessing metal disappearing from people's bodies.

Very exciting. Despite all the testimonials I remain reserved and skeptical. I have seen angels and demons, but the "sightings" have been few and far between. I attempt to be open and non-judgmental and, yet, I want to be discerning as well.

As the evening unfolds, Dr. James Maloney informs us that there is a huge angel standing next to him and calls a woman up from the audience. He starts to speak some things to her and she starts writhing in what appears to be emotional pain and suffering. Dr. Maloney looks at the audience and states, "It's demmonnnic," in an almost condescending tone.

The woman is "freed" of whatever is binding her and she returns, weeping, to her seat. Watching from the audience, I sense that Dr. Maloney is not being very loving or honoring to the woman, which raises more questions for me about deliverance. Was the demon on her? In her? How does he know? Did the angel tell him? I wonder if I need to be able to see an angel to help deliver people and it leaves me with greater confusion about psychology and counseling.

Later, I approach Dr. Maloney and introduce myself as an LPC.

"You're a counselor, huh?"

"Yes, and I have a question. What did you do with all your psychology stuff once you learned about the supernatural realm?"

"Oh, I threw all that stuff away," he says with a wave of his hand.

Dr. Maloney's response confirms what I'd been learning over the past couple of years: I realize that I've been counseling people struggling with demonic oppression. People need more than counseling…they need spiritual help. It made me angry. I want justice and his answer makes me want to fight even more.

* * *

In the Army, soldiers study and learn how to recognize the enemy, how they operate, and identify the vehicles they use. I needed a better understanding of my real enemy and his role in sickness and disease. Remembering how I misinterpreted the word pregnant, I investigated the root words and meanings of disease, sickness, death and illness. I discovered that the root words originate from "dis" and some of the definitions included "god of the underworld, evil, wicked, and sick." I believe healing is God's will…but…why isn't everyone being healed? Does healing include mental illness?

When I examined more root words, I discovered that pharmacy comes from the Greek root word "pharmakeia" which means practicing witchcraft, "utilizing demonic powers and sorcery through the administering of drugs or potions." Wow…interesting. That helps to explain why many of the drugs used to treat mental illness don't cure the illness; they only suppressed the symptoms.

I choose to believe that all sickness, disease, mental illness, pornography, negativity, lies, sorrow and pain are works of the devil. It helps to solidify what I learned at the "Power and Love" conference. I was told that "God does not need disease and sickness to remove us from the world." They also pointed out that there are no diseases in heaven, so—of course God wants everyone healed. I'd want the same thing for my children.

God uses all things, but really wanted me to trust Him first. I learned to trust Him when I went off my own medication. The doctors said I would die...and I didn't. We do live in a world full of evil, sickness, disease and death. I acknowledged the usefulness of medicine and the wisdom of receiving healthcare, but now I knew where it all originated from.

On the other hand, if all sickness and disease are from the devil? Why were so many Christians sick? I continued to be surprised when I learned that some leaders, pastors and teachers or their spouses...were sick. Didn't they know it was a spiritual battle? What about their authority?

*   *   *

I wanted to help deliver people, so I sought training. I couldn't find a lot of people who conducted deliverances. I'd seen and experienced what the Holy Spirit did in *moments* what took me years to counsel people to break free from. People prayed for each other in church, but deliverance was rarely mentioned. I believed it should be a central theme. Prior to moving to PA, I thought deliverances only happened in movies. Do deliverances require an angel like Dr. Maloney claimed he had with him? If so...how do I get one to work with me? Is that Biblical?

*   *   *

I do not fear demons, because I believe in God's power. I trust in my authority and who God says I am. However, I encounter many Christians, who I believe to be rooted and grounded in the Word of God, who are fearful. "If you step out, the attacks will be greater," is a statement I heard more than once. This confuses me since I know 1John 4:4 states that "greater is He that is in you (me) than he that is in the world." I also know the Gospel of John and the authority I have as a Christian because the Most High God lives and dwells within me. As God renews my mind, He teaches me that I am just as "anointed" as any other Christian.

I met with "professionals" in the field of deliverance and sat in on their lectures and talks, read some of their books and even had a two-hour conversation with a man many of the families recommended. I was seeking guidance, wisdom and wanted to learn from his experience with deliverance.

The man I interviewed focused on my social history and kept asking specific questions about my sexual abuse. It felt very icky. I finally confronted him and reminded him that I was not there for him to counsel me, but for me to learn about deliverance.

I told him that I was not afraid to confront demons. He told me that I "should" be.

"But...God doesn't give me a spirit of fear but of power, love and a sound mind." I respond, quoting 2 Timothy 1:7. "If I'm fearful, I'm not trusting God."

Two hours later, I left the meeting even more confused. I guess I need to ask God...not man.

*   *   *

What I discovered was a lot of misinformation, many discrepancies and inconsistencies, and different "streams" of thought. Every time I found a leader I thought was Biblical and had the answers, God would highlight a serious concern or lack of integrity in the person, or their ministry. Some people were unavailable, or unwilling, to answer my questions. I read several books, but many encouraged memorizations of lengthy prayers and techniques. I felt confused, frustrated, and overwhelmed with the conflicting information...but it didn't stop me.

*   *   *

Our family continued to pray for people, but Ben and I began to notice some disturbing patterns that were hard to ignore. Some people who experienced healing after prayer sometimes later exhibited an increase in pain, pain located elsewhere in their bodies, or even a torment of emotional, spiritual and physical attacks not only for themselves, but sometimes in their families as well. Several people who were healed had their symptoms return, yet they refused to be prayed for, and it seemed, that they became solidified in their beliefs that healings were **not** for today. A close friend diagnosed with bipolar disorder lived four joy filled months free from medicine and voices, but then they returned with a vengeance.

We knew people needed ongoing support, discipleship and deliverance, so we searched, but could not find, local ministers to refer people to. As a result, Ben and I decided to enter the battle ourselves. The first "planned" deliverance Ben and I participated in was requested by a young woman named Barb that Ben met through praying for people at work. Barb identified herself as Charismatic and believed she needed deliverance, based on numerous demonic occurrences happening in her home and manifesting in her life wreaking havoc.

Ben and I drove into the beautiful countryside of PA for our very first experience in helping someone be set free from demons. In anticipation of a movie-like experience, I felt excited and cautious at the same time.

Prior to the meeting, we consulted with people in Bible study, read manuals and books, listened to teachings, and received counsel from peers. And then we did everything backwards. We forgot the anointing oil and didn't start off in praise and worship. We also did things that seemed right at the time...

Knock. Knock.

Barb flings open the door and welcomes us inside. Her long, flowing, brown hair is pulled back loosely, tied in a bun and she's dressed in an oversized peace T-shirt and leggings. She introduces us to J.C., her 13-year-old daughter, and we chat about school and their pet cat.

We decide to start off in prayer together, but Barb stops Ben half-way through. She whispers to me that we are making the demons angry. I was observing Barb while Ben was praying and had watched as her lip curled up quite unnaturally. Barb doesn't want her daughter to be present during the deliverance, so she sends her to visit a neighbor before we enter into prayer again.

I take the lead, sit down directly in front of Barb, as she seats herself firmly in an oversized arm-chair. Ben pulls up a chair off to Barb's right. Finally, we start. As we pray together, and ask the Holy Spirit for help, the names of the demons are revealed to Barb. As Barb "hears" the names she tells me and I order them to leave. It is calm, orderly and all seems to be going well—until I tell Barb to forgive.

She refuses. "No!"

"What?" Surprised by the refusal...I glance at Ben who shrugs his shoulders.

"Umm...forgive," I falter.

"No!" she states again, glaring at me. The intensity in her eyes startles me.

"Umm...okay, well...hhmmm..." I respond, my mind searching...praying silently. "Okay...well, I stand in the gap for Barb right now and I speak out forgiveness in Jesus name!"

As I speak, Barb's eyes widen in sudden fear and her head rears back.

"I forgive John in Jesus name..." I continue with names of other people who have harmed Barb. I keep going as she squirms and writhes in her chair. Eventually she starts speaking out forgiveness.

It is as though my speaking forgiveness for her, loosens her tongue. She is able to take over and speak forgiveness for people I don't know and also ask for her own forgiveness. The whole deliverance visit lasts about an hour and she appears genuinely joyful, but also expresses her concern that the demons might not be "all gone." I don't know how to answer or assure her that they are.

We discussed the deliverance with Barb in the weeks and months following our visit to her home. Barb expressed a deep gratitude that I had allowed the Holy Spirit to lead me to speak forgiveness for her. Barb reported that she didn't feel like she had control over her tongue—until I stood in the gap for her and spoke it first.

Barb enjoyed her renewed life and began to experience success and told us she felt free and alive. She enjoyed a powerful lifestyle, prayed for people, built her support system and joined a local church. However, Barb struggled with several ongoing close relationships and frequently expressed anger towards her neighbor, close friends and her daughter. Over time, the demons returned–coupled with severe medical problems. Barb ended up needing a wheelchair for a while, but no matter how many times we prayed for her–it didn't help. We did not live close enough to minister to her daily, although in the beginning we tried. She lacked skills and knowledge that we were unable to provide for her, because of the distance. We too were learning and growing and didn't have the answers. Despite our efforts to keep in touch, we lost contact with her as time went on.

*   *   *

"I feel such love and compassion coming from you," states Claire as we are both leaving the Bible study/prayer group.

"Thank you."

"I want to be more like that, but I'm too scared," she says.

"Scared of what?" I ask, looking up at her oval shaped face surrounded by her beautiful curly blonde hair.

"I'm afraid people won't like me back," she responds with tears glistening in her eyes.

Knowing fear and anxiety are not from Jesus and are spiritual attacks, I offer to pray for her.

She gratefully accepts and I clasp hands with Claire who is almost six feet tall.

"Right now in Jesus name I take authority over fear and anxiety!" I state confidently.

Immediately Claire pitches straight backward on the carpet–screaming all the way.

Stumbling, I try to break free from her grasp, maintain my own balance and not step on her all at the same time. Miraculously, I manage to remain standing and continue my prayer, "I tell them to GO right now in Jesus name!"

The whole scene is dramatic, quick and somewhat confusing. The two other women in the room rush over to us and start praying in what sounds like war tongues. They start spiritually binding demons and sending them to the abyss.

A few minutes later, Claire rises up off the carpet, reports feeling free, and visibly appeared vibrant. She told me she didn't remember much about what happened, but said that the voice was not her own, and the screaming was terrible for her to endure. We exchanged information as I desired to keep in touch with her and learn from the experience as much as possible.

I kept in contact with Claire for several months. During that time, I learned more about her, and her situation. She was living with her father at the time and struggled to forgive him for small offenses and negativity. Claire reported frequent spats with him, siblings, friends, and told me that she had also been hurt by ministries. She was unwilling to consistently speak forgiveness for the accumulated wrongs and, over time, she reported an increase in fear and anxiety. Claire also lacked communication and interpersonal skills, and I was not able to minister to her on an ongoing basis, to teach her what I knew. It appeared that Claire not only struggled spiritually, but emotionally, interpersonally, and would have benefited from learning some basic interpersonal skills. Her situation became worse and she left home to live in a group home. At times, she called in the middle of the night requesting prayer. It worked— but only for a while.

*   *   *

The more I tried to help people, the more it seemed to resemble placing psychology on top of spiritual problems. It seemed like I had just traded one form of counseling for a spiritual form of counseling. Except worse—because what I was doing now seemed to be producing even worse outcomes than secular counseling.

I want structure, ethical guidelines and accountability. As a result, the desire for a consistent way to minister, deliver, set, and keep people free—kept growing inside of me: urging me, challenging me and filling me with zeal. There had to be a supernatural way to help people and keep them consistently free from demons.

* * *

One night, I wake up in the middle of the night. With my heart and mind focused on God, I speak in tongues. Within minutes, I feel the tangible presence of the Holy Spirit. The hairs on my arms stand up and goose bumps spread down my body. The air is thick and I feel calm and peaceful. While praying in tongues, I feel an immense surge of power course through my body. It feels like I've been struck by lightning.

My body jerks and twitches.

It hurts.

Despite the pain, I feel more powerful than I have ever felt. The electrical power surge intensifies. In that moment, I connect with God's heart. I experience the intense, awesome, amazing, tangible love He has for people. My heart aches and feels like it doubles in size.

I start to feel overwhelmed emotionally and physically. It is intense and too much for me to bear. As soon as I start to think that I can't take it anymore...it stops.

I feel empty and weak.

I experienced God the Father's heart aching and breaking for His people. I wept for hours before returning to sleep. The experience inspired me to write the letter you read on page 110.

* * *

The next morning, I attempted to convey my experience— to describe the overwhelming massive feelings of love to the women in my Bible study. It did not go well. My zeal and lack of ability to describe my experience in words caused some of the women to be uncomfortable and one lady told me that she thought there was something "wrong" with me. I agreed that I lacked wisdom, but I didn't agree that there was something "wrong" with me. Although I disagreed in the moment, the seed of doubt her words planted remained.

* * *

Ben and I agreed that we needed more training, education and guidance. So, after living with Mom-mom and Pop-pop for almost three years, we decided to move. We chose Randy Clark's Global School of Supernatural Ministry (GSSM) in Mechanicsburg, Pennsylvania.

GSSM consists of structured presentations from itinerant ministers paid to present their teachings, ideas, theories, or revelations to students. The primary goal of the training is to introduce students to minister in the supernatural and develop a supernatural lifestyle centered on healing. Our time in the school included a ministry trip to Brazil for ten days.

Right before our trip to Brazil, I walked by two people at the school praying for a man on a couch. I noticed it was Steve, an acquaintance, and I observed that what the people were doing was not consistent with what I'd read and experienced. Steve is normally a vibrant man in his mid-twenties with a strong spiritual life, love for people and desire to worship Jesus. I knew him to be filled with life and love...

*   *   *

"Life, life, life." The lady prodded Steve with her hand poking him in the chest.

Steve is lying on his back and appears near death. His eyes are closed and his skin is pale. Another man, with a scruffy beard, is holding his legs to keep Steve from sliding off the leather couch onto the floor. He is mumbling some sort of prayer and it sounds like he is speaking in tongues.

I don't recognize the two people praying over Steve, but it doesn't appear to be effective, and it sure doesn't look like it is producing life. Standing directly over the couch, I look Steve in the face and command him to open his eyes.

Steve's eyes fly open, they meet mine and in a very childlike voice—not his own—he inquires, "Daddy?"

Immediately, I take over the situation and tell the couple to step back and stop touching him.

"In Jesus name I ask Holy Spirit well up inside of Steve," I continue in my prayer and I take authority over fear, anxiety and speak love into him. In a few minutes Steve is upright on the couch and able to recognize me. Sitting down next to him on the couch, I sense what God wants me to tell him next.

"Speak out forgiveness."

"No!" Steve responds and closes his eyes again. His head dips and his shoulders sag along with his refusal.

"I stand in the gap right now for Steve and I speak out forgiveness for his mother, I speak out forgiveness for his father, in Jesus name."

As I speak, Steve's eyes fly open. I see terror as his eyes widen, reminding me of a deer caught in the headlights of an oncoming car. As I speak, I watch his eyes clear. His eyes focus on me and he obediently takes over in the prayer and speaks forgiveness for several other people.

Later, Steve and I discussed the deliverance. Steve shares with me that when I spoke out forgiveness for him, the demons inside his head began screaming—right before they left him.

* * *

Ben and I spent ten days ministering in Brazil with GSSM. We witnessed numerous healings, deliverances and I saw angels. It was an exciting time and I was intent on learning all I could about the spirit realm.

Riding on the ministry bus with our team, I observed an interaction between two team members that did not sit well with me. I had a gut reaction to a male and female sitting in front of me apparently playing around with the power of the Holy Spirit.

It was disturbing—lacked honor—and sounded almost sexual. As I sat in the seat behind them, I averted my eyes in an attempt to block out what was occurring right in front of me. As I sat there, I remembered my authority and began to pray and spoke out against their behaviors. In moments, both people were silent and started reading from their Bibles.

I discussed my concerns with one of the ministry leaders. She told me that I was growing in discernment, encouraged me to trust my gut feelings to determine if behaviors and manifestations, were Holy or demonic.

Later, during a ministry time, I came upon the female from the bus as she was praying for a man. She looked up at me from the floor with fear in her eyes. She had her hand on the man's chest and her arm was moving unnaturally. It was moving snake-like and matched the man's writhing's.

Although I helped her—and the man—I judged her and others in my heart. I questioned behaviors, actions and choices that the ministry team members were making. I believed that since I could "control" my reactions and not be "drunk in the Spirit" like the others were, that they needed to act more mature.

A short time later, God taught me a serious lesson about the limits of my control...

* * *

Ben and I are seated in chairs on the right side of an open room set up in rows facing a large stage. The floor is concrete, the walls are brightly painted, and we are seated approximately six rows from the front. It is during our ministry trip in Brazil and we, along with our interpreters, are here for a training about words of knowledge. Ben and I have heard the teaching several times and are not really excited about sitting through it again.

Randy starts by playing a video advertisement of a conference called "The Voice of the Apostles." As soon as the music starts, the familiar cramping in my stomach starts. It intensifies, becomes more painful, and I feel the urge to get down on the floor. As I slide off of my chair, my knees hit the cement floor–hard. I curl up on the floor hugging my abdomen trying to be discreet.

Ben and I have been through this several times before and he has learned to **not** focus on me, because there is nothing he can do. His job in this situation is to be aware of what is going on around us, to figure out what may have triggered the feelings so we can discuss what happened and try to determine what God is doing through us.

Following the short video, Randy's assistant stands up and reads a passage from Ephesians about love. Randy informs us that he believes God is encouraging him to do a baptism of love before the planned training.

The entire time, I am on the floor. Travailing is painful. It feels like childbirth and, when it is over, I feel exhausted so I decide to rest on the floor while Randy continues with the shortened version of his training.

The session ends and Ben tries to help me up, but my muscles will not cooperate. In fact, I am unable to even lift my head up off the floor. I start to weep—and panic—as I tell Ben of my paralysis. Internally I start a dialogue with God, promising that I will do better about asking for help from others, asking for forgiveness for judging others, and basically trying to negotiate a release of some sort—so I wouldn't be embarrassed. A lovely British lady came over and prayed for me and my anxiety changed to peace…but I still couldn't move. I wasn't embarrassed any more, in fact, it seemed kind of funny.

The bus arrives and we need to leave. Randy walks by and tells Ben, "Pick her up and get her on the bus."

It was extremely embarrassing—and funny—at the same time when four men came over and each picked up one of my limbs. As they lifted me up, my head flopped backwards. It took another person to hold my head up as they carried me out of the building. The bus had to circle the block so they plopped me down on the sidewalk into Ben's arms.

When it returned, the guys again lifted me up, carried me onto the bus and deposited me into a seat. I immediately started sliding off the seat. Ben kept me from falling, and remained by my side. When we arrived at the hotel, one of our friends obtained a wheelchair to help transport me to our room. It was a lot less conspicuous than having five people carry me through the lobby.

My paralysis lasted for a few hours. The whole experience was confusing. I repented for judging others and for believing that I had all the answers. I also gained an even greater appreciation for my husband. God was teaching me the importance of walking in love.

There were many more supernatural occurrences, powerful prophesies, and unexplainable events that we experienced. We questioned, read, and prayed our way through some very confusing situations. Many times, we didn't understand until later. Some we still don't understand. We were new to the supernatural healings, miracles, sightings and lifestyle and we wanted to know everything.

* * *

As I spent more and more time in prayer, questioning, and fellowshipping, I began to notice "an anything goes" mentality when it came to the Holy Spirit. I was told that the "Holy Spirit is a big boy" and will do what He wants to do. Other people described Him as a gentleman. Many did not appear to be able to recognize the difference between a Holy or a demonic manifestation.

The prevalent teaching on discernment was, that if there was a spiritual manifestation, and the person got up off the floor rejoicing—it must be from God. If they got up and they weren't joyful, closer with God, or reported an unpleasant experience—then it wasn't. But, there were only a few people willing, able, or available to help, if it wasn't deemed to be "of God."

I'd experienced the reverential fear and awe of the power of God when He scolded me in the bathroom stall and when I was helpless on the floor. I felt saddened when I witnessed an almost cavalier attitude towards the power of the Holy Spirit. In my seeking I read a book by J. Lee Grady called "The Holy Spirit Is Not For Sale." In his book, he described many of the disturbing events that Ben and I were encountering and questioning. His book validated my concerns of idolizing "anointed" leaders, throwing Holy Spirit "fireballs," and the apparent lack of purity in ministries and itinerate ministers. I started praying for an increase in wisdom and truth.

*   *   *

I knew God the Father loved me and valued relationships, but I struggled with how to have a relationship with the Holy Spirit. What kind of relationship could I have with a Ghost? A genderless Spirit? An It? I'm a visual person and was struggling with the image of the Holy Spirit. I've studied the brain and knew that what I was struggling with, was creating a frame of reference I could relate to—but I didn't have any.

Many people identified the Holy Spirit as an unseen force dwelling outside of themselves or "falling on them" during a service. I questioned their discernment and judged people in my heart. Although I struggled, I thought I knew more than most, based on my knowledge. However, I learned in a very personal way how to tell the difference...

*　*　*

When I was out there examining what other people were doing wrong, I lost sight of God and started to operate from pride rather than love and service. And when I operated from pride, it allowed old familiar self-destructive and demonic thought patterns to emerge. I believe it was the spirit of suicide. At one point, I tried to cut myself and Ben had to restrain me and cast off the demon.

When Ben "delivered" me that day, it was intense for both of us. Following the experience, I felt vulnerable, immediately repented, and created a list of people I needed to request forgiveness from. I contacted each one and was grateful for the opportunity to humbly ask for—and receive—forgiveness for the way I acted over the years. My list was long and my bag of stones was large. Many forgave, some were confused, and some had already died, so I had to speak it out in my bedroom.

Since then, the suicidal thoughts have resurfaced a couple of times, but they no longer have any power over me. I shined the light of Jesus on those demons and they had to flee, in Jesus name! Remember, not every thought is your own.

In Matthew 6:14-15 and Matthew 11:26 Jesus says forgive, or you are not forgiven. I began to understand some of the reasons why forgiveness is so important to God. Asking for forgiveness—and speaking forgiveness—keeps us humble, cleans our hands and allows us to have a pure heart.

*　*　*

Forgiveness is an act of war in the spirit realm. The demons hate it; they know the power of it. I also learned from these experiences—and realized too late—that while we were helping people to some degree by casting out their demons, we were not able to provide the ongoing training or support needed to help renew their minds on a daily basis.

Sadly, none of the people we "helped" remained free. I found, yet again, people either lacked a willingness to forgive, lacked skills to adopt a new mindset, didn't know their identity, or didn't have a firm grounding in the amazing love of God. Once again, Ben and I felt responsible for the outcome of their lives. We were the ones who had helped free them, but we didn't know how to help them after they were "released." As a result, we created some of our own "walking wounded" and for that we repent. Please forgive us, forgive us, forgive us.

We renewed our commitment to learn a better way; it had to be out there somewhere. So we continued seeking, learning and growing in wisdom. We didn't realize that our zeal and desire for more would cause discord, stress, and fights in our relationship. But God knew…which is why he rooted and grounded our relationship in love and forgiveness in 2009.

* * *

For a season we attended a local church and there was a little homeless man that "latched on to us" because we gave him money from time to time, prayed for him and loved on him. George was a little un-kept, dirty at times, and when we attended—we hugged him and told him he was awesome.

One Sunday, I attended church alone and George approached during worship. I knew he was there, but I was struggling inside with being joyful and loving him unconditionally. I was judging his outsides. I immediately began to experience the cramping feelings inside, I got down on the floor and rocked and prayed. I asked God to cleanse my heart and NOT allow me to get up off the carpet until I could genuinely love George and see him the way that Jesus did. I needed some Jesus glasses…quick…because George was not leaving and I did not want him to feel rejected by me.

I asked for God's help through forgiveness. "God judge me first. Please forgive me, forgive me, forgive me…" I started to feel genuinely loving towards George. "I forgive George; he is only doing what he knows to do. Truth is attractive. I forgive, I forgive, I forgive George." As I continued in my simple act of obedience, I began to feel genuine love for George and the cramping feeling in my stomach subsides.

I sat up and looked at George with genuine loving "Jesus eyes" and was able to love him non-judgmentally. George is not bad. As a baby I'm sure he did not want to grow up and be homeless. That probably was NOT on his list of things to do. But, it was only through a simple act of obediently speaking forgiveness—and asking for forgiveness—that I was able to feel pure and holy inside enough to be loving towards George so that my words were not hollow.

* * *

I had to be willing for God to judge me first. I knew I was not "feeling very loving" towards George. But, instead of blaming it on him, his outward appearance and personal hygiene, I had to look at myself first. As a result, I added a daily request in my prayers. I asked God to judge me first so I could love more perfectly.

Forgiving ourselves, cleaning up our messes—and our hearts—has become a daily habit my family does out of obedience. When the more difficult hurts, offenses and injustices occur they are easier to handle because we practice daily cleansing. We don't put it off until later when we "feel like it" —we 'get er done" now. It's easier that way.

* * *

The more I forgave the cleaner I felt inside. The more I forgave, the closer I felt to God and became even more zealous as my love grew. When I forgave freely, my capacity to love others grew. I witnessed it in my children as well. If they argued, I had them sit across from each other and use a DBT skill called broken record, which is repeating several times; like a broken record repeats. "I forgive you, I forgive you, I forgive you." Then repeatedly ask for forgiveness as well. "Please forgive me, forgive me, forgive me." Following this simple rule out of obedience, allows freedom for them to love each other the way God loves and sees them.

* * *

Once I realized the power of forgiveness, I asked the Holy Spirit to lead and guide me to remind me of people I had not fully forgiven from my past. My mom was brought to mind. I spoke out forgiveness for her as I viewed her life and behaviors through Jesus glasses. I tried to see her from God's perspective. She was one of His amazing creations who had her own prisoner of war experiences, her own hurts, pains and sorrows. I know that she struggled and was afraid. As I thought about her life and the pain, sorrow and heartache she endured, my heart softened even more. I compared her apparent "blindness" of my abuse to the blinders used on horses.

When we travel through Lancaster County, PA, we pass many horse drawn buggies. Many have what are called "blinders" attached to their bridles to restrict the horse's vision. The eyes of a horse are on the sides of their heads and my friend Jerry Cooper, who owns a horse farm in SC, describes horses as "thousand pound scaredy cats." Horses are easily spooked by anything new. The blinders help the horse keep focused ahead and not be distracted, scared, or "spooked" by events happening around them.

I love horses. Putting blinders on horses does not change their nature, it sometimes adds to their fear, because their vision is restricted. Artificially restricting their sight sometimes causes more anxiety. They are forced to only focus on what is ahead.

The driver of the buggy sometimes uses a whip or switch to keep the horse moving ahead, facing forward—in fear and obedience. My mom was taught like that. The evil one put "blinders" on my mom so that she couldn't see what was going on around her. She still got hit, but was forced, and trained, to keep moving forward in fear, obedience and deception. I believe she was not able to see what really happened to me as a child. The devil had placed blinders on my mom through pain, loss and tragedy.

As I pondered the similarities between blinders and how Satan works, I forgave in a more genuine way. As I forgave more from my heart, the "eyes" of my heart were opened and I was able to notice in scripture things I had not noticed before. Every time I forgave, a veil (or blinders), were removed from my eyes and I was able to notice an aspect of God I hadn't noticed before—a truth that had been hidden from me. As a result, God led me to a spiritual truth that I was not quite prepared for.

{ 24 }

LOVE OF A MOTHER

"**A**AARRRGGGHHHH!" I scream out loud as my fist slams into the dashboard. My Jeep faces an empty playground at a deserted church in Fountain Inn, South Carolina. It's the middle of the afternoon and rain is pouring down—like the tears streaming down my face.

"God, why do I always have to be the one to forgive?" I cry out in anguish. "It's not fair!"

Feeling the familiar cramping and tightening in my gut, I wrap my arms around my abdomen and rock back and forth.

Ben and I are fighting, again.

You are not allowed to run this time. It's time to stay and fight.

"What do you mean? That's all we've been doing is fighting! I don't understand!" I'd even packed a bag this time. Thoughts start flowing as quickly as my tears. I could just leave, disappear, not have to go back, it would be easy, I didn't need much money, I could just leave, my kids would be fine without me; better probably…without all the fighting.

I know it is Satan trying to influence me in my weakness, so I do my best to ignore the words, but it's been over two years of fighting and I'm tired.

"God, I'm so tired of fighting with Ben," I sob. "Please help me."

I am.

"What do I do?"

You are not allowed to run this time. It's time to stay and fight.

"Why?"

Because it's Truth.

"I don't want this if it means the end of my marriage with Ben."

You are not allowed to run this time. It's time to stay and fight.

"I forgive, I forgive, I forgive…forgive me…forgive me…forgive me…I love, I love, I love." I recite as my tears subside and I submit to truth. As I speak out in obedience I am reminded in my heart that Ben is **not** my enemy. My fight is not against Ben, it is against powers and principalities. Satan is the one trying to split us up.

You asked for this.

"What, the fighting?"

You asked for this.

"I asked for what?"

Truth. I immediately know what God is talking about. The truth about the Holy Spirit.

I sat for hours in the parking lot that day before returning home. That was the last time I tried to run. I heeded God and I chose to stay and fight, to do whatever it takes.

* * *

Ben and I participated in GSSM together until God told Ben to leave in November and then me in January. Just like that, I was not allowed to go back. In my searching I wanted to enroll in other schools, but God consistently cut off all opportunities. During this time, Ben bought me Jay P. Green's book "The Interlinear Bible Hebrew English and Greek." I compared passages and words and was amazed at how different verses translated from one language to another. A different kind of fire was lit inside of me and I realized God was directing me to learn Hebrew. Apparently God forgot that I flunked Spanish in high school. Despite my misgivings, I was obedient. Almost two years into studying Hebrew and the root words, God revealed to me that the Holy Spirit is…feminine. What?

* * *

The Holy Spirit's femininity was a constant source of disagreement between Ben and me for many months. I consistently showed him documents, research and writings that validated a feminine Holy Spirit and how it was translated out of the Bible. Eventually, Ben started identifying the Holy Spirit as "Mother," even before I did.

I didn't want the Holy Spirit to be feminine. I associated power with the Holy Spirit and I didn't think of females being very powerful. It also forced me to look at the relationship with my own mother again. My mother was strong willed, but she had never been there for me in the tough times. How am I supposed to trust a maternal spirit I can't even see? Trusting the Holy Spirit was harder than believing in God as my Father.

The Bible says to honor your Father and your Mother and you will have eternal life (Ephesians 6:2). Honor both, not just one. How can I honor my Mother if there isn't one? I honor God the Father and God the Mother Holy Spirit. It was easy to believe that Jesus loved me. It took a lot more to believe God the Father loved me, but I continued to struggle with trusting the Holy Spirit. It was easier when I believed that the Holy Spirit was masculine. As I examined the scriptures, my identity became clearer...

I was birthed, formed and fashioned in love. God the Father and Mother loved me and created me. God loved me and when I made a choice and believed in Jesus, I accepted my inheritance, my birth rite. And when I was baptized in the Holy Spirit, She convicted me, purified me and filled me with zeal. I am loved. I was loved in the beginning and I am loved now.

The war is between the love from my heavenly family versus the fear in the world. God didn't give me a spirit of fear. I choose what I focus on.

{ 25 }

THE BATTLE

The battlefield is in my mind and the battle is for my beliefs and what I focus on. I have a choice as to what I focus on...the amazing love of my Father and Mother in heaven or the fear in the world? I will become (or manifest) whatever I behold. In the world today, just about everywhere I go, or look, something tries to instill fear in me. A fear that I either lack something, or something is "wrong" with me, and it needs to be fixed in order for me to be happy or healthy.

Whatever it is, it usually accompanies a way to fix me...enticing me to buy something, read something, take a pill, follow advice, come to a service, attend a conference or class, purchase a product or whatever it may be. Satan is around trying to use someone, somewhere, to get me to be afraid. Whatever "it" is, if it is based on fear, or negativity, then it is NOT what God wants for me.

My fight is not against flesh and blood. That means my enemy is not my parents, neighbor, spouse, children, or anything made of flesh. **My fight is not people.** Satan uses people to hurt people. I don't want to help him! I refuse to be mean, fight, or say bad things about people. I strive to speak loving, uplifting words.

Interesting! [handwritten note]

*   *   *

I was struggling with a choice. My hair was thinning, falling out, and not growing back. I noticed the thinning for years, but it became so noticeable that I looked old and sickly. I was aware that it was directly related to the lack of thyroid in my body. But...I believed that I was healed...God "wrote it on my heart." It was my testimony. Why wasn't it growing? I promised God that no matter what happened with my hair, I would always praise Him—but I really like my hair. I tried all the battle tools that I taught people and yet my hair continued to fall out.

Medicine isn't bad, but I felt like a hypocrite for even considering taking medicine. Over time, my self-consciousness grew, I hated having my picture taken, and the way I looked influenced whether or not I spoke to anyone in public. I went from praying for people, enthusiastic, and outgoing to being introverted and silent. More and more of my time was spent in front of the mirror and researching hair growth techniques. I don't wear a lot of make-up and don't spend a lot of time on my hair. My feelings about my hair interfered with how I looked, what I wore, and I stopped enjoying riding in my Jeep with the top off.

My inner conflict was even worse. Am I not trusting God's word? Have I failed? I fought so hard to convince others that I was healed and no longer needed medications. What would I say? I thought about all the people that haven't been healed. I know there are many Christians who believe in healings, trust God, and are sick or dying. I realized that I'd judged them in my heart. "God, please forgive me for judging them."

* * *

"Do you think God's mad at you?" my friend Terry asks.
I pause. My tears subside as I consider her question.
"No...but."
"Then don't worry about it. God uses all things."

* * *

We live in a sick, diseased and dying world. The battle was for my attention. I was more focused on my appearance than on God. My hair loss caused me to examine my "belly button" and figure out what was "wrong" with me. Was I harboring un-forgiveness? I checked my heart. Satan uses all things too...I made a choice.

* * *

"I decided to go back on my medication."
Incredulous, Ben looks at me, "What?"
"Not out of fear of dying," looking at him intently. "I want my hair to grow back."
"But, I thought you were healed?"
"Me too...," I respond. "Me too."

* * *

I seek God in prayer and He assures me that He is **not** mad at me. My identity as a powerful spiritual daughter of God…does NOT change. It's not what goes into me that defiles me—it's what comes out. I want to profess God's heart wherever I go and taking my medicine doesn't change my identity.

I chose to believe that my identity and authority does not change. God taught me that it was possible to live without medicine and He is not mad at me. I chose to take my thyroid medication so I could focus my attention on other people rather than on my hairline. God couldn't use me if all my attention was focused on me. The battle was for my attention.

{ 26 }

WEAPONS OF WARFARE

There are many weapons our family uses to help us to be positive, focus on God, and rejoice in all things. We love to praise and worship, have an attitude of gratitude and love one another. We focus on it daily and confront each other if we slip into negativity.

You cannot overcome negativity with mediocrity. Everywhere we look it surfaces, and if it were easy to combat, the world wouldn't be so consumed by it. In our striving to live powerful, effective, spiritually grounded lives, Ben and I have found that one of the most effective weapons against negativity is a radical attitude of gratitude—especially in the face of things we don't want.

One day, I was struggling with the negativity being spoken around our house and it was trying to get in my spirit. I refused to submit and broke out into a radical attitude of gratitude.

*   *   *

I burst into the bedroom. "Thank you God for paint on the walls!"

Slam goes the door.

Derik, eight years old, is laying on the bed reading a book. He looks up.

"Thank you God for clothes on the floor!" I start pointing at random objects as I rant. "Thank you God for books," my eyes scan the room. "Thank you God for windows, thank you God for window shades, thank you God for socks, thank you God for underwear. Thank you God for computers."

"Um…Mom?" interrupts Derik, "Did you just thank God for underwear?"

"YES I DID! AND THANK YOU GOD FOR ELASTIC BANDS IN UNDERWEAR CAUSE IF WE DIDN'T HAVE

ELASTIC BANDS IN OUR UNDERWEAR—THEY WOULD BE DOWN AROUND OUR ANKLES!"

We laughed.

It worked.

I overcame negativity with a radical attitude of gratitude.

*   *   *

Two very powerful weapons we use daily that build up rather than destroy are the "Great I Ams" and the "Great You Ares." (Remember the land of Ur?) The "Great I Ams" is modeled after the positive affirmations used in psychology, but affirm our spiritual identity. The "Great You Ares" confirm someone else's identity as an awesome creation loved by God. We speak them out to our friends and family, the people we spend time with, and where there is often the most discord.

*   *   *

"Carter honey, say your Great I AMs." He and Derik have been fighting.

"I don't feel like it, Mommy."

"I know…that's exactly why I'm telling you to say them."

He rolls his eyes, stands, and places his hand on his heart. "I am awesome. I am amazing. God the Father lives in me…Mother Holy Spirit lives in me…I look like Jesus, and I'm awesome!" Carter half smiles.

"Feel better?"

"Yeah, kind of," he says.

"Say them again…louder."

*   *   *

We are talking about speaking truth and life and not allowing the evil one to use us as his mouthpiece. It is a bright Sunday Morning and soon Carter is rejoicing and speaking out "Great You Ares" to Derik.

"You are awesome, you are amazing, you are the best brother," Carter rattles off quickly.

Derik joins in and starts to try and out-speak Carter, "You are creative, you are smart, you are the best brother."

"You are a great soccer player, you are smart!" Carter continues.

This goes on for a few minutes, soon the boys are laughing and smiling at each other and have forgotten why they were fighting.

We notice that when our kids have not been repeating their "Great You Ares" as part of their morning and evening routines, they end up fighting more frequently. In our house we do not agree with the idea that our children will fight just because they are boys. We believe that is a lie from the pit of hell. There is enough negativity and hate in the world and I will not let it invade my house!

We are not perfect and we make mistakes in our family, but we agree quickly and ask for forgiveness. When the boys do fight, we sit them down and before we ask them to tell us what happened, we have them speak out, "Forgive me, forgive me, forgive me." We also say, "When we are pointing a finger at someone else, there are three pointing back at us." Judge us first, God.

Over time, I began to believe in how great God says "I Am." It is no longer just a psychological exercise to overcome my past; it is a truth I believe to my core and I want everyone to experience this same kind of love of self. It has proven helpful in establishing my children's identities—and I encourage you to do the same.

Hang a sign in your room and put a note in your car to remind you to speak out the truth about God's amazing love for you, and begin speaking it to others as well. Root yourself in your identity of love. Change your internal dialogue of negativity based on fear of what the world may say about you, in the future, or a lie that was spoken about you in the past. You are who God says you are...awesome! And, I challenge you to tell others as well. Tell people they are awesome...just because God made them that way. It'll make their day...I promise.

{ 27 }

FIRST AID

I spent time volunteering for a church collecting clothing donations for fire victims during the outbreak of house fires in Coatesville, PA, in 2009. I encountered a woman there with knee problems and she allowed me to pray for her healing. She experienced an immediate healing and was very touched by my prayers. A couple weeks later, I saw her again and she informed me that her knee pain had returned and asked me if I could pray for her again. I knelt before her and placed my hands on her knee.

"In Jesus name I command this knee to line up with God's word. I speak healing to her knee in Jesus name." Glancing up at her, I see her shaking her head no.

"Holy Spirit I ask you well up inside Jill and gently remind her of anyone she needs to forgive—right now in Jesus name."

I wait.

Jill starts talking. "Well, I don't really think so, maybe my neighbor. I have been kind of mad at her lately. I guess I could forgive her."

Crackle, crackle, crackle.

"What was that?" I ask puzzled.

From my kneeling position on the floor I look up at Jill. My hands are resting gently on her right knee. She looks down at me in confusion. She'd heard the crackling too.

"I don't know," she says.

I removed my hands from her knee and she takes a step back and begins to bend her knee back and forth. "It's my knee! It's healed!"

I wasn't even praying at the time. It was her forgiveness that led to her healing.

*   *   *

When Carter was six years old he was playing at the pool and a little boy pushed him down. He came to me crying, holding his arm and favoring his shoulder. I prayed for him and he forgave the little boy. Carter told me that he felt better and the pain had gone away. He went back and sat by the pool, but didn't really swim after that. Interesting thing about praying for kids' pain to go, they won't lie to you and tell you right away if they are still in pain.

A couple days later, Carter was still favoring his arm a little, so I took him to the doctors to have it X-rayed. Carter's collar bone was broken. I was shocked. I remembered how painful mine was from my youth and how I wasn't able to even breathe without pain. I immediately started feeling extremely bad for not being a good Mom and taking him right away. But, we had prayed, and even though it was broken, he only had a little bit of pain in the evening.

Carter was upset because we had just purchased Hershey Park passes for the summer and had plans for an amusement park, roller-coaster-riding summer and he would have to be in a sling for at least six weeks. We kept praying over it and I asked Carter to forgive me for not taking him sooner.

When Carter came to me in pain at the pool, I used my prayer—first aid spray—when what Carter needed at that time was love from his mother. I basically did what my own mom had done to me. She had sprayed me with first aid spray and told me "you'll live" and sent me on my way. I genuinely asked Carter to forgive me for not acknowledging the pain he was in, and the desire in his heart for love and comfort. Judge me first God.

Smiling at me, Carter says, "I forgive you Mommy."

That was Saturday. Sunday morning, Ben is leading us in devotions at home. Carter is on the floor of our living room in Camp Hill, PA, and Carter raises his hand in the air.

"Yes Carter?" Ben asks, then looks at me puzzled as tears race down my cheeks. He glances back at Carter and realizes he is raising his right arm, the one with the broken collar bone, straight up in the air. Our home breaks out in praise and radical gratitude! Carter is healed! Two days later we celebrate by riding rollercoasters at Hershey Park. I still have the X-rays and Carter is quick to share his testimony. I love that kids are quick to tell how God healed them!

* * *

Forgiveness is directly related to physical, emotional and psychological healing. Satan hates it when we forgive, especially when we don't feel like it. So, I challenge you to experiment for yourself. If you are experiencing any kind of medical issue, say a quick prayer and ask the Holy Spirit to lead and guide you about who you could forgive–just do it–even if you don't believe it will make any difference. Anyone that comes to mind just speak out loud and say, "I forgive."

Forgiveness releases your enemy from a debt they owe, but even more importantly, releases you from carrying around their debt in your heart. You always have a choice, whether to pick up another stone to carry around, or just drop it by the wayside and unload your heavy burden. I choose to radically forgive. "I forgive, I forgive, I forgive…forgive me, forgive me, forgive me."

Sling your bag full of stones at the giant of un-forgiveness, lighten your load, and step into your destiny. It is your birth rite and your identity and the only thing standing in your way is un-forgiveness.

{ 28 }

RELEASE YOUR ENEMY

I spent eight hours with my brother Jimmy on Black Friday in 2013 sifting through forty-year-old documents stuffed in a box filled with emotions when out tumbled a man I never knew.

He was a handsome, courageous young teen that starred in a school play in the early 1960's. He was a U.S. Marine Corps soldier who served during the Vietnam War. On 16 Nov. 1965 he began his artillery training. As I examined the documents, a picture of a young marine with a desire to do well formed in my mind. The young man was a military driver with aspirations of becoming a Marine officer someday. On that day, in November, his 43 lines of handwritten notes were done in pencil and the tightly written words on the old carbon copies were still legible. I saw how he carefully formed the missing vowels, dollar signs and consonants the ink had missed. I could almost picture a motivated private aptly listening, yearning to learn that the weight of a projectile from a 105 Howitzer was 33 lbs. and $58.30 the cost for one green smoke round. I learned that, in 1965, a gun salute from a 105 Howitzer cost the government approximately $70.00.

I never knew this man, because the identity that I described above, was stolen from him during the war and replaced with anger, addiction, and a hardened heart. He was someone who wrestled with his own un-forgiveness. The man who tumbled out of that box married my mother in 1972 and became known to me as my perpetrator. I dragged him around with me for years, not realizing I could release him from the debt he owed.

The documents touched my heart and helped me to see him as a person who had dreams, aspirations and a desire to do well. I caught a glimpse of who he could have become. But what really made me weep was the tattered Geneva Convention card issued on 21 August 1965 by Lyndon B. Johnson titled

"The Enemy in Your Hands" that described the required treatment of Vietnam prisoners of war. I'd felt like the enemy in this man's hands for so long—it was time for my release. "I forgive, I forgive, I forgive."

I wept for James and a life marred by the evil one who used him to kill, steal and destroy. I wept because he was born innocent like every human being is. As a child I'm sure he didn't dream of growing up to become an alcoholic and a perpetrator. I wept because when God told me to forgive him after my mom died in 2004, I ignored the message. My step-father died on the streets... alone. "Please forgive me, forgive me, forgive me."

I wept because I could have been a light for him and I was too busy holding onto my own bitterness. I wept because I love him, not for what he did to me, but because of his identity...my father...a child of God. I don't know if he ever came to know Jesus; I pray he made it to heaven because I love him.

I found James's grave in January 2014, in Biloxi, Mississippi. I stood there and asked for forgiveness, weeping, because I finally found freedom. I honored him in my heart. No more stones.

{ 29 }

TIME TO FIGHT

So, what stones are you hauling around? What battles do you continue to fight—and lose? Who have you refused to forgive for the unthinkable, unimaginable things they did to hurt you? Allow my journey to light your way to a new sense of freedom, light and joy. I can attest that only one act—forgiveness—has made all the difference. And, with forgiveness, arises an identity based on unconditional love.

Throughout the first half of this book I shared with you how I fought to obtain my identity through worldly means. I was rejected from birth and the words spoken about me, and to me, by my family, friends, classmates and others, shaped an identity I believed to be bad, sinful, stupid, retarded, unworthy, rejected, poor, unloved, and ugly.

I was baptized Lutheran when I was nine, but the Bible was never taught in our home. Religion did not provide an identity I was able to maintain because I didn't understand it. I didn't feel loved. I was taught to fear God and believed that He makes me sick if I reject him and only loves me if I do certain things right.

Books offered a temporary escape for me as I vicariously lived my life through characters in stories. I embraced those glimpses of other worlds, but at some point, I had to stop reading and live my life—a life of pain and anguish.

I tried to escape negative labels by escaping into books, alcohol, drugs, unhealthy relationships with men, and ultimately into the Army. Although I picked up some positive labels along the way, alcohol and drugs further reinforced feelings of rejection, depression and negativity. I witnessed first-hand how alcoholism and addiction damaged every relationship it touched one way or another. Alcohol and drugs provided temporary escapes—with negative consequences—and moved me further away from the love and acceptance I was seeking.

My Army identity was positive and helped to create a value system of honor and integrity, but it was all about performance and obedience as a means of acceptance. I did it, and did it well, but it still lacked in love.

I tried to obtain an identity through marriage. My first marriage was about appearances. We pretended things were okay in public, but in private would joke sarcastically and call out the negatives. Our marriage became a presentation of the right car, clothes, job, education and church, and love could be taken away at any moment.

Parenthood didn't provide the love I desired, because I had no clue how to love unconditionally. I tried to raise my daughter to feel loved by being as loving as I knew how and to protect her from my past. But I drove her away with my beliefs and my choices and the words that I spoke.

Education didn't fulfill me either. I graduated in the top of my class with a Master's Degree in counseling psychology. I learned and worked in the most challenging environments and with some of the most challenging clients. I gained favor because I performed well and was accepted by peers, colleagues and clients. Love was still lost.

Nor did psychology, counseling and self-help books provide what I needed. I participated in counseling sessions, retreats, and conferences to help me deal with past issues, self-esteem, forgiveness, relationships, and spiritual concerns. I worked the twelve-step recovery model (though I never labeled myself an alcoholic) to improve myself and make my life more workable, but still no glimpse of an identity birthed in love.

Having a healthy marriage didn't provide unconditional love either. Even when the other person is psychologically healthy, supportive, kind, loving, amazing, and awesome, there are limitations. The love is there even when we fight, but there is always the knowledge that divorce is a choice any human being can make. What happens to the love? Does it go away?

Money didn't solve my identity issue either. Ben and I both had very lucrative careers and—according to one financial advisor—could be millionaires if we would have continued working in our chosen professions. We gave money away, lent money, funded numerous ministries, and when we needed something, we were able to afford it. We never had a problem with finances. It was quite a change from growing up in poverty and lack, but, regardless of my ability to access money, it still left me yearning.

Being a Christian and "turning my life over to God" didn't work either. I tried to find the formula to make it work. I studied my Bible and memorized scriptures. I regularly attended church, taught Sunday school, created ministries of outreach, did works, volunteered, went on mission trips, drove the church bus, planned church activities, opened our home to strangers, prayed, and "did" the things recommended for us to do. It sometimes even made relationships worse because I wore my "Christian badge" and judged others as being okay only if they would accept Jesus, or be sinless.

Even when I was being of service, an instrument of God, I could only love people as much as the resources I had to give away. I could help them through psychology. I could educate them. I could lend them money to help in their situations, I could tell them about church, the Bible, or God, but I had no way of helping them to consistently "feel" loved by me or by God, because what happened when I left? I could only be a loving friend or counselor to so many people and only to a certain extent.

It was only when I began to forgive in obedience that I started to feel God's amazing love for me. Once I started to feel it, I wanted more. The more forgiveness I spoke, the stronger the love was. Now, my beliefs and my identity are not based on what anyone says or thinks about me. Even if you say that you love me, what happens to my identity if you change your mind? I know who I am, and *whose* I am. I choose my identity based on the ever faithful, unending, always the same, word of God. God's words and promises are never changing. I am worthy of God's love.

We are all like Abram living in the land of Ur ("you are") but God is calling you out of that old identity and calling you into the land of the "Great I Am." He is trying to tell you that He created you as good in the beginning and that has **not** changed. God's love is unwavering, and you are an amazing, awesome, wonderful creation. Father and Mother of all that is living are telling you that you are loved. They love you, They love you, They love you. You are worthy. That will never change.

*   *   *

Thank you for reading this book. I pray it has touched your life, but most of all, I pray it has released you to forgive. I pray it leads you into an amazing, loving relationship with God, Jesus and the Holy Spirit. As we end this part of our journey together, I want you to know that I love you and you are awesome, wonderful, and amazing. That will never change. I love you and I believe in you.

I leave you with a challenge…forgive freely, live your life with boldness and be a warrior. Forgiveness is an act of war and I challenge you to speak it out of obedience every night before you go to bed. "I forgive, I forgive, I forgive, forgive me, forgive me, forgive me, I love, I love, I love…"

Release the enemy into the hands of God and you will be free from having to be bound to something to which you were not created to be bound. Let your captives go and you will be free—free to live, to love, and to laugh. Let forgiveness reign in your heart. Let forgiveness flow from your mouth. Let forgiveness spring forth in your life. Let it be a model in your home… a moral standard…a character-building habit…a lifestyle choice.

Practice forgiveness and it will grow deep roots in your heart, in your family, in your home, and in your yard. Practice forgiveness with your children and it will reign at your child's school, on your street, in your neighborhood, and in your city. Let forgiveness reign in your life and you will change your state and the nation and the world.

Let it reign…Let it reign…Let it reign.

EPILOGUE

Growing up I learned obedience based in fear. In the military I learned obedience through self-discipline. In psychology I learned obedience through wisdom of man, and in the spirit realm, I learned obedience through love. I speak out forgiveness through obedience, not because I am fearful, self-disciplined, or because it is something that will "work for me" as a technique to get what I want; I speak out forgiveness because I desire and crave the amazing love of God. The cleaner my heart is, the more room there is for God. I desire more of God so that I can love, love, love the hell out of everyone I meet. I want to be love, speak love, act in love, and spread love wherever I go. My motto is, "Everything done in Love, Honor, Integrity and Truth. In Jesus name."

Ultimately, I cannot take you farther than I am willing to go and I cannot give away what I do not have. I love you, I love you, I love you…

*   *   *

As I stare at the Kevlar of the soldier in front of me, I utter a small prayer. *Please God…I think I want to live.*

"ONE MINUTE!" the Jumpmaster yells.

We shuffle closer together heading towards the gaping hole in the C-130.

"GREEN LIGHT! GO, GO, GO!"

My heart pounds. Despite my fear, I shuffle quickly towards the door. I thrust my static line at the Jumpmaster; I let go, turn to my right, do a little hop, grip my reserve with both hands, tuck my chin into my chest and start my count. The sound of the engines is deafening as the fierce wind grabs hold of my body and I'm yanked horizontally from the plane. My body clears the plane and the shock of the static line yanking my canopy jerks me violently…I forget to be afraid. Within seconds, I'm swinging from side to side and my hands reach up to grab my risers. The hot sun is blinding and my eyes focus. I am floating in the air and for the first time in my life I feel completely free…and alive…

As we land the parachute of this book, completing our perfect PLF, I encourage you to freely give what you have received and I promise you will feel more alive than you have ever felt because you will be free. Free to be who God created you to be…Love.

Prayer of Forgiveness

Dear God,

I forgive, I forgive, I forgive! Please help me to forgive freely. Judge me first God, so that I may love You more perfectly. Please forgive me God for any time that I may have acted that way. Please remind me of any time that I may have caused someone else pain so that it is easier for me to forgive this person for the pain I am feeling right now.

I want to be discerning God; not judging Your creations as lacking, but remembering that all people are Your creations and I want to love them as You love them—as amazing and awesome! They are fearfully and wonderfully made! Help me to see them with Jesus glasses.

Help me to remember that my fight is not against flesh and blood and that person would not have acted that way if they had been filled with Your amazing love. Let me love them more perfectly so that I may do Your will in loving them, because You first loved us. Any time I am pointing out a behavior that someone is doing or has done, convict me first God. Help me to ask forgiveness for me first. If I am pointing a finger at someone else, then there are three pointing back at me. Forgive me, forgive me, forgive me…I forgive, I forgive, I forgive…I love, I love, I love…In Jesus name.

Help me to do everything in Love, Honor, Integrity and Truth. Love in Jesus name.

Amen

About The Author

Tina Genaro is a veteran of the U.S. Army and a licensed professional counselor since 2005. She is currently in private practice and treats adolescents and adults. She resides in Virginia with her husband, Ben, their two sons, and two cats. "The Enemy In Your Hands" is her first book.

Tina desires for her personal journey of faith to inspire, encourage and educate people. Her passion is for people to know that they are loved by God and for people to discover God's plan for their lives.

Please contact her by email at tinajgenaro@gmail.com or visit her on Facebook at Tina Genaro LPC LLC.

PRAISE FOR JULIE LAWSON TIMMER

Five Days Left

"An extremely talented writer."

—Jodi Picoult, *New York Times* bestselling author

"I sat down with this book after dinner, and when I looked up, it was 2 a.m. and I had turned the last page. My only regret was that there weren't a hundred more pages."

—Jacquelyn Mitchard, *New York Times* bestselling author of *The Deep End of the Ocean*

"An authentic and powerful story."

—*Kirkus Reviews* (Starred review)

"Absorbing, deeply affecting, and ultimately uplifting, it heralds the arrival of an author to watch."

—*Library Journal* (Starred review)

"Timmer handles delicate, controversial issues with deep insight into human nature, and ultimately renders a story that will stay with readers long after they reach the last page."

—Amy Hatvany, author of *Heart Like Mine*

"A stunning debut about the impossible things we do for love. Heartbreaking yet uplifting, *Five Days Left* is a book I won't ever forget."

—Sarah Pekkanen, bestselling author of *Catching Air*

"This novel feels as true as life."

Untethered

ALSO BY JULIE LAWSON TIMMER

Five Days Left

Untethered

MRS. SAINT
and the
DEFECTIVES

A Novel

Julie Lawson Timmer

LAKE UNION
PUBLISHING

Text copyright © 2017 by Julie Lawson Timmer
All rights reserved.

No part of this book may be reproduced, or stored in a retrieval system, or transmitted in any form or by any means, electronic, mechanical, photocopying, recording, or otherwise, without express written permission of the publisher.

Published by Lake Union Publishing, Seattle

www.apub.com

Amazon, the Amazon logo, and Lake Union Publishing are trademarks of Amazon.com, Inc., or its affiliates.

ISBN-13: 9781477819968
ISBN-10: 1477819967

Cover design by Kimberly Glyder

Printed in the United States of America

*For Elizabeth Lloyd, our "Mrs. Saint," whom we loved
and miss.
And who was nothing like her fictional namesake, save
for the generosity, the elegance, and the low wooden fence.*

Chapter One

It was only when Markie saw her husband's hands clasped around another woman's breasts that she finally acknowledged their problems weren't ones she could hide any longer. Except that wasn't completely true. Though it shamed her to confess it, the truth was that if she had seen them—his hands, the breasts that weren't her own—in the privacy of their bedroom or in some tawdry motel room she had burst in on, she might not have admitted it still. There had been other women before, and since the only people who had known were Markie, Kyle, and his mistress-du-jour, it had always been an easy secret to keep. An easy reality for Markie to pretend away.

Lipstick stains on collars, the smell of perfume she didn't wear—why dwell on these things when they could be shoved aside instead, leaving her free to continue her charade as a happily married woman? An enviably married woman, in fact. Kyle couldn't keep a vow or a job, and he spent more than he earned and borrowed more than he admitted to, but he was handsome and fit and sexy, and Markie could tell from the looks on the faces at the dinner parties and black-tie casino nights so popular with the private-school crowd they ran with that there wasn't a mother at Saint Mark's Prep who didn't wish she could go home with him.

But secrecy was no longer an option now. Markie had seen them—the hands, the breasts—on the screen of a phone held by one of the members of the Saint Mark's Mothers' Club, a phone being huddled over, ogled at, by five other members as they sat, spandex-encased and Botox-injected, at a booth in a swanky restaurant near the school, whispering and shushing and pointing and not-entirely-smiling-with-glee-but-sort-of. And she knew that by the time she had raced home, screamed up the driveway, stormed into the house, and finally confronted her husband, it would be all over Saint Mark's and her workplace (which were one and the same). All through the ranks of the Mothers' Club and the staff and the students, one of whom was Markie and Kyle's eighth-grade son, Jesse.

After that, it would be only a matter of time before the rest of the truths she had ignored—Kyle's many other infidelities, his maxing out of credit cards Markie hadn't even known they had, his emptying of their checking account, their savings account, Jesse's private-school tuition fund, his college fund—surfaced. And even if that particular level of detail wasn't shared around the Saint Mark's campus, around their neighborhood, their town—Markie wasn't about to reveal such facts, and surely Kyle wouldn't air his complete list of sins—it would become clear, when Jesse didn't show up on campus the next fall, that *something* had happened to them financially. And that whatever it was, it was as mortifying as the fact that the photo of Kyle's hands, the other woman's breasts, and their joining together had made its way through the phones of every person Markie would never be able to face again.

❧

Kyle left that night. It was right after Easter. Jesse had a quarter term to go before the end of the school year. Thanks to his father, they had no money to pay for it, so Markie had swallowed pride and bile and accepted a Loan of Many Attached Strings from her parents. The

minute the Saint Mark's school year ended, she listed their house, now deep underwater. To keep it in shape for showings and to fulfill one of the many conditions of her parents' charity, she moved back into her childhood bedroom in her parents' home, Jesse into the guest room, for the summer.

She didn't last a week. Her parents, Clayton and Lydia, had never approved of Kyle, who did nothing for their status at the club—no impressive letters after his name, no fancy alma mater for them to casually drop into conversation, no promotions to mention offhandedly over cocktails or golf or bridge. But they approved even less of divorce. There was a child involved now—their grandson. Not to mention all the years they had spent convincing their friends that Kyle was, in fact, worthy of their daughter. Now what were they supposed to tell everyone?

"And it's not as though we can say you're doing so much better without him," Lydia told Markie, eyeing her daughter's recently added weight, her not-recently highlighted hair ("We don't show our roots, dear, no matter how badly off we might be"), and the old yoga pants and baggy T-shirts she wore constantly, having no other items in her closet that fit anymore and no money to replace them. "We could do a little shopping trip, maybe," Lydia offered. "Though I don't know how much black we'll find in the summer, and really, at this point, I think dark colors are your best friend, don't you?"

They approved only slightly more of their grandson, whose teenage ways they interpreted as just this side of criminal. "All this lying about," Clayton sputtered. On their second day, he rapped on Jesse's door at six thirty in the morning. "The sun's up—why aren't you? Ha ha ha." Another rap. "I'm joking, son, but I'm also not. Up and at 'em. Your grandmother's got breakfast on the table, and I've got a big lawn you can mow. Let's give those muscles a shot at making an appearance, shall we?"

"And the video games," Lydia fretted. "Aren't you worried he'll turn into one of those, you know, Columbine-type kids? He already looks the part." Jesse was as thin as their daughter was heavy. Clayton and Lydia took equal offense to both conditions.

After dinner on their second day, Markie retreated to her bedroom, claiming exhaustion, and sat in the middle of the floor, a bottle of wine and a decade's worth of diaries open beside her. She read, in loopy, purple handwriting, about the "amazing" career she saw herself in, the "perfect marriage" she planned to have with the "very successful, very hunky" man she was sure she would meet "after college, when I've already seen the world and figured myself out and decided what I really want in a husband." The "gorgeous" house she would live in, which would be "even bigger and more beautiful than my parents' place."

She woke the next morning with her face glued by tears and alcohol to the pages of one of her notebooks. When she dragged herself to the kitchen in search of coffee, Clayton was waiting, pacing. He took in her unbrushed hair, her puffy, bloodshot eyes, and her untied robe and cleared his throat. "I think we need to talk about the way the two of you are handling your . . . situation," he said.

On their fourth day, Markie, desperate, applied over the Internet for a job in a town about forty miles from their old house. The company was in a hurry to fill some new positions that sounded low-level and mind-numbing, but it meant that after the online application and a brief phone interview the next morning, the job was hers. Plus, it was a work-from-home position, perfect for someone so mortified about her fall from marital, societal, professional, and financial grace that it was difficult for her to face her own son, let alone the rest of the world.

On the fifth day, she hunched over her laptop and scoured the listings for rentals she could afford on the measly piece-rate wage she would be making. Another loan from the First Condemnatory Bank of Clayton and Lydia Wofford would have killed her. To her surprise, she

found a landlord willing to cut a deal. On the sixth day, she broke the news to her parents.

And on the seventh, she loaded Jesse back into the car and sped away, to the promise of a town where no one knew her, a job she could do in seclusion, a house she planned to invite not one single guest to, and a life she could tread lightly on the emotionally safe surface of. She planned on going through the motions rather than becoming truly engaged, while she licked the wounds caused by her own bad decisions and waited for the shame that filled her from the top of her skull to her furthermost toenail to recede. Assuming it ever would.

Chapter Two

Jesse inched his way slowly down the wet truck ramp, sliding one foot back, then the other. Markie followed him carefully, trying to match her forward steps to his backward ones in both length and pace. At a different time, she might have suggested they call out their movements to make sure they were in sync—a simple "Right, left," or "Now, now." But he was rationing his words lately, and she knew if she asked him to blow a few dozen on Saturday morning, it could be Monday before he spoke again.

They had managed to get all the smaller things into the house before the rain started. They were leaving the heaviest items for Kyle, who promised he would be there by nine. He had missed the loading process at the old house earlier. A "thing" suddenly came up, he told Jesse by text—they should get the neighbors to help put everything on the truck. He would catch them at the new place to help unload. Jesse wouldn't admit he was upset with his dad for flaking out. For a while, he wouldn't even admit Kyle wasn't coming.

But by ten, he had stopped looking down the street for signs of his father's car, and at ten thirty, he climbed into the back of the truck, where Markie was studying her watch and trying to keep her anxiety in check. She had until noon to return it to the rental place or she would be out another hundred dollars for the late-return penalty. Since Kyle

was as diligent about paying child support as he was about being places on time, every penny mattered.

Jesse caught his mother's worried expression and quickly turned away, and Markie braced herself for the scowl she knew she'd see when he faced her again, the narrowed eyes and curled lip that said, *If you knew we couldn't manage things on our own, why did you kick him out?* The boy had become a master of disdainful looks, reproachful head shakes, and long, accusatory exhales.

It would be so much easier, Markie thought, if he would voice his displeasure out loud, tell her precisely what his issue of the day was with her. She could stick up for herself then—not that she felt she had any defense, but there might be some hole in his argument that she could dig herself out of, some inaccuracy in his reporting of the facts that she could set him straight on. At the very least, she could bust him for using a disrespectful tone. What could she say in response to an aggrieved sigh?

To her relief, when he turned back to her, his expression wasn't reproachful but pensive, even sincere. Scanning the waiting bed frames and mattresses, the couches and armchairs and the large wooden table, Jesse clasped his long, thin fingers together and lifted his spindly, pale arms over his head in what he presumably thought was an athlete's stretch. "No problem, Mom," he said. "We can handle it. We're, like, totally fine."

Markie let go of the breath she didn't know she had been holding. This was the thing about Jesse: just when she thought he was going to incinerate her with a death stare or walk off in a huff, he would say something nice instead or smile at her, sometimes even pat her on the arm. He was like the little girl in the childhood poem, the one with the curl on her forehead—"When she was good, she was very good, and when she was bad, she was horrid." Markie had a new respect for the fictitious little girl's emotionally exhausted parents. The vacillations were so draining.

She regarded Jesse sideways, a brow arched. The other thing about him was that he was fourteen, and over the prior twelve months, his body had done the bubble-gum thing, getting thinner as it stretched longer. His arms were thicker at the elbows than the biceps, his legs wider at the knees than the quads. He was embarrassed to wear shorts, and the jeans he was sweating in on that humid first day of August sagged low, not because it was the fashion, but because there was no tush to hold them up. No belt, either: the last time Markie offered to buy him one, he declined, telling her in typical Jesse-ese, a language that allowed only short phrases and abhorred elaboration, "Belts aren't a thing, Mom."

He wore small, round, wire-frame glasses, which, combined with his smooth, pale face, made him look a little like a young John Lennon. (When he was in elementary school, she was allowed to say Harry Potter.) His dark bangs would have completed the look if he weren't tossing his head sideways every thirty seconds to keep them off his forehead. He was a kid who would be picked first for some kind of academic challenge, in other words—a geography bee, a who-can-name-the-kings-of-England-in-date-order contest. Maybe, in his coolest moments, a video-game competition. But something physical, like unloading a truck full of furniture? In the rain, in ninety minutes, with a fortysomething, sagging-in-the-middle mother for a teammate? Not a chance.

But in addition to generously offering up seven words and the trace of a reassuring smile, Jesse gave Markie this certain look, one he had first used the day his father left. It was a push-pull of confidence and desperation, of let-me-take-care-of-you-Mom and please-don't-doubt-me-or-I'll-doubt-myself, of man of the house and frightened little boy. It made Markie's heart simultaneously burst with pride and break with sadness each time she saw it.

"Sure, we can handle it," she told him.

So there they were, saggy-middled mother and bubble-gum-limbed son, inching down the slippery ramp of the truck, their heavy wooden dining table suspended between them, both determined for different reasons to pretend that the weight of it wasn't killing them. That the morning hadn't added another mark in the long column of disappointments they had both suffered at the hands of Markie's ex-husband and Jesse's father. That lugging the rest of their heavy furniture off the truck and up the puddled walkway and through the narrow side door of the rented bungalow, on their own, in the rain, in an hour and a half, would be remotely possible.

Both pretending that, on the matter of the moving truck, just as on the matter of their life in general and their ability to function properly since Kyle left, they were "like, totally fine."

Jesse had barely reached the level pavement of the driveway and Markie was still slipping her way precariously down the ramp when a flurry of activity and noise poured out of the side door of the house next to theirs. A tiny white-haired woman marched outside, her hand raised as though she were hailing a cab.

"Arrêtez!" she called as she stomped across her lawn toward Markie's.

She hadn't gotten far before two men—one older, taller, and thinner, the other younger, shorter, and wider—rushed out the door after her, quickly overtaking her. The younger one extended his hand to her, but she shooed him off with a wave and yelled, *"Vas-y! Vite!"* He spun away and raced ahead, joining the older man in jumping the low wooden fence that separated the two properties.

Markie craned her head slowly to look over her shoulder, curious to see what the men were running toward but aware that sudden movement could send her, the table, and her son plummeting off the ramp. Seeing nothing out of the ordinary behind her, she swiveled her head back around the other way to find that the men were now almost in her driveway, and the woman, who was easily seventy-five years old

and couldn't weigh one hundred pounds, had marched herself through a gate in the fence and was storming across Markie's yard.

"Arrêtez!" the woman yelled again. "Stop! Put that table down *maintenant*! This instant!"

The table's legs clunked hard on the ramp as Markie dropped it. Jesse let go of his end, too, and stood frozen in place, his arms raised at high right angles, hands open wide. As the woman made her way across the patio at the back of the bungalow, the two men reached the truck. The younger one—midthirties, Markie guessed—clad in faded jeans, a T-shirt, and a ball cap, approached Jesse and said something Markie couldn't hear, and the boy shuffled sideways, hands still raised, giving up his end of the table.

"Madame," the older man said to Markie, with a small bow. *"S'il vous plaît."*

He was dressed more for a business meeting than for racing across lawns and over fences, with pressed suit pants, a dress shirt, and polished loafers. He levered stiffly forward and arced a hand through the air toward her, as though she were a princess climbing down from a carriage, he her devoted footman. She let him help her make a clumsy jump from the top of the ramp to the ground, and when he saw she was safely deposited, he placed one foot on the ramp and stepped up as easily as though it were a distance of mere inches rather than feet.

Gripping the table, he nodded at the younger man, who nodded back, and together they trotted down the ramp, up the walkway, and into the house. The entire trip took them a fraction of the time it had taken Markie and Jesse to move halfway down the ramp. By the time the men were inside, the old woman had made her way to Jesse, and taking him by the elbow, she led him to his mother, planting him in place beside her. He scowled and rubbed his arm, but he didn't move from his assigned spot.

From the closer vantage point, Markie could see she had been generous in her estimate of seventy-five years and one hundred pounds—she

should have added ten years and subtracted as many pounds. The woman wore an expensive-looking linen suit, and diamonds flashed from her ears, collarbone, and a few fingers, making Markie wonder if part of the reason she seemed so cross was that she and her equally well-dressed husband were being kept from some important event. Before Markie could tell the woman they needn't have disrupted their plans, a jeweled finger wagged in her face. But only barely—the tiny woman had to stretch her arm high to get it close to Markie's chin.

"The small boxes, I was prepared to let you take," she said in a thick French accent. "Even *avec la pluie*—with the rain. And then *les autres petites choses*—the other small things. Those lamps, the pillows, your suitcases, and the such."

Markie and Jesse exchanged glances. It was clear their new neighbor had been watching as they unloaded the truck.

"*Mais, une table?*" she continued. "*Et . . .*" She leaned around them, peering into the truck at the couches and bed frames waiting to be carried inside. "*Non. Ce n'est pas raisonnable!*" She put one blue-veined hand on Markie's arm, the other on Jesse's, and steered them to the giant oak tree on the lawn beside the driveway. They could hear the rain pelting the canopy of leaves above, but not a drop made it through. "We will wait here," she said, "in the underneath, and let them finish."

Jesse seemed thrilled for the break, but Markie checked her watch and said, "I appreciate the help. I really do. But I have to get the truck back in less than an hour. So we need all hands on deck here, including the four of ours." She indicated her hands and her son's, and motioned for the boy to go with her to the truck. He widened his eyes in protest, and she was about to snap, "Jesse—now!" when the hand on her arm clamped more tightly.

"*Non,*" the woman said, with a single hard shake of her head. "This will not help. You will be getting in their way only."

She pointed to the walkway leading to the bungalow, where the older man was practically running with Jesse's futon mattress on his

head while the younger one trotted along behind with an ottoman balanced on a TV stand. The elder worked his way into the house and was outside again, holding the screen door wide, by the time his partner reached him.

"Thanks," the younger man said.

The other responded, *"De rien,"* before jogging back to the truck.

As much as Markie resented being held hostage under her own (for the length of her lease term) tree, she realized the woman was right—she and Jesse would only interrupt the men's choreography. She could see inside the truck, and she was amazed at the progress they had made already. Thanks to them, she was certain to make it back to the rental place in time. Plus, her son was enjoying the rest, and the truth was, she and her aching muscles were, too. So she stood under the oak tree with Jesse and their petite captor and allowed her weary body to enjoy the break.

From time to time, she saw the older man look over at the woman, who lowered her chin or turned her head or raised a shoulder, each gesture garnering an understanding nod from him, after which he issued a soft-voiced command to the younger one. *She's an ancient infield coach in jewels and pumps,* Markie thought. *Even better: she's Yoda in a St. John suit.*

Smiling to herself, she tried to catch Jesse's eye to let him know she had something funny to tell him. She could picture his slow, tilted nod and half grin as he said, "Nice one, Mom." But he was staring down the street, and when he turned back to her, his lips were twisted, his way of cutting off a frown before it could take hold.

Markie realized, too late, that he must have been on watch again for Kyle, and that the self-congratulatory grin on her face was not the right response for a boy whose father was now more than two hours late. He untwisted his lips, allowing his frown to fully form before it morphed into a scowl, and Markie could hear the words he wasn't

saying: *We wouldn't have needed his help moving in the first place if you hadn't divorced him and then sold my childhood home!*

Before she could readjust her mouth into a more sympathetic shape, he let out a huff and turned, and she could tell he was about to walk away. Distance and silence: Jesse's two answers to any conflict lately. He took a step, but before he could take a second, the old woman reached out her other hand and caught him by the back of his shirt, and to Markie's surprise, Jesse took a step backward, returning to his original position.

"Oui," the woman said, patting his arm. "You will stay." He nodded obediently, but he didn't look at her, and he would not meet his mother's gaze.

To break the tension, Markie tried to introduce herself and her son to her new neighbor, but she could only get out "By the way, my name is—" before the other woman gave a quick, emphatic shake of her head and raised an index finger to her lips.

"See-lonce," she whispered, gesturing with her chin to the men on the ramp as though they were competitors at a golf tournament and any noise might cause them to miss the championship shot.

My God, she's bossy, Markie thought, more amused than irritated. It was one thing for the woman to assume Jesse would obey; he was a child. But for her to expect another adult to accede, particularly an adult who (unbeknownst to the older woman) had spent decades perfecting the art of ignoring her own parents' commands, was so unreasonable it was funny. Markie flashed the woman a magnanimous smile. *She has no idea who she's dealing with.*

"I really must get back to it," she said, taking a step toward the house. She wasn't eager to resume carrying things, but she could hold the door open for the men, at least, direct them where to set things down, clear a path for them among the boxes and other items she and Jesse had tossed haphazardly inside the door earlier.

The grip on Markie's arm tightened. *"Attendez.* Wait."

Had it sounded like another command, Markie might have laughed and walked off, but the woman's words were quiet this time, with no hard edge of instruction. Her mouth was softer, too, no longer set in a ferocious line, and as she tracked the men's movements, Markie could see a certain brightness in her eyes, the kind Markie's own took on when she watched Jesse do something clever.

"Attendez," she said again, even more quietly, the word more a declaration of wonder than a command, and because Markie knew how lovely it was to feel what the other woman seemed to be feeling, she stopped trying to talk or move. Instead, she looked down at the gray-white curls, immaculately set, of the person forcing her and Jesse to stand there together, and she smiled.

The "common" in "common enemy" was a start. It would give Jesse and her something to talk about later, at least. Something to shake their heads at and laugh about: the crazy old neighbor lady who spied on them for who knew how long before bolting out of her house to bark orders at them in French. How she held them captive for so long despite being half Markie's weight and a quarter Jesse's height. The way she managed, with nothing more than a series of well-timed nods, one or two words, and the grip of a hand, to choreograph both the rapid unloading of a moving truck and a brief détente between a reticent teen and his mother.

Chapter Three

Markie parked the car and lifted the bag of groceries from the passenger seat. After offering profuse thanks to their three unexpected helpers and excusing herself to return the truck, she had dropped it back at the rental place, reclaimed her car, and stopped to splurge on fancy sandwiches from the shop a few blocks away. Tuna and veggies for her, with mayo on only one side, as she was on another halfhearted kick to lose her post-divorce pudge. Nothing overly ambitious, though, and in fact, as she pulled away from the store, she decided that if she could find the cooler they had unloaded from the truck earlier, she would dig out the mayo she had brought over from the fridge in the old house and smear some on the other side. It had been an emotional morning. She was entitled to cheat a little.

A three-meat sandwich for Jesse, with spicy mustard. At the last second, she had them wrap some lettuce in foil and put it in the bag. They hadn't been eating all that healthily lately, but she told herself if Jesse put the lettuce on, she could feel okay about his nutritional input for the day. Kyle was the only one who had ever bothered putting real meals together. For a while after he left, she had kept up the habit of buying heads of broccoli, bags of carrots, a few zucchini—all of which she would toss in the crisper and then forget about while she and Jesse zapped another frozen pizza or opened bags from the drive-through.

A week or two later, she'd notice the stench in the fridge, pick the slimy things out, and throw them in the trash. Then she'd head back to the grocery store, telling herself she needed to feed her son better, and go through the process again. But she couldn't afford to waste good money on food they weren't eating, so she finally gave up the charade, and for the past few months, she had been bypassing the produce section altogether and aiming straight for the freezer aisle.

There was no better enabler of a highly processed junk-food diet than a teenage boy, especially one with no desire to talk while he ate. If they were having proper meals together, actual sit-down, use-cutlery, discuss-the-day dinners like they used to have when it was still the three of them, she might have been inspired to carve up a roasted chicken from the grocery deli, at least. Rip up some iceberg lettuce, toss in some grape tomatoes. Maybe heat a can of corn.

But she had stopped trying to force words out of her son months ago, and while she was at it, she gave up pretending that "just being together" while they ate was helping their relationship. The biggest smile Jesse had given her in months came the night she suggested he might want to eat his pizza alone, in front of the TV, while she enjoyed hers with a book in another room. Their communication had sunk to the same pathetic level as their nutritional one, in other words, although if you counted "Have a good day/You too," as conversation and pizza sauce as a vegetable, both of which parenting lows Markie had begun stooping to, they weren't faring so badly.

At the bungalow's side door, which was half wood (on the bottom) and half window (on the top), Markie was reaching for the knob when the French-speaking woman who had accosted them earlier suddenly appeared on the other side of the window. She smiled at Markie and held up a drinking glass.

"What—?" Markie began, stepping inside and into the small family room, where her neighbor had clearly found the boxes marked GLASSES/DISHES.

Markie couldn't believe it. She had been able to laugh off the woman's bossiness earlier, but seeing her here, inside the bungalow, rooting through their things, wasn't funny. It had been a dreadful morning, loading what was left of her broken life into a rented moving truck, having to tear her son away from his only home, seeing him keep his faithful, fruitless lookout for his father. Sure, it was helpful to have the truck unloaded, and Markie was grateful, but for the past several hours, she had thought of nothing but sitting in the family room, alone, with her feet up, while Jesse hid out downstairs with his sandwich and his phone.

"Ah," the woman said. "*Vous êtes arrivée.* You are back. We were . . ." She trailed off and glanced at the glass in her hand. "And then Fraydayrique needed water." She pointed behind her, to the dining/living room combo on the other side of the kitchen. "Come."

"I don't mean to be rude," Markie said, "and I appreciate all your help earlier, but I'm afraid I'm really not in the mood for—"

But the woman appeared not to hear. She turned and headed toward the kitchen, which adjoined the family room, made a quick stop to fill the glass at the sink, and then continued through the archway that led from the kitchen to the dining room/living room combo. Markie heard some loud commands in French, followed by the supplicating voice of the older man, whose name was evidently "Frédéric."

In the kitchen, Markie dropped her grocery bags on the counter and sighed.

Footsteps thundered on the basement stairs, then the basement door opened, and Jesse stepped through into the kitchen. He reeked of aftershave, which Markie pretended not to notice, the same way she had been pretending his weekly shaving routine was something more than wishful thinking. She used the task of unpacking the food as an excuse to turn away from him.

"What's going on?" she whispered, nodding toward the living room.

"She wouldn't leave, Mom," he whispered back. The "Don't blame me" was implied. "I told her we were going to take our time getting things organized, but she wasn't having it." He turned back to the living room. "Actually, it doesn't look half bad. You should check it out."

Markie glared at the archway. She wasn't about to prance through it, gaze excitedly around, and praise the meddling Frenchwoman for her handiwork. She had moved here to be left alone, was desperate to be alone, not only today, but for the foreseeable future. She had a past to reconcile and a future to sort out, and she couldn't do either without solitude. She wanted no intrusions—no new friends, no old ones, either, and certainly no overly helpful neighbors. She huffed and turned back to the groceries.

"What?" Jesse asked, in a voice casting her as the complaining child, him as the patience-strained parent.

"Nothing," Markie said. "It's been a long day." She set her sandwich in the fridge, handed him his plate, and stepped toward the archway and the living/dining room beyond. "I thought we could use a break from pizza," she said.

"I never need a break from pizza," he said. "But this is super sweet. Thanks."

She pointed to the pile of romaine beside his sandwich. "Eat all the lettuce."

"Whoa," he said, volunteering half a grin. "Health nut."

"I'll go thank them and send them on their way."

She managed only half a step through the archway before running smack into her neighbor, who held the empty water glass aloft in victory, the creases around her mouth jumping back to make room for a wide smile.

"Fraydayrique had not had enough to drink," she said, and the expectant way she beamed at Markie suggested he was a shared concern of theirs.

"I, uh . . . ," Markie began.

The woman took Markie's hand and pulled her back through the archway into the kitchen.

Markie extricated her hand and put it behind her back. She would brook no more gripping and tightening and holding in place from this woman. "Look," she said, "it was very nice of you and your husband and son to help us. We're extremely grateful. But we can take it from here—"

"Och." The woman waved dismissively in the direction of the living room. "Those ones do not belong to me. That is not my boy. And my husband—my Edouard—he is dead to me."

"Oh," Markie said. "Then who—?"

But the old woman had turned to look at Jesse, who was sitting on a stool at the kitchen counter. Markie turned, too, and caught the perplexed look on his face.

"Qu'y a-t-il?" the woman asked. "What is it?"

Jesse studied his hands as he placed his palms flat on the counter, side by side, then slid them slowly away from each other. "I, uh . . ." He cleared his throat. "You said, 'dead *to me.*' I think you mean just 'dead' unless what you mean is that he did something to make you—"

"He is dead to me," the woman said, punctuating her answer with a sharp nod, as though that took care of the issue.

"Yeah," Jesse said, "but that still doesn't really clarify the . . . thing . . ."

But she turned away from him, toward Markie, and Jesse shrugged and reached for his sandwich.

"Vous êtes Markie," she said. "Chessie has told me."

Markie glanced at her son, who pointed a finger to his chest and mouthed, "Chessie." Markie smiled at him, and the woman snapped her head around to see what the boy was up to. He dropped his finger and looked at the floor.

"He tells me this is your actual name." She looked at Markie through eyes narrowed by suspicion, waiting, it seemed, to hear the boy had been lying. When Markie only nodded, the woman clucked and

patted her arm sympathetically. "*Moi, je m'appelle* Angeline St. Denis. This is *S-A-I-N-T* and then *D-E-N-I-S*. But you will call me 'Mrs. Saint' if you are not prepared to pronounce 'St. Denis' correctly. And since you are American, I assume you are not. So. Mrs. Saint, if you please."

Markie opened her mouth to give "St. Denis" a try, and Jesse, who was fully aware of his mother's stubborn refusal to be told she couldn't do something—a trait he shared—shook his head and sliced a finger across his throat.

"Saint Dennis," Markie said, ignoring him. He winced.

"Och! *Non!*" Mrs. Saint dropped Markie's hand, set the empty glass on the counter, and shook two fists at the ceiling, as though cursing the universe for allowing such an imbecile to move in next door. She glared from mother to son in a way that made it clear Jesse had made the same attempt earlier.

Jesse lifted his hands above the counter, palms up, and mouthed, "I warned you."

"*Ce n'est pas* Deh-niss," Mrs. Saint said, dragging out the word in an overly American accent. "It is Duh-nee." She paused dramatically and then repeated, "Duh-nee. And it is not Saynt, like the ones who go marching in. It is only San, with the *t* being a . . ." She tilted her head upward, searching for the English word in the kitchen ceiling. "Suggestion," she said finally. "The *t* is a suggestion." She looked at them each in turn again, daring them.

Jesse turned his hands so his palms faced the old woman. "I'm good with 'Mrs. Saint.'"

Mrs. Saint beamed at him like he had just announced he got into Harvard, and they both turned to Markie, who was determined to try again. Now, with the pronunciation lesson, she was certain she could get closer. She had taken French in high school—her accent wasn't bad. And she'd be damned if some four-foot-nothing Frenchwoman was going to stand in their kitchen and try to scare them out of trying

to speak a language that didn't belong to her any more than English belonged to Markie and Jesse.

She glanced at her son, ready to press her lips into a smirk in response to his having handed over his stubbornness badge so quickly. But her mouth fell open in disbelief instead. Mrs. Saint was rubbing her hand up and down his forearm in pride at his compliance, and Jesse, who wouldn't let his own mother so much as tousle his hair anymore and claimed not to care what anyone thought of him, was smiling at her as though her approval was all he had ever wanted. He leaned toward her in a way that said, "Keep rubbing my arm," and Markie was certain if she gave it another minute, he'd start to purr. She had been trying for the past five months to get this boy, so plainly in need of a hug, to accept any kind of physical affection.

"Mrs. Saint it is," she said.

The old woman's smile split her face in two, and with the hand not already assigned to Jesse, she took Markie's and squeezed it again. *Fine,* Markie thought, *I'll allow this one last squeeze.*

"Bienvenue!" Mrs. Saint said. "Welcome to the neighborhood!" She looked at them each in turn and smiled wider. But only for a split second, and then her expression of delight was gone, her formerly wide, bright eyes now turned narrow and dark. *"Alors,* Chessie tells me there is no dog."

"We're not a dog family," Markie said.

Mrs. Saint pursed her lips in a *We'll see about that* manner, then lifted Frédéric's glass from the counter, filled it, and held it out to Jesse. "He should have another," she said, nodding toward the archway.

If Markie were the one to hand him the glass and give the veiled instruction to take it to a man he barely knew, Jesse would stare dumbly at her until she realized her mistake and lowered it back to the counter. Alternatively, he might cock his head as though she were temporarily insane, giving him an order. Or snicker, finding humor in her delusion

that he would ever obey. He would most definitely not smile, reach for the glass, say "No problem!" and make a beeline for the living room.

When he was gone, Mrs. Saint leaned toward Markie, motioning for her to bend down so they would be closer.

"Boys only wear that much cologne when they are trying to cover up something else," she whispered. "While you were out to buy the lunch, he was outside in the back. Fraydayrique believes he . . ." She raised two fingers to her lips in a *V*, holding an imaginary cigarette.

Markie straightened, took a step back, and shook her head. "Absolutely not."

"A dog will keep a boy out of trouble," Mrs. Saint said. "The responsibility. Also to keep him company, *non*? He seems a lonely one."

"He's not in trouble," Markie said, "and he's not lonely. He has lots of friends in our old neighborhood."

"Only these lots of friends are not here, in your new neighborhood," Mrs. Saint said. She seemed about to say more when the sound of something being scraped across the wood floor came from the living room. *"Attendez!"* she called, bustling past Markie. When she was almost through the archway, she turned back and put a finger on the side of her nose. "We will discuss it later. The trouble. And the lonely. And also *le chien*—the dog."

"I don't think there's anything to discuss—"

But Mrs. Saint nodded to herself, as though her own agreement were all that mattered, and tore off into the living room, doling out instructions in two languages as she went.

Chapter Four

Markie's new living room was only slightly larger than her old master bathroom. She knew this, of course, from her walk-through a week earlier, but she hadn't been too concerned about it at the time. Sure, it seemed a little cramped, but you don't get a clear picture of a space when it's empty, she told herself. It would seem bigger when it was furnished.

But now, her grandmother's spindle-leg love seat, chair, and coffee table (the only valuable pieces of furniture she hadn't sold) were arranged, and the room that had seemed small during her walk-through felt positively claustrophobic. She couldn't breathe suddenly, and she thrust a hand out to grasp the back of the love seat while she coaxed her lungs to fill and her legs to rescind their threat of buckling. Mrs. Saint and her helpers rushed toward her, arms extended, but Markie waved them off.

"I'm fine, I'm fine," she said, though her gasping betrayed her. "It's just . . ." She shook her head. How could she explain it?

It was "just" that even the strongest conviction that she would be better off no longer married did not, it turned out, provide immunity against the shock she felt in realizing that she was, in fact, no longer married. And although there had been reminders around her all day—the rental truck, the boxes, the sight of their old house, their neighborhood,

and then the entire city in her rearview mirror—it was the puny living room, so sad-looking compared to the cavernous, cathedral-ceilinged space in her old house, that punched her hardest in the gut.

"Would you prefer for them to arrange in a different way?" Mrs. Saint asked. "We thought this would be best for entertaining. Because every seat can see well the fireplace." She swept a hand, indicating.

Markie considered the arrangement and knew her neighbor was correct. She also knew it was irrelevant whether the furniture was arranged to accommodate company—after she ushered out the three people standing before her, she and Jesse would be the only ones who set foot inside the bungalow for the length of their tenancy. There was no need to share that out loud, though, so Markie smiled, told them it was perfect, and, hand extended, crossed the room to finally introduce herself to the two men who had done so much work for her.

Frédéric said his name the way Mrs. Saint had—"Fraydayrique"— as he took her hand in both of his and bowed deeply. Markie moved to Frédéric's companion, who hesitated before finally resting his hand limply in hers.

"And this is . . ." Mrs. Saint said, dragging out the last word, her gaze fixed on the younger man until he finally caught on.

"Oh! Bruce!" he said, diving his stubbled chin to his chest and shaking his head as though he could never get that one right, the whole state-your-name-when-meeting-someone-new thing. His cheeks were red, either with embarrassment or shyness, and he seemed to Markie like an oversize, socially awkward child. It was the same way Markie felt when she was around her parents' friends at the club, with their inside jokes she didn't understand, their standards for appearance she never seemed to meet. Despite her ambition to avoid all personal connection, she felt an instant kinship with Bruce, and she patted him on the arm, smiled warmly, and said, "It's very nice to meet you, Bruce."

Directing her attention to Frédéric as well, she said, "Thank you so much for your help. We lost our moving team at the last minute.

Without the two of you, we never would've gotten the truck unloaded ourselves and returned on time."

"*Non, non,*" Frédéric said, waving her gratitude away. "But it was our play-zire. We were more than happy."

Markie took in his formal attire and wondered how happy he could be to have foregone his other plans in order to perform heavy labor for a woman he had never seen before. Bruce, his jeans and T-shirt worn-looking and ill-fitting, had presumably not been invited to whatever affair the elder two were planning to attend.

"So you're French, too," she said to Frédéric.

"French *Canadian*," Bruce corrected, and Mrs. Saint reached over and gave his arm an approving pat. He beamed.

"I am," Frédéric said. "But corporate America beat out most of my accent over the years. Angeline suffered no such pummeling."

The expression he directed at Mrs. Saint was so openly adoring that Markie almost said, "Aw," out loud. How nice, she thought, that the woman had found love after her late Edouard. But Mrs. Saint frowned and turned to the window, and Frédéric, his smile collapsing, stared at his loafers.

"Bruce would like to ask you about the tay-lay-vi-zions," Mrs. Saint said.

Bruce pointed to the two TVs that sat on the invisible threshold where the tiny living room met the minuscule dining area. "We wasn't sure which goes where, since one's . . . you know . . . bigger."

"Oh." Markie swatted the air. "Please leave the rest. You've done more than enough. Jesse and I can take it from here." She extended her arm toward the archway and the side door beyond. "I'm sure you've all got things you'd like to do. We're really quite able—"

"But Fraydayrique has brought with him his hammer!" Mrs. Saint said. "His picture-hanging nails, also." She pointed to a toolbox Markie hadn't noticed before, sitting on one of several large boxes grouped

together in the corner, all marked Artwork. "And also there is the entire kitchen to unpack!"

Markie dismissed the boxes of art with a flick of her hand. "I'm not going to bother with those. Jesse'll carry them to the basement later, along with most of the kitchen things. But thank you so much. You've gone above and beyond your neighborly duties." She moved her arm again to show them out, resisting the urge to jab her finger repeatedly toward the door until they got the hint.

"I should move them TVs, though," Bruce said. "They're pretty heavy."

He had seen Jesse's stick-thin limbs, in other words, and he had also seen the boy's middle-aged, out-of-shape mother. And he knew there was no way those two were hoisting those sets anyplace. He shifted nervously, waiting for her answer. The look on his face was so earnest, so hopeful, it seemed a refusal might crush him.

"Sure," Markie said, letting her hand fall to her side in defeat. "That's very kind of you. The big one and the stand go in Jesse's room. The smaller one goes in mine."

Mrs. Saint made a noise as Bruce pointed to the ceiling. "Big room for you and small for him? That's how we done the beds."

Markie started to answer, but she was distracted by Mrs. Saint's reaction to the TV-in-bedrooms idea. She wanted to tell the woman she was aware it was a parenting no-no. She knew Jesse would stay up too late watching. She knew not having a common set meant she wouldn't even be able to pass off their mind-numbing tube watching as "family bonding." But she also knew her son, and she knew what he needed right now, and it wasn't mother-son togetherness or a bunch of rules about screen time.

She had already tried pleading the TV-and-video game case to her parents, though, and they had not been moved. No way was she about to prostrate herself in front of another judge, and certainly not one she had known for only half a day. So she told Bruce, "Actually, he's taking the room in the basement," and before Mrs. Saint could register

her disapproval about that as well, Markie added, "That's the room he requested. He's had a very rough year. I said yes."

Bruce redirected his finger from the ceiling to the floor. "Move the bed frame before I go?" he asked. "Can pull the cable down from the family room, too."

"That would be lovely about the bed frame," Markie said. "No need on the cable, though. Not in the budget right now." She shrugged as though the lack of cable wasn't going to be a huge disappointment to her son—huge enough that she still hadn't found a way to break it to him—and fluttered a hand in the air. Ho-hum, no big. "He's got one of those gaming systems he can hook up." She moved her waving hand in the direction of the family room. "I think I saw it near the side door."

"Le pauvre," Mrs. Saint said. "To have a rough year at such a young age. Divorce, *non?*"

Markie didn't know if the other woman was legitimately asking if she was divorced as opposed to widowed, or if she was merely confirming what she already knew. It seemed entirely plausible that she might have extracted the information from Jesse while Markie was at the store. The thought annoyed her, and although she felt childish doing it, she ignored the question and pretended not to feel Mrs. Saint's eyes on her.

Bruce cleared his throat, and Markie was certain it was his way of telling her no one denies Mrs. Saint a response. Had it not been such a stressful day, and had she not recently spent seven days being bossed around by her parents, Markie might have confirmed that, yes, she was divorced. Instead, she pressed her lips together. It was her house—she would decide whom she'd answer. She felt a frowning toddler rising up within her, arms crossed, feet stomping, and she lowered her head so the others wouldn't see her cheeks flush with embarrassment at her own behavior.

"Let me just check on that gaming system," she whispered as she scurried past the three of them and through the archway.

⚜

Finally, they were leaving. Markie thanked them again and received a shallow bow and a drawn-out *"Madame"* from Frédéric, a quiet "Okay, bye"—after prodding by Mrs. Saint—from Bruce, and all of this, from Mrs. Saint:

"Are you certain about the art? I have a housekeeper, she is called Patty, who has a real sensation for art. She could help you arrange on the walls. It would be so much nicer than the empty.

"And what about the kitchen? Chessie says frozen dinners always. Pizzas and the such. Made in a microwave and not even a real oven! My Ronda—she does the cooking for us—she could make some things. Casseroles and so on. Also we have vay-gay-tay-bles in the garden. She could bring to you. She could organize the kitchen, also.

"But what about patio furniture? I saw none from the truck. I have *quelques* extra. I will have Frédéric and Bruce carry over later.

"And what of *le pauvre*, Chessie? He should at least have the cable, *non*? I feel it is included in the rent after all. You will check your lease. If it is not said so in there, you will telephone to the leasing agent, who I think has left it out only. The landlord will pay for it. This I am sure about."

Markie declined each of the woman's offers, except for the idea to check about cable. She was certain she had asked the leasing agent about it and was told it wasn't included, and she couldn't imagine her neighbor knew better, but it was worth a shot for Jesse's sake. Mrs. Saint nodded, satisfied to have landed one. She seemed about to say more, but Frédéric tapped her shoulder and gestured to the doorway, and to Markie's surprise, Mrs. Saint followed him out. Markie smiled gratefully at him, and he winked.

"We will discuss another time the art and the foods and the kitchen," Mrs. Saint said as she made her way through the door and across the patio.

Markie shook her head and blew out an exasperated puff of air, but she couldn't help smiling at the retreating back of the elderly woman

who had just sacrificed the better part of a day, and whatever fancy event she and Frédéric were planning to attend, for the sake of a new neighbor. Markie still wanted nothing to do with her, but she might be willing to admit the woman was more charming than annoying.

Mrs. Saint reached the low fence and made her way through the gate before turning back. She lifted a hand, and Markie raised hers in a wave. But instead of waving, Mrs. Saint held a finger in the air. "*Et aussi*, we will discuss *le chien.*"

Before Markie could form the thought, *Nope—definitely more annoying than charming*, Mrs. Saint nodded once, turned, and bustled through the garden toward her own side door. Markie was tempted to stand on her tiptoes and peer over the fence to see if the flowers were parting to make way for the old woman as she went.

Chapter Five

Overnight, four wicker chairs appeared on Markie's patio, along with a glass coffee table and a moveable umbrella on a stand. It was a beautiful set, far nicer than anything she could have afforded. She was admiring it when Mrs. Saint came out, and Markie ran to the fence to meet her.

"It's gorgeous," Markie said. "You're very generous. But it's too much. I can't accept it."

"*Non, non.* Not too much. Two for you and Chessie, and two to entertain." Markie was about to explain what she meant by "too much" when Mrs. Saint added, "Anyway, I could not use. I already have." She gestured to her three-season screened porch, crowded with two love seats, a large coffee table, and a number of chairs.

There was no furniture in Mrs. Saint's yard, though, Markie noticed, and following her gaze, Mrs. Saint said, "Only I don't sit out from the porch. Because the sun." She pointed to the sky and the round yellow enemy hanging there. "That is why the umbrella." She wagged a finger. "You must make sure to stay under. And especially Chessie."

It didn't add up, of course. If Jesse and Markie could avoid the sun with the umbrella, so could Mrs. Saint. And "could not use" was explained less by the crowded porch and more by the fact that there

were still store tags on the table, umbrella, and chairs. Markie suspected her neighbor had sent Frédéric and Bruce out to buy it all right after they walked out the bungalow's side door the day before.

Mrs. Saint wouldn't hear of sending the men back to take the furniture away, and Markie gave up for the moment, but later, she wondered if she should try again. What was the etiquette of returning a gift like that, though? If Mrs. Saint refused to send Frédéric and Bruce to collect it, should Markie and Jesse carry it back over the fence themselves?

There was a difference between graciously declining a gift and unceremoniously depositing it at the giver's doorstep. It was too expensive a present in Markie's view, but then, she didn't wear thousand-dollar suits on the weekend or keep an entire staff of people employed. Maybe, when it came to housewarming gifts, patio furniture was to Mrs. Saint what a small potted plant was to Markie.

She penned a thank-you note that afternoon, had Jesse add his signature, and asked him to deliver it himself so he could add his in-person thanks as well. He returned to the patio with a dumbfounded expression and dropped into one of the other chairs.

"She said we're welcome. She said she gives all her new neighbors a gift."

"Nice," Markie said.

He held up a hand to let her know she hadn't heard the rest of it. "She said she's keeping herself and Bruce and Frédéric and the rest of them out of our way for a while. Giving us time to settle in. She said she'll check on us later."

"Later today, you mean?"

He shook his head. "Later, like in a few weeks."

"Wow." Markie ran her hand over the wicker armrest of her chair, which suddenly seemed like an even more generous gift now that it came with three weeks of quiet rather than the daily storming of the fence she had been expecting.

Jesse, gazing at Mrs. Saint's house as though trying to figure out if he had really gone over there and heard the words he thought he had heard, or if it had been a dream, said, "Yeah. I know."

⚜

Markie walked downstairs around eight on Sunday night to find that Jesse had dutifully begun their Sunday-evening Skype call with her parents. Her son, knowing these conversations weren't easy for her, had taken it upon himself to initiate them. Every week when she heard the bloop-bloop-bloop of the computer call starting, she reminded herself that this gift he was giving her was worth several days of one-word answers and contemptuous glares on his part.

She loved her parents. She truly did. So much that for years she had dragged her husband and son to see them every Thanksgiving, Christmas, and Mother's and Father's Day, to be greeted the same way each time: a knuckle-breaking handshake for Kyle as Clayton looked over his son-in-law's shoulder at the car in the drive and said, "We were certain this would be the year you'd be able to spring for airline tickets. Well, maybe next year—but only after you take lessons from my daughter in how to hang on to a job. Ha ha ha. I mean, it's only funny because it's true, am I right?"

A pat on the arm for Jesse, followed quickly by "Whoa there, mister! Shoes off before you take another step. Remember how things work here. Now tuck in your shirt before your grandma gets a view of you. No collar, huh? Well, we'll have to make do for now, but Lydia will want to go buy you something better before we go to the club, of course."

A hug and kiss for Markie, along with a nod in Kyle's direction, and "Still keeping this guy around, huh? Say, I figured out his secret to marrying up—having in-laws who live too far away to talk sense into their daughter." Hardee-har-har. And welcome home.

Clayton, whom Kyle had long ago dubbed "the Commander" (never to his face, of course), would then corner his son-in-law in the kitchen to pour drinks and pour on more insults, Jesse would tear upstairs to hide in the guest room with a book or handheld game, and Markie and her mother would settle in the living room to wait for the tray of cocktails, Markie in desperate need of hers and getting more desperate by the second.

"Don't let him destroy anything up there."

"He never has before, Mom."

"He's a lot . . . ganglier now, though." This with a frown, as though the boy were growing for the sole purpose of spiting his grandmother.

"I'm sure he'll be fine."

"But you'll check on him in a few minutes. Or send Kyle up. Just to be sure."

"Fine, Mom."

"Now tell me. Are you still working?"

"You know I am."

Heavy sigh. "But surely you wouldn't *choose* to work if you had the option of staying home and being a mother?"

This was some of Lydia's best work—a single bullet that could splinter into multiple fragments and hit more than one target: Markie, for sacrificing her child's delicate psyche by "dumping" him in one of those—shudder!—"daycare places," and Kyle, for failing to earn enough money that his wife could stay home with their son.

"I'm a mother even when I'm working, you know," Markie would try.

"Oh yes, I suppose that's true, from a technical standpoint. But you know what I mean, dear. Real mothering."

Cocktails would finally be served, along with an assortment of cheeses and backhanded compliments. One of Lydia's go-tos: "I always admire your generation, the way you're not at all concerned about your appearance."

When Markie and Jesse were there for their miserable week right after Kyle left, her mother put a reassuring hand on Markie's arm and said, "I think it's just as well you've let yourself go, dear. This isn't the time to be worried about how much weight you've gained or what your hair looks like." That didn't stop her from offering to get Markie in to see her stylist, though. "Only because we'll be eating at the club while you're here. If we weren't going to see anyone we know, it would be fine."

Jesse also spent considerable time in the crosshairs of his grandparents' criticism during that visit, making his initiation of the weekly calls all the more generous.

"You can't stay in the guest room all day, dear, with the door closed and the drapes pulled. It isn't healthy." Lydia to Jesse, when he emerged for a glass of milk.

"It's what teenagers do, Mom." Markie, taking the carton from Jesse so he could escape the kitchen with his full glass.

"It's not what you did when you were his age." Lydia.

"That's because no way would I let a kid of mine hole up like that, all antisocial." Clayton, clapping a heavy hand on Jesse's shoulder and steering him toward the kitchen table. "Your grandmother doesn't need a mess on the carpet in the guest room." As if the boy were incapable of drinking without spilling or had plans to turn the glass upside down and watch its contents splash onto the floor while he cackled maniacally, his eyes glowing red.

"Say, why don't you sit right here and read the front page so you'll have something to talk about when the McLarens and Wilsons come for dinner tonight." Clayton again, indicating the newspaper lying open on the table. "You didn't say boo at the club last night. I tried throwing you those softballs about the president, and you didn't even swing. Let's make a better showing this time."

"I'm not really into politics, Grandpa." Jesse, paging through the paper until he found the comics section.

34

"It's all those video games he plays!" Clayton, to the McLarens and Wilsons at dinner later, after more failed attempts to get his grandson to sing for his supper. "They've melted his brain so much, the only part of the paper he can understand is the funnies! I'll tell you what, he's so addicted he had to bring his own gaming system!

"God forbid he go a few weeks without it. We've got that great big pool at the club, the tennis courts, an award-winning golf course, and all he wants to do is sit inside in the dark and play on that blasted TV all by himself!" As he complained, he flashed his teeth at Jesse as though it were all a big, friendly joke between them.

Later, when the guests were gone and Jesse was upstairs taking a shower, Markie asked her parents to lay off. "It's a different world than when I was his age. There's more pressure at school and everywhere else. Kids need space to unwind, escape. Especially ones who're still reeling from their parents' divorce."

"Good riddance to bad rubbish, I say," Clayton said. "Surely the boy recognizes you're both better off without the dead weight. Did you tell him where the rest of his private-school tuition went? And all his college money? Did you tell him about the . . ." He wrinkled his nose at the thought of having to say the words *affairs* or *adultery* out loud. "About the rest of it?"

"Of course not, Dad. Jesse doesn't need to know all of that about his own father."

"Still and all," Clayton said. "It's been a few months now, and you know my motto: 'Chin up, move on.' What the boy needs is more discipline, not more coddling. Tomorrow I'm taking him down to the club, see if I can set him up with a job for the summer. A couple of months washing dishes with the Hispanics will make him appreciate his station in life. You think those people have the luxury of moping in front of a PlayBox, or whatever it's called, when things don't go their way?"

Markie had seethed the entire drive home while Jesse, from all appearances, had forgotten about it by the time they pulled onto the

interstate. "They're old," he said. "You've gotta let them say some stupid stuff." Now he was chatting with them over the Internet like his time with them in the summer had been filled with praise and hugs.

Markie took a five-dollar bill out of her wallet and set it on the kitchen counter. The boy deserved to walk up to the sandwich place around the corner on Monday and treat himself to something better than microwaved pizza rolls. She watched in awe as he leaned against the kitchen counter, laptop in front of him, and laughed generously at another of Clayton's jokes.

She didn't know if it was a teen thing or only a Jesse thing, but even on his grumpiest of days, he could always scrounge up some cheer for his grandparents, the same way he had morphed from tired and annoyed to charming and affectionate with Mrs. Saint the day before. She had seen him do the same with their former neighbors, and while her first feeling used to be resentment that he could smile for other people but not his own mother, she had been working on replacing that emotion with something else.

She knew most teens broke out of their sullen phase at some point, but she wasn't sure about the ones who, in addition to having to deal with the regular and painful-enough aspects of being a teenager, were also saddled with the humiliation and heartache of their parents' very public breakup. She couldn't tell herself with certainty that Jesse's bitterness would be gone in six months, or a year, or by high school graduation, or ever. She didn't want him to grow up to be one of those people who are permanently in a bad mood, and especially not because of something she had done. So when she saw him smiling, laughing, and offering words without the listener having to drag them out of him, she tried to feel grateful that someone was getting him to be sociable and tried not to care that the someone didn't ever seem to be her anymore.

Jesse chatted away as he walked around the house, holding his open laptop high in the air, facing away from him so its camera could feed his grandparents images of each room. It was their first tour of the

bungalow, and if Markie could manage it, a virtual tour would be the only one they ever got. It would take her at least the duration of their half-year lease to build up enough emotional reserves to see them in person again.

As her son worked his way from room to room, Markie could hear her father exclaiming in the overly cheerful, paternalistic way he reserved for the young and the elderly—and, she guessed, the Hispanics at the club. She could also hear him using words like *tiny* and *cute* and *starter home*. These words did not hold a complimentary place in Clayton Wofford's vocabulary.

Lydia's tight "Mmm-hmm's" let everyone know she was no more impressed than her husband. Jesse rounded the corner into the living room, and Markie heard her mother say, "Oh, and there's mother's spindle-leg furniture." She punctuated the statement with a sigh, and Markie knew what it meant: while some parents might love the idea of their children making use of family heirlooms, Lydia saw it as a sign of failure.

The Woffords had avoided cocktail hour at the club for a full month after Markie broke the news. "Imagine what that was like for us," Lydia told Markie later. "Not that our reentry was a piece of cake. All the questions! You wouldn't believe how critical some people can be."

"Is that my daughter in the corner of my screen?" Clayton asked. "Zoom in!" It was his latest joke, ever since Jesse explained that they didn't need to put their faces up to the screen to be seen, and that when they did, the view from his end was "Um, a little more detailed than I think you want other people to see. As in, I can see right inside Grandma's nose right now."

Lydia was horrified, but Clayton had tried to turn it into a "bit" that they'd all do together—you "zoom in" close to the camera and show me your nose hairs, I'll zoom right back and show you mine, hardee-har-har. There can't be tension as long as someone's laughing, right?

"In all seriousness, though, Markie," Clayton said as Jesse stood beside his mother, leaving her no option but to join him in the frame. "You need to do a walk-through to check that everything's as advertised—"

"And if it's not," Lydia cut in, "you could use that as an excuse to back out. Take another look for something in a . . . different area." She meant a better area. The bungalow's zip code would impress no one. Plus, how would Markie show everyone in her old circle that she was doing just fine if she lived too far away for them to see? It was one thing to have them run you off, another altogether to let them keep you away.

"All moved in, Mom," Markie said. "And I dare you to tell Jesse he has to load and unload another rental truck sooner than six months from now."

Jesse shook his head, and Lydia smiled, nodded, and backed out of the frame to "go check on the tea."

"Like I was saying," Clayton continued, "you need to make sure the tub drains okay, toilet doesn't run, faucets don't drip all night. The key is to assess it all now and make a list of anything that's not up to par. In fact, Jesse, why don't you take me around with the computer? We can have a look-see, come up with a punch list. It's not something your mom needs to be bothered with anyway."

For a while, Markie had tried telling herself that her father's belief that women didn't, and shouldn't, know about certain things was the explanation for how Kyle had been able to spend their entire savings and their son's school fund without her noticing. Lydia had never once questioned Clayton about money—Markie was only acting the way she'd been brought up. But she had made her way through all the stages of How Did My Life Come to This? and she had passed finger-pointing long ago. She was standing in a minuscule, badly furnished rental house, sixty-eight dollars in her pocket and not much more than that in the bank, an angry boy beside her and newly disappointed parents in front of her, for one reason: her own willful blindness.

"We should really give the fuse box a once-over, too," her father told Jesse.

"Actually, Grandpa, our neighbor already checked all that stuff for us," Jesse said. And because he knew his grandfather, he added, "I mean, not our neighbor, but her friend—a man."

Markie leaned out of the sight of the laptop camera and lifted her brows with curiosity.

"One sec, Grandpa." Jesse lowered the computer screen to take himself out of the frame. "Frédéric," he whispered. "Before you got back from the store, Mrs. Saint told him to make sure everything was set right. Tighten the fuses or something, and the kitchen sink sometimes leaks, and she wanted him to make sure it was better. That's why he brought his toolbox over."

"How would she know about those things?" Markie asked.

He shrugged. "Maybe the last person who lived here complained to her or whatever."

"I missed the dining room," Lydia said, back now from fake-checking the fictional tea. "And your room, Jesse."

"Here, I'll show you again, Grandma." Jesse jogged back through the kitchen toward the archway, Clayton laughing too heartily at the way the picture jumped on their end.

"Rough seas!" he called. Jesse laughed along, and Markie took the five-dollar bill off the counter and replaced it with a ten. Let the boy upgrade his lunch tomorrow—he could add chips and a soda.

A while later, he returned to the kitchen, no laptop in sight.

"Thanks for doing that," she said. She pointed to the ten. "For you. For lunch tomorrow. Should be enough for a six-inch sub, chips, and a drink. You remember seeing the sandwich place when we drove in, right? A block that way, and then about one and a half to the right?" She pointed in the general direction.

He looked at the bill but didn't take it. "You don't have to."

"I want to."

"I don't mind talking to them," he said.

"I know, but still. I mean, I love them, you know I do. And they've helped out a lot recently, and I'm grateful. But . . . some family dynamics are difficult, that's all."

Jesse reached for the ten and shoved it in his front pocket. "I'll skip the chips and pop and get a foot-long." He smiled and gave her a gangly hug. "We can split it."

Chapter Six

They had been in the bungalow for two weeks, and while all kinds of activity had been taking place on Mrs. Saint's side of the low wooden fence, none of it had spilled over onto Markie's property. Their elderly neighbor, true to her word, had been giving them space to settle in.

And settle in they had. The scattered shoes near the door, stacks of dishes on the counter, and the overflowing recycling bin in the corner made it look like they had lived there for months. They had only unpacked the things they would need for six months. In Jesse's case, this meant he had upended all of the boxes marked J—BEDROOM onto his floor and tossed the empties into a corner of the basement, where they would wait until it was time to move again.

Markie had stacked her unloaded boxes in a tidy pile beside Jesse's leaning tower of cardboard, and she'd filled another corner with all the still-packed boxes they had decided not to bother opening. Anything they wouldn't need during the span of their half-year lease remained entombed: the artwork Frédéric was ready to hang on their first day; most of the kitchen tools Markie had collected over the years (none of which were required for zapping frozen meals in a microwave); the board games they used to play after dinner.

Jesse had begun ninth grade only a few days after they moved in. So far, he had nothing good to say about his new school. The teachers were

"pretty terrible," his classes "totally boring." He had met a few friends, including a guy named Trevor who was "sort of cool." The others were "not so bad, some of the time," but they had all known one another "for like, ever," so it had been hard for him to break in.

The walk home from school was "miles too long" and "way too hot." Markie kept suggesting he take the bus, but he told her buses for high-schoolers weren't a thing, which meant either that there weren't any available or that there was no way he was about to take one. Either way, he was still walking.

She had offered him a ride that morning, as she had done every morning since school began, but he gave her a pained smile, which maybe meant rides from moms weren't a thing, either, or maybe meant he couldn't stand the idea of being in the car with her. She didn't want to think about it for too long, so she smiled and laughed and waved and told him to have a great day, all in a way that made her seem more manic than motherly. She was certain that by the time he reached the end of their walk, he would be at least a little happy about school, if only because it would give him an eight-hour break from the crazy woman he lived with.

Since he left, she had been sipping her coffee on the patio while she gazed with forced serenity around the yard and told herself everything was fine, it would be this way even if he were back at Saint Mark's, where he had attended from kindergarten through eighth grade. Teenagers never liked the start of the school year, whether they were surrounded by strangers or by the friends they had been with since they were learning to tie their shoes.

Markie walked inside, refilled her cup, and chose one of the many stacks of files covering the dining room table to carry back out to the patio, where she had been working most days. They were having an oppressively hot August, and she was trying to save money by running the air-conditioning only at night. The humidity was at an all-time high, but there was a breeze on the patio and shade from the umbrella,

and she had been telling herself every day that those were fine working conditions. That it was comfortable on the patio, not stifling.

That reviewing claim file after claim file for Global Insurance Company was gripping work, not a mind-numbing, humiliating demotion from the high-profile position she had recently held as director of development for Saint Mark's. That Jesse's identity as Student No. 2432 at the overcrowded urban high school she had enrolled him in wasn't a shattering fall from the ivy-covered, marble-staircased, khaki- and blazer-filled bubble of Saint Mark's.

But she hadn't fooled herself, and she hadn't fooled her son. The reason the dining room table was available for her stacks of work files was that Jesse was still carrying his microwaved frozen dinners down to his bedroom every night to eat in front of his TV, his phone, or his gaming system. Or to stare at the wall, for all Markie knew, but in any case, he was still not interested in eating with her or in having the kind of dinnertime conversation they used to have.

Or any kind of conversation. Markie got a "Hey, Mom" when he arrived home from school and a "Night, Mom" when she called good night down the basement stairs, but most days she didn't get more than that. Some days she got less—a grunt after school, the sound of thunder on the basement stairs, and a slammed door at the bottom.

The nothing-but-grunts-and-slammed-doors days, she guessed, were the ones when he couldn't reach his father on the phone. Any failure of Kyle's to connect was Markie's fault, in Jesse's mind, not Kyle's. There was no "I can't believe he can't make time for me, his own son." It was only "I can't believe you drove my dad away." Not that he ever said it out loud, but she could tell.

Sometimes, because he was a good kid who felt guilty when he had been hard on her for too long, she got a full-toothed smile, an offer to zap her plate of pizza for her, a sincere "Thanks, Mom," for some small thing she had done for him. And then *she* felt guilty, because she knew he had forced himself to be friendlier than he wanted to be.

It wasn't that she was one of those moms who made excuses for her kid's bad behavior. When he bit a girl at daycare when he was two, she didn't laugh it off and say, "Kids will be kids," or talk about how he was simply one of those toddlers who "used his mouth to explore." No, she told the daycare teachers and the little girl's parents that it was a terrible thing her boy had done. And then she glared at Jesse all the way home, sitting there in his car seat in his matching yellow-and-blue tow-truck shirt and shorts with his chubby flushed cheeks, and she told him he had better not ever do it again.

She didn't make excuses for her own bad behavior, either, and that was why she didn't blame her son for saying so little to her before he disappeared into the basement every day after school. Because she knew she was the one who had caused all of this: Jesse's surliness, his demotion to public school, her crappy claims-review job, the tiny house, and the tinier bank account that didn't even allow her to run the air-conditioning during the day.

She had caused it all by doing one terrible thing: she had looked the other way.

⚜

There had been clues—not for their entire twenty years together, but for the last few. Suddenly, Kyle was always having her sign documents, which he described in terms that were equal parts minimal and vague. *"It's just something for the mortgage. You know, since we're co-owners." "It's a bank form—don't worry about it." "It's for the mutual fund. So they have our signatures."* She might have asked for more details, but he always managed to choose the moment she was racing around the house, searching for her purse and keys, late for work. So she would nod at his opaque explanation, scrawl her name, and rush out the door.

She brought the mail in one day and found a FINAL NOTICE statement from the power company. It was an administrative error on the

company's part, Kyle said. Of course he had paid the bill on time—hadn't he always? In fact, he expected a follow-up letter soon, apologizing for the screwup. When she asked him about it later, he said he had thrown the written apology away. *"Only a petty person would hang on to something like that."* Anytime she went to fetch the mail after that, he had already gotten to it.

These things were odd, sure, and it was true he had always had a propensity to spend too much money, but he had taken care of the finances for almost two decades and nothing had gone wrong, so why would she suddenly start asking questions seventeen years in? As for the women, the simple truth, however lacking in brilliance, was that she didn't want to be cheated on, so she refused to consider that it might be happening.

Kyle suddenly had a work trip every other week, though he'd had none in years past. He wasn't at the same company—he never stayed in one place long—but he always held roughly the same position (software sales), and it wasn't like he was moving to better and better jobs, with ever-increasing salaries and travel budgets. So how was it that his work travel kept becoming more extravagant? Maui one month, the Florida Keys another. There was even talk of Paris. *"Too bad Jesse and I can't tag along." "Yeah, too bad. But he's got school and you've got work, so I think it's best if I go alone . . ."*

What possesses a woman of above-average intelligence to look the other way and keep her head locked firmly in that direction? To blindly accept, "Don't worry. I've got the bills handled. The investments, too. We're in great shape," and to never ask to see the statements? To keep her nose averted so she wouldn't catch the scent of perfume—a kind she doesn't wear—on her husband's suit jacket? Markie could answer for only one such woman, and her answer, one that filled her with shame now that she had acknowledged it, was: appearances.

Every morning she stepped over Kyle's lipstick-collared shirts on the faux Italian marble of their bathroom floor, walked into the attached

garage of their highly leveraged McMansion in their too-expensive subdivision, and slid, blissfully ignorant, into her entry-level (leased) German sedan. She hummed a self-satisfied tune as she made her way several blocks west to her office at the school or, depending on the day, a few subdivisions east to the massive home and sculptured gardens of Headmaster Deacon, where she was the life—and, as the director of development, the hostess—of regular fund-raising luncheons, garden parties, and silent auctions designed to bring more money into the most moneyed private school in their part of the country.

She was the epitome of the kind of parent who was attracted to Saint Mark's, the kind the school wanted to attract more of: well bred, well dressed. Well matched—Kyle Bryant was a stunning-looking man, and since no one suspected what Markie was trying so hard to ignore about the health of their bank account and their marriage, everyone assumed they were the perfect couple. People wanted to be Kyle and Markie Bryant, and if they couldn't achieve that, they wanted to be near the Bryants, to have their kids attend the school that threw parties that would include the Bryants. She was living the life her parents lived, the one they so desperately wanted for her. The one they had raised her to believe she wanted for herself.

Markie came across as more school ambassador than employee. Surely a woman who dressed like her, who lived where she lived, who danced like that with a man that handsome didn't actually *need* the job but only wanted to find a way to put her university degree, along with her considerable social skills, to good use. It wasn't true. They were private-school parents only because of the work ethic of Markie's grandfather, who had died when Jesse was four, leaving a sum large enough to send him to Saint Mark's and then to the private college of his choice. The bequest would pay for Jesse's education, but nothing else—the Bryants' mortgage and car payments and everything else counted on two full-time salaries.

Markie would never forgive herself for the fact that, at the time of her grandfather's death, she was more irritated with her father than she was grateful for her son's inheritance. "I want your word you'll put it into a separate account, marked specifically for Jesse's education, so . . . nothing can happen to it," Clayton whispered to her inside the lawyer's office. Had he followed with "Cough, cough—Kyle—cough, cough," his meaning would not have been more clear.

Surely this was one of those occasions a psychologist would have a field day with, where a child cringes at a parent's observation not because it is unfair and untrue, but because it is precisely the opposite. In the end, it turned out Clayton had given his son-in-law too much credit, not too little. He thought the fact the money was in an account expressly named "for the benefit of Jesse Clayton Bryant" would keep Kyle from pilfering it.

While Clayton and Lydia held their son-in-law solely accountable for his family's downfall, Markie refused to let herself off that easily. Kyle's conduct was reprehensible, but she had sins of her own. She had never set out to collect cars, real estate, and couture the way some of the members of the Saint Mark's Mothers' Club did, but she did make sure she had the basic possessions required to back up their membership in the private-school social circle her grandfather's gift had gained them entry into: a vaulted-ceilinged house in the right neighborhood, a car with an acceptable hood ornament, and a few expensive suits and pairs of shoes.

She wasn't greedy about it, and she didn't fund any of it with a single cent of her son's money. But she used "My son attends Saint Mark's" to buy her way in, and once she was there, she did what it took to stay. When she figured out people thought she had taken the development job as a means of keeping herself busy rather than paying the bills, she chose not to correct them. She liked having people believe she had the portfolio to be one of the idle rich but the work ethic to forbid herself such sloth. It made her seem that much more principled.

It made her marriage that much more enviable. Sexy, good-looking men like Kyle were even sexier and better looking when people assumed they were single-handedly providing the luxury cars and designer ward-robes and monthly highlights their wives were able to take for granted. Markie had never been the kind of head-turner Kyle was, but in the golden glow of his presumed success, she felt taller, slimmer, more attractive.

She rode so high on her artificial, installment-plan-purchased Golden Couple reputation that she couldn't see—she chose not to see—that the footing underneath had become unstable. But who would want to face the truth? The divorcing couple around the block, the older pair up the street who had run into financial trouble and now had to put off retirement—those weren't the people at the top of the invitation list for the best dinner parties in the Bryants' exclusive neighborhood. They were the ones whispered about at those gatherings, with words that claimed sympathy but eyes that said something less charitable.

So what if the hostess at every party flirted with Kyle when she thought Markie wasn't looking? So what if he flirted back? Wasn't that simply good manners? "My wife is in the other room" could be enough to get them stricken from the list when it was time for the next event. And surely Kyle would never do anything to embarrass her in their own town.

Chapter Seven

In April, Markie ran into a group of school mothers having lunch at one of the exposed-pipe-and-brick-wall wine bar/bistro places that dotted the upscale streets at the tasteful commercial edge of their neighborhood, a few blocks from Saint Mark's. She was there to meet a donor; they were there to kill the hours between their post-school-drop-off Pilates session and their before-school-pickup fair-trade coffee klatch in the school's courtyard.

There were five of them at a table with six chairs, all huddled over a cell phone. One of them saw Markie and nudged the one beside her, who looked up and nudged the next, and so on, like a group of living, bleached-blonde-and-Botoxed dominoes. In each of their expressions, pity jostled for position with scorn, and when the first one said, "Oh, hey there, Markie," it was in the tone of a doctor about to deliver the news that the chemo hadn't worked.

"Ladies!" Markie said, taking her time to reach them while she ran a few speeches over in her mind to address whatever it was they were so ineffectively trying to pretend they hadn't been discussing: *Jesse would never cheat on a test/steal a classmate's phone/break into one of your liquor cabinets/sell pot during lunch hour. I'm sure it's a mistake. If he confessed, he's covering for someone else—one of your boys, perhaps.*

She inclined her chin toward the phone, covered now with a diamond-adorned hand. "What's this?" They exchanged glances, and she could hear the telepathic debate: *We can't show her. / Well, we can't very well* not *show her now—she knows it has to do with her. / I don't want to be the one to do it. / Fine, hand it to me and I will.*

Finally, one of them offered her the phone, swiping it as she raised it toward Markie. "I'm trying to get back to the first one," she said, as a series of photos carouselled across the screen. Markie thrust her hand toward the phone, but the other woman held the device out of her reach and kept swiping. "I really think it's easier to take if you start from the first one and work your way—"

Markie snatched it from her. If her child was about to be expelled—

But the pictures didn't show Jesse sliding a baggie to a classmate over the lunch table. Or angling his head to see the answers on someone else's test paper. Or chugging a bottle of Chivas in the butler's pantry of one of their houses.

They showed Kyle. In a bathing suit. On a beach framed by palm trees. Standing behind a woman wearing only the bottom of her bikini, her big, bare breasts spared from total exposure only by his widespread hands. The woman's arm reached out, presumably holding the phone and snapping the selfie as she tilted her head back and grinned up at him. Kyle's mouth formed a Cheshire cat's smile, and his eyes, half-closed, completed the expression that any adult would immediately recognize as the contented fatigue of a man who had just gotten laid.

Markie dropped the phone and heard it clatter on the table as she spun toward the door. But she couldn't take a single step in retreat, because at the end of her turn, she crashed into a woman who was heading for the empty chair at the table. Markie wouldn't have thought she could possibly feel any more agitated, but this was the one woman in their social circle whom she truly disliked.

She was the woman who headed up the Mothers' Club, and as Markie had complained to Kyle many times, because of some weird

competitive streak or superiority complex, this woman had slowly pitted their Saint Mark's jobs against each other when they should have been working in concert. She was the only woman whose dinner invitations Markie was tempted to decline.

She was also the woman whose breasts Markie had just seen up close on a cell phone.

"Markie!" she said. "You're joining us? Terrific! Like I said in my last e-mail, the Mothers' Club could use more help with this year's—"

It was then that the woman looked past Markie toward the table of her waiting friends. Her fake enthusiasm faded immediately, and before Markie could think to run past her and out the door, she saw the other woman's eyes narrow, then darken with something Markie couldn't readily name.

Of course Kyle was home when she screamed into the driveway moments later and tore through the front door. It turned out his "What's on your agenda for the day?" every morning that week had been less about taking an interest in her life and more about determining when he could take a midday nap on the family-room couch without being caught jobless. She must have known that before. She must have sensed it in the tone of his question. Now, after her humiliation in the restaurant, she had—finally—lost her motivation to continue to overlook it.

"Let me see the account balances," she said, clicking the TV off and slamming his laptop cover closed over his poker game. "Right now. All of them."

It should have offended him that she asked about the money first, the women second. He should have felt the sting of that, and being Kyle, he should have manipulated that rejection into some kind of sorrowful accusation that Markie's lack of jealousy showed how passionless their marriage had become, and that's what had driven him to it.

Or maybe she should have been the one to feel hurt when he didn't start by begging her forgiveness and pledging his undying love, but

instead went straight to justifications and defensiveness. But that was the thing about their relationship: forgiveness-begging and love-pledging had long become things of the past. Now it was only about finger-pointing and blame-deflection.

They had been so close in the beginning. So crazy in love with each other—and despite what Clayton and Lydia had said, it had absolutely been true love and not "a grown daughter's childish rebellion against her parents." True love, true lust, of the flush-faced, pounding-heart, fluttery-stomach, "can't take my hands off you, can't stop thinking about you, can't spend a day without you" type.

Back then, Markie couldn't believe her luck. Charming, popular Kyle Bryant, in a different league from her in terms of sex appeal (a different stratosphere, really) wanted plain old unremarkable her? So smitten was she, so flattered by his attention, that it was no effort to excuse a few red flags. So he was a little immature, somewhat flaky and irresponsible, not very good at owning his mistakes, and not particularly ambitious. As the youngest of five and the only boy, he had been coddled like a little prince. What chance had he been given to grow up?

And look at the good traits a childhood with four sisters had given him: he was sensitive, understanding, more willing to share his feelings than any other guy she had ever known. And he was incredibly romantic, forever sweeping her up in long embraces or producing flowers or lighting candles even when they were only having boxed mac and cheese while she studied and he flipped through pages of a magazine. She decided those were the things that mattered most. Look at her parents: her father might have been upstanding and duty-bound since he was five, but where was the passion? If Markie had to choose between dependability and romance, she'd take the latter.

But that was *before* the kid and the big mortgage. Before she realized that it's oh-so-easy to devote your heart, mind, and body to another person when you're both *in college* and there's so little stress in your lives. Romance and passion and long talks into the night can carry the day

when there are no bills to pay, no jobs to hold down, no middle-of-the-night feedings, no debates about attachment parenting and discipline techniques.

After all those things, after all the pressure and stress the grown-up responsibilities brought with them, after all the tears from her about needing a real partner instead of a second child, the (broken) promises from Kyle about how, this time, he would finally begin to act like one, after all the fights when, ultimately, he threw up his hands and said she was expecting too much, things changed. "Crazy in love" was downgraded to "in this together," which sank, eventually, to "We owe it to Jesse" and "What would people think if we split up?" For more years than she could count, staying together hadn't been about the feeling they couldn't live without each other, but only about their son and how it would look if the Golden Couple revealed their tarnish.

Kyle's explanation for the mess he had gotten them into was—no surprise to Markie—immature, illogical, and devoid of personal responsibility. As for the repeated job loss, "Look, Markie, *you're* the one who wanted me in all these big-shot sales positions. *I* never said I had what it took to do that kind of thing. I'd have been happier working construction; you know how much I loved those summer building jobs when we were in college. But you wanted a successful businessman for a husband, so I faked it at every company for as long as I could. *For you.* I could've told you they were all going to figure it out after a while."

As for the money, "It's always been so important to you to have all the things everyone else at Saint Mark's has. You think I wanted to be the one to tell you we couldn't afford all that stuff?" And as for the women, "*You* try living with someone who's so much more responsible and successful and such a better parent. It erodes your self-esteem completely! If I hadn't found *some* way to feel good about myself, I'd have ended up depressed, or worse. You think *that* would've been better for our son?"

The mortgage company was unimpressed with Markie's promises that if they would merely give the Bryants a slight extension, she could make things right. Because by then, unbeknownst to her, Kyle had already requested the maximum number of extensions allowed to enable him to divert their monthly mortgage payments to stave off the collection agencies breathing down his neck about the credit cards and home-equity loans that were even more delinquent than the house note. They were all done granting extensions on this account, a mortgage representative told Markie over the phone, in a tone that made it clear just how many times Kyle had called them and how annoying he must have been. But here's what they would do: they'd give Markie and Kyle six months to either pay up or get the hell out before they initiated foreclosure proceedings.

Markie couldn't pay. Their "rainy day" fund was gone, along with Jesse's school account. Enter Clayton and Lydia and their Loan of Many Attached Strings. In hindsight, Markie wondered if borrowing tuition money to keep Jesse at Saint Mark's a few months longer might have been more an act of cruelty than compassion. Word had traveled through the student body that not only had his parents filed for divorce in the wake of a financial crisis, but Jesse's father had worked his way into the bedrooms of most of the Mothers' Club over the course of his son's nine-year tenure at the school.

There had been vague rumors before—ones Markie had studiously ignored—but in the spirit of upper-crust discretion, the gossip had been tastefully squelched before it had been allowed to gain legs. Apparently, once it got out that the Bryants were no longer financially capable of remaining in the Saint Mark's circle, it was decided that they should also no longer be afforded diplomacy.

If Markie had paid attention to her husband's financial shenanigans, she could have put a stop to them before they got so out of control. If she had acknowledged the lipstick stains, the scent of someone else's perfume, the alibis that didn't add up, she could have called him on his

infidelity, made him renew his vow of faithfulness. If she had stopped to think about it, to piece together that the money and the women were signs of a deeper problem, she could have dragged him with her into counseling, locked the door, and insisted that they not leave until they had worked out all of their issues, recommitted themselves to each other, their family, their son.

Were it not for her willful blindness, she could have spared Jesse the humiliation of trading private school for public, five thousand square feet of living space for nine hundred, family dinners with both of his parents for traded weekends via court-ordered visitation. Relative anonymity among his Saint Mark's classmates for the infamy of being "that kid whose parents self-destructed."

The night they told Jesse about the divorce, Kyle pulled the boy aside to say he was sorry about how things had turned out. He didn't fess up to the maxed-out credit cards, the secret refinancing of the house, the unpaid mortgage statements, his pilfering of Jesse's education account. He certainly didn't mention the Mothers' Club.

What he said was that he had "tried to reason with your mother," but that it hadn't worked out. "What can I do, pal? I guess she just doesn't want to be married anymore."

When Jesse relayed this to his mother later, he said it in a tone that suggested he wasn't entirely sure his father had been completely honest with him. Markie studied her son carefully as she considered her answer. The boy knew his parents—he knew his father's impulsiveness, his occasional immaturity, how it sometimes seemed like there were two children in the house, Markie the lone parent. He knew, deep down, that she would never have given up on her marriage, on their family, unless his father had committed some major matrimonial infraction.

But it didn't matter what the boy knew, deep down. What mattered was what Markie saw in his eyes, in the set of his mouth: *Don't tell me what he said isn't true. Don't tell me your side of it. Don't tell me anything that will make me question my father, a man whose dependability has*

always been a fragile, fleeting thing in my life. Because I will not survive that.

Markie patted his hair and kissed his cheek. And did not set him straight. Instead, she let him believe what his father had said, that the blame for the dissolution of their marriage, their family, Jesse's entire world, lay at her feet.

And that was why, in addition to avoiding their former neighborhood, her job at Saint Mark's, the Mothers' Club, and every other person, place, or thing that reminded her of their past life, she was also avoiding her own son. Or letting him avoid her, as the case may be.

Chapter Eight

The side door slammed shut as Markie raced downstairs to say good-bye. "Damn!" she said to the empty kitchen. She should have skipped the hair and teeth brushing. The day before, she had managed to fit those in and still make it to the kitchen as Jesse was making himself a sandwich for breakfast, though when he saw her, he dropped the knife, abandoned the open jars of peanut butter and jam, grunted "Bye," and walked out of the house, a backpack in one hand and two plain pieces of bread in the other. He must have adjusted his schedule this morning, timing it so he could slip out before she got downstairs.

A couple of weeks earlier, after their first Skype call with her parents from the bungalow, she had made the mistake of interpreting Jesse's hug, and his offer to split a sandwich with her, as an invitation for her to take another shot at bridging the gap between them. "Listen," she had said, placing her hand on his, "Mrs. Saint thinks maybe you were smoking outside yesterday when I was out buying lunch. Is that true? Are you smoking?"

He yanked his arm out of her reach. "We haven't even been here a whole weekend, and you've already got the neighbors spying on me? Nice trust, Mom."

"I didn't ask her to—"

But he was already halfway down the basement stairs. At the time, she had tried to work up some fury about his walking out on their conversation, but she couldn't manage it. *That* was the shot she had decided to take to bring them closer? Accusing him of sneaking a smoke in the yard? She didn't blame him for being angry with her for that. She was furious with herself about it. She wasn't two-full-weeks-of-silent-treatment furious, but then, she wasn't a teenager whose life had been recently upended.

Now she watched from the living room window as he walked down the block, his pack slung over his right shoulder. Her head started to pound, and she headed for the coffeemaker. She pushed the button on the machine and reminded herself that it was Friday, at least. She had an annoying trip to make to her company's downtown headquarters later, but after that, she would be able to relax. She was ahead on her work for the week, so she was planning to knock off the minute Jesse got home from school.

She wanted to fix things. Maybe they would walk down to the sandwich place for dinner. Catch a movie, even. Her first Global Insurance paycheck had hit her bank account the day before—finally, they could live a little. There had to be some new video game he was after, or maybe some new style of hoodie or jeans that everyone wore at school. They could stop for those things after the movie. Yes, it was bribery. Right now, she wasn't above it.

Later, peering into her tiny closet, she averted her eyes from the main clothes rod on which her nicest suits and dresses hung—all too tight now, thanks to her post-divorce carb-fest. Hanging on a hook behind the door was the sole businesslike item she owned that still fit: a green dress she had purchased shortly after Jesse was born.

She still remembered the day she bought it. By the time she had loaded Jesse into his car seat, gotten them to the mall, and made her way to the dress department—finally, not the maternity department!—she calculated she had four minutes to shop before he woke and hollered

for milk. She grabbed three dresses from the rack and settled on the first one she could fit into—a trendy-looking green scoop-necked item that she loved in the dressing room. When she got it home and under regular light, she discovered the color leaned toward neon, and on closer inspection, the scooped neck seemed to scoop slightly to one side. No matter, though—it didn't have an elastic tummy, so to her, it was high fashion. She had worn it constantly.

Now she took the dress off its hook, slid it on, and regarded herself in the mirror, wrinkling her nose. She was amazed Kyle had let her out of the house in such an atrocious article of clothing all those years ago. She couldn't believe she was about to let herself do it again today, and for the fourth time in as many weeks, no less, as she had now been to the Global Insurance office that many times, having started her job before they moved to the bungalow. Climbing into the decidedly not flashy, definitely not European, used car she had bought for $500 after she lost her fancy leased one, she told herself that on the upside, even if someone from her old life were to see her, they would never recognize her.

Downtown, she fought traffic to reach the loading bay at the back of the Global Insurance building, where two shipping department guys would remove the boxes of completed files she was returning and replace them with a new set while she performed her requisite check-in on the fortieth floor. In the elevator, she held her breath and pressed the number. *In, out, fast,* she whispered to herself—the mantra she had developed after her first miserable trip to the building. There were only a handful of work-at-home employees at Global Insurance. The rest of the company's vast army of claims processors worked here, in the downtown headquarters, between floors thirty and forty. Markie had only seen the fortieth—the floor occupied by Claims Review and Appeals Processing—but her manager, Gregory, assured her the others were identical, each an enormous square space with a perimeter of offices and an interior filled with cubicles, cubicles, and more cubicles.

Markie had heard of "cube farms" before. The fortieth floor was more like a cube prairie. Across its great expanse, claims reviewers (this was Markie's job—and it was a quiet one) were interspersed with appeals processors (involving telephone calls). This meant that in one cube, a person might be trying to read silently, while directly beside him someone else squawked loudly into her headset, explaining at several decibels greater than necessary why it was that although Global Insurance was most definitely "On Your Side!" and "Here for You!" it could not, sadly, pay that particular claim.

On her first trip to the office, standing on the perimeter of the cube prairie with Gregory and listening to the sound of shuffling paper and keyboards clicking and people coughing and sniffing and sighing and chairs moving and file drawers opening and closing, Markie had thought of the farmers in biblical stories watching as clouds of buzzing locusts swarmed toward them. *This must be what it sounded like,* she thought, *the droning noise of impending doom.* She had scratched her arms and checked the collar of her neon-green dress, shaking the fabric to set free the insects she was sure had crawled under the polyester and onto her skin.

Now, stepping out of the elevator, she tried not to look at the cube prairie as she racewalked down the long hallway and into the office of the wordless, humorless woman who collected everyone's completed log sheets each week and handed them new ones. Markie didn't know the woman's name—the nameplate outside her door said only Log Sheets. On Markie's first visit to headquarters, Gregory had pointed out the office and explained the log sheet–swapping process, but he claimed not to have time to make introductions. Markie suspected he might be afraid of the woman. If she thought less of him for it at the time, she didn't the following week when she stood on the threshold of the woman's office and offered a cheerful "Good morning!" only to be met with a pinched-face glare as the Log Sheet Lady growled, "I don't do small talk."

Markie set her sheaf of papers in the in-box on the corner of the Log Sheet Lady's desk, then stood quietly, staring at her sandals. She almost committed the sin of letting out a sigh at the sight of her own chipped toenail polish, but she caught herself in time and waited soundlessly as the woman first checked carefully over the ten pages of completed columns of notes and figures, then made unintelligible marks in a small notebook before reluctantly handing over a new sheaf of blank sheets.

In Markie's view, more than simply being an exercise in sartorial humiliation and interpersonal unpleasantness, her weekly trips to headquarters were a ridiculous waste of time. Surely, she had suggested to Gregory, it would be more efficient to have all the files scanned and available online, to have Markie submit her log sheets over e-mail, and to have the Log Sheet Lady send new ones the same way. The claims review department was singularly focused on churning out as many closed claims as possible (preferably with DENIED stamped across the front). Indeed, Gregory's entire bonus structure hinged on the number of completed files his team members reported each week. Wouldn't everyone involved be better served if Markie spent her Friday mornings at home, adding another dozen or so files to her weekly numbers count?

But streamlining the work-at-home process wasn't a priority, Gregory had insinuated, though he refused to come right out and say it. Hiring a few dozen work-at-home employees was the brainchild of Global's human resources department, as a response to shareholder dismay about the company's being passed over by a number of "preferred employer" lists. It was bad for PR to have the company excluded from those lists, many of which focused on how much flexibility the workplace provided for its employees.

Global's leadership agreed to give the program a try, but they hadn't completely bought into the idea, and for that reason, some of the clunky aspects of the program, such as the weekly in-person file-and-log-sheet swap, weren't likely to be ironed out anytime soon, or possibly ever. Markie had begun to suspect that management was hoping the

work-at-home employees would find it all so frustrating that they would finally give up and agree to take up residence in the cube prairie. The company would still earn a place on the various lists for having "offered" the flexible positions, and it would have all its rank and file downtown, under the close supervision of managers like Gregory.

She could imagine the rhetoric in the future press release: "We at Global Insurance have generously offered flexible work situations to a number of employees, and some have tried it. It is a proud reflection on the unique esprit de corps we have developed in our office that each of our work-from-home employees has opted to give up their flexibility in order to join their fellow Global comrades in our downtown headquarters." If Markie hadn't been desperate to hang on to her work-from-home privileges as a means of hiding from the world, she might have been tempted to fight for them as a statement against corporate oppression. But reclusiveness was her current focus—she would leave employee subjugation for someone else to rail against.

Stepping out of the Log Sheet Lady's office, Markie aimed herself toward the two glass exit doors at the end of the hallway. Before she had taken more than a few steps, she heard Gregory call her name from somewhere deep in the cube prairie, and without thinking, she made the dire mistake of stopping midstep. Now he would know she had heard him—there was no way she could race to the exit, pretending she hadn't. Next week she would be more strategic.

As the considerably sized Gregory puffed and sweated his way down the corridor, Markie studied her fingernails and pretended not to notice how long it was taking him to shuffle his heft the final forty feet that stood between them. She knew she should close the gap herself, spare him the effort, but she was hopeful that having to cover the entire distance would cause him to associate physical discomfort with trying to talk to her so that next time he wouldn't bother. She also knew she deserved to go straight to hell for such thoughts and hoped her

pre-divorce displays of compassion would make up for her post-breakup grumpiness.

Finally, Gregory reached her, doubling over, hands on knees, to catch his breath. After half a dozen wheezing gulps, he straightened. "Whoo! Maybe I need to add more steps to my Pep Walks!" He held out his wrist to show her the electronic step-counter he wore. Not surprisingly, his wasn't the subtle black she had seen on other men, but the same garish hue that colored the walls of the fortieth floor, the surface of every desk, the cushions of every chair, and even the ceramic sinks and toilets in the bathrooms: Global Insurance purple.

"Purple is energizing!" Gregory had told her during her office tour. She thought "vomit inducing" was more accurate, but she kept the thought to herself, sparing herself the chiding from Gregory that such a comment would be considered, according to the Glossary of Global Insurance Terminology, "Morale Oppositional" or "Potentially Team-Dismantling." In Markie's four weeks on the job, she had not demonstrated satisfactory use of GI terminology, despite countless hints from Gregory that her Recommend for Retention Rating would skyrocket if, in addition to her higher-than-average Claims Review Completion Levels, she would demonstrate a willingness to exhibit Full On-Boarding with the GI Way.

"Nice," Markie said, indicating his step-counting device.

Gregory clasped his hands over his head and attempted a side bend, but the weight shift put him off balance, and he had to thrust an arm out against the wall of a nearby cube to catch himself. Recovering, he patted the cube wall as though he had been making a planned inspection of it all along, and then he shuffled back into the center of the hallway. He wiped a great deal of sweat from his forehead, checked his step-counter again, and smiled.

Markie was crushed that the work of chasing her down seemed to have made him feel pride rather than agony, but maybe she should have expected it. Gregory fancied himself an athlete. His office was filled with

the kind of motivational posters that compared work ethic to physical endeavor. On her tour, he had pointed out his favorite, centered over his desk: under a photo of an eight-man rowing crew was a caption that said, WHEN WE ALL PULL TOGETHER, WE ALL SUCCEED!

"That's us, here at GI," Gregory told Markie that day. "And I'm like the player-coach. You know, pulling the wooden . . . thingie, right along with the rest of my, uh . . . boat fellows." Whereupon he had made a motion with both arms that was nothing close to rowing or canoeing or any other sport, water-based or otherwise.

"How's it going, Gregory?" Markie asked, giving him a warm smile to make up for her earlier uncharitable thoughts.

"Good, good," Gregory said. He scanned the hallway, the cube prairie, and his own shoes, looking for something else to say, before finally settling on "You?"

Poor Gregory, she thought. As verbally inept as he was, she knew he would like nothing more than for the two of them to have a long, meaningful conversation. He had told her that he viewed his direct reports as friends more than employees. He considered them family, even, having no wife, no kids, no life, really, outside of work. If he spent all day taking Pep Walks and Networking or Mind Mapping or Info Sharing in the cube prairie and didn't get his own work done, no problem—he would just stay until seven, or nine, or midnight, and finish up.

"It's worth it, for the, you know, to be close to people," he told her. Worth it only to Gregory—on prior visits, Markie had spied him from the hallway as he hoisted himself along the rows of cubes, and she had seen the panicked looks on people's faces as he got closer, the frantic moves to pick up the phone and fake an important call, the mad dashes out the other end of the row for a pretend bathroom break.

"I'm good, too," she answered.

"Good *like your numbers,*" he said, grinning. "You're going to have the highest of the whole team by next week." He leaned closer. "I had them give you more files this go-round. That's good for you *and* for

me." He blinked—she was pretty sure he meant to wink—and rubbed his thumb and forefinger together. "Not to mention good for GI. But a little bump in our checks is nice, right?"

"It sure is."

"You should splurge next payday," he said. "Get yourself something new." He indicated her green dress, then touched the collar of his golf shirt, which was, naturally, Global Insurance purple. It was also quite new looking, with a crisp collar and a row of buttons that lined up neatly instead of veering west like the neckline of Markie's dress. Her face reddened at the thought that even Gregory dressed better than she did.

"I'm afraid my next paycheck's already spoken for," she said. "And the one after that. And . . ." She made a rolling motion with her hand to complete the idea.

He cocked his head to the side, confused by her gesture, but she had already said enough. She was not about to list for him her many creditors and payment deadlines and interest rates and penalty fees. Or tell him about her strategy of financial self-flagellation: if anyone was getting anything new in her house, it was the fourteen-year-old who had done nothing to warrant having his finger pinched so many times by constantly tightening purse strings, not the forty-five-year-old who had let them get into that condition.

They stood awkwardly for a few moments while Gregory tried to think of something more to say, and Markie tried to conjure up an emergency that would allow her to leave, stat.

"Oh!" she said, patting her purse. "Was that my phone?"

"I didn't hear—"

"Yes, I think it was." She rooted through her handbag, pretended to find her cell, and fake-read a terrible message on its screen. "Oh no!" she gasped. She looked up at Gregory with simulated panic in her eyes. He didn't catch on, so she added, "Something terrible happened!"

"What happened?" he asked.

She turned away, artificially distraught, and raked a hand through her hair, hoping the dramatic gesture would serve to both distract him and give her time to think of some awful thing that required her to rush home immediately. She couldn't think of anything, so she went with "I know! You're right! I have to get home right away!" Turning, she headed for the exit doors. Gregory started to walk with her, so she picked up her pace, losing him in fifteen steps.

"What is it?" he called after her. "What happened? Markie?"

"I will!" she called back, waving without turning around. "I will drive carefully! Thanks! You're a great help, Gregory."

⚜

This is how the universe punished Markie for pretending there was a disturbing message on her phone earlier: she got a disturbing message on her phone. She had finished her last file for the day and was waiting for Jesse to get home so they could start their mother-son night out when he texted to say he wanted to hang out with Trevor after school. Maybe even stay for dinner at Trevor's house. He would be home by ten. Was that okay?

Trevor, whose name I've heard exactly one time, but whose face I've never seen? she wanted to text back. *This boy I haven't met, whose parents I know nothing about, expects your mother to have no problem with your spending the entire afternoon and evening there? Is Trevor's father going to drive you home, or do they intend to have you walk, alone, in the dark? What are these people* thinking, *these so-called parents of this so-called Trevor, letting a ninth grader walk home by himself? Tell me the address, and I'll come and get you at ten. Or right after dinner. Better yet, why don't you just tell Trevor that tonight's not going to work out?*

At Saint Mark's, she had known every child, every family, every parent's occupation. She had most of Jesse's friends' mothers on speed dial, could get to their houses with her eyes closed. It was time to remind

her son of this, she thought as she reread his text. She would do it over dinner that night as they reconnected. They could leave Trevor of the Negligent Parents to invite some other unsuspecting kid over while she explained to her child that he needed to take things a little more slowly when it came to his social life. She wasn't at all comfortable with this insane public-school laxness where kids made plans willy-nilly with people their own parents had never even laid eyes on. He had to give her some time to catch up.

I'm not so sure, she finally texted back. I've never met Trevor.

?? Jesse replied, and because Markie had an honorary PhD in Interpreting Teenage Boys, with a major in the Naturally Quiet subset and a minor in the Recently Turned Sullen, she knew exactly what "??" meant: *This again, Mom? First you grill me about sneaking cigarettes in the backyard, and now you don't trust me to choose my own friends? What's next—you going to check to see if my toothbrush is wet after I tell you I've brushed?*

She set her phone in her lap and closed her eyes. He was adapting to his new surroundings, making friends. Did she really want to interfere with that, to tell him to hold on just one minute, let's stop this forward advancement and rewind things to how they used to be? This was how things were *now*. And if that made her nervous, if that made her feel uncomfortable, then she was going to need to suck it up and learn to be nervous and uncomfortable.

Never mind, she texted back. Ten is fine.

Chapter Nine

One morning the following week, as Markie lowered herself into one of her patio chairs, a stack of files cradled in her arms, she heard the door from Mrs. Saint's house to her screened porch open and close, the scraping of chairs on the wood floor, the clatter of dishes being placed on the coffee table, and the voices of the elderly woman and the four members of her staff as they prepared to sit down. Coffee hour was about to begin, and Markie could predict exactly how the next sixty minutes would go.

She hadn't set out to memorize the daily goings-on across the fence, or even to take note of them. She had no interest in getting to know her neighbor or the elderly woman's household employees or how any of them went about their days. Her goals were to be alone at her own house and to maximize her income by reviewing as many claim files as she could. But the fact was, it was impossible to live or work in the bungalow without hearing almost every word spoken next door. Mrs. Saint had half an acre at least, but her house sat so far back from the street that it was mere steps from the low wooden fence that separated the two yards. Markie's property was tiny—there were only a few feet of lawn space between the house and the property line. This meant that neither Markie nor Mrs. Saint could have a conversation

in their yards, or even inside their houses if the windows were open, without the other hearing.

Markie had taken to whispering to Jesse when they spoke on the patio and to making sure her kitchen window was closed before she called down the basement stairs to let him know the pizza was ready, or that she was going up to her bedroom to watch TV, or any other announcement that might elicit a disapproving finger wag from her neighbor. She made work-related phone calls from the patio from time to time but never personal ones—those she took inside, from the corner of her bedroom farthest away from her neighbor's house.

Mrs. Saint took none of those kinds of precautions, however, and that was why Markie could predict not only how coffee hour would go, but the rest of the day as well. First, Ronda, the cook, would produce a tray of baked goods, apologizing about how undercooked or burned or misshapen they were, while everyone would tell her it all looked wonderful. But halfway through the meeting, when Ronda went inside to fetch more coffee, the others would huddle together and discuss in hushed voices how terrible the day's scones or muffins were and how they planned to get rid of them. The least offensive ones could be rendered somewhat edible by smothering them with jam, while the worst would be tossed out the door and onto the lawn for Bruce to collect later and bury at the bottom of the compost bin behind the garage.

Next, Mrs. Saint would ask Bruce, Patty, and Ronda what they had planned for the day, and no matter what answer they gave, she would offer suggestions for amendment: Do this thing first, the other second. Spend more time on that one than you did last week. Markie noticed that Mrs. Saint rarely asked Frédéric how he intended to spend the day, and when she did, it didn't seem she was doing it to provide a critique, but only to make conversation. After the meeting ended, Frédéric and Bruce would confer outside the screened porch for a few minutes while the sounds of running water, clinking dishes, and Ronda's humming would float out the kitchen window. Markie would have thought

cleaning the kitchen might be something on Patty's list, but she was trying not to let herself deliberate over the proper division of tasks between the cook and the housekeeper.

Several times during the day, Mrs. Saint would check on everyone's progress—Markie could hear her voice ringing out through the house or yard as she pointed out errors and made suggestions for fixing them. Most of the fixes seemed to require Frédéric's oversight, so Markie heard his voice often, as well, as he checked in on the others and tried to help them avoid disaster before it was too late.

"That kind goes in the shade, not the sun, remember?" she had heard him call to Bruce when the other man was poised to plant a shrub in the wrong spot in the garden. "You have to unplug the iron *every time*," she had heard him remind Patty—not that this one had stuck, as Markie heard him say it almost every day. She had lost count of the number of times she had heard his low, gentle voice in the kitchen, followed by Ronda crying, "Oh, you're right! I can't believe I did that again! It's completely ruined!"

At the end of the day, Patty would leave in a frantic hurry, claiming she was going to be late for some evening activity that everyone seemed aware of but no one ever named, while Ronda, Bruce, and Frédéric stayed to eat dinner with Mrs. Saint. Markie found the fact that her neighbor took all of her meals with her employees to be equal parts endearing and controlling—which, she had decided, was the perfect description for the Frenchwoman herself.

Markie was opening her first claim file when she heard her neighbor's voice. "So. You will join us for coffee today?" She was at the fence, gesturing to the screened porch behind her, where the others were still getting set up. "It has been some long time now."

In the three weeks since she and Jesse had moved in, Markie had exchanged polite waves with Frédéric and a few sentences with Bruce, but she hadn't yet met Ronda or Patty, or Patty's young daughter, Lola, who appeared at the house after school and on weekends, or Patty's

mother, Carol, who came only rarely and never stayed long. And she hadn't heard a peep from Mrs. Saint, until today. True to her word, the older woman had given them time to settle in.

Markie raised her coffee cup. "Thank you, but this is my caffeine quota for today, I'm afraid." With her other hand, she lifted her file. "And now I'm on the clock."

"But are you paid by the hour with such a job?" Mrs. Saint moved a hand to her hip and tilted her head, and Markie felt like an eight-year-old who had been caught shoving all her dirty clothes under the bed.

She also felt a small amount of irritation at Bruce, to whom she had once revealed the nature of her job and the fact that her pay was piece rate. As the groundskeeper not only for Mrs. Saint but also for the bungalow's landlord (something he had shared with Markie during her first week living there), Bruce was always outside, often hovering nearby. Thankfully, he seemed as uninterested in conversation as Jesse, but one day he ambled close to the patio and confessed he had been wondering about the stacks of files she was always working on.

Recalling how socially awkward he had seemed the day she met him, she wanted to reward him for his effort in initiating a conversation, so she told him a little about her job. She didn't want him to think she was slacking by stopping to chat—no matter how little she cared about insurance claims review, she was determined to bring her trademark work ethic to it—so she had also explained she was paid by the file, not the hour.

"I mean, I've started work for the day," she told Mrs. Saint. "And I don't like to stop once I've started. Trying to harness momentum."

"*Oui*," Mrs. Saint said, nodding with understanding. "Because this is a job much more boring than your last. So it is hard to keep excitement."

Markie was stunned—she hadn't shared any such information with Bruce. Noticing her shock, Mrs. Saint said, "Chessie tells me, when he

71

is walking home from school last Friday." She pointed in the direction of her front door, out of Markie's sight.

Markie widened her eyes in disbelief. Jesse hadn't mentioned being intercepted by their neighbor as he walked home. Most likely because he hadn't thought much of it, she told herself; it probably seemed like a coincidence to her naive son that the old woman happened to be out front at the precise time the high school kids were walking past. *Leave us alone while we settle in, my eye.* Markie told herself that later she would order Jesse to take the bus home from now on or find a different walking route. Perhaps she should tack on a threat of some kind—the loss of his precious gaming system, for starters—if he so much as aimed an eyeball in their neighbor's direction again, let alone revealed another fact to her about himself, his mother, or life inside the bungalow.

The porch door banged shut, and the old woman turned to peer through the screen. They were all sitting now, waiting. "So you will keep up the working for now," she told Markie. "And I will come over in"—she consulted her watch—"two and a half hours. When it will be time for a break."

Markie felt her body sag and hoped it wasn't apparent to her neighbor. She had so wished Mrs. Saint's I'll-give-you-time-to-settle-in would last longer. "I don't take breaks" formed on her tongue, even though every morning she stood, stretched, adjusted the angle of the umbrella, and took her time carrying her coffee cup inside. If she was feeling exceptionally guilty about her general inactivity, she made a trip—sometimes even two—around the outside of the house.

Other days, she stood at the kitchen counter and paged through a magazine or read a chapter of a book before returning to the patio and the claim files that awaited her. She did all of this at roughly eleven—the exact time Mrs. Saint had said she would come over. Markie swallowed the fib, and before she could think of a better excuse, the old woman nodded once, turned, and walked away.

Chapter Ten

Two and a half hours later, Mrs. Saint deposited a gift basket at Markie's feet and eased her tailored-suit-clad body—houndstooth check, with a silk blouse and heels—into one of the other patio chairs. It turned out she and Frédéric hadn't been wearing formal clothes on Markie and Jesse's move-in day because of some special event, but simply because that was how they always dressed. Each time Markie had seen Mrs. Saint since then, the older woman had been wearing another expensive suit, and Markie had watched in amazement as Frédéric helped Bruce with any number of hot, dirty jobs—digging up bushes in the hot son, kneeling in another part of the garden to replant them—while clad in suit pants, a dress shirt, and loafers.

"So," Mrs. Saint said, arranging herself so her back was ramrod straight, her legs angled back and to the side and crossed neatly at the ankles. "You will come for coffee another day. Get to know everybody. They are all eager to talk with you."

"I'm really more of a start-the-day-in-silence type," Markie said.

"For lunch, then."

"I'm afraid I'm not very social these days." Markie gave what she hoped was an unapologetic smile, her way of putting a friendly but emphatic end to the discussion.

"Because the divorce."

Markie's smile wilted. She wasn't about to exchange confidences with a woman she barely knew. "Because we won't be here long," she said. "Our lease is up at the end of January. So there's no point."

"But do we not all need a community, no matter how long or short we are in a place?"

"I have my son."

Mrs. Saint nodded in the manner of someone who wasn't convinced, but Markie made a show of staring at the cloth-covered gift basket until the other woman left the matter alone and followed her gaze.

"Muffins," Mrs. Saint said. "Half made by Ronda and half from the store." Lowering her voice, she said, "She tries hard. But I wanted to bring some others, just in case. I put a jar of jam, too. And, also, Ronda has sent you a gift."

She reached under the cloth and extracted a small square box made of Popsicle sticks, handing it to Markie. It was a tiny replica of the bungalow, complete with accurately placed windows and doors, and even the half story for the main bedrooms and bathroom. It had been painstakingly crafted—not a single gap showed between the sticks, there wasn't one stray blob of wood glue, and the pieces forming the half story were precisely cut to allow a snug fit for the roof. There were even curtains on the upstairs windows.

Markie had seen Ronda several times as the cook crossed the lawn to take a drink or snack to Frédéric and Bruce, or to ask Frédéric for help with something. Her perfectly round, permanently flushed face sat atop her equally circular body, making her look, even from a distance, like a risen loaf of bread dough. Markie regarded the wooden house and tried to picture Ronda's thick fingers constructing something so precise. *It must have taken her hours,* Markie thought, pressing a hand to her chest. She had received plenty of lovely gifts in her lifetime, but no one other than her own son had ever given her something handmade, until now.

Turning the structure in her hands, she located the side door, which was attached by two minuscule hinges and propped open. Two small cloth figures were affixed to the door, one in black pants and twist-tie flip-flops, the other in denim pants and a T-shirt. "How adorable! Is this me and Jesse?"

"*Mais oui*. She is a faith healer, Ronda. Or so it is what she says. Which I do not know about this, honestly. Magic and special powers for things, I am not so sure. She likes to send luck to people by making totems such as this. Of course, no one of us can say that when the good thing happens, this was because of the totem rather than a person's own hard work and the fate of the world. And when the good thing does not happen, well, she of course cannot explain.

"But"—she dipped her chin—"this is a thing she feels very strong for. And so we have gotten used to seeing her totems all over the everywhere. This"—she gestured to the house—"is to bring you luck in your new home so that you will have a long, happy time here." She reached out and touched the paper faces of the dolls. "You see? They smile. And also"—she moved her finger to the figures' pipe-cleaner arms—"they hold hands. So we will hope that Ronda does have some powers, *non*?"

Markie bit back her annoyance. What did Mrs. Saint think she knew about Markie and her son? What exaggerated story had she relayed to her employees about them, to make Ronda think they needed some magic totem power to help them connect with each other?

"Well, she's done a lovely job of the house," Markie said, "and it was a cute idea to include the dolls. But we're fine, my son and I. Quite fine."

Mrs. Saint smiled thinly, and Markie felt like a child who had just told a wild story to her patient grandmother. She ignored the feeling and pressed on. "And we're leaving soon, like I said. So while I'm sure it'll be a happy stay for us, it won't be a long one."

Mrs. Saint set her chin and looked away as though she knew better about whether they'd be leaving soon or not, and Markie fought the

temptation to ball her hands into fists and say, "And you can't stop us, either!"

"Anyway," Mrs. Saint said, "Ronda has been having this sit in the kitchen, waiting. She wanted to leave it outside the screened porch so it would be closer to you and bring you luck sooner. But Patty reminded that Bruce might step on. This has happened many times with gardening totems she has made for him."

"Well, it was very thoughtful of you," Markie said. "And of Ronda. The muffins and the little house and the time to ourselves. We're pretty introverted, Jesse and I. Not everyone understands that. You have more visitors in a day than we do in a month."

Mrs. Saint craned her head to look at something on her side of the fence, and Markie suddenly heard Bruce and Frédéric behind her, discussing something about a wheelbarrow and mulch. She was tempted to ask Mrs. Saint to confirm the theory she had developed, that Frédéric played the role of general contractor rather than regular employee. But that would violate the rule she had set for herself: *Stop being curious about them.*

"It must be a nice thing to have so much help," she said instead. "Keeping up with a house can be so physically tiring."

"Och," her neighbor said. She leaned close and whispered, "Sometimes I think the most tiring thing is to fix all their mistakes!" She indicated the basket, with Ronda's muffins and the store-bought replacements.

Before Markie could stop herself, she leaned in, too, and whispered, "But if they're not good at their jobs, then why—?" She clapped her lips together, trapping the rest of her question. She did not care. She could not. She would not.

The older woman had guessed, though, and tilted forward even more, beckoning for Markie to do the same. When their heads were almost touching, she whispered, "*Mes défectueux*, they are all in need of help. But who wants to be told this straight in the face? Or to be

handed charity? So I give my help by asking for theirs. And by paying for honest work. Not always good, but honest."

Markie heard the men's voices receding as they walked to the end of the driveway for their first load of mulch. Keeping a watchful eye trained on her yard, Mrs. Saint, her voice still low, said, "In the past, with *les autres*, I was very strict, always demanding for them to learn to do it right the first time. I wanted them to move on, get real jobs, with bosses who would not allow for the repeating of so many things. Those ones, they worked for me only for one month, two months, before I push them out, to a better life, on their own."

The men's voices got louder, and Mrs. Saint put a finger to her lips, glancing casually around the patio to make it seem, in case Frédéric and Bruce looked over, that she was merely enjoying a pleasant morning at the neighbor's and not talking about them. While they waited for the men to deliver the mulch and then retreat out of earshot for another load, Markie shifted in her chair and surveyed her neighbor's house and yard, both understated yet immaculately maintained.

The house was a ranch of unimposing size, but its gray exterior walls were so rich, its white window trim so crisp, Markie suspected it must be repainted at least once a year, if not more often, and possibly hand-washed in between. The lawn rivaled the golf course at the Woffords' club for flawlessness, and the garden beds along the fence and the side of the house, while filled with local plants and flowers rather than anything showy or exotic, were tended with the sort of care Markie would expect if Mrs. Saint's home were open to the public.

Markie had no idea what Mrs. Saint was paying everyone, but if she had enough money to employ a staff for years, surely she could afford to live in a much nicer part of town where the homes were truly impressive. If it were Markie at seventy-five or eighty years old with that kind of wealth, she would upgrade immediately and cruise into her final chapters in a tony area with fancy new zero-lot-line

condos—maintenance-free construction, no landscaping or yard to keep up, and neighbors who didn't turn over with each lease term.

Behind her came the sound of shovels scraping the bottom of the wheelbarrow, then the squeaking wheel of the vessel as someone pushed it back to the driveway. Mrs. Saint watched them go, then leaned in again. "Now I am much too old for this, for pressing them to get better and find somewhere else to go. I am much too . . ." She tapped two gnarled fingers over her heart.

"Oh!" Markie said. "Are you ill?"

Mrs. Saint frowned at the fingers on her heart as though she hadn't realized they were there, and then she dropped her hand, and her gaze, to her lap. "I get tired more easy, is the thing I mean. Because I am older. This is all."

Markie doubted this was all, but she wasn't about to push on a personal health matter despite her suspicion that if their roles were reversed, her neighbor surely wouldn't allow her the same privacy. "Well, you and Frédéric get around pretty well, I'd say," she said instead.

Mrs. Saint's head snapped up, and her dark, narrowed eyes told Markie it would have been better to push about her health than comment on her age. "Och! But he is much older than I am!"

Markie managed to keep from saying, "Nice try!" or arching a skeptical brow, but the old woman must have detected her disbelief anyway, because she said, "Many people find it a surprise. But this is why smoking is a bad idea, I tell to Patty. Frédéric has never done, and I have all the years along. So this is what I get for that: people think me the same age, when I am a complete ten years younger.

"Can you believe there are even people who ask to me what it was like in the Second World War? As if I lived in that time?" She stared at Markie with practiced incredulity, waiting, it seemed, for Markie to verify the ridiculousness of such a notion. Or, more accurately, to indicate she had bought the charade.

"It takes a lot of work, to do the training of many people," Mrs. Saint said, evidently eager to move off the topic of her age. "I have not the stamina for it now. Also, I am not so able anymore to keep up with all these details of who is looking for help, what are the skills they want, where the applications must go, and the such.

"*Alors*, these ones"—she gestured toward her house, indicating the helpers in and around it—"I think maybe they will never be able to leave me. Not unless they decide to teach themselves to do their things correctly and then find a new job on their own, locating the place and giving the application and all of it. But I do not think these are things that will happen.

"Frédéric tries to fill into my shoes, but he is not stern enough." She shook her head, but there was more affection in the gesture than frustration, Markie thought. "Always he has been too forgiving, that man."

Mrs. Saint's left hand moved to her right, and she touched the wedding band she wore on her right ring finger, the universal sign for widowhood. Watching, Markie recalled the older woman talking about her "Edouard" and wondered if one of Frédéric's too-forgiving acts had been to let Mrs. Saint know she was free to pine for her late husband forever and never return Frédéric's affection.

"He insists on impossible things from himself," Mrs. Saint continued, "but then he lets others . . ." She frowned, sighed, and said nothing more.

They were silent for a few moments, Mrs. Saint lost in thought and caressing her wedding band, Markie regarding the old woman with a curiosity she tried, and failed, to extinguish.

"Anyway," Mrs. Saint said, "because I cannot help them like before, and he never could do it all himself, I have been hoping someone else would come along someday to take up the job."

She considered Markie for such a long time, and with such intensity, that Markie felt her head reflexively shaking no before she even heard what Mrs. Saint said next: "This is why I was so happy to hear

that a young woman was moving in beside. Someone with a working-at-home job, especially, who would be around always. Someone with more energy than I have."

Still moving her head from side to side, Markie pressed herself against her seat back, as though by creating a greater distance between them she could guard herself from the outrageous request her neighbor was hinting at. She couldn't believe this woman! Not only had she obviously extracted Markie's age and employment information from the bungalow's leasing agent, but she had made the unilateral decision—before Markie even arrived on the scene!—that the new tenant should be the one to take over as employment counselor for her apparently unemployable staff!

Markie eyed the Frenchwoman and wondered what other information she had squeezed out of the agent. The number of personal questions on the housing application had been so alarming that had she not been so desperate to get Jesse and herself out from under the thumbs and judgmental glances of Clayton and Lydia, she would never have filled out a single line. Even with her urgency to find a place, she'd had second thoughts after hitting "Send" on the online application. Did she really want to deal with such an overreaching leasing agent?

Plus, the place was more than she could afford and required a full-year commitment. She had been offered the Global Insurance job only that morning—she couldn't be certain it would work out for an entire year, and even if she could be sure, a hefty rent payment was a big risk for someone who was paid piece rate instead of a guaranteed monthly wage. She listed her concerns in the "Notes" section of the rental application and reminded herself that things happen for a reason: if they rejected her because of her financial instability, it wasn't meant to be.

Within an hour, she heard back: they were willing to reduce the monthly rent by 10 percent, waive the security deposit, and shorten the lease term to six months with an option to extend. If those new terms appealed to her, all she had to do was send a check for the first month's

rent, and the place was hers. Having recently been hoodwinked on the financial front, Markie was suspicious. "That's very generous," she wrote back, "but would you mind telling me why you're so willing to cut such a deal?" The place had been vacant for some time, the agent replied, and the landlord was eager to fill it. Satisfied, Markie put a check in her parents' mailbox that night.

"I'm afraid I'm not the help you were expecting," Markie said, her voice firm, her position nonnegotiable. She indicated the stack of files beside her chair. "I have so much work. And . . ."

"And a boy," Mrs. Saint said.

Markie couldn't tell if the older woman was being understanding or if she was pointing out that with only one child, Markie had plenty of time to serve as the new outplacement coordinator. "And like I said, we're moving soon, so there wouldn't be time anyway."

"It is only that I worry," Mrs. Saint said. "What would they do if anything happened to me?"

She steepled her fingers, and as she bent her head to study her hands, Markie considered how endearing it was for Mrs. Saint to care so much. The woman might be nettlesome, but she was also selfless.

"I'm sure you worry," Markie said. She wasn't getting involved, but she wasn't without compassion. "Maybe there's a community organization that could help. Some kind of job-skills training center or something."

"Yes." Mrs. Saint looked up. "This is a good idea. I will look into."

"Good," Markie said. "I hope you find something." Eager to move the conversation away from the subject of her own involvement with Mrs. Saint's employees, she said, "So you've been doing this for a long time, it sounds like. Hiring people to work around your house, coaching them, helping them get jobs?"

"My Edouard has provided me with more money than I need. And we have all learned, have we not, that we are to help our neighbor? This is a way I could help."

"So it's a religious calling?" Markie asked. Confusion registered on the older woman's face, so Markie explained. "'We are all to help our neighbor,' you said. I thought maybe it was some sort of instruction from the Bible or something. And I guess I assumed you were Catholic, since you're from Quebec. I'm sorry if that was—"

"Mais oui," Mrs. Saint said. "Catholic. Of course. But this is not something I have learned from a Bible anyway. Only something I have learned from life."

"Well, it's a lovely idea, helping a neighbor," Markie said. "And I'm sure there are plenty of people like you who do it for reasons other than religion. It's a way of giving back, isn't it? And that can be especially appealing to someone who received a great deal of help themselves once—"

"Of course not!" Mrs. Saint dropped her hands and pressed so firmly on the arms of her chair that it seemed she was about to stand and leave. She didn't move, though, and after a moment she composed herself. "Of course not," she repeated, this time more quietly.

Markie considered pointing out that she only meant her statement to be generic—she wasn't suggesting this was the case for Mrs. Saint specifically. Given the violent reaction, though, it felt like the wiser choice to leave it alone, so instead she said, "Well, it's extremely thoughtful of you. Lots of people have plenty of money, but they don't use it on anyone but themselves."

Mrs. Saint swatted the compliment away and turned from Markie, pretending to examine the shrubs bordering the patio, while Markie added "humble" to the list of positive attributes she was starting to appreciate in the older woman. She would still prefer to avoid Mrs. Saint for the remainder of her time in the bungalow, but there was no denying the fact that the woman was doing a great amount of good in the world. More than Markie ever had.

More than her parents had, too, as far as she knew. How many worthy causes could have been aided with the amount Clayton and Lydia

spent on annual country club dues, she wondered, before she checked herself and her hypocrisy. Hadn't she told herself only moments ago that with the kind of money Mrs. Saint had, her own investment would be in a swanky condo? And hadn't she had that thought mere moments before she advised her neighbor in no uncertain terms that she would not be signing on to help?

"Where did you meet them?" she asked. "Frédéric and Bruce and Ronda and Patty? And all the others over the years?"

It wasn't curiosity, she told herself. It was simply polite conversation. It was also a preferable focus for her attention than her own selfishness. From the way Mrs. Saint immediately interrupted her faux study of the shrubbery and turned to speak, Markie could tell it was also a more appealing topic to her neighbor than the subject of her generosity.

"Bruce, I met when he is getting fired from the gardening and hardware store he is working at," Mrs. Saint said. "I am walking out of the place with Frédéric, and the manager was giving some very rough words to Bruce, and then he opened the door and pointed him to the outside, like he was an unwanted cat!" She narrowed her eyes. "We never have gone back to that one.

"And so, there were we, walking out at the same time with him. And Frédéric was having a struggle with a new wheelbarrow and many bags of things. So he took up a step with Bruce, and he pointed to the car, and he said, 'This is my lucky day, *monsieur*, because I need someone strong to help me with some jobs, and it seems you are now available.'"

"*Frédéric* hired him?" Markie asked. "But isn't Frédéric one of—?"

"He knew I was about to. And he knew it would feel better to Bruce if he is asked in such a way as that, by a man who needs help with some jobs, rather than an old woman who might only be having sorry feelings for him. And so he came with us, and he has done the garden and lawn ever since. Also now your lawn and garden, as you

know, since the landlord of your house also hired him. He is a very . . . hard-working gardener."

She wouldn't dare say he was a good gardener, Markie thought, or an efficient one. Over the past three weeks, she had seen Bruce plant, then dig up and replant elsewhere, about a dozen small shrubs, half a dozen taller bushes, and several armfuls of hostas. This after Frédéric or Mrs. Saint pointed out that, alas, he had put shade lovers in direct sun again or had forgotten that Mrs. Saint wanted taller things here, shorter ones over there.

"And Frédéric?" Markie asked. "Where did you meet him?"

"And then Ronda," Mrs. Saint said, ignoring the question, "I saw her crying in a diner."

"You mean, she'd just been fired, too? You have some timing!"

"*Non*. She was not being fired, but she was being yelled at for her whole shift because she is not enough fast on her feet. She tells me this when I sit beside her in the booth. I order tea, and I sit with her, and she tells me these things. Also that she is distracted often of times by this faith healing thing she has.

"She thinks she sees visions and the such, and each time she stops to focus on that, even if there is something on the stove she should be giving her concentration to. Of course, she was not very good enough of a cook for them to tolerate when she is slow or distracted. And so, maybe she would be better at a place where it is not so important if she is this way. This is the part I told her."

"And at your house, she doesn't need to be fast or focused," Markie said.

"Or good!" Mrs. Saint whispered, her eyes almost disappearing in the wrinkled folds around them. She bent forward, her body shaking as she giggled noiselessly. "Oh, I should not," she said, gasping for air. She straightened and covered her disobedient grin with a palm until it fell into an appropriately sober line, then cleared her throat. "Patty and her little Lola, I have met in a food pantry."

Younger than the others, Patty was tall and super skinny and pale and pockmarked and long-haired and gravelly voiced. Several times a day, Markie saw her slouching outside in the corner where the porch met the house, one hand in the back pocket of her painted-on jeans, the other holding a cigarette. Sometimes she carried an old metal lawn chair out of the garage and plunked herself down, stretching her long legs and tilting her face to the sun while her cigarette dangled from one hand, sometimes falling to the ground as she dozed off.

Patty's daughter, Lola, was in second grade this year, a fact Markie assumed the entire neighborhood was aware of, since the girl had spent three days shrieking with joy about it before school resumed. She was a shorter version of her mother—thin and pale, with stringy, dirty-looking hair always fighting to escape its messy ponytail. Each time Markie saw her, Lola was in some strange outfit—a dress on top of jeans, shorts over leggings, a long skirt matched with a bikini top.

Also each time Markie saw Lola, the girl was alone, wandering aimlessly around the yard. It made Markie feel sad for her. Did she have no friends she could invite over, no toys to play with? A lonely child herself, overlooked by parents focused more on whether their daughter impressed their friends than whether she was happy, Markie had felt an instant connection to Lola, despite having seen her only from afar. One afternoon when Lola was digging with a stick in a patch of dirt behind Mrs. Saint's garage, humming a forlorn-sounding tune, Markie had to force herself inside and up to her room to keep from inviting the girl over for lemonade and a round of one of Jesse's old board games.

It seemed to Markie that Patty regarded her daughter as more of an amusement than a responsibility. Several times Markie had seen Patty languishing on the metal lawn chair while inside the screened porch, Bruce or Ronda tried to cajole Lola into finishing her homework or having an apple instead of another handful of cookies.

"Don't you agree, Patty?" the others would call.

"If you say so," Patty would answer with a shrug and a flick of her cigarette, to show she really had no dog in the fight.

"They came in at the end of my shift," Mrs. Saint went on. "The moment I saw them, I knew—" She clamped her mouth shut, cutting off the rest of her sentence, and shook her head. Then she took a deep breath, let it out slowly, and muttered, "I am getting tired."

"You knew what?" Markie asked.

Mrs. Saint looked down, suddenly very interested in whether she had gotten dirt on her shoes. "I knew they needed help. This is all."

It was clear that wasn't what Mrs. Saint had known when she first saw Patty and Lola, but Markie decided not to press. It wasn't like her neighbor would admit the truth anyway, given her track record of disclosure thus far, and accusing her of dishonesty hardly seemed like the right thing to do during their first real conversation.

"The tables all were empty," Mrs. Saint went on, "and there was not many food left, but they were happy for a place to sit. Patty was not in such a hurry to go back home. They live with her mother, and that woman has . . . challenges. Patty was telling to me all the list of where she was taking Lola every day, only to get a break from this mother. So I make the suggestion to spend time at my house instead of all these places they are going where a young child does not need to be so all the time. I already had the others to help, but you can always find more things, *non*? Vacuuming and the such?"

Markie looked sideways. The only time she had heard the vacuum running inside, Patty was outside, smoking and sunning on the old metal lawn chair.

"Or helping Ronda to remember to look at the pots so there is not so much boiling over every time," Mrs. Saint said. "And cleaning up in the kitchen when things get spilled on the floor, which is a thing Ronda is doing always. And then later, I suggest maybe it would be very better in the school over here for Lola, not the one near their apartment, and Patty agreed. So, that is why those two."

"And then Frédéric?" Markie tried again. She was as annoyed with herself for asking again as she was with her neighbor for not answering the first time.

"I have a special skill, you see," Mrs. Saint said, "in finding what thing a person needs most in their life. Noticing what is their *défaut*, which is to mean their . . ." She turned her hands over and examined her veins for the English translation. "Flaw. I am good at seeing what is the flaw they have that needs to be fixed and then helping them to fix it. Sometimes people want to agree about this, and sometimes they do not. But this is a thing I am good at."

Mrs. Saint gazed around the patio, looking everywhere but at Markie, who was certain the woman was thinking of the many terrible failings her new neighbor possessed, starting with forcing her son, "*le pauvre*" Jesse, to suffer the deprivations of life without five daily servings of vegetables or a dog. Markie wanted to roll her eyes at the lack of subtlety, but instead, feeling defensive, she decided to attack from another angle.

"Did you say *défectueux*?" she asked. "When you first started telling me about them? And does that mean what I think it does? Because, I have to say—"

"*Oui. Défectueux.* Or to say in English, I think, day-fec-tif?"

"De-fec-tive," Markie corrected, dragging it out not to accentuate the correct pronunciation but to make clear how inappropriate a term it was.

"Defective," Mrs. Saint repeated, nodding her thanks for the English lesson and missing the rest of the point.

"Don't you think it's a rather insulting label?" Markie said.

"Och"—Mrs. Saint waved a hand—"I would never say it *to* them. Oh, and here comes Bruce with his mulch. I guess Frédéric has started on something else."

Markie, unwilling to let the matter drop, leaned closer and whispered, "But to even say it *about* them—"

There was a loud noise behind her then, and Bruce said, "Oh, for Pete's sake!" Mrs. Saint winced, and Markie turned in her chair to find the gardener standing beside an overturned wheelbarrow and looking glumly at an ugly swath of dark mulch that now covered two square feet of Mrs. Saint's formerly pristine lawn. Muttering, he righted the wheelbarrow, dropped to his knees, cupped his hands, and started scooping the offending dirt back where it belonged. It was a finely mixed substance, though, and much of it sifted through his fingers. At the rate he was going, it would take him hours to clean it up.

Markie swiveled back around, expecting her neighbor to be wincing still, or even jumping to her feet, ready to bark instructions for a faster cleanup. But all traces of displeasure were gone from the older woman's face, and instead of leaping up and shouting, she sat still, watching him silently—almost, Markie thought, contentedly.

After a moment, Mrs. Saint called, "Or a shovel?" She pointed to the side of the garage, where a shovel leaned against the outer wall. "Would it be more quickly, do you think?"

There wasn't a trace of annoyance in her tone, and she leaned forward, her expression eager, as though she had no idea if a shovel would be faster and was waiting for him to solve the dilemma for her.

Bruce followed the aim of her finger to the shovel and considered it for a moment. "I think a shovel will be faster," he announced. He retrieved the tool, and after he had deposited two shovels' worth into the wheelbarrow, he faced his employer again. "I'll have this cleaned up in no time. Don't worry."

Mrs. Saint spread her arms wide, palms out. "Why would I worry?"

Bruce beamed and resumed his work as Markie took in her neighbor's pensive face. She could almost hear Mrs. Saint's internal plotting as the old woman constructed a plan involving Frédéric and a trip out to the yard after Bruce left—there would be a flashlight, Markie imagined, and possibly a pair of tweezers. She could almost hear the curse words Mrs. Saint must surely be thinking to herself, too. There was no way

such an affront to her perfect grass wasn't causing a significant degree of mental anguish.

But if any of this was going on inside the older woman's head, none of it was apparent from the outside. Rather, there was a softness around Mrs. Saint's mouth and a brightness in her eyes as she watched Bruce work. It was the same expression Markie had noticed on move-in day when her neighbor stood under the oak tree, watching the two men unload the truck.

"Look," Markie said, her voice low, "it's clear how much you care about all of them. You've given them jobs, you give them no end of second chances. You're worried about their future without you. And all of that is really sweet. It's just that it feels . . . not right, your calling them your defectives. I know it's none of my business, but—"

Mrs. Saint patted Markie's knee. "I apologize. I am not one for . . ." She made a circular motion with her hand as she tried to recall the correct English phrase. "Making a mincemeat with my words. They need help, these ones, in different ways. That is all. Or even to say it a different way, they each have a break—they each are broken. And if a thing is broken, you say it is defective, *non*?"

"Well, you say that about *a thing*, sure," Markie said. "You don't say it about *a person*."

Mrs. Saint pursed her lips and nodded, but not in the manner of someone conceding a point. "What is your way of helping people?" she asked.

I leave them alone, Markie wanted to say. *I don't storm over within moments of their arrival and take over their move-in process, accuse their children of sneak smoking, criticize their TV-viewing habits, and suggest they need to improve their nutritional intake and get themselves "un chien."*

She went with a less confrontational truth instead. "I . . . I haven't been big on volunteering recently. But I, uh, always helped with the school's Earth Day project every year. And there were other, um, campus

cleanup days and that sort of . . ." She gave up. "It's not easy to find extra time, with a son and a divorce and . . ."

"Of course."

Mrs. Saint's smile and the tone of her voice let Markie know she owed her neither an explanation for her dismal record of community service nor an apology for jumping on her word choice. Markie felt something relax in her chest as the defenses she had instinctively kept up around her neighbor eased a little. Maybe it wouldn't be terrible to get to know her a little better.

"The first time I heard Lola's voice in your yard," Markie said, "I assumed she was your granddaughter. Do you have any? Did you and Edouard have children?"

In an instant, Mrs. Saint's smile disappeared. *"Non."* She bowed her head and pretended to study the wicker weave of her armrest, her fingers tracing the ropy strands. Her anger was so palpable that Markie wanted to kick herself for asking such a personal question.

"I'm sorry," she said, reaching to touch the older woman's knee. "It's none of my business. I shouldn't have asked."

Mrs. Saint snapped her head up, moved in her chair to escape Markie's touch, and stretched her lips into an artificial smile. *"Non, non.* It is nothing. I am only, as I said, becoming tired. I think I should be returning home." She stood, and Markie rose, too.

Mrs. Saint pointed to the basket. "In some days, I will send Lola to fetch this. She has been very much wanting to meet Chessie. It would be nice for them to play outside together."

"Jesse's in ninth grade," Markie said. "Lola's in second."

Mrs. Saint shrugged. "Homework together, then. Lola is needing help always, and the rest of us are not so good at all the maths and such. I am sure Chessie could do. This would be good for the both, I think."

Markie felt her cheeks begin to catch fire. First the woman wanted Markie to be her unpaid Assistant in Charge of Defectives, and now she

wanted Jesse to tutor their offspring? And who did she think she was, telling Markie what was good for her own son?

Markie lifted the basket and stepped to the door. "The best thing for Jesse is what he's been doing—spending time with the kids at his new school, making friends. Ones his own age."

Mrs. Saint's lips twisted sideways, and Markie could tell she was about to speak. She didn't want to hear it.

Pushing the side door open, Markie said, "I'd better get these muffins inside, out of this heat."

Mrs. Saint nodded and moved toward the fence. "And I will send Lola—"

"No need. We'll get the basket back to you."

"Oh yes. You could have Chessie—"

"*I* will bring it to you," Markie said firmly. "Thanks again. And please give my thanks to Ronda."

She stepped inside and closed the door before Mrs. Saint could say they would discuss it later.

Chapter Eleven

On Monday, Markie woke to the staccato sound of rain on the roof. She groaned—she would be confined to working inside—and after reading the clock on her bedside table, she swore. It was 7:09 a.m. She had overslept.

"Bye, Mom!" Jesse called from the side door, and now she smiled, his cheery farewell enough to erase her annoyance at the weather and her oversleeping.

She reached for her cell phone and texted him, apologizing for not being downstairs in time to say goodbye. She signed off xo, and for the first time in several weeks didn't immediately regret having pushed her luck.

Her phone dinged a moment later with his response: No worries. You too. xo

On the weekend, they had finally gone on the deli-and-movie date she'd been planning. It hadn't exactly been a chat-fest. Jesse didn't say much about Trevor or the nameless "other guys." He said even less about the fact that, as they were driving to the deli, Kyle had texted to cancel their plans for Sunday brunch. "It's whatever. He's really busy." But they ate an entire meal at the same table, trading at least three dozen words, they laughed at all the same parts in the movie, and on the way home,

when Markie said she'd had a great time and would love to do it again, he said, "Same."

Markie looked out her bedroom window and saw her son walking toward the curb, where a car idled. The driver, a boy who didn't look much older than Jesse, jerked his chin in greeting and called something Markie couldn't hear. Jesse returned the chin lift and climbed into the backseat beside two shadows she couldn't make out, and they pulled away.

Presumably, one of the other passengers was Trevor. Or was he the driver? She had assumed he and Jesse were the same age, but she hadn't come out and asked the question. Should she have? And if Trevor was only a ninth grader, was that his older brother behind the wheel? Or a friend? Was it someone Jesse knew, maybe from past rides? He hadn't complained about the walk home from school lately—was this why?

She reached for her phone. She needed to remind him of their rule that he ask her before accepting a ride from someone she hadn't met. But instead of typing a message, she set the device back down. The conversation could wait until he got home. She would hate for the kids in the back to see his "mommy's" admonition on his phone screen.

In the bathroom, she washed her face and studied her reflection in the mirror. Should she have the discussion with him after school? He was in high school now, so maybe the ask-before-getting-into-a-car rule should be retired. She could imagine a vehicle full of impatient teenagers rolling their eyes as he stood on the curb, pecking away at his cell phone and saying, "Just let me get clearance from my mom first." She wanted him to have friends, to be close enough to a few kids that he could ask for a ride if it was raining, or even if it wasn't. Maybe she should keep quiet.

In the kitchen, she filled the kettle, ground five tablespoons of coffee, and dumped them into the French press. As she waited for the water to boil, she peeked out the window above the sink and wondered whether Mrs. Saint would hold her morning meeting inside the house,

given the weather. She pressed her forehead against the window glass and peered into the porch, trying to discern whether the cushions on the porch chairs were cloth, in which case they would be too damp to sit on, or vinyl.

The porch was in shadow, so she squinted harder, until the screaming kettle roused her, calling her attention not only to the boiled water, but also to the fact that she had been spying. She spun to face the stove top, pouring water into the press and crossing her arms as she waited for it to steep. She didn't realize she had turned around again until she felt the cool glass of the window against her forehead.

Cursing, she ordered herself into the dining room and reached for the curtain. Before she could pull it closed, she saw a tall, thin shadow cross the window in Mrs. Saint's unlit living room, and she wondered why Frédéric would show up early on such a day. Surely there would be little for him to do, few outdoor tasks for him to supervise and correct, given the rain.

At ten, she rose from the dining room table and her neat stacks of files and stretched her arms high, swiveling her head right, then left, to work out the kinks. In the kitchen, she transferred the remaining muffins from Mrs. Saint's basket to a plastic container and peered outside. The rain hadn't stopped, but it had let up significantly. Crossing the wet lawn, she forced herself to fix her gaze straight ahead, not allowing a sideways glance into the porch. If coffee hour had taken place out there while she was working on the other side of her dining room curtain, she didn't need to know about it.

Mrs. Saint answered the door. Markie was surprised—she had expected Ronda or Patty to answer.

"Only the others are gone," Mrs. Saint said, noticing the look on her neighbor's face. "I sent them out on the errands."

Markie held out the basket. "I wanted to thank you again for this. And to thank Ronda."

"You could come in and wait for her. They might not be long." She stepped backward and opened the door wider.

Markie didn't move, nor did she allow herself to peek inside. "Thank you, but I really have to get back to work," she said. "And look, I forgot to do it when we talked the other day, but I also wanted to thank you for the idea to call about the cable. I checked with the leasing agent a few days after we moved in. You were right: it was included in the lease after all. Not in the actual document—I checked before I called. They somehow left it out. The leasing agent couldn't say why. Anyway, Jesse was thrilled."

Mrs. Saint nodded. "Except that sometimes I think it was a mistake to tell it to you. Because too much TV is going on. I did not realize how it would be."

Markie cocked her head sideways, puzzled. "How would you know how much TV—?"

The old woman pointed across the fence to the egress window that led from Jesse's basement bedroom to the side yard. "The lights from the TV. They do the . . ." She opened and closed her hands twice. "Into the too-late hours."

Stop spying on him and you won't have to be disappointed about how much TV he's watching, Markie wanted to say. Instead, she went with, "Well, it's only the first month of school, and they seem to be easing in pretty slowly. When his homework ramps up, the TV will go off. Although, like I've told him, the ability to work with noise in the background isn't a bad one to have. TV, stereo, roommates talking, whatever. So even when his schoolwork starts getting harder, I can't say I'll be too strict about whether he keeps the set on, as long as he's getting his assignments done."

Mrs. Saint pursed her lips at this, and Markie could tell the other woman was deciding whether to argue the point now or leave it for later. Markie decided for her, stepping away from the doorway and

turning for home while she forced herself to remain calm. Why had she bothered to offer the woman an explanation?

"Thanks again for the lovely basket," she said with exaggerated cheer, raising her hand in a wave as she stepped lightly toward the bungalow. *I will not storm across the lawn like an angry child.*

"And have you met the boys who picked him up this morning?" Mrs. Saint asked.

"Nope," Markie said, not turning, not stopping. "He's in high school now. He doesn't have to ask me every time he gets a ride from someone."

"It is only that Frédéric is seeing those ones before, in the downtown. He recognizes the car."

Markie refused to slow her pace. "I trust my son. He's very responsible for his age, and he knows better than to—"

She clamped her mouth shut. She was done explaining herself, done defending her child to this woman, to her parents, or to anyone.

As she stepped inside the bungalow, she heard the creaking of Mrs. Saint's door as the woman began to close it. Before Markie could congratulate herself for finally getting in the last word with her neighbor, Mrs. Saint said, "I am sure you already have rules for the special window."

⚜

When Jesse got home, Markie asked about the friends who had driven him.

"Just Trevor and the guys."

"I'd love to meet them sometime."

He winced. "They're not taking me to the prom, Mom."

"Kids don't meet their friends' parents these days?"

"Uh, no." He reached into the cupboard for a box of cereal.

"Well, maybe you want to have them over sometime. Just to hang out, not to meet me, specifically."

He scanned the family room and kitchen and the doorway that led to the unfinished basement and his cramped bedroom. "Here?"

She was shocked by how much his question hurt. Or was it an accusation? She decided to leave it alone. She wanted to leave Mrs. Saint's comments alone, too, especially after the smoking-in-the-yard fiasco, but she couldn't.

"Mrs. Saint seems to have some concerns about them. Do you have any idea what she's talking about?"

Jesse thrust his hand into the cereal box and shoved a handful of honey-covered Os into his mouth. "None."

"She said Frédéric ran into them downtown, and, I don't know, saw them doing something he didn't like, maybe? She didn't give any details except that he recognized the car."

He scoffed. "It's a Ford Fusion. Do you have any idea how many of those there are around here? Wrong guys." Carrying the box with him, he reached in for another handful as he walked to the basement door.

"Oh, hey," Markie said, pretending a thought had come to her out of the blue and had no relationship to his friends or her chat with their neighbor. "I was thinking, do we need to talk about the egress window? Like, when and why you'd open it?"

Jesse stopped at the door. "What's an egress window?"

"In the basement? The big one, in your room?"

"That thing opens?"

Markie was torn between feeling like a great mom for having such an un-devious child and feeling like a negligent parent for going so long without telling him how to save himself in the event of a fire.

Chapter Twelve

It gave Markie no joy to know it, but Kyle had not risen to the occasion as a divorced dad. Instead of spending every other weekend with his son, as the parenting schedule allowed, he showed up late on the occasional Saturday or Sunday morning, took Jesse to lunch, sometimes (but rarely) adding a matinee or some other short excursion, and returned him before dinner. Most weeks, he didn't show at all. Sometimes he texted to cancel, but not always, and Jesse had spent a lot of time standing in the driveway, a flat hand over his eyes like a visor, peering down the street for a car that never came.

"It's just that he's really busy right now," Jesse would tell Markie when he gave up waiting and returned to the house. "He wanted to come, but he got caught up with something."

The "something" changed often—Kyle was helping a buddy move or paint or put on a new roof or pave the driveway. Or he was focusing on his new job or traveling for work. Or getting ready for an interview, after he "decided to leave" his last position. The end result was always the same—another week gone by with Jesse not seeing his father.

Markie wasn't one of those divorced women who liked to nod, self-satisfied, as she listed for herself all the ways in which her ex was disappointing their son. She and Kyle were over, but Jesse and Kyle would never be. She wanted them to have a good relationship. She wanted her

son to be able to count on his father. For that to happen, though, Kyle had to become reliable—not his strong suit.

It had been endearing at first, his flightiness and the scatterbrained way he meandered through life. In college, she was his wake-up call during final exams, his external conscience when the bar beckoned more loudly to him than the library. Her friends made fun of their dynamic, calling her "little mother" and him "wayward son," but she liked the roles they had fallen into. After a childhood of being deemed incompetent by perfection-seeking parents, it made her feel good to be the responsible one in the relationship, the person with the answers, the master plan. Plus, she assumed this must be the way of life for all beautiful people: as compensation for their good looks and charisma, they were allowed to let their far-less-captivating partner handle life's boring details while they, unhindered by such trifling concerns, floated about, charming everyone. She was the backstage director who worked so hard to make the star shine and without whom there could be no show. She was needed. And that made her feel secure.

Marriage didn't change things. They would plan a dinner party, and when the appointed date arrived, Markie would be dashing madly around the house getting everything ready, while Kyle, having lost interest in place settings and wine pairings, would wander off to the gym. There would be frantic calls from her, sincere apologies from him, along with a last-minute shower and change of clothes as their guests were arriving, or often after they had already come.

She would be frazzled and anxious and wondering if the entire night would be a failure, and then he would burst into the room, hair still damp, smiling and laughing and greeting their friends as though it were perfectly natural for him to make such a late entrance. Within thirty seconds of his dazzling arrival, the party would be on its way. Markie would begin the night thinking she wanted to strangle him and end it gazing at him over the candlesticks and wondering how she had been so lucky to find such a man.

In the early years, she'd refused to let it bother her. Some people were made to manage all the mundane details of life, she told herself, while the beautiful people like Kyle were meant to breathe animation into it. Markie was social enough, but she didn't have a fraction of what Kyle had when it came to entertaining, whether it was adults for dinner or Jesse's ten best friends for a sleepover or just the three of them at home on a weekend. She was invitations and polished silver and perfect place settings. Kyle was music and dancing and backyard bonfires and ice-cream sundaes for dinner. She could never take on his role. Why expect him to do hers?

After she had collected more years, though, along with colleagues, bosses, and neighbors, some of them rivals with Kyle in the charm-and-sex-appeal department, she realized it wasn't a Beautiful People Thing that prevented Kyle from participating in the tedious workings of their household; it was only a Kyle Thing. And whether because of learned helplessness or advanced age or a rebellion against the unceasing demands of adulthood, it got more pronounced over time, until a formerly endearing quirkiness started to look, to Markie, like unappealing flakiness. The more she pleaded with him to act his age, the more childish he seemed to become, and over time, the "trifling minutiae" he couldn't be bothered to invest in went beyond events of little consequence like dinner parties or parent-teacher meetings and expanded to things like work deadlines, job interviews, and commitments he made to Jesse.

The inevitable ending to which it all led—Kyle's ignoring the bills, their budget, their wedding vows—should have been something Markie saw coming. The fact that she had ignored the warning signs was completely on her. It should also have been, she thought, the nadir to which he allowed himself to sink, at least where Jesse was concerned. But unfortunately for Jesse, his father's rock bottom was apparently still a few fathoms away. Even an event as sobering as divorce hadn't convinced Kyle to deflakify, and that was on him.

Since their split, she had tried a few times to get him to see things from their son's point of view and step it up in terms of regular phone calls and showing up on time (or at all). But his response was always the same: He and the kid were doing fine. They were men. They didn't need hours together to gab. They sent texts every few days, had the odd meal together here or there. They were good.

She told him she wasn't so sure, that texts and calls might be enough for Kyle, but Jesse needed more from his father. She had learned, though, that there was no person in the world a man was less likely to take advice from than his ex-wife. She had the feeling that when she discussed this topic with Kyle, her words sounded to him like those of Miss Othmar, the unintelligible teacher from *Peanuts*.

Despite her pleas, he had not increased his visitation with his son, nor had he increased the frequency of his texts and phone calls or gotten better at showing up when he said he would. This was why Markie was pretending to read a novel on the patio one Saturday morning in late September when really she was holding her breath, squeezing her eyes shut, and saying a prayer that this time Kyle would come through.

Moments earlier, Jesse had walked down to the driveway to wait for his dad, his backpack slung over a shoulder. "See you in the morning, Mom," he had said, not making eye contact, and Markie, relieved he wasn't looking at her when she spoke, called up her most confident voice and told him to have a great time. She heard a car pull into the driveway, and at the same time, Mrs. Saint's side door opened.

"Hey, Dad," Jesse called. He said more, but Markie couldn't make out the words. A row of shrubs between the patio and the driveway muffled the sound and blocked her view. She rose and was tiptoeing over to snoop through the branches when she heard Mrs. Saint call out behind her.

"Good morning to you, Markie!"

Caught, Markie jumped away from the bushes and turned to face her neighbor, who stood in her doorway in an expensive-looking suede

suit and matching shoes, examining with uncertainty the dew-damp-ened grass that lay between them. Markie called "Good morning" back and lifted a hand in greeting.

The gesture was lost on Mrs. Saint, who was now staring over Markie's head. Her property was on a higher elevation, and from her vantage point, she could see over the top of the shrubs to Markie's driveway beyond. Jesse must have looked up, because Mrs. Saint raised a hand to wave before directing her gaze back to Markie. Holding a finger in the air, she studied the wet grass again, and Markie, realizing the other woman must have something to tell her but didn't want to yell or ruin her shoes, headed toward her. She was wearing her usual dollar-store flip-flops—she should be the one to make the trek. Mrs. Saint started at the same time, though, and they met at the fence.

"Today is a good time for you to meet Ronda," Mrs. Saint said. "She has had not a nice week, and I think talking to someone quiet, like you—" She stopped speaking and craned to see over Markie's head. "Oh! Chessie is arriving home, I see. I thought before that he was going."

"He *is* going," Markie said, not bothering to look. "His father's taking him overnight."

Mrs. Saint frowned. "*Alors*, I do not think this is so."

Markie whipped her head around in time to see Kyle's car backing out of the drive. His window was down, and he was saying something Markie couldn't hear. Jesse, still standing in the driveway, nodded once, but she couldn't make out his response. A second later, Kyle sped away. Long after the car was out of sight, Jesse stood there, unmoving, staring down the street. Then he wrenched the pack off his back, slammed it to the ground, and kicked it, sending it sailing several feet. Snatching it up by a single strap, he stomped toward the house, head down.

"Och," Mrs. Saint whispered.

"Sweetheart," Markie said, when Jesse reached the side door. "I'm so sorry." She had learned to stop there.

Jesse, his hand on the doorknob, kept his head lowered. "It's fine. It's just that he has this all-day meeting in, like, an hour, and it's really important. He tried to get out of it, but he couldn't."

"Do you want . . . something to eat, maybe?" Markie asked.

But he was through the door now, and she knew that by the time she made it inside, he would be in his room, lost in one of his video games, the volume turned up loud.

"The thing about a dog is, a boy will hug it."

The words were whisper quiet, and because of the accent, and the fact that Markie was facing the opposite direction, it took her a second to figure them out.

"He will bury his face in its fur. And he will cry if he needs to. Even if he cannot allow himself to do this in front of another person."

Markie didn't have the energy to argue about it, especially now, so she decided to simply say goodbye and that meeting Ronda would have to wait for another day. "I think it's best—" she began, spinning around to face her neighbor. To her amazement, the old woman's eyes were shining, and she was holding two fingers to her lips to keep them still.

"I must go," Mrs. Saint whispered. She turned and made her way back to her house, stepping through her side door and into her sitting room. A moment later, the sitting-room window lowered, and the curtains closed.

Markie marched into the bungalow, snatched her cell phone from the kitchen counter, and dialed her good-for-nothing ex-husband. It went to voice mail. Kyle made it a practice to never listen to voice-mail messages, but she didn't care—she cursed at him until a beep informed her she had used up her allotted time.

Chapter Thirteen

Markie had been working in her dining room for the past two weeks, avoiding Mrs. Saint since the episode with Kyle in the driveway. She didn't want to hear more about how Jesse needed a dog, and she didn't want to have to lie, either, which was what she imagined it would take to get the woman to let the idea go. "Oh, everything's fine—he and his father made up the same day."

Everything wasn't fine. Kyle hadn't shown up since, and if he and Jesse had been texting or calling each other, Markie wasn't aware of it. Kyle never responded to the voice mail she left, though she didn't blame him. She had tried to talk to Jesse about it, but he only said, "It's whatever," and changed the subject.

Usually, the new subject involved his going out with Trevor and his other new friends. His phone dinged constantly with texts, and he now had plans every day after school and most evenings after dinner. Plans of the unspecified, teenage type: "Nothing. Nowhere. No one. Just Trevor and the guys."

It was like the name of a band—Trevor and the Guys. Or a single entity, many-headed, multilimbed: Trevorandtheguys. She didn't know if Trevor was the sole person named because Jesse was closest to him, or because Trevor was the leader, or for some other reason, and she didn't want to blow it by asking. Jesse was annoyed with Kyle for once, not

with her, and while she took no pleasure in the former, she found great relief in the latter and wasn't interested in having it change.

Plus, the boy was home when he was supposed to be, and he was getting his homework done. So she kept her questions to herself and said, "Sure, sounds good." "See you at six." "See you at ten." "Have a great time." And because work was going well, she tried to add, "Here, take a ten," as often as she could.

Markie was rinsing her lunch dishes at the sink when she spotted Ronda alone in the side yard, no boss in sight. This was her chance to thank the woman for the Popsicle-stick house and the muffins, and she tore toward the fence to find the cook carrying Patty's rickety old folding metal lawn chair out of the garage.

"Would you like one of these chairs?" Markie called, an arm extended behind her, toward her much more comfortable patio furniture. "It's the least I can do after you sent that lovely house over."

Ronda smiled broadly and lumbered over.

"Thank you for that, by the way," Markie said as she waited for the woman to reach her. "I'm sorry I haven't made it over before to thank you and to meet you. I was . . . well, there's no excuse, really." Finally, Ronda was at the fence, and Markie extended her hand. "I'm Markie. You're Ronda, right? Or did I just thank the wrong person?"

"Nope, I'm the one," Ronda said, and her voice was so quiet Markie had to lean closer to make out the words.

Ronda shook hands, hers thick and warm. It was soft, too, as were her flushed cheeks, and Markie thought of the Lycra-encased members of the Saint Mark's Mothers' Club, who spent countless hours and dollars in the quest for the dewy-pink glow Ronda had acquired for free by making a two-minute trip from the house to the garage to the fence. It made her love the fleshy cook instantly.

Holding on to Markie with one hand and fanning her face with the other, Ronda said, in her tiny voice, "Oh, land! Wrestling with that old chair!" It seemed an impossible incongruence, Markie thought, the

largeness of Ronda's body and the smallness of her voice. "But at least I won!" She pointed to her victim, sitting obediently open in the sun.

Finally releasing Markie's hand, Ronda said, "We've all been so eager to meet you. And to meet your boy. Especially Lola. She's so excited about having a playmate next door. You should've seen her when Mrs. Saint said she'd spoken to him a few times on his way home from school. She about blew her top! She wanted to leave school early so she could be standing out at the front, too." She chuckled briefly, then leaned closer and, serious now, said, "She knows she's not allowed to knock on your door and seek him out. Not until you've shown you were, you know . . . ready."

Markie decided to ignore the part where Mrs. Saint had indeed been standing outside, waiting to intercept Jesse, not just once but "a few times," and went straight to setting expectations for Lola's interactions with him. "I hope someone will warn her that high school kids aren't really into playing," she said, striving for a tone that was as kind as it was firm. "I wouldn't want her to get her hopes up."

Ronda smiled, undaunted. "Too late for that, probably. And thanks for the offer of a chair, but it's for Lola, not me. And I don't think you want her smearing her chocolate into your new cushions."

As if on cue, the door from the screened porch opened and Lola appeared, wearing a short, summery dress with jeans underneath and an old hooded sweatshirt, unzipped, over top. Holding something aloft in one hand, the girl jumped from the top step down to the grass, sailing over the four wooden steps that led down from the porch and landing with her bare feet planted together, both arms high in the air.

"Nice!" Ronda called. "I'd give it a nine point five." To Markie, she said, "We let her watch the Olympics this summer. She's been doing that ever since."

Lola snapped her head toward the fence, her mouth open.

"You didn't notice anyone else was out here?" Ronda laughed. "Why am I not surprised? Put a Hershey bar in your hand and watch the rest of the world disappear."

At the mention of it, Lola gazed lovingly at the chocolate bar she held, then turning back to Ronda, pointed at the chair, her expression inquisitive.

"Yes, I put it there for you," Ronda said. "Your mother says I should only give you fifteen minutes, though, and then herd you back in for homework. You want a glass of water?"

"No, thanks." Lola shivered and pulled her sweatshirt closed.

"I thought your mom was going to fix that zipper," Ronda said. Lola shot her a look, and Ronda said, "I know, but even a few safety pins would keep it closed. She doesn't have to actually *sew*. Leave it here when you go, and I'll see what I can do."

Lola nodded and climbed into the chair, crossing her legs. Using her free hand, she brushed her stringy, dirty-looking hair out of her eyes, and Markie tried not to think of how much she could accomplish if the girl would let her take a damp cloth and a hairbrush over.

"Oh!" Ronda said. "Our manners! Lola, this is Mrs. Saint's new neighbor, Ms. . . ." She peered at Markie and asked, "What should she call you?"

"Markie is good. Hi, Lola."

Lola smiled shyly. "You have a boy."

"Yes, I do. His name is Jesse. He's older. He started ninth grade this year."

"I started second."

Markie almost said, "I know, I heard," but caught herself, and instead asked how she liked school so far.

"I like *after* school better. Ronda gives me these sometimes." She held up the chocolate bar. "And Frédéric lets me help him do stuff."

"But not today," Ronda said. "You have that reading work sheet, and then your mom needs to get going early. So there's not much time."

Lola didn't need to be told twice, and in about two seconds, she had the candy wrapper torn off, rolled into a ball, and shoved into the pocket of her jeans.

"That girl would eat five of those bars if I let her," Ronda said. "She once told me she'd had chocolate for breakfast, lunch, and dinner over the weekend. On both days! She doesn't have too many rules at home. So I've got to be a bit strict with her here, keep her to a bar a week."

"I wonder what her dentist thinks about her eating so much chocolate," Markie whispered.

"That's what Mrs. Saint's always saying every time I give her some. But then Frédéric reminds her what it was to be a child with a rare piece of chocolate, and she backs down." Ronda smiled.

"Mrs. Saint certainly has a lot of opinions," Markie said, leaning toward Ronda conspiratorially. "I'm surprised to hear she ever concedes a point, to Frédéric or anyone. By the way, how did she meet him? I've asked her a few times, but she always acts like she can't hear the question. For someone so interested in everyone else's story, she's certainly reluctant to reveal her own!"

Ronda's smile sagged, and her eyes told Markie there was no point in anyone trying to get her to utter a negative word about her employer or in expecting her to reveal information the Frenchwoman didn't want others to know.

"I imagine most people that age have a little mystery to them," Ronda said lightly. "All that life! I know I'd find it hard to keep all the details straight, even if I wanted to let people know everything!"

Markie didn't buy it, and Ronda must have been able to tell, because she gave an apologetic smile. But she didn't offer anything further, and Markie could see it would be futile to push.

They were both quiet for a few minutes, and then Ronda said, "I can tell you this, though. She may come out swinging hard, but on the inside, she's really an old softie."

Markie pictured Mrs. Saint sliding into the diner booth beside the crying Ronda, putting an arm around her, tut-tutting as she brushed hair out of Ronda's eyes and told her she needed to find a job that wasn't so demanding. "I could use a cook myself," she heard the old woman lie.

"She has really helped the others," Ronda said. In response to Markie's look of confusion, Ronda said, "Bruce, Frédéric, Patty, and Lola, I mean. They needed a place, and she made one for them. A job and a good salary. Even meals; that's where I come in." She jabbed a thick finger into her breastbone.

"She wanted to make sure they were eating three good squares. People on hard times, sometimes they let that go first, you know. But if someone just makes up a plate for them, they'll eat it. So we serve a nice hot breakfast, a good lunch, and then dinner. To make sure they're taking care of at least that part of things."

"Right," Markie whispered. She waited for Ronda to add the part where her cooking wasn't all that good, where she was distracted so easily that she let pots boil over, so Mrs. Saint had to bring Patty in to help with the mess. The part where Ronda needed a place, too, where she was *this close* to losing her job and Mrs. Saint came to the rescue just in time. The part where she wasn't merely cooking *for* Mrs. Saint's Defectives but *was one of them.*

But Ronda was finished talking. The door from the house to the screened porch opened then, and Patty called through the screen, "Lola! We've got to bolt! I'm already running late!"

Seeing Markie and Ronda at the fence, she called, "So, there she is. Our reclusive neighbor."

"Patty!" Ronda chastised. To Markie she said, "Sorry. No filter on that one."

"It's fine," Markie said, waving to Patty, who was walking toward the fence. She wore skintight jeans and a low-cut blouse, and like her daughter, she was barefoot. Markie extended her hand. "I'm Markie. Neighborhood recluse."

109

Patty shook with one hand while the other reached into her back pocket, extracting a pack of cigarettes. She pulled one out between her teeth, pushed the pack back into her pocket, fished a lighter out of another pocket, and then dropped Markie's hand so she could cup the flame in both hands. Markie watched her, entranced—not by Patty's simple act of lighting a cigarette, but by the authoritativeness of her movements. Everything about this woman seemed out of place, from her seventies-style feathered hair to her inappropriately sexy outfit, to the regularity with which she seemed to shirk her work duties and her child, yet she moved and spoke and carried herself as though she belonged exactly where she was and was conducting herself precisely as she should be.

"Just ribbing you," Patty said, inhaling, then angling her face up to let a long trail of smoke out without blowing it into the other women's faces. "Mrs. Saint told us you weren't much for company just yet." Jabbing a thumb over her shoulder where Lola sat, she said, "I hope she's not the one who finally brung you out from under cover."

Lola looked up at the accusation, then bobbed her head back down to her chocolate bar.

"No," Markie said, "it was me. I came out. I wanted to thank Ronda for the muffins and the little house."

"Totem," Patty corrected, and Ronda blushed.

"Oh yes. Totem. Of course." Markie turned to Ronda. "Sorry."

Ronda waved the apology away. "It's fine. Really. I know Mrs. Saint probably already told you she has no use for—"

"I loved it," Markie said. "The little . . ." She struggled to recall if Mrs. Saint had used a special term for the dolls. "Figures? Of me and Jesse? They're adorable. I can't tell you what it meant to me that you took the time to make it. I don't think I've ever received such a thoughtful gift before."

Ronda beamed, and Patty gave Markie a grateful smile and said, "Wasn't it incredible? Ronda spent hours." She turned to the other woman. "How many, do you think?"

"Oh, I didn't keep track," Ronda said. "I was just happy to do it. I hope it brings . . ." She tilted her head toward Mrs. Saint's house, as though reluctant to say the next thing, in case her boss overheard. "Luck," she whispered.

"I'm sure it will," Patty said. "Don't you think it will, Markie?"

"It already has. I've met the two of you today. And Lola."

Patty scratched out a laugh. "She meant it to bring *good* luck." Putting a hand on Ronda's shoulder, she said, "Frédéric wanted me to remind you that you were going to get dinner started early tonight. He has to go out for a while."

"Oh yes, that's right," Ronda said.

"So, where's Frédéric off to after dinner?" Markie asked.

One of the many unusual things she had noticed about the daily schedule on the other side of the fence was the fact that most weekday afternoons at a little before two, Frédéric left, returning about an hour later. They were all aware that he left, calling goodbye and greeting him when he returned, but as with Patty's evening activities, the details of Frédéric's daily sojourn went unmentioned. Markie had spent more time than she wanted to admit watching, trying to sort out where it was that he went every day. And equally weird, why it was that the only time Patty's mother, Carol, seemed to come over was during that precise hour when Frédéric was gone. The two things didn't seem to have any connection, yet they only ever occurred in tandem.

Patty took the time to stub out her cigarette, light a new one, and blow a long curl of smoke above her before looking directly at Markie and saying, "Who knows?"

Markie felt her cheeks flush as though she had been caught doing something lewd.

She opened her mouth to apologize for treading where she wasn't welcome, but Patty turned to Ronda and spoke before Markie could. "He says you can leave the dishes. He'll do them when he gets back. That way, he can drive you and Bruce home right after dinner, on his way."

"Oh, that's very nice," Ronda said, still looking at Lola. "I'll stay and finish, though. He shouldn't have to."

"As long as you don't take too long, I think," Patty said. "Frédéric wants Mrs. Saint to lie down after you eat, and she won't if people are still here."

"Is she ill?" Markie asked.

"No!" Ronda said.

It was the first time Markie had heard the cook speak loudly, and she might have concluded it was a reflexive, head-in-the-ground response by an employee unwilling to admit her boss was sick, but Patty said, "She's just tired, and he suggested she should take a nap, and she said she had too much to do before dinner, so he said fine, take one right after dinner, and she promised him she would."

Patty stared expectantly at Ronda, who was still languishing against the fence, watching Lola. Finally, Patty put a hand on the cook's arm and in a gentle voice said, "So? Can you get dinner started early, you think?"

"Oh yes, yes, of course!" Ronda said, laughing. "I lost my train of thought for a few minutes there, didn't I? Yes!" She pushed herself off the fence and walked to the side door. "I just need to think about what I should make," she said, possibly to herself, as she reached the door.

"I think you've got a recipe on the counter," Patty called after her. "Something with pork chops?"

"Oh yes, that's right. The pork with the . . . what was I going to do with it?"

"Mushroom soup," Patty said. "Can's on the counter. Sounds real good. If there's any left, save some for my lunch tomorrow?"

Ronda turned and beamed. "I'll be sure to."

"And that," Patty whispered to Markie as they watched Ronda go, "is one of the reasons Mrs. Saint has too much to do before dinner. Getting the simplest meal on the table takes forever. If we're not reminding her she's got something on the stove, we're helping her clean it all up after it boils over."

Patty laughed and shook her head at Ronda's receding form. "I love the woman, I do, but sometimes she takes more getting after than that one." She pointed to Lola, still eating, in her chair. "You about done?" Patty asked her daughter. "Because we really got to bounce in a minute here. Mrs. S said Carol could swing by and get us today, but our window won't be open too long."

It was then that Markie realized she hadn't seen or heard Frédéric the entire time she had been outside. Given how tight-lipped Patty had been about the man's evening destination, Markie knew better than to ask about the Carol/Frédéric coincidence. She would have to solve that mystery another time. Or better yet, she would try harder to ignore it.

"What if you go with Carol and I stay with Frédéric?" Lola asked between bites.

Markie waited for Patty to chastise her daughter for saying "Carol" instead of "Grandma," but Patty only laughed and said, "Nice try."

Then again, Patty hadn't referred to Carol as "Mom." They were an intriguing pair, this decidedly nontraditional mother and daughter, though Markie tried to deny to herself how interesting she found them.

"Finish up and then go pack up your stuff," Patty told Lola. "You'll have to get that reading or math or whatever done at home. You know Mrs. Saint's going to ask about it tomorrow."

Turning back to Markie, Patty said, "Why they've got to bore them all day with it and then send it all home to bore them some more, I don't understand. But then, I'm not a shining example of a scholar. For starters, I'm not supposed to use the word 'boring' when I'm talking about school and homework. Or so I'm told."

She rolled her eyes dramatically, arcing her head in the direction of Mrs. Saint's house to make it clear where the instruction had come from. "She thinks I should hire someone. Not to help her actually do it, just to remind her. She's smarter than Carol and me together. She could do all the work if she had someone who kept on her about it. And it ain't about to be me."

Markie feared the conversation was heading in the same place Mrs. Saint had hinted at some time ago, with Jesse being hired as Lola's tutor. "Maybe Carol can remind her tonight while you're out," she said to Patty.

"Ha!" Patty barked. "By eight, someone will have to remind Carol that Lola's in the apartment with her. And who the kid even is." She curved her fingers and thumb in a circle as though she held a bottle, then tilted the invisible object to her mouth.

Markie's mouth dropped open as a car horn sounded from the front of Mrs. Saint's house, unviewable from where they stood.

"That's her," Patty called to Lola. "Scoot! Quick!" She pointed to the corner of the house. "You run around that way and tell her I'm coming, and I'll grab your bag on my way through. Don't let her take off without me!"

She gave Markie a quick wave and jogged to the screened porch, depositing her cigarette butt in a tin can near the steps before she raced up them, into the porch, and through the sliding doors to the house. Lola watched her mother disappear, then gazed plaintively at what was left of her chocolate bar. Sighing, she popped the last bit into her mouth, jumped to her feet, and ran to the front yard, wiping her fingers on her dress as she went.

⚜

Markie had her solitary dinner in the family room while Jesse ate his downstairs in front of a video game. Setting her plate aside, she picked

up the novel she had been trying for weeks to read, but two pages in, she found herself distracted by the sounds of machine guns and explosions coming from below. Giving up on the book, she went to the basement door. "Jesse?" she called. He didn't answer, so she tried again.

The gunfire stopped. "Yeah," he said, in the way of someone hoping the conversation would be short so he could go back to what he was doing.

She had been thinking of asking him if he felt like going out for ice cream, but it seemed like a silly idea, suddenly. He was fourteen, not ten. She tried to think of an alternative—a slice of pie at the sandwich shop? A walk around the block?—but talked herself out of each.

"Mom?" Jesse called, and his impatience was obvious. "My game will reset if I don't—"

"I was just going to say I'm going up to bed," she said.

He laughed. "It's seven thirty."

"I'm taking my book. I'm going to read for a while."

"Night," he called, returning to his game so quickly that her own "Good night, Jesse," was drowned out by warfare.

Upstairs, she lay, fully clothed, on her bed and stared at the ceiling. The muffled sounds of gunfire rose through the heat vents, reminding her of the impotent effort she had just made to connect with her son. God, she had made a mess of their lives. She opened her novel, scanned a few paragraphs without taking them in, and let it fall to the floor. Nowhere in her teenage diaries had she written that one day she planned to be incapable of making a single relationship function properly, including with her own child. She shut off the light, closed her eyes, and willed a blanket of sleep to spare her from having to spend another conscious minute with herself.

Chapter Fourteen

"So out with these ones again," Markie heard from the other side of the fence as she sat in her patio chair one afternoon, work files on her lap. She had just said goodbye to Jesse after he had raced into the patio after school to dump his backpack and ask if he could hang out with Trevorandtheguys, to go "likely nowhere" and do "pretty much nothing." She turned toward the fence, a cavity-inducing smile on her lips. *Your disapproval doesn't faze me.*

"At least no driving these days," Mrs. Saint said. She must have seen them waiting for Jesse on the sidewalk. "Not that boys cannot chase after the trouble on their own foot."

"Brian's car has been in the shop," Markie said, ashamed at how proud she was to show off her knowledge, not only of the driver's name, but the fact that his car was having troubles. She stopped herself from repeating what Jesse had told her a few days earlier, that it might be something with the transmission. But she did permit herself to add, "It's a Ford Fusion, by the way. Very common around here."

"It is only that Frédéric and Bruce are finding things hidden near the trees," Mrs. Saint said, lengthening her neck to peer at the wooded area behind her garage. "And so it seems maybe they have been back there."

Markie laughed. "I think Jesse and his friends are a little old to be playing with toys in the woods. Whatever Frédéric and Bruce found, I'm guessing Lola's the one who left it."

"Och, but it is not toys. It is cans of . . ." The old woman held up a hand, and with her index finger she pressed an imaginary nozzle. "The spraying kind of paint. Also the ends of cigarettes. They have found these things in the morning time when they did not see them the evening before, and so it seems they are being left there very late."

"Jesse's home by ten every night," Markie said, feeling her voice stiffen. Mrs. Saint craned her head to stare pointedly at the egress window, and Markie felt herself arch up as something inside her snapped. She could not have made it more clear that what she wanted above all was to be left alone, yet other than those first three weeks of blissful silence, she had been intruded on almost daily by this woman! And on every occasion, although Markie had desired desperately to turn her unwanted visitor away at the fence, she had instead forced herself to be polite—friendly, even—despite the fact that on most days she could barely summon the emotional energy to carry on a conversation with her own child.

And what had she gotten from Mrs. Saint in return? Not respect or time alone, but only "Ochs!" and head shakes and criticisms and accusations. It would have been excruciating enough for her to have to deal with a neighbor who was nonjudgmental and uncritical; to have to bear someone so nosy and opinionated was torture. Why had she made herself suffer through this?

"Look," she said, her voice low, her eyes boring a hole into the old woman, "I am done with your accusations. He's smoking, his friends are up to no good, he's sneaking out late at night to play with spray paint? I mean, what else—"

Mrs. Saint chuckled and shook her head as though Markie were a peevish child complaining about things she didn't understand. "*Non, non,* but I am *for* Chessie, of course, not *against.* I like him very much.

And the same is for Frédéric. He feels very worried. *Le pauvre*, with no father around—"

Markie popped out of her chair and stood ramrod straight. "He has a father!" she heard herself screech as her hands balled into tight fists. Mrs. Saint flinched at the noise and opened her mouth to speak, but Markie beat her to it. "They had a misunderstanding that time you saw his dad drive away without him! A simple misunderstanding, like people have! It wasn't some big trauma that caused my son to go from perfectly well-behaved boy to sneaky, smoking, spray-painting hoodlum! You've blown it all way out of proportion!"

The old woman moved to speak again, but Markie held up a hand and went on. "I don't know what your problem with me is. Maybe you don't like single mothers, or maybe you don't trust teenage boys, or maybe you're just bored. And obviously, you didn't get the message when I said it the first time, but I don't want . . ." She waved her hand at Mrs. Saint and the fence. "All of this! So you need to take your . . . whatever it is . . . somewhere else. And leave me and my kid alone!"

She waited a beat for emphasis before marching to the door and yanking it open. As she stepped inside, she allowed herself a brief glance toward the fence, and to her delight, her neighbor appeared completely cowed—head down, hands clasped together. Markie fought the urge to throw her head back and cackle. She was stepping inside when she heard the woman clear her throat. She froze and waited—she couldn't wait to hear this apology.

"Of course, a dog would bark if someone was trying to sneak out the special window."

Markie ground her teeth, stomped inside, and slammed the door.

⚜

She woke in the night to a thud and the sound of voices. At first she thought she must have left the TV on, but when she opened her eyes,

the room was dark. The clock read 11:40 p.m. Instinctively, she reached for Kyle.

She hadn't sobbed, night after night, at the sight of his empty spot in her bed. Nor had she fallen asleep clutching his pillow, or stared miserably into her closet, gripped by regret over the lack of men's shirts and pants and shoes. The absence of aftershave in the bathroom didn't depress her. But she had missed him desperately when it was late at night and a lightbulb flickered and then burned out, or the fridge motor kicked on suddenly, waking her. Or when the house creaked—or, like now, thumped.

And lately she had noticed the void when she wanted to complain to someone about Jesse's bad-temperedness. Many times she had reflexively turned sideways to roll her eyes to Kyle after a particularly rude glare or grunt from her son and had been surprised and saddened to find he wasn't there. That was her own doing, though, as was the fact that there was no girlfriend she could call and vent to anymore, either. Her mother may or may not have risen to fill the role of confidante, but Markie hadn't given her the chance. The thing about setting your life up so you could be completely alone was that you ended up completely alone. And while most of the time that suited Markie just fine, there were times when she wondered if it had been the right thing to do. Like when her kid was acting terrible. Or when she was blaming herself for being the reason her kid acted terrible. Or when her house was making noises in the night.

Markie expected that if Kyle missed anything about her, it was probably something equally bland and passionless, like her organizational skills or the way she folded laundry. It made her feel disappointed in both of them, and she vowed to encourage Jesse to hold out for a partner whose absence would cause the complete annihilation of his soul. He should never settle for someone who could be replaced by a good home alarm system or a dry cleaner. She listened for another

minute and then, hearing nothing, pulled her hand back from the empty space, rolled over, and drifted back to sleep.

Hours later, a loud knock woke her, and now she was truly frightened. The clock read 3:30 a.m. There was another knock, and she wondered suddenly if it was Mrs. Saint. Maybe she had hurt herself somehow and needed a ride to the hospital. Or lost power. She tiptoed to the window overlooking Mrs. Saint's house and looked out. There was a light on in her neighbor's sitting room. Had the old woman left it on before making her way across the yard in the dark?

A louder sound rang out—they were banging now, not just knocking—and Markie realized it was coming from the front door. It couldn't be her neighbor, then—she would never walk around the house when there was an entry much closer. Kyle wouldn't show up without texting first, especially at this hour, and Jesse's friends surely wouldn't choose three thirty in the morning to make their first appearance. It couldn't be anyone they knew. Whoever it was must be at the wrong house—a drunken neighbor, maybe.

She realized she had never talked to Jesse about what to do if there was a thud in the night, voices, a knock on the door. Specifically, she had never told him that whatever he did, he shouldn't answer. It could be some crazed criminal who gained entry into unsuspecting homes by knocking at an hour when people were too tired to question and instead just opened up.

She sat up. He usually slept through anything, but what if this had woken him, too? What if he was getting up right now, making his way to the door? She jumped to her feet and flew downstairs. Sneaking past the front door, she checked the basement, letting out a long, relieved breath when she found it was dark and silent. Jesse must be sleeping through the racket, thank goodness.

Eyeing the front door again, she took a timid step toward it, then another. A narrow strip of glass ran the full length of the wood frame on either side. The glass was thick, like the bottoms of soda bottles, its

purpose more about aesthetics and letting in a bit of light, less about providing a clear view outside. But if she got close enough to the glass, she would be able to make something out, at least, and with the outdoor light on and the interior ones off, she would be able to see who was there without being seen herself.

Holding her breath, she stepped to the narrow window and peered out. There was a police car parked at her curb—its lights weren't flashing, but she could easily identify their silhouettes on its hood. A police officer, his dark uniform distinguishable even through the thick glass, stood on the doorstep, his arm raised, ready to bang again. Markie was flooded with relief.

Until she opened the door and got a clearer look at the squad car: there were two boys in the backseat, and one was her son.

Chapter Fifteen

Five of them, including Jesse, had been caught spray-painting Levin Pharmacy, a few doors down from the sandwich shop. Markie couldn't believe it. Not only the illegality of the act, but the incongruity of it. Their first week in the bungalow, they had met the Levins, a lovely older couple whom Jesse, true to form, opened up to immediately. He had even offered to make trips to the pharmacy himself when they ran out of paper towels or soap or milk.

"I don't mind," he insisted. "Mr. Levin's funny, and Mrs. Levin's like a grandma—you know, a typical one, always friendly and happy to see you and handing out cookies and stuff." Not like Lydia, in other words.

The pharmacy was a stand-alone building, and they had managed to tag three of its four sides before the squad car pulled up. Jesse's handiwork was confined to the pharmacy's alley-facing back wall, behind a dumpster. His tag—one straight line about six inches long—might have gone unnoticed, the officer told Markie, as Jesse might have himself, had he not walked to the front of the store, hands up, when he heard the police arresting his friends.

The officer asked Markie to follow the squad car down to the station. Jesse was released into her custody that night, with orders to return on Monday morning to speak to the judge. Because of his age and the fact he'd never been in trouble before, he was likely to be treated under

the juvenile code, the officer explained. With luck, he'd get a warning, and his file would be destroyed. The same was true for Trevor, who also had a clean record.

"Judge Hegarty usually gives kids one free pass," the officer told Jesse. "But don't ever show up in front of him again." He pulled Markie aside and said, "Keep him away from the other three guys. They're always on our radar, and that's not a place your kid wants to be." Those three would be almost certain to get probation, since this wasn't their first time at the station. They'd be ordered to make restitution to the Levins for the damage, too. The oldest two, both juniors and clearly the ringleaders of the operation, might even face charges as adults.

Driving home, Markie tried to loosen her death grip on the steering wheel, to relax the taut muscles that strained so tightly her forearms were shaking. She took deep breaths, held them for a count of four, and let them out slowly while she told herself to wait, calm down, take the time to get home and into the driveway before she let him have it. If she started in on him now, when her rage was at its peak, she might not be able to stop herself.

She watched him as he sat slumped against the passenger-side door, his mouth trembling, his left hand covering his eyes. Was it true remorse or an act? The thought that he might be faking made her want to let go of the steering wheel with her right hand and smash him, a solid backhand to the chest. It's what her father would do. Not sure how to express your disappointment? Show it.

She had never struck her son before, but God, it was tempting right now, and it would spare her the task of having to sort through the hadron collider of thoughts racing around in her mind, smashing into each other and against the inside of her skull. What was he thinking, sneaking out in the middle of the night with a bunch of teenage thugs? Vandalizing that lovely couple's property? When had he turned into that kind of person?

He wasn't the only subject of her rage, though. She was furious with the other boys, too, for coming up with such an asinine plan and dragging her son into it. He was an idiot to go along with it, but that's all he had done—gone along, and probably because they let him know if he didn't, he could find another group to hang out with. They had preyed on his new-kid status, and she hated them for that. *Pick on someone with your own criminal background.*

And then there was Kyle. Unreliable, selfish, non-child-support-paying, good-for-nothing Kyle. The image of her ex-husband made her chest and neck burn with ire—now *there* was a guy who deserved a good clobbering. Their son needed a strong, responsible father figure, especially now, and what he'd gotten was a useless, spineless man-child who couldn't keep a single promise. And it wasn't only how Kyle had acted since the divorce. It was everything he'd done leading up to it—everything he'd done to cause it. How could he expect their son to operate within the boundaries of his mother's house rules—let alone the law—when Kyle himself had cheated, lied, and stolen his way out of his own marriage?

And what about Markie herself? Didn't she belong at the top of her own hit list? How stupid could she be, putting an angry teenager into a room with an escape window and assuming he'd only use it in an emergency? Letting him trot off with kids she knew nothing about, accepting his "nothing" and "nowhere" answers? If her son deserved a dressing-down for choosing the wrong friends, for going along with their illegal schemes, didn't she deserve one, too, for her negligence in allowing him such freedom?

She had spent weeks telling herself she was doing the right thing in giving him a wide berth, telling Mrs. Saint that he was a smart kid, a responsible one, a boy who would never pick bad kids for friends, would never sneak out at night, would never do the things the Frenchwoman had accused him of. She had yelled at the woman today, for God's sake, screeching at her about falsely accusing her faultless son. Had she really

believed he was as innocent as she had claimed, or had she only wanted to believe it to make things easier for herself?

He was so quick to turn silent, so willing to stay that way for days. She had been desperate not to give him a reason to do it. Things were much nicer in the bungalow when she said, "Yes, go ahead. Of course, you can spend time with kids I don't know / ride in strangers' cars / have dinner with a family I've never met." The air in the house was easier to breathe when she stifled her concerns, pretended all was well. *He's a good boy. He's a teenager now. He's in high school. He's old enough to make his own decisions.*

Sure, he had always been good *before*, but he'd had different friends before. Hadn't she sensed something was up with this mostly unnamed group of boys? Hadn't she wondered if Frédéric was right and it was Brian's Fusion he had seen downtown? Hadn't she known, somewhere deep down, the perils of being a new kid, especially one whose self-esteem had been gutted so completely by the bad behavior of his parents? Wasn't Jesse the precise sort of child most susceptible to getting in with the wrong crowd, doing whatever it took to be accepted?

She felt her body relax, saw her elbows bend, her arms no longer ramrod straight against the wheel. It was no longer such an effort for her to breathe steadily. The desire to hit him, even to yell at him, had passed. "What's shocking to me," she said, "is that you *like* Ben Levin. And Sharon. You've been in their store a dozen times, and you've always said they were so nice—"

"I know!" he cried, and the noise was like an animal caught in a trap.

He pressed both palms to his ears, and she could see his arms trembling with the force. It wasn't an act, then. He wasn't a different kid. He was a confused one, a conflicted one, one who had made a huge mistake. Her heart didn't break for him, exactly, and she wasn't anywhere close to feeling bad for him—he was a perpetrator here, not a victim. But something inside her shifted a little.

She wanted to push, to ask him if he had spoken up, suggested they find entertainment of a legal form, or at the very least pick a different target and leave the Levins alone. If he did and they ignored him, he should think about that, about what kind of friends they were. And if he had been afraid to speak up, he should think about that, too. Not that she'd allow him anywhere near them after this—not the three worst ones, anyway. She'd have to think about Trevor. But she told herself to go no further here. She wasn't in the right frame of mind for a dispassionate discussion about his choice of allies, and neither was he.

They drove a few more blocks before he finally dropped his hands to his lap. Out of the corner of her eye, she could see him wiping away tears. He put his glasses back on, shoved his hands under his thighs, and kept his gaze trained on his shoes as she made the final turn onto their street.

"So how long am I grounded for?"

Markie considered the question as she pulled into the driveway and turned off the engine. They were home now, safely parked in the driveway. Finally, she could let him have it. She could feel her father's "This is not how I taught you! This is not what I expect of a child of mine! As long as you're living under my roof . . ." creeping up her throat, pressing against the backs of her teeth.

She swallowed the lecture and turned to her son. "Why don't we both go to sleep now, and tomorrow, when we're not so exhausted, we can talk about consequences." She looked at him sharply, ready to retract her statement if she saw even a hint of an I-got-away-with-it smile on his face.

He nodded, his mouth a self-reproaching line. "Okay." His hand moved to the door handle, but instead of pulling the lever, he let his fingers rest there. "Thanks, Mom. For picking me up. And for not trying to make me feel worse than I already do."

Inside, he stumbled down to his room. He forgot to close the basement door, and Markie could hear his soft snoring in less than a minute.

She pushed the door shut, poured wine into a mug (as her stemware was still boxed up), and retreated to the family room couch. The rage she felt in the car had altered, and so had its targets. Yes, Jesse was to blame for his actions, and he would be punished. For starters, she would send him to the Levins' store tomorrow to apologize in person. If they didn't want to hear it—and who could blame them if they didn't?—she would make him write a letter. After that, well, she was still thinking.

But was she really going to aim all of her ire at a fourteen-year-old boy? Or his slightly older compatriots, none of whom had a completely developed frontal cortex? Kyle was old enough to know better, but had she honestly thought he would act any differently? Could she expect anyone who knew her ex to buy her line that all this time she had been counting on *him* to show their son the right way to manhood?

Markie refilled her ceramic mug with more wine. Jesse hadn't been a leader at Saint Mark's, but he wasn't a novitiate, either. If someone had come up with the asinine idea to sneak out in the middle of the night and vandalize a building, he would have had more than enough clout to decline without fearing a loss of social position. But those weren't the kids he was dealing with anymore.

Because his mother had wanted out.

Away. To start over in a place where she could stop at the gas station without worrying that people would see what she was driving now. Run to the grocery store without suffering the pitying looks from across the produce aisle, the whispers in the deli line. *"Years, evidently, right under her nose, and she never had a clue." "Highly leveraged, all of it. I hear even the furniture was rented."*

She hadn't been able to move quickly enough. She had been in forward motion since the moment she discovered the extent of Kyle's betrayals, on the fastest track she could find to escape the scene of her plummet from grace. File divorce papers. List the house. Find a rental in a new town, a new school for Jesse, a job where she wouldn't be recognized—better yet, where she wouldn't even be seen.

No sobbing herself to sleep over the loss of what might have been. No lying in bed in the mornings, paralyzed with fear about whether she could make it on her own after all those years being part of a couple. No pausing to consider Kyle's admissions, finally, his pleas for a second chance, his promises he would do better. No time in reverse or even neutral. Move, move, move.

It was for the best, their clean break. New life, new start. She was doing it for both of them so they could move on. And she had moved on—from a passionless marriage, from the constant threat of financial destruction, from the lingering suspicion she was being lied to, cheated on, from the nauseating fear that at any moment she would be discovered for the poseur she was. Jesse, though, had merely moved.

Markie stood, sloshing white wine over the side of her mug. She set it on the floor, shook her hand to fling off the drops, and paced to the side door. She checked the lock, checked it again, and paced to the kitchen counter. What had she been thinking, pulling him away from his friends, his classmates, their neighbors, the world he knew? Away from his father, most of all. Things would have been miserable if she'd stayed with Kyle, but weren't they miserable now anyway, especially for Jesse? Kyle might not have been Father of the Year while they were married, but he was there, at least, most of the time.

She stepped to the door again, turned right, stepped to the wall, right again, stepped to the couch, right again, lapping the room until she was back at the door. She had assumed she could do it on her own, play the role of father and mother. She thought she had such intuition, such a sense about how to handle him. They were so much alike, she had told herself. His needs would be teenaged versions of hers: solitude, quiet, a judgment-free zone, dinners on his own, TV in his room, no forced conversation.

Back off, she had told herself. *Give him space. Don't push, don't coddle, don't crowd.* It was the wrong call. Obviously. He needed something else, something different, something more than she was providing. But

she had no idea what. More of Kyle? She couldn't fix that, not now. She could try—she had been rehearsing for some time the next torrent of curse words she would leave on his voice mail—but she knew better than to think it would help.

More discipline? She couldn't bring herself to mimic her father, or even her mother, for that matter. Military school? She hadn't had a child just to send him away, though, and it was the same concept her father followed: tear them down to build them up. She wouldn't do that to Jesse.

She did another lap of the family room, then another. Should she eat more crow, borrow money from her parents, suck it up and move back to their old neighborhood, where the fathers of his friends could spend time with him, show him how men should act? Put him back into Saint Mark's, where he already belonged and didn't have to prove himself?

But *did* he belong there now? What if he had even more to prove after what had happened? Plus, did she want to uproot him again, so soon after doing it the first time? She had already run from their troubles once. Did she want to run a second time? Was that the kind of example she wanted to set for him?

She had no clue where to go from here. Her own strategies hadn't worked, her parents' tactics weren't ones she was willing to attempt, and while she was certain there must be something between the two extremes, she had no idea what it was. She hadn't thought it through enough before she told Kyle they were finished. She had seen red, blown up, pointed to the door, and told him not to come back. Everything else was just details.

She had not once considered whether she could actually pull off all those details. She hadn't taken the time to think about what it would take for a single mother to raise a teenage boy. She had acted impulsively because she couldn't stand pretending anymore. Because she wanted

out, she wanted better. She, she, she. At what point, if ever, had she considered her son—what *he* wanted, what *he* needed?

Markie poured one more mug of wine and returned to the couch. She took a few sips, then set the cup on the floor, wrapped her arms around her waist, and rocked forward, then back. *This is my fault,* she told herself. *All my fault.* She curled onto her side, her arms still wrapped around her waist, and cried herself to sleep.

Chapter Sixteen

Sun through the window in the family room door woke Markie, and soon after, her throbbing skull let her know she wouldn't be rolling over and drifting back to sleep. Her watch revealed what her head had already told her—it was almost eleven, she was hung over, and it was hours after she usually ingested her daily two cups of coffee. She would be paying for this all day.

She stood, stretched, and kicked over her half-full mug of wine as she stumbled toward the kitchen. Cursing, she wet some paper towels, carrying them back to the family room to dab up the spill. She was on her way back to the kitchen to dispose of the soggy, sour-smelling mess when there was a knock at the door. She turned slowly—her head wouldn't allow sudden movement—to find Mrs. Saint peering in the door's window.

Markie's head pounded harder. She needed to hang a curtain there, she told herself, so she could pretend she wasn't home when the neighbor knocked. Mrs. Saint motioned for her to hurry, then looked down at the ground, checking, it seemed, on whatever it was she had come to deliver. Markie told herself to get it over with fast: accept what the old woman was offering this time—partially uncooked cinnamon rolls from Ronda, a badly potted houseplant from Bruce, or some household item Mrs. Saint felt they couldn't live without and had ordered Frédéric

to go out and buy—say thank you, and send the woman on her way. After that, she could devote herself to starting the coffeemaker, locating the ibuprofen, and lying quietly until Jesse woke. She had an important conversation planned with him, and she would be of no use if she felt like her skull was about to shatter.

She opened the door, and before she or her neighbor could speak, a blur of black-and-white fur reared up, its huge paws hitting Markie in the chest. She stutter-stepped backward to maintain her balance, and her head, not happy with being jostled so fast and without warning, screamed at her. She gently pressed a palm to her temple as the dog, its front feet back on the floor now, pushed its rib cage into her legs and licked her other hand, her wrist, her forearm—its entire body wagging.

She pulled her hand away and held it out of the dog's reach, but this only made it bark, a piercing sound that tore through her cranium. It jumped up, trying to reach her hand, and let out another excruciating bark as it rose onto its hind legs, planted its front feet on her chest again, and dove its snout into her armpit. Markie glared at Mrs. Saint, hoping the older woman would read *Get this thing off me and out of my house* in Markie's eyes so she wouldn't have to injure her head by saying the words out loud.

"She is the Australian kind of sheepdog," Mrs. Saint said. "A pure one, even, which is rare for finding at a dog pound. But she arrived yesterday only, and because Frédéric has been very early this morning, before anyone else had a chance to see her, this is why he was able. They are very intelligent."

Markie pushed the dog off her chest, and it barked, ran around her, barked again, and ran in the other direction. "And very active," Mrs. Saint said. "So she will take a lot of Chessie's time for training and exercising. A big responsibility." She held a leash toward Markie.

Markie refused to take it. "A lot of *Jesse's* time?" she said.

She couldn't believe it—now the woman expected Jesse to walk her dog for her? And then it hit her. Her brain, caffeine deprived, wasn't

processing quickly. Of course the woman wasn't there to show off *her* new dog.

"Ohhhhh no," Markie said, backing away from the woman and the leash. "No, no, no!"

"*Mais*, do you not now agree he needs something to occupy his time?" Mrs. Saint asked. "Or someone who will love him like this?"

She nodded to the dog, now licking Markie's hand, hitting all the spots between her fingers before moving on to her wrist and then her forearm. She had given up trying to keep them under her armpits, since it only made the dog jump up and bark, and her head couldn't take either.

"*I* love Jesse," Markie said, and even in her compromised mental state, it sounded as ridiculous as Mrs. Saint's expression conveyed. Man's best friend is not his mother.

"And also this," Mrs. Saint said, holding out her other hand to offer a folded piece of paper.

The dog's records, Markie assumed. She was curious, nothing more, so she took the paper. But when she opened it, she saw a to-do list, a dozen or so jobs to be done around Mrs. Saint's house. The words "Help Frédéric with" preceded at least half of the tasks.

"I know he has a father," Mrs. Saint said, raising her hands in defense. "It is only that Frédéric has been saying he could use some help. He would pay Chessie for the work, of course."

"*Frédéric* would pay?" Markie didn't know why she was asking about this detail, since she wasn't about to let her son spend a minute on the other side of the fence.

"Och, I mean of course *I* would pay him," Mrs. Saint said, as though one thing were the same as the other.

Markie waited for an explanation, but Mrs. Saint turned, pretending to check on something at the door. When she turned back, Markie handed her the list.

"No. Absolutely not. Jesse has enough on his plate with schoolwork and friends."

"But surely you do not still like these friends?"

Markie was about to lie when Mrs. Saint added, "Frédéric saw."

"Saw what?"

Mrs. Saint pressed her lips together and lowered her chin slightly. *Let's not do this,* she seemed to be saying.

"So Frédéric was at your house at three in the morning?"

Mrs. Saint lowered her chin again—this wasn't about where Frédéric spent the night. But she fake-checked the door again, and while her head was turned, she said in a thin voice, "He saw the graffiti at the pharmacy. When he was there first thing, for the paper. He spoke to Ben and found out who."

Liar! Markie wanted to scream, but her head wouldn't permit it. Mrs. Saint turned back from the door, but she wouldn't make eye contact, and instead, she glanced from the leash, which she held in one hand, to the list in the other, and extended both again.

Markie ignored both items and basked in the glow of victory. *I've caught her!* She wanted to push the woman on this, this Nosy Parker who was always so eager to push everyone else on everything. But the dog had tired of licking her and was now back to running circles around her, trying to get her to chase it; and Markie, sensing another round of barking coming on, cradled her head in anticipation. She needed the dog to stop, and she needed coffee—those were her priorities. Mrs. Saint's secret relationship with Frédéric would have to wait.

She turned to the kitchen, waving a hand vaguely in her neighbor's direction to let her know she was done talking. She was headed for the coffeemaker when a thumping on the basement stairs created a new assault on her brain, and a second later the door burst open, and Jesse stood in the opening wearing only jeans, his hair a mess, glasses clutched in one hand.

"I thought I heard barking," he said, in a voice that showed he knew that couldn't possibly be what he heard.

He pushed his glasses on, peered around the kitchen and family room, and spotted their visitors. "Oh, hey! It *was* barking!"

The dog, on hearing the new voice, barreled through the kitchen toward the boy, and before Jesse could prepare himself, it leaped up, planting its front paws on his chest. The skinny teenager was no match for the running dog, and he toppled over backward, landing hard on his nonexistent rump. All Markie could see of her son was his jeans and bare feet as the dog stood over him, its tail wagging furiously.

She heard panting and licking, and "Hey! Hey! Stop!" and prepared herself for the moment when Jesse recovered from the shock and started complaining, maybe even cursing, about the unexpected assault. She wouldn't blame him for being angry, and she glared at Mrs. Saint herself, ready to add a few choice words to her son's. The dog was out of control. It was a wonder Jesse hadn't hit his head and gotten a concussion or stumbled farther backward and all the way down the stairs.

But Jesse's protests gave way to giggling, and soon his hands appeared on each of the dog's sides as he first patted its fur, then buried his hands in it. The dog's legs folded as it lay flat on top of the boy who, still laughing, lifted his head off the floor and peered over the animal's back at Markie and Mrs. Saint. This exposed his neck, which the dog immediately attacked with its long tongue, sending Jesse into hysterics.

His "Stop! Stop!" was the same fake protest Markie had many times heard before, when he was a little boy, begging her and Kyle to stop tickling him while at the same time hoping they would keep it up. His hands moved up the dog to the crest of its back, where they joined, his fingers interlacing as he hugged the animal close. Markie could see his head moving side to side as he burrowed his face into the dog's fur.

She dreaded turning back around and facing Mrs. Saint, who would surely be smiling smugly, waiting for Markie's concession that the older woman did indeed know what was best for Jesse. She gritted her teeth and

faced her neighbor, and she was shocked to see that the old woman's eyes were glassy, not triumphant, and her lips, which didn't seem to know if they should form a happy arc or a regretful one, trembled from one shape to the other. She was looking at the boy and the dog, but at the same time, she seemed to be looking through them to some other place and time.

Was it her own childhood she was remembering? Markie wondered. Or one she had once hoped to witness and never did? Markie recalled Mrs. Saint's curt *"Non"* when she had asked about children. But was *curt* the correct word? Or was it that the topic was a painful one for her neighbor, and she simply hadn't wanted to discuss it? Not every woman is heartbroken to not have children, but plenty are.

How did I overlook that possibility? Markie asked herself. Why had she allowed herself to leap straight to a conclusion that was completely devoid of compassion? And she had done the same thing with her neighbor's evasiveness about the topic of how she knew Frédéric; for all she knew, there could be an equally reasonable justification for why Mrs. Saint didn't want to discuss it. Yet all this time, Markie had been irritated by her refusal to answer. She had been five parts suspicion and zero parts sympathy. So eager to blame, so slow to try to understand.

God, Markie thought, *when did I become so hard?*

She regarded her son, still laughing as he hugged the dog. She didn't want a dog. But then, she also hadn't wanted to give things another try with Kyle, and now he had dissolved into vapor in his child's life. She hadn't wanted to borrow more money from her parents to keep Jesse at Saint Mark's, either, or to stay in town near his old friends, so she had moved him away, stuck him in a big public school with a new batch of kids—and look how that was turning out.

She reached for the leash. "But that's all," she said firmly. "No jobs for Jesse." She pointed to the list in the woman's other hand and shook her head.

Mrs. Saint tucked the paper away in her jacket pocket, and Markie waited for an indication that the bossy old woman was thinking to

herself that the dog was not all, in fact, and there would indeed be jobs for Jesse. But Mrs. Saint's wistful expression didn't change, and when she withdrew her hand from her pocket, it clutched a tissue, which she touched to the inside corner of each eye.

"I have left food and bowls outside the door," she whispered, turning to leave. "And Frédéric will come soon with a cage—I mean to say a crate—in case you . . ." She bowed her head and gave up the end of her sentence. Reaching the door, she gave Markie a quivering smile, then let herself out.

Markie rushed to the window and watched as Mrs. Saint made her way slowly home, stopping several times to lift the tissue to her eyes. Frédéric appeared then, carrying a dog crate out of the garage. When he saw Mrs. Saint, he stopped midstride, dropped the crate, and ran to her, a hand extended. Markie waited for the old woman to wave him off, annoyed, but instead, she allowed him to take her arm.

When she was safely on the other side of the fence, the old woman tilted her head and rested her cheek on his chest. Markie's jaw dropped, and her mouth stayed open for a long moment as Frédéric and Mrs. Saint stood there, his lips moving as he said things that made her nod her head or shrug or lean harder against him. From time to time, she raised the tissue again, until finally he took it from her and touched it to her eyes himself.

Markie couldn't breathe. Her own eyes filled, and as she reached up to wipe them, she realized her head no longer pounded. The ache had moved to the left side of her chest.

Finally, Mrs. Saint extricated herself and continued toward the house. Frédéric called something after her, and she held up a hand without turning back, then let herself in the side door and disappeared while he remained at the fence, staring after her. He pressed the tissue to his own eyes and held it there for a moment before he shoved it in the pocket of his dress pants and trudged, slump-shouldered, to retrieve the crate.

Chapter Seventeen

The dog was finally, blessedly, asleep. Jesse had wrestled with her for an hour in the backyard, then fed her and took her for a long walk. She was on high energy for all of it, with no signs of tiring, and Markie wondered what feat of strength it would take for him to force her into her crate. But when they returned from their walk, he simply pointed to the bed waiting inside the metal enclosure and said, "Crate," and she walked in happily and plunked herself down, exhausted. When he latched the door closed, she looked up, mildly curious, and then laid her head back down. She was snoring moments later.

Markie sent him immediately to the pharmacy to apologize to the Levins, telling him their discussion about consequences could wait. She had no intention of being home alone when the animal was fully rested and back into jumping/running/barking/licking mode. Along with the food and bowls, Mrs. Saint had left a long tie-out leash for the yard, a luxurious-looking dog bed and matching blanket, a thin file about "Angel" that the pound had handed over, and a book about Australian sheepdogs. Markie glanced at the table of contents, and when she saw the chapter titled "High Intelligence, Higher Energy," she closed the book, frowned at the sleeping animal, and silently cursed her neighbor for forcing on them the exact thing she didn't need in her life right then.

She decided that when she and Jesse did get around to their consequences discussion, part of it would include a threat that if the dog became too much for her son to handle, they would take it straight back to the pound. Her capitulation had come during a moment of mental weakness, brought on by her hangover and caffeine withdrawal. Now that she had partially cured herself with two cups of strong coffee and three ibuprofen, she was thinking more clearly, and she was prepared to set some firm limits.

At about the time she was beginning to wonder how things were going at the pharmacy, Jesse walked in. She didn't have to ask how it went: he was crying. She stood and opened her arms, but he evaded her hug and flopped onto the family room rug beside the crate. He unlatched the door and Angel rushed out, ready to play.

"No," he told her quietly. "Just lie down." To Markie's surprise, the dog folded her legs, landing on her stomach, and nestled her nose into his neck. He pushed her gently on her side and buried his face in her furry chest, and Markie silently cursed her neighbor again—for forcing on them the exact thing her son needed in his life right then.

She gave him what she hoped was enough time, and then asked, "So I guess the Levins didn't want to listen to your apology?"

"They listened," he said, his voice muffled by the dog's coat.

"Oh! Good. But then why are you—"

"He was devastated, Mom!" It wasn't easy to make out his words, but he had his face pressed into the dog for a reason, so she wasn't about to ask him to sit up and face her so she could hear him more clearly. After a while, Jesse rolled his head away from Angel and looked at his mother with red-rimmed eyes.

"He's almost eighty," he said, "and of course he has that German accent. I never added it up before." He made a guttural noise then, his mouth twisting in self-hatred. "I'm such a jerk!" He waited for her to catch on, and when she didn't, he said, "Have you heard of Kristallnacht?"

"Oh my God," she said, and now *she* felt like the jerk.

"He told me all about it. He said it was the most terrifying night of his life!" Jesse cried, his voice in splinters. "They lost everything, including the store his father had spent a lifetime building! And guess what kind of store it was? A pharmacy!"

"Jesus."

"And we had to go and fucking *spray-paint* all over the store he built here! I am such an asshole!"

He didn't apologize for the language, and Markie made no comment about it as she watched him pull the dog closer, its wide, pink tongue lapping across his eyes over and over as his rib cage jumped up and down with his sobs. Finally, his body stilled and the pink tongue moved to his neck. He cleared his throat and spoke in a voice he struggled to keep from breaking.

"Mrs. Levin told me that when the police called them last night, they both drove straight over to look, and for the entire ride over, they held each other's hands and cried. She said when Mr. Levin saw the store all covered with paint, the whole thing came back to him so loudly he actually covered his ears. He could hear it like it was happening again, right there—rocks going through windows, and people crying and yelling in the streets.

"And he could see it, too—old men getting beaten up right in front of everyone, his sister crying, his parents shouting at them to hurry up and pack, they were leaving right away—" Jesse's voice cracked, and his whole body shook. He sniffed, dragged an arm across his nose, and tried to compose himself.

"He set it up inside to look just like his dad's. The pharmacy, I mean. His parents never saw it. They never made it out. Only he and his sister did, and before he left, he promised his dad he'd do this—set up another store, make it look exactly the same. Carry on what his dad had started. Mrs. Levin told me she's known all along that he's more proud of the store than he was when their kids were born. And

it's never bothered her, because the kids were for the two of them, but the store was for"—his voice broke again—"everyone who came before them."

He rolled onto his back and raised his right arm high into the air before bringing it down fast, slamming his hand on the floor. It made a loud *thwomp!* on the area rug, and Markie gasped—if he had done that on the wood floor, he surely would have broken bones. Before she could ask if he was okay, he rolled back onto his side and shoved his face into Angel's fur again. The dog wagged her tail and licked the top of his head as he howled into her chest.

It was shameful, what Jesse and his friends had done to Mr. Levin's store, what they had put that lovely old couple through. But as she watched her son crying into his dog's fur, she felt no shame. Jesse had sucked all of that emotion from the air inside the bungalow, leaving none for her to grab on to. Instead, she felt sadness that this sensitive boy felt lost enough, insecure enough in his new friendships, desperate enough to do whatever it took to cling to them, that he had allowed himself to go along with something that was anathema to the person he really was.

After what felt to Markie like an hour, he finally stopped crying, sniffed, and rolled onto his back again, folding an arm behind his head and looking at Markie with swollen, bloodshot eyes.

"I have an idea about a punishment. It's not purely grounding, though, so I don't know what you'll say."

"Try me," she said.

"I thought I could get a job and give the money I earn to Mr. Levin. The police said some of the guys are going to have to pay something to him anyway. But I don't know if it'll be enough to cover all the damages. Mr. Levin told me he paid two of his employees a thousand dollars to go down there in the middle of the night and cover it up, so by the time anyone came in early today, it would look like it always did."

So, Markie thought, *Mrs. Saint had been lying after all. Frédéric couldn't have seen the graffiti when he went for the paper that morning.* Jesse went on.

"He probably could've gotten it fixed for a lot cheaper, but he had them paint the entire outside instead of just covering the graffiti. He didn't want people to look at the store and see something had been covered up. He didn't want people to guess at what someone might've written—"

"Oh my God! Did they write—?" Markie started, her chest suddenly filled with ice.

"No!" Jesse shot up from the floor onto his knees. "None of us even knew their . . . background. The guys were just being idiots, doing their usual tags, nothing to do with the Levins at all. And I would never! Do you think I would—?"

"No," she said. "But I didn't know about the others."

"They wouldn't, either," he said, still on his knees. "Anyway, I don't know if the money will cover all of that. And even if it does, I want to pay him back, too." He looked up at her, his eyes pleading. "When I'm not working I'd be at home, grounded. I *should* be grounded—I *want* to be. I'm just asking to be ungrounded for, like, a few hours a day, a few days a week, until I've given him the thousand dollars. And in exchange for being let out for work, I'll be grounded for the whole time it takes me to pay him, even if that's a longer time than you would've said."

"It'll take you a long time to earn that much money on your own," Markie said. "Months. Do you think the other guys will want to pitch in? The ones who don't end up with restitution orders, I mean? Trevor?"

He twisted his lips. "Doubt it."

"Do you want to ask?"

"Nah. Pretty sure they'll think it's a stupid idea."

She pressed her top two teeth hard against her bottom lip. *And this doesn't make you reconsider whether these are kids you want to be friends*

with? But she said nothing. Push too hard to get kids out of your child's life, and he'll only pull even harder to keep them in it.

"So are you saying yes?" he asked.

"I want to hear what the judge says first," Markie said. "It's not a given he'll let you off completely, and he might have something in mind of his own."

"Trevor's dad talked to a lawyer," Jesse said. "He said he's, like, ninety-nine percent sure we're going to be fine." He started to smile, but then he seemed to think better of it. "I mean if the judge lets us off easy."

"Grounded," Markie said, "except for going to and from work. And before your grounding is over, we're going to have a long discussion about how much time you'll be spending with those older boys. The ones who led the entire operation."

Jesse snapped his head up, his mouth open, ready to protest. He seemed to talk himself out of this, too, and instead he said quietly, "They're not bad guys, Mom."

"Still."

He turned away from her, and she could see the muscles in his jaw working as he struggled to control his emotions. "They're also my ride to school and back. Not to mention the only people I really know at school. And Trevor's still going to be with them all the time, so if I can't be around them—"

"We don't have to do this now," she said.

"It's not like they're getting pulled into the police station every week. So I'm not sure why . . ."

His voice had changed from the plaintive tone he had used to tell her about the Levins to the touchy one that usually signaled an impending day or two of radio silence. It wasn't much consolation to Markie that she had the upper hand here. It had been a terrible weekend, but there was a silver lining within her grasp—a newfound closeness between them, a greater degree of mutual respect, where she didn't

lower the hammer like her father would have, and in return, he didn't shut her out completely. If she kept on about Trevor and the guys, she would strip all the shininess out. "You know what," she said, "let's just forget about it for now. I was thinking out loud, mostly, and I shouldn't have done that. We can talk about it later, when you're done being grounded. Okay?"

He turned back to her, a grateful half smile on his lips. "Yeah," he said.

Bullet dodged, Markie thought. *For now, and possibly forever.* By the time he found someone willing to hire a fourteen-year-old, then got in enough hours to earn $1,000, Trevorandtheguys would hopefully have tired of waiting for him and dropped him from the group. She didn't believe for a second they were the only kids he knew at school, nor did she worry that if he weren't part of their little posse, he would spend the rest of high school friendless.

❖

"The thing is," Jesse said on Monday night, coming up from the basement, "there aren't a lot of people who'll hire ninth graders." He had appeared before the judge that afternoon, and to their tremendous relief, he was given a firm warning but nothing more, his file destroyed. Free to charge ahead with his voluntary restitution plan, he had been on his computer most of the evening, looking for jobs.

Markie looked up from the dining room table, where she was filling out her log sheet and organizing files for the next day. "True," she said, trying not to gloat. Operation Keep Him Away from the Bad Kids was proceeding exactly as she had hoped.

"So I think my best bet is Trevor's dad."

Her heart sank. "Trevor's dad will hire you?"

"Yeah. He owns a lumberyard. Trevor works there sometimes, like weekends and in the summer. I just talked to him, and he said a couple of guys quit and his dad could use some help. It's a lot more, you know,

physical than I really want, but the pay is, like, amazing. I could pay Mr. Levin super fast."

"I'm not so sure—"

"It would only be me and Trevor," he said, rushing in. "None of the others. And we'd be working the entire time, except for, like, a five-minute break now and then, which we wouldn't even leave the yard for. I'd go straight there and come straight home after. Trevor's in trouble, too, so he's not allowed to go anywhere but school, work, and home anyway. And I promise I'll walk Angel every day before school, like I did today, so you won't have to deal with her."

He had taken the dog out for so long that morning that Markie worried he might be late for his first class. He made it in time, though, and Angel was so tired from the outing she dozed most of the day. She fussed twice, and Markie put her on the tie-out, but there were no hijinks—the exhausted dog trotted obediently from the crate to the leash and back again. Markie could hardly complain—it was good for her get up and move around every few hours anyway, and the brief interruptions hadn't interfered with her ability to get through a respectable number of files.

Jesse looked at her imploringly, and she turned away, unable to withstand his earnestness. He had found himself a job, and a physical one at that—talk about self-imposed penance! How many teenagers would go to such lengths to right their wrongs? What reasonable parent would stand in the way?

She tried to stifle her disappointment. This was not the months-long job search she had been hoping for, the long delay she was counting on to keep him safe from the influence of the other boys. He would be plugged into the group as much as ever if he spent afternoons and weekends with Trevor. So much for distance, for them getting tired of waiting for him.

"So can I?" he asked.

Markie racked her brain for alternatives, anyone who might hire a fourteen-year-old. People she knew from their former life—she would force herself back over that creaky bridge if she had to. People Kyle knew.

"Oh!" she said, having suddenly remembered Kyle's friend Danny, who owned an office supply store.

Kyle had shown up with him at dinnertime about a year earlier, explaining, as she hastily set another place at the table and redistributed their three-person meal among four plates, that they had been pals since high school and lost touch. "Until we literally smacked into each other in an aisle in his store a few hours ago! And I couldn't very well just shake his hand and say, 'See you in another twenty years.' So I dragged him out for a few drinks and told him he had no choice but to come have dinner with us."

Danny, who had looked sheepish when Kyle claimed "a few drinks," also seemed surprised that his old friend hadn't called or texted his wife hours earlier to let her know about their dinner guest. But Markie told him it was fine, he should stay, and by the time the meal was over, he was clasping a hand on Jesse's shoulder and saying the boy should look him up if he ever needed a job.

"You seem a lot more upright than your old man," he'd joked.

Kyle had laughed, too, and said, "No, really, I meant it—I'll get the next round for sure," but Markie had a feeling that the afternoon's drinks weren't all Danny was talking about.

"I have an idea," she told Jesse. "But I need to check into it first."

"So I should tell Trevor no?"

"For now," she said.

Markie sent her text the moment Jesse returned to the basement: **Kyle, we really need to talk about Jesse. Call me.** She had tried him a few times on Sunday, to no avail, and Jesse had had no luck reaching him earlier in the day before they left for court.

Two hours later, as she was getting ready for bed, her phone dinged with his response.

Been tied up. Call you first thing in the AM.

Chapter Eighteen

Markie checked her watch after Jesse left for school the next morning: it was just after seven. Knowing her ex and his loose interpretation of the phrase "first thing," she predicted she could get a few hours of work done before she heard from him, so she ushered Angel into her crate, settled into a chair at the dining room table, and opened her first file.

She hadn't even read two sentences when the crying began. "Hush," she called. "Go to sleep."

The crying didn't stop, and by the end of the first paragraph, it changed to a high-pitched howl. Markie cursed her own softness—she had let Jesse get away with only a half-hour walk this morning, since it had seemed darker and colder than the day before. No more mercy, she told herself. He would need to start wearing a thick sweatshirt and a reflective vest from now on.

"Fine," she said, unable to ignore the howling, "but just for a few minutes."

In the family room, she unlatched the crate, and the prisoner, over-joyed at her release, leaped up. The force knocked Markie backward, and her tailbone hit the wood floor, followed by the back of her head. She gasped in pain as the dog trotted over her and tore through the kitchen. Markie could hear the sound of nails scratching on hardwood

and furniture being knocked into—and over—as Angel made her way past the dining room table and into the living room.

"Angel! Come!" Markie begged feebly, in too much agony to yell.

She eased herself to her feet, using the arm of the couch as a crutch, in time to see Angel shoot around the corner from the front hall, her paws paddling frantically as she lost her footing on the kitchen floor.

"Crate," Markie pleaded, pointing.

And praying—there was no way she would be able to chase the dog down if she took off again. Angel, thank goodness, obeyed, and Markie slid the latch closed. "You can whine and cry all you want. You're not coming out again until Jesse gets home."

As if on cue, the dog pressed her snout through the top bars of the enclosure and howled. Hands over her ears, Markie limped back to the dining room and tried to resume working. Ten minutes later, the dog hadn't let up, and Markie, cursing, carried her file upstairs. She closed her bedroom door and lay on the bed on her stomach—it was a better position for her bruised tailbone anyway—and started over on the first sentence.

The howling continued, and Markie turned her radio on, cranking the volume to drown out the dog. The music hurt her already-sore head, though, and after fifteen minutes she realized she still hadn't made it past the first paragraph. This wasn't the route to a healthy paycheck or to maintaining her work-from-home status.

Glaring at her too-thin bedroom door, she wondered if she dared let Angel out long enough to fold up the crate and carry it down to Jesse's room. It didn't seem possible in her condition, and anyway, she remembered lying in bed and hearing the gunfire and shouting from Jesse's video games through the heating vents. The boy had quickly agreed to keep the sound off. She could expect no such cooperation from the dog.

She was staring, unseeing, at her file and wondering how she was ever going to earn a living under these conditions, when Kyle called. "You wanted to talk?"

Angel howled again, and Markie winced. "Can you meet me someplace?" she asked. "Somewhere over here would be great—I've got a lot of work to do, and I'm behind already."

"Yeah," he said, drawing out the word, and she braced herself for a complication. "The thing is, I'd need to get a cab, so distance is a bit of an issue. Can you come here?"

"What happened to your car?"

"Long story, but there's a coffee shop near my apartment. On Water Street. You know the one?"

She thought of the stack of unread files on her table and sighed. "Meet you in thirty minutes?"

❧

He stood when she reached the table, reaching his arms out stiffly, awkwardly, more Dr. Frankenstein's monster than ex-spouse. She had no idea what he expected her to do—turn herself sideways and squeeze between them?—so she leaned around and pecked him on the cheek. They put their orders in with the barista, and when they sat down, Markie apologized that she didn't have much time, so she was just going to jump right in.

"Brace yourself," she warned, and then she described everything that had happened in the past three and a half days, from the thump in the night to the banging on the door to the squad car, the new dog, the judge, and blessedly, the warning and the destroyed juvenile file. She relived it all in the telling, and as she spoke, her heart pounded, and she pressed her thumb and forefinger against the bridge of her nose to stop the tears that were threatening. When she was finished, she looked up through

her fingers to find Kyle was mirroring her—finger and thumb against the bridge of his nose, head down.

"I know," she said gently. "It's a lot to take in. And so disappointing. I cried—"

It was then that she realized he wasn't crying. He was laughing.

"You think it's *funny*?" she said, and a couple at a nearby table looked over. She ignored them and repeated the question, louder this time.

He looked up at her, guilty, and tried to stop laughing.

"I don't believe this!"

"Oh, come on," he said, reaching for her hand. She moved it away. "Nothing happened to him, right? Record destroyed, you said? So then, no harm, no foul. And you've got to admit . . . I mean, think about it! He's hidden behind the dumpster, completely out of view. Safe! But he has to be all God-and-country about it and give himself up! I mean, it's funny! He couldn't be a criminal if he tried!"

Markie stood, purse in hand. "I didn't drive all the way—"

"No!" he said. "Don't go! I'll stop!" He stood, too, and took her by the arms. "Please. I'm sorry. It's just so . . . classic Jesse. 'Here I am, Officer! Arrest me, too!' I mean, any other kid would've crouched down in the dark until the cops left and then hightailed it out of there. And who else but Jesse would've come up with the idea to pay the old man back? I know he's been cranky with you for the past few months—with both of us. But it's times like this when a person's mettle shows, and I'll tell you what—our boy's got some."

He pushed her gently backward and down, until she was seated again. Sitting, too, he said, "I know you were worried—*are* worried. But think about it. He came home *crying*, you said. He wants to earn *a thousand dollars* and give every cent of it to this man. This is not a kid who can stomach crime. He's wielded his last can of spray paint, I guarantee it."

"I don't know about that," Markie said. "But I do know I'm not thrilled about him working with this . . . Trevor. So I was thinking maybe your friend Danny could hire him at his store. To stock shelves or whatever. Remember when he was over? He loved Jesse, and when he was leaving, he told him—"

"Yeah," Kyle said, dragging a palm across his chin, "I'm not sure that's going to work."

"Why not? Can you at least ask him before you—?"

"The thing is, Danny and I are . . . sort of on the outs at the moment."

"Why?"

"He says I owe him money."

She looked at the ceiling, then back at him. "Which means you *do* owe him money."

"So he says."

"Is there some reason you won't just pay him back?" she asked, but before he could answer, she stopped herself. "Never mind," she said. "I don't want to hear it. I'm done hearing your lame excuses—"

"Can we not do this here?" he asked quietly, looking around the shop.

Markie slumped in her chair. "Fine. Do you have any other friends who might hire him? Ones who're still talking to you, I mean?"

"Seriously, Markie. Can you not? With the attitude?"

"I need help here, Kyle, and so does your son."

"Kyle?" the barista called from the counter, and Markie watched as he jumped up and flashed the woman his most enchanting smile. At the counter, he leaned toward her to pick up the lattes and said something in a low voice. The barista threw her head back, laughing, and said, "I can see I'm going to have to keep my eye on you." Markie turned away.

Kyle set their lattes on the table, and she took a sip of hers while she waited for him to sit. Still standing, he cleared his throat. "You, uh, have any cash? It came to nine forty, and I only had a five."

"*Nine dollars* for two coffees?" she asked.

She reached for her wallet and gave him a ten. He paid the barista and sat again. "Look," she asked, "could you at least come over every other day or something and walk this crazy dog of his? If he's going to be out looking for a job, then putting in his hours, plus staying up on homework, he's not going to be able to get up at five every morning and tire it out. And I can't have it tearing up my house and howling while I'm trying to work."

"I'm really not a dog person, is the thing," he said.

"Neither am I!" she said. "But it's not just about the dog, Kyle. You're Jesse's father. He needs you. Not only to take Angel for walks, but to just be with him. Spending time, talking, doing father-son things. He's spiraling. Can't you see that?"

"Well, I'm really not set up to have him over at my new place," he said. "It's small. I don't even have a TV. And the fridge is one of those dorm room ones that hardly hold any food; the kid would starve. And I can't imagine you really want me coming around your place every other day. You divorced me, Markie. You wanted me out of your life."

It was a typical Kyle move, blaming his bad behavior on her, and she opened her mouth to call him on it. But his body seemed to have sagged, suddenly, and his face, normally bright with optimism, seemed weary. Markie changed course, and instead of berating him, she softened her voice and said, "We've known each other forever, you and I. We have a son together. I never imagined we would stop being in each other's lives. You can come to the house. To walk the dog or just to hang out with Jesse. It's fine with me." *Fine* was a stretch, a very long one, but she was willing to extend herself for her son's sake.

Something in Kyle seemed to break then, and his body and face both crumpled. Markie had never seen him look so broken. She felt her exasperation melt away as compassion took its place. She tried to think of something encouraging to say to him, but before she could come up with anything, he leaned forward, his voice low and unsteady, and

said, "The thing is, I don't blame you. Look, I know I'm not a guy who spends a lot of time on self-examination, but even I'm not too dense to have given a bit of thought to why my wife didn't want to be married to me anymore. I screwed up. I know I did. I'm . . . what was the word you used? Flaky?"

She started to apologize, but he waved her off and went on. "And you were right," he said. "I'm a complete flake. Always have been. The only time I was anywhere close to being a stand-up guy was when I was with you. On my own, I'm . . ." He looked away for a long moment before facing her again and whispering, "I'm a fuckup. I know I am. I mean, for God's sake, I just had to ask my ex-wife to help cover two measly lattes. Yeah, I owe Danny money, and a few other people, too. I got fired last week, and I'm not sure if there's a job around here I haven't already been hired for and canned from. Plus, I'm hardly a shining example of fidelity or honesty or any other moral you'd want to pass on to a kid. So what the hell do I have to offer Jesse?"

Markie moved to speak, but Kyle held up a hand to stop her. "He takes after you, thank God," he continued. "I know he had this one huge lapse of judgment with the spray paint, but we both know that's not who he really is. He's a grounded kid, an honest one, a responsible one. He's going to be a good man. I agree with you that he needs to get away from these guys he's been hanging out with. They're a bad influence. But so am I. He's better off without me."

"Kyle," Markie said, reaching for his hand, "you can't believe that's true."

"We both know it is," he said. He stood. "I need to get out of here."

"Wait!" Markie said, rising as he made his way to the front of the shop. "We *don't* both know it's true! I think—"

But he was gone.

❧

Jesse jogged up the walk, tossed his backpack onto one of the patio chairs, and, out of breath, asked if she had checked into her job idea. His sincerity filled her with regret. They were failing him, she and Kyle. She needed to do better.

"I did, and it didn't pan out. I'm sorry."

Her words were almost drowned out as Angel, trapped inside in her crate, resumed the deafening protest she had kept up most of the day. Jesse ran inside and reappeared a moment later, the dog leashed. He held her off with one hand as she jumped up, desperate for attention, and used the other to fish his cell phone from his back pocket.

"So I can call Trevor and say yes?"

Markie was tempted to tell him, look, it was a lovely gesture, his promise to pay the Levins back, and she was proud of him for even thinking of it, but the entire thing was getting a little too complicated. Maybe a handwritten letter of apology would be an adequate alternative. How long could he avoid the wrong path if his workmate was one of his co-vandals? Damn her ex and his uncanny ability to burn bridges with every colleague and acquaintance he'd ever known! If not for Kyle's unpaid debt to Danny, there would have been an alternative that kept Jesse's conscience strong while also keeping him away from Trevorandthehoodlums.

"Mom?" Jesse said, holding his phone aloft. "Can I? Call him? His dad's there until five today, and he told Trevor I could come in and—oh, hi, Mrs. Saint!" He waved, and when Markie turned to look and saw no one, he explained, "She was on the porch, but she just went inside."

Markie bowed her head in defeat and sighed. She couldn't believe what she was about to suggest, but anything was better than letting him spend more time with Trevor the spray-painting twit. Taking a breath, she gestured across the fence and said her next words as fast as she could, before she lost her nerve.

"Go talk to her. She has a list of things Frédéric could use help with. When she first told me, I didn't think you'd be interested, but,

obviously, things have changed. The list wasn't all that long, but I bet if you tell her what you're trying to do, she'll add to it."

"You *want me* to talk to Mrs. Saint?" he asked, incredulous. "You want me to *work for her*?"

Markie chastised herself for the sighing and muttering she had done about their neighbor in her son's presence. From now on, she would keep her griping to herself.

She nodded. "It would probably be a lot less physical than the lumberyard."

A self-conscious smile flickered over his lips. "I was starting to worry about that, to be honest. Trevor's a lot bigger than me. But you really think she'd come up with more stuff? A *thousand bucks'* worth?"

"I do."

"That's, like, crazy."

Before Markie had a chance to reconsider whether perhaps Trevor might be the lesser of the two evils after all, Jesse took off across the patio, Angel running behind. She watched as they sped across the lawn, jumped the fence, and sprinted the rest of the way to Mrs. Saint's side door. Jesse knocked, and a moment later, Frédéric answered, bowing stiffly in greeting. He exchanged a few words with Jesse, then called over his shoulder.

Mrs. Saint appeared, opening her folded piece of paper and holding it out to Jesse, who took it with one hand and held the dog's collar with the other as she pulled to get in the door. Markie waited for Mrs. Saint to point to the screened porch or the tie-out or some other place where Jesse could secure the animal so she wouldn't sneak into the house. But the older woman stepped back, pulling Frédéric with her to make room, and beckoned the boy and his pet inside. The door shut behind them, leaving Markie alone, gawking at her neighbor's closed door.

Chapter Nineteen

The thud of a closing door woke Markie at 5:45 on Wednesday morning. She panicked for a moment, recalling the last time she'd been woken by a noise in the night, but a moment later she heard Angel whine from the sidewalk outside her window. Peeking out, she saw them walking down the street, Jesse holding plastic bags in one hand, the leash in the other, as the animal tugged, trying to get him to move faster. He resisted and forced her to walk beside him at his ambling pace, and Markie grinned. The boy might want a dog, but he did not want a morning jogging routine. Angel would have to get used to the fact that her owner was a video gamer, not a runner.

She was finishing her second cup of coffee when the two of them came panting in an hour later.

"I tried getting up earlier," he said, "I really did, but I just couldn't do it. Sorry. I know you think she needs to be out a lot longer." He collapsed on the floor, struggling to muster the energy required to unhook the leash. "Even the hour killed me." He closed his eyes and appeared to be settling in for a nap.

"Jesse," she said, "it's quarter to seven."

"Ugh," he groaned, lifting himself slowly. "I've got to get Lola in fifteen minutes."

As Markie predicted, Mrs. Saint had been more than willing to add to Jesse's list until it resembled a work order that would total $1,000 over several months. Some things she would come up with as she thought of them, she told him, but others she added right then as he stood in her sitting room, Angel at his feet. The new items were all Lola-related: walk her to school in the mornings on his way to high school (a block from the elementary), walk her home in the afternoons, take her along on his after-school walk with Angel, help her with homework.

"How's that for easy money?" he said when he returned from talking with his new employer. "She'll pay me for basically walking myself to school and walking my own dog!"

Mrs. Saint was worried the girl wasn't getting enough exercise, she told Jesse. Plus, she sensed Patty needed more breaks from Lola, as did the others, including Mrs. Saint herself.

"And here I am," he said, "looking to earn some cash. So it's all, you know, a win/win or whatever. 'Shooting the single bird with the identical bullet' is what she said, actually."

"I told her I didn't think a ninth-grade boy would want to hang out with a second-grade girl," Markie told him. "I'm sure it wouldn't be a problem if you asked her for other jobs instead. I saw the list, and it was all Frédéric's stuff. Maybe Bruce has some things."

"I don't mind," he said, and she was shocked.

When he had first seen Lola on the other side of the fence shortly after they moved in, he begged Markie not to make him go over and introduce himself.

"I mean, I sort of mind," he admitted. "But Mr. Levin minded what we did to his store, so who am I to mind what I have to do to pay him back?"

"I'll feed her," Markie said, gesturing to the dog. "You go shower."

"For real?"

"You can't be late on your first day of work. Not for any job, even one for a neighbor." It sounded so much like her father that she felt

compelled to add, "And I'm proud of you. For what you're doing to make things up to Mr. Levin. So I want to help."

"Proud," he repeated, as though he had possibly heard her wrong. "Not ashamed that I have something to make up to him for in the first place?"

She thought back to Sunday morning and how she'd had the sense that he had extracted all the shame from the atmosphere around the house. Her father, whose spirit had now settled into the kitchen, having heard her mini-lecture on the importance of timeliness, rose inside her. Clayton could find stray pockets of shame between the particles of oxygen and nitrogen suspended around them if he had to, after which he would trot them out in the form of "I can't believe a child of mine would stoop this low," or "How will your mother and I show our faces at the club after this?"

Markie drowned his presence in a mouthful of scalding coffee. "Proud," she said, pointing to the basement door. "Now, shower. Hurry."

"You're the best, Mom."

One point to Markie. One to the French Canadian, for the dog and the job. Zero to Clayton the Commander.

⚜

As it turned out, an hour-long stroll was not enough to tire Angel for the day, and before she finished her first file, Markie knew there was no way she would be able to work with all the fussing going on in the other room. By ten, she had been through half a bag of dog treats in an effort to bribe the animal into being quiet. She had stuck all of Angel's toys through the metal bars, had reached in to pet her, and out of sheer desperation, had even sung to her.

Nothing worked, and Angel had gone from whining to crying to barking and, finally, howling. The windows were open, and Markie

couldn't help hoping the noise was disturbing Mrs. Saint, too. She was tempted to let the dog get louder to teach her neighbor a lesson. But she couldn't afford another two-file day like Tuesday, so she clipped Angel's leash on, opened the back door, and let the overly energetic animal drag them both to the tie-out.

"You have a time-out, young lady," she growled as she switched the leash for the tie-out clip and stomped away.

She heard Bruce's voice as she reached the door. "Sounds like someone's not behaving well."

"She needs way more exercise than we thought," Markie told him. "And Jesse is physically incapable of getting up early enough to make that happen. I haven't gotten a minute of work done since Monday. I don't think Mrs. Saint realized how high maintenance she'd be. This breed is . . . something else."

"Oh, she knows her dog breeds," Bruce said, glancing at the dog, who was busy digging a deep hole in the middle of the yard. "I'll take care of that hole later. And hey, I bet Patty could walk her sometimes. She could go way longer than an hour since she ain't in no rush for school or nothing in the mornings. She's fast, too. Got those long legs. Probably make a big difference." He turned to Mrs. Saint's house. "You want me to get her out here to talk about it? She could start today, I bet."

For Markie, the notion of even more traffic over the fence was worse than the thought that Angel might keep her from ever reviewing another file. It made her chest tighten to think of it, and in her anxiety, her next words came out snappish.

"I thought she had a job," she said.

She heard the irritation in her voice and was appalled at her own rudeness. Bruce wasn't responsible for any of this. He didn't appear offended, though, and Markie considered the fact that he seemed not to read social cues very well. Maybe his mess-ups on the job were more

about not hearing the subtleties in communication than they were about not being a capable gardener.

But he deserved no less respect because he wasn't easily offended. "I'm sorry," she said. "I've just had it with this today." His expression showed he still didn't follow, so she moved on. "Anyway," she said, "I can't afford a dog walker on top of her food and . . . everything else." She gestured with the leash to indicate that it, too, had come at a price, along with the crate, the bowls, and the toys. But it hadn't, of course, and neither had Angel herself. Mrs. Saint had provided it all. "Well, the food," she corrected herself.

"Oh, you don't got to worry about her food," Bruce said. "I'm planning to stop for a new bag every other week when I'm over there at the nursery. Pet store's right beside. And you wouldn't need to pay Patty, neither. I'm sure Mrs. Saint would just make it part of her job. She's always looking for ways to add, you know, variety. Patty's not one for doing the same thing over and over."

Markie shook her head. The last thing she wanted was for Angel to become part of Mrs. Saint's master plan to keep her so-called Defectives occupied.

"I couldn't let her walk my dog without paying her for it myself," she told him firmly. "And I can't afford to pay her for it. So Angel gets a time-out on the tie-out. And that'll have to do."

Four more time-outs and a lot of begging, chasing, and cursing later (but very little file reviewing), Jesse arrived home, dropped his backpack, and dove onto the area rug to unlatch the crate door. Angel leaped out, and he fell back dramatically, pretending to be pinned underneath her.

"How was she?" he asked.

Markie glared at him, but he was too busy with the dog to notice.

"How'd the walks to school and back go?" she asked.

"Not as bad as I thought. Lola isn't one of those talker girls like I was worried she'd be. She'll answer questions, maybe say one or two other things, but other than that, she keeps to herself."

"Sounds like you." She didn't add "lately." She wondered if he even remembered a time when he spoke in paragraphs, or even sentences longer than about five words.

"Even though she didn't say a lot, I could tell she liked the company. I get the feeling she's kind of lonely."

Markie regarded her son. In the past few days, so much of the real Jesse had shown through the grumpy teen veneer. She would never say it to him, but it struck her that messing up in a major way was exactly what he had needed in order to reset himself. She thought about Kyle's unexpected contrition at the coffee shop and wondered if he was going through a similar thing. She hoped so, for his sake and for their son's.

"Are you going to help her with homework today, too?" Markie asked. "Or maybe that's not every day? I can't remember how much schoolwork you had at her age."

"Every day. I guess she's a really crummy reader, so there's always that to practice. Plus, today she's got a math work sheet."

Markie pictured Jesse sitting at the table in Mrs. Saint's kitchen, trying to explain math to Lola as their neighbor hovered nearby and attempted to pry information out of him about his mother or commented about his too-baggy jeans or his too-long hair.

"That's a lot of time to be spending over there," she said, trying for a casual tone. "Homework with Lola, and also the chores with Frédéric?"

"I think the stuff with him will be mostly on the weekends," he said. "But maybe some afternoons, I guess. That a problem?"

"No. I'm just thinking that you and I aren't the most social, and there are a lot of people over there. All the time. Just wondering if you're up for that, or if maybe it'd be better for you if you and Lola . . ." She pointed to the dining room. "There's a big table in there."

He shrugged. "I guess we could bring her work sheets and stuff over here. Ronda was heading out to buy stuff for cookies, but I can just ask her to bring them over once they're done. I'm sure she won't mind."

Markie envisioned the large cook coming across the yard with a plate of cookies, gripping it carefully in two hands as Bruce ran in front to help her, Frédéric walked behind with two glasses of milk, Patty tagged along to remind Lola to be back in time for them to head home for her secret evening plans, and Mrs. Saint brought up the rear, ready to supervise the correct placement of cookies onto plates, the wiping of milk mustaches off upper lips.

Once the old woman was inside, she would surely amble into the living room to check on whether Markie had hung any artwork yet—which would lead to her tsking and och-ing and motioning for Frédéric to run back for his toolbox and for Patty and Bruce to fetch the art from the basement while Ronda rooted through the cupboards to see if there was something she could make them for dinner.

"On second thought," Markie said, scratching arms that suddenly felt like they were covered in poison ivy, "if the job Mrs. Saint offered was for you to help *over there*, then I guess you need to do that. Don't want to be asking for concessions on your first day."

"Ooookay," Jesse said, clearly confused by her 180-degree change but not at all interested in the cause of it. "That works, too." He jumped up, retrieved Angel's leash, and snapped it on. "I'll bring her back in a bit and grab my history book," he said. "I've got a quiz tomorrow. Get this: Mrs. Saint says part of my tutoring job is *to do my own homework* in front of Lola. I mean, I won't get it all done, since I have so much more than she does, but I can do a bit of it, like looking over history. Cool, right? I mean, who gets paid to do their own homework?"

"It's very generous, that's for sure," Markie said.

He reached the door, but instead of opening it, he turned back. "Oh, do we have any Hershey bars? Lola says she'll do all her homework without complaining if I give her one."

"We don't," she said, "but you don't want to teach her to do homework for a reward anyway. You want to get her to do it *for herself,*

because she *wants* to learn, *wants* to get good grades—the same reason you do all of yours. That's why Mrs. Saint's paying you to look at your history notes over there. She wants your work ethic to rub off on Lola."

"Oh, yeah. That makes sense." He smiled. "So, like, you and Mrs. Saint are totally on the same page, huh?"

He was out the door and across the patio before Markie could form the thought, not for the first time, that having him spend his afternoons with Trevor might have been the safer choice after all.

Chapter Twenty

The fact that Jesse wasn't hyperbolic about his first week with Lola—it was "okay," she was "not a bad kid," their walks home were "still fine," tutoring her was "maybe a little more annoying" than expected "but not as awful as it could be"—made his report the following Sunday, about his first afternoon with Frédéric, that much more notable.

"It was, like, amazing!" he told Markie as he collapsed on the family room floor a little before six o'clock on Sunday evening.

He was physically exhausted but mentally amped up, so while his limbs were motionless, his mouth was the opposite. He lacked the energy to push Angel away, so as he gave Markie a rapid-fire play-by-play of his afternoon, the dog licked every inch of skin she could find. Markie was shocked into muteness at the number of words voluntarily leaving her son's mouth, and she could only sit, openmouthed, and listen.

"We replaced a fifth of the fence! A fifth! Just us! In only three hours! That means taking out the old part, carrying all the new wood over, measuring it all. Oh, by the way? Frédéric's a total perfectionist, to an *insane* degree. We checked every measurement, like, a hundred times. Then we had to cut it all. Some we did with a handsaw right at the fence, and some stuff, the bigger posts, we carried into the garage,

where he's got this totally cool workshop set up where a second car would go.

"That's a ton of work! When he pointed out the section of fence he wanted to finish, I figured it would take us twice as long as it did. Oh, and I did the handsaw! I sucked at first, Mom, like, so bad. And you should've seen Frédéric, trying to pretend I was doing a decent job so he wouldn't hurt my feelings. He had to look away a few times after I butchered a few of the little rail pieces. He had extras, though, luckily."

He dropped his voice here, although they were the only two in the room. "He told me he bought extras, and then he told me he thought it would be Bruce helping him, and then he shrugged. Which I'm guessing means he expected Bruce to mess up, and he planned ahead for it. But he wouldn't come right out and say that. Just like he wouldn't let on that I was messing up.

"He'd say things like 'Perhaps on the next try you will take a little more time to get the saw at the right angle before you start to cut' or 'I always find that checking my work as I go is helpful, rather than speeding through and finding I have gone off the line.' He's like, the world's most patient teacher."

Markie considered this. Perhaps that was the answer to Frédéric's almost-daily disappearance.

"Do you think he's a professor?" she asked Jesse.

Earlier, she had formed an idea he might be a consultant of some sort. She hadn't considered teaching—until now. There was a community college in town and also an extension campus of the state flagship university. Maybe he taught at one of those places? "Did he mention anything about teaching? Or where it is that he goes every afternoon?" Jesse looked at her quizzically, and she quickly explained Frédéric's regular sojourn and how she couldn't get a straight answer about it from the others.

"Nuh-uh," Jesse said. "He didn't say anything about it. I don't think he's a teacher, though."

"Why not?"

"He just seems too . . . I don't know, shy or something. He seems a bit . . ." Jesse looked at the ceiling for the right word and, not finding it easily, shrugged, letting the thought dissolve.

Sad, Markie wanted to finish for him. *Defeated.* Those were the words she often conjured when she thought of Frédéric. It was as though he had once held a far higher position than handyman and general foreman to a group of fellow Defectives, and he was constantly aware of that. Or was she imagining things? Had her own fall from professional, social, and financial grace made her see things in Frédéric that weren't there?

"Why are you so obsessed about where he goes, anyway?" Jesse asked.

"I'm not," she said. "I'm just taking an interest in our neighbor."

Jesse laughed. "Since when?"

"I find him to be an intriguing person, that's all," she said. "But never mind. Go on with your story. What else did you do over there?"

"Oh, right. Let's see . . . oh yeah, we took one of the big posts to the garage for him to cut with the table saw, and I asked him if I could learn to use it sometime, and he was like, 'I always think it is best to master the less complicated tools first.' Can you believe that? Unreal, right? I mean, I don't even know why I asked about it, but once it came out, I expected him to laugh at me and say, 'Nice try!'

"Anyway, I got a little better with the handsaw after the second hour, and by the end he was smiling at my cuts and telling me, 'Good job.' And then, when I was leaving just now, he told me that maybe next Sunday he'll try me out with the big posts on the table saw! How awesome is that?"

"That's great," Markie said. "I had no idea you'd actually like that kind of thing. Carpentry, I mean."

"I know! It's way more fun than I thought it would be. Frédéric said he felt the same way. He was an engineer—did you know that?

Designed landing gear and a bunch of other stuff for airplanes. Total desk job, he told me. That's why he's always dressed that way, I think, like he's going to some important office job, because for so long that's what he did. I mean, I didn't ask him, but that's my guess."

So he could be a professor after all, Markie thought. Engineering was a brainiac thing, not a comedy routine—a shy person could teach it. Given the regularity of his outings, it made total sense. A consultant's hours would vary more, wouldn't they?

"Never lifted a hammer until after his career was over," Jesse went on. "He never owned a handsaw even, let alone all the stuff he's got set up in the garage. And he says there's even more in the basement. I really hope he'll show me sometime. He didn't offer, so I didn't ask. Anyway, it was so cool!"

Markie laughed at his excitement. "You make me want to get out there and replace a section myself. I should call you Tom Sawyer."

"And it's straight-up addictive, too," he said. "I mean, I can't wait to go at the next section. I never noticed before, but now I can see how old the wood is, where it sags in places, where parts are broken. I wanted to keep going until we'd gotten rid of all the old, broken stuff and put up all the new wood. I told him we could keep going—get half of it done today and finish it all off next Sunday. But he says Mrs. Saint won't let him work past four on weekends."

"But it's almost six," Markie said. "So was she away for the day, or—"

"Oh, we knocked off two hours ago," he said, and she smiled at his use of what must surely have been Frédéric's phrase. "We've been sitting in the garage talking all this time. Then he had to go, because Mrs. Saint wanted to be sure he ate dinner. Isn't that funny, how she's like that? With a quitting time and making sure he eats? And she must've sent Ronda out with water for him five times an hour.

"She'd carry this big pitcher out and look at his glass, and if it wasn't empty yet, she'd stare at it until he finally walked over and drank it. It

reminds me of how Mrs. McLaren is with Mr. McLaren. Remember at Grandma and Grandpa's club last summer? She was always handing him sunscreen or water or telling him to move his chair into the shade."

Markie considered the fact that in seeing this kind of doting, Jesse hadn't been reminded of his grandparents. Or his parents. Neither Markie nor Lydia had ever been a fraction as solicitous with their husbands as Mrs. Saint was with Frédéric, and in the few months she had known him, Frédéric had proven himself to be more devoted to his employer than Markie could recall Kyle or Clayton being to their wives. And then there was the fact that the time, attention, patience, and encouragement Frédéric had given Jesse that day had been so much more than the boy had received from his own father or grandfather in at least half a year. It was plainly something Jesse had been starved for, given the animated chatter it had inspired. For that reason alone, Markie decided, she would love Frédéric forever.

"So," Jesse asked, "what's for dinner? I'm starved."

"Frozen pizza?" she suggested. "Or we could heat up—"

"Because Ronda made this enormous pan of lasagna." He sat up, the thought of food having evidently restored his energy, and separated his hands to show how big the lasagna was. "I'm talking *gigantic*. Not sure why she made so much, 'cause she made a point of telling me they'd never get through it over there, and that if you and I wanted to take a few pieces off her hands, it would be a help more than anything."

He was on his feet, pointing toward Mrs. Saint's house. "Since we were only going to have frozen pizza . . ."

Markie shrugged her consent, and about ten minutes later, he returned with two heaping plates and three containers.

"For lunch tomorrow," he said, putting two of the containers in the fridge. "This one"—he nodded to the third—"is salad. I told her we're not much for green stuff, but she said Mrs. Saint wouldn't let her send dinner without it, so . . ." He shrugged, reached for two plates from the cabinet, and set a piece of lasagna on each. With two forks, he

portioned salad out of the container onto the plates. "I thought about just tossing it, but I get this funny feeling Mrs. Saint would figure it out. Is that crazy?"

Markie looked at him blankly, refusing to admit she didn't think it was crazy at all.

"Oh, and there's this." He reached into his back pocket and extracted a figure made of Popsicle sticks and wool, which he held up. "It's Angel. I'm supposed to put her with the house." He set the totem beside the little house Markie had put on the kitchen windowsill.

Later, they Skyped her parents, and Markie was relieved to turn the entire thing over to her son as he took his grandparents through the same repair-the-fence play-by-play he had blurted out earlier. Clayton was impressed.

"A man needs to learn to use tools sooner rather than later," he boomed. "So I owe this Frédéric chap a thank-you. So does your father. He's actually quite handy with tools himself, your dad, though I don't suppose he's taken the time to show you that."

Markie would have jumped in to defend Kyle, but Jesse, who either never recognized her parents' digs at his father or never bothered to take offense to them, had moved on. After he and Frédéric were finished with the fence, he announced proudly, there was a long list of other jobs, staring with "tinkering with Mrs. Saint's car a little, since it's been running a little rough." Markie was sure he had no idea what this meant, but she loved that he pretended to.

"A man should be able to repair his own vehicle," her father propounded. "And if he can't, it's not the right vehicle for him. So how is it that you came to be hired by this neighbor, anyway?"

"I . . . I . . . ," Jesse stammered. "Uh . . ."

"We've just gotten to know them," Markie said, as though that answered the question.

She had been in many situations where lying to her parents would have been the easier thing, but she had never been able to do it, so

she had gotten good at making short, true statements in a way that made them sound authoritative. If her parents ever wondered about the vagueness of some of her explanations, they were too proud to ask for elaboration.

"Well, then," Clayton said, and he started to ask Markie about extending the lease on the bungalow, since his grandson clearly loved his new job next door and was obviously benefiting from it. She was saved by her mother, who interrupted to ask Jesse about his schoolwork, and thus relieved, Markie took the opportunity to slip out of the camera frame.

"I've got a history test tomorrow, actually," Jesse said, "so I'd better go. I'll see if Mom . . ." He glanced over the laptop screen to find Markie making an X with her forearms and shaking her head. "Right," he said, "so . . . that test. I'd better get back to my books. We'll talk to you next week, okay?"

Not half an hour later, Markie was reviewing files at the dining room table when Jesse and Angel came thundering up the basement stairs. She asked how the studying was going, and he announced he was finished.

"Is Lola rubbing off on you, rather than the other way around?" she asked. "You usually spend hours preparing for tests. Especially history."

"Yeah, but it's World War Two."

"And?"

"And Frédéric was alive during World War Two. He was a kid, but he, like, totally lived through it. I mentioned I had a test on it tomorrow, and every minute we weren't talking about how to rebuild the fence, he was telling me about the war. Didn't I tell you that? I thought I did. Then again, I was a little delirious when I got home. I just drank three glasses of water in the basement bathroom! Anyway, I looked over my notes from class, and there's pretty much nothing that'll be on the test that Frédéric and I didn't talk about."

How wonderful it would be if he were this animated every time he came back from helping Frédéric, she thought, and then quickly she told herself not to get carried away. This was Jesse she was dealing with: as much as he had obviously loved his time with the older man, he could just as easily return home livid the following week and storm down to his room, ignoring her for the rest of the evening. Today could be as good as it got.

Seize the opportunity, she told herself. *Find a way to continue what he's started. An entire evening of talking and laughing together would be such a treat!* "Hey," she called, "you want to see if there's something on TV?"

Jesse said something, but she couldn't hear, so she stood and followed him to the kitchen. He was bent over the counter, inhaling another piece of lasagna.

"I didn't hear what you—" she started before she noticed the cell phone bolted to his ear.

He held up a finger. "Hold on a sec, Trev." He looked up at her impatiently.

"I was asking if you wanted to find a show or something," she said.

He smiled at her as though she were the ungainly girl with a back brace, he the quarterback, and she had just asked him to the homecoming dance, and he shook his head. As she walked back to the dining room and plunked down in her chair, dejected, she heard him say, "Sorry about that. So what were you saying?" After a few "Uh-huhs," she heard his dishes clatter into the sink, his footsteps on the basement stairs, and his bedroom door closing.

Chapter Twenty-One

Markie was savoring the last few sips of her fair-trade coffee. It was the only good cup she'd had in months, the eight-dollar bag of on-sale beans one of the first treats she had allowed herself since Kyle left. After months of store-brand sludge, it tasted like melted heaven, though she could imagine her old friends laughing at the use of "treat" to describe it, her bargain coffee from the endcap display. They wouldn't have taken a second look as they headed down the aisle for their sixteen-dollar-a-pound bags. But she had allowed herself twenty dollars for "splurge" items at the grocery store, and after committing twelve of those to Jesse's favorite deli beef jerky, it was the endcap coffee or nothing.

She took another sip and looked at her waist, admiring the way her yoga pants now gaped there. Another few weeks of star-level file review like the two she had just completed, which would mean another few paychecks like the one she had received this week, and she might allow herself a new pair, one size smaller. Angel whined from her crate, and Markie smiled—smiled!—and told the dog she would be with her in a minute.

"Let me just finish this, girl, and then I'll get my runners on."

A couple of weeks earlier, after a few more mornings watching Jesse drag himself up from the basement to take the dog out before school, Markie had finally let him off the hook, telling him he could sleep until the last minute on weekdays, and she would take over the morning walks. His homework had started to pile up, and with his Lola-related obligations during the week and his Frédéric-directed ones on the weekends, he had been staying up later and later to get his schoolwork finished. The early walks were killing him. And killing his mood—gone were the mile-a-minute descriptions of the projects he was working on with Frédéric, and back were the grunting and stomping and slamming of doors.

Spending her first two hours of the day walking a dog she never wanted wasn't Markie's idea of the good life, but forcing her son to do it at the expense of his health was even less appealing, as was forcing herself to deal with his irritability. And after two weeks, Markie had to admit that the new routine was, in the broken English of their neighbor, "shooting the single bird with the identical bullet": Jesse was better rested and far more pleasant to be around; Angel was getting enough exercise to keep her quiet the rest of the day, allowing Markie to regain her position as leader of Gregory's team; and her post-divorce pudge had started to fall away.

She was avoiding her reflection in the mirror less and less. She was getting frequent e-mails from Gregory, congratulating her for her A-player status at Global Insurance. And she was getting regular thank-yous from Jesse, often with the added bonus of a full-on smile or a hug, rewards that, more than her ever-loosening clothes and the attaboys from her boss, kept her motivated to pull on her running shoes and snap on the dog's leash every morning.

It made her feel guilty, how surprised Jesse seemed that she had been willing to take on this chore for him. "The day we got her, you told me if I couldn't manage it all by myself, she'd have to go back to the

pound," he said. "And you're not exactly the kind of mom who makes empty threats."

One of the things she had gotten from Clayton and Lydia was follow-through. When Jesse was little and she started counting "One . . . two . . . ," he knew better than to let her reach "three." Markie wouldn't have thought twice about whether Clayton and Lydia would have forced her to return a dog in the same situation. Hell yes. But she had thought far more than two times about her own threat, and she assumed Jesse knew that when it came down to it, she would never do something as extreme as that. Did her son believe she was as rigid as her parents?

Something in the way he approached Angel's afternoon walks made her think he did view her as that unbending. "I'm really sorry, Mom," he told her after his first week trying to walk Angel with Lola alongside. "I don't think it's doing a lot of good. Lola's so freaking slow, Angel could probably do an army crawl and still keep up."

The girl was like that on their walk to and from school, too, and it was driving him crazy. They had to leave much earlier than he wanted to in the mornings, and they were getting home so late in the afternoons that it was hard to fit in Angel's walk and Lola's homework before Patty rushed the girl home. "I'm going to ask Mrs. Saint to take the dog walking off my list," he said. "I'll just do it on my own after dinner every night."

But the following Monday afternoon, he was home from school as early he used to be when he was walking alone. Markie asked how he'd finally managed to get his charge to walk faster.

"I didn't," he said. "I piggybacked her." She couldn't believe it, and he saw it in her face. "Desperate times," he said, shrugging, and before she could respond, he told her he would be back in a minute and raced inside. He returned sometime later with a cobweb-covered scooter and helmet he had dug out of a box of old toys in the basement. "I don't know why I didn't think of this sooner."

That afternoon, after their tutoring session was over, he attempted to teach Lola to ride the scooter. Markie could hear them from the patio, bickering like siblings as they went up and down the sidewalk, Angel running behind, yapping. "I'm not sure it's going to save us any time," he told Markie later. "She falls off every few feet, and then she spends about ten minutes griping, and I've got to practically beg her to give it another shot. She's not nearly as into it as I thought she'd be. Which is weird. I've seen a bunch of kids her age ride scooters to school. You'd think she'd want in on that, but . . ." He sighed. "Guess we'll be walking again tomorrow."

She didn't have to ask him how the walk went the next day—he was stretching and rotating his neck as he walked in the door. "Maybe the scooter lessons will go better today," she said, trying to cheer him up.

"Guessing they will," he said as he made his way to the basement door, "because I think I might have figured out what the problem is." He was back upstairs soon after, stuffing a wad of bills in his jeans. "Leftover birthday money from Grandma and Grandpa," he said, seeing her expression. "I'll be back in a bit. I told Lola to let Mrs. Saint know I'd be there a few minutes late today."

He left, and when he returned, he was carrying a brand-new scooter—bright pink with white-and-yellow daisy decals; white, pink, and yellow streamers on the handlebars; and a matching helmet. "I took a closer look when we got to her school this morning," he said. "She'd have been the only girl riding an old black scooter with a scuffed-up boys' helmet."

"Jesse!" Markie said, standing. "You *bought her*—?"

He put a finger to his lips and gestured across the fence. "I want to surprise her."

She watched as he carried them across the lawn and over the fence. When he was about five feet from Mrs. Saint's side door, he stopped and put his arms behind his back, trying to conceal the gifts. He had only taken a single step forward when the door burst open and Lola came flying out.

"I been waiting for you!" She threw herself at him, hugging him around his waist, and Jesse, laughing, dropped the surprises to the ground as he staggered backward, trying to regain his balance.

"These are for me?" Lola said, falling to her knees. Not touching them, she looked up at Jesse, waiting, and the look of disbelief on her face made Markie lift both hands to her throat. Jesse nodded, and Lola dove for the scooter, clutching it to her chest as she rolled on the grass, kicking her feet and screeching.

"Yeah, you're nuts," Jesse said, and Markie could see the corners of his mouth pull down as he tried not to smile. "And no going even six inches on that thing without wearing your helmet."

Lola stopped her rolling and screeching, let go of the scooter, and snatched up the helmet. She put it on, buckled it closed, and jumped to her feet. "I'm calling them Pinky!" she said. "The scooter *and* the helmet!"

"Sounds like something you'd come up with."

She put a hand on her hip. "Or I could call them *Jesse!*"

He brought a fist down gently on the top of her helmet, pretending to clobber her. "And I could take them both back to the store."

She squealed and clutched her helmet tightly to her head. "Let's go show everyone!"

Grabbing the scooter, she ran for the side door, but instead of turning the knob, she withdrew her hand from it, spun around, raced back to Jesse, and threw her arms around him again. "You are the very best one!" she said, before she released him and turned back for the door, a hand extended behind her.

Shaking his head, he said, "And *you* are the very weirdest one."

But he took her hand and let her drag him to the door, and when he turned back to Markie to wave goodbye, he was no longer trying not to smile.

❖

Markie swallowed her last luxurious sip of coffee and set her cup in the sink. She let Angel out of her crate, picked up the leash, and said the magic word—"Walk!"—before realizing she had dumbly forgotten to change out of her pajamas. Commanding the dog to stay put, she ran up to dress. Not surprisingly, Angel followed, amped up by the sound of her favorite word and not happy about the delay.

"Okay, okay!" Markie told her, pushing the animal off her as Angel nudged. "I'm going! I'm going! Get off me!" she said as they approached the top of the stairs, and the next thing she said was, "Oh no!" as the dog pushed too hard, knocking Markie sideways and down.

The first thing to hit the floor at the bottom was her left ankle. She heard a loud snap, and in the same instant, she felt a bolt of excruciating pain shoot from her leg to the top of her head. Crumpling, she howled in agony, cursed, then howled some more. The dog, sensing trouble, whimpered and sat nearby.

"*Now* you decide to sit still?" Markie shouted.

She was launching into a second round of cursing when there was a knock at the side door. The French accent came shortly after. "Markie? Is everything okay? We have heard a lot of noise!"

Angel made a move for the door, but Markie shot her hand out and grabbed the dog's collar, holding her in place. "Shhhh!"

Mrs. Saint knocked again, louder this time, and Markie gripped the collar tighter and pressed her other hand over her own mouth to keep herself from crying out as the pain in her ankle went from unbearable to torturous. Finally, the knocking stopped, and moments later came the sound of the neighbor's side door opening then closing.

Slowly, and with a new and ever-fouler swear word at each step, Markie limped her way into the family room, trapped the dog in her crate, and retrieved her purse and keys from the kitchen. At the last second, she grabbed the broom, too, and used it as a crutch to help her hobble to the kitchen window. Coffee hour was still in full swing. If she

limped out to her driveway now, they would see her through the screen and come running over.

So she waited, fighting her tears and watching her ankle get bigger and purpler until finally, after what felt like an entire day, the group on the porch stood, collected their dishes, and made their way inside. It was a shorter walk to the car from the side door, but that route was in plain view of Mrs. Saint's house, so Markie snuck out through the front, taking her broom-crutch with her. Thanking God the break was in her left ankle and not her right, she tossed the broom and her purse into the car, lowered herself in, and drove as fast as she could to the hospital.

Chapter
Twenty-Two

Her ankle wasn't broken, but that wasn't much consolation. With a sprain so extreme, the treatment was almost the same: crutches, a splint, a prescription for painkillers, and orders to stay off her feet as much as possible for the next several weeks. Markie slept the rest of the day in a pharmaceutically enhanced daze. When she woke, it was dusk, and Jesse was sitting on the floor at her feet, a basket beside him.

Inside was a get-well card, signed by everyone next door.

"Lola drew you a picture, too," he said. "It's on the fridge. And Ronda sent over a casserole. She wants me to take her back a list of your favorite meals, and she'll make those next, starting tomorrow." He rummaged in the basket for a notepad and a pen and handed them to Markie.

She pushed them aside. "I can manage to get from the freezer to the microwave to zap pizza."

He brought a large bell out of the depths of the basket and set it beside her. "From Mrs. Saint. She says as long as you keep the kitchen window open, she'll be able to hear if you ring this, and someone'll come right over." Markie tried to push the bell away, too, but he shoved it back. "Come on, Mom. I'm gone all day. What if there's an emergency?"

"Like what?"

"I don't know," he said. "But I don't want to sit in school wondering about it, either. Just keep this handy, and ring it if something comes up." She made a face, and he made her promise.

"Patty says she can come over and walk Angel in the mornings," he said, and before Markie could protest, he added, "but I told her I'd take that over. Already set my phone alarm."

He slept through his chiming phone on eight of the next nine weekdays, though, so Markie spent the better part of two weeks trying to figure out how to maneuver on crutches with a thick plastic boot strapped around her left ankle, how to balance her pain medication so it was enough to keep her leg from throbbing but not so much that it would prevent her from working, and how to bribe an underexercised dog into lying quietly so Markie could maintain her A-player status at Global and the paycheck that went with it.

She succeeded at none of these, which was why on the following Friday, her last file-swap trip of October, she was hobbling feebly on her crutches toward the exit doors on the fortieth floor, praying she would make it out without running into Gregory. She was halfway down the hall when she heard his voice from deep in the middle of the cube prairie.

"Markie?" She quickened her pace. "Wait! Was that Markie?" she heard him ask.

She couldn't fathom whom he was talking to, since she had managed, in her three months of employment, to avoid interacting with a single coworker outside of Gregory, the Log Sheet Lady, and the two guys in the loading bay.

"Hey, Markie, hold up there a minute!"

He was at the end of the hallway now, behind her. She was so close to the exit doors she could feel the cool metal handle against her palm. If her numbers for the past two weeks hadn't been so pathetic, she might have kept going. Even with crutches and a splint, she could be safely

behind the closed elevator doors by the time he made his way the length of the hallway. She couldn't abide a pep talk from this man.

But she couldn't afford to get on his bad side, either, so she stopped, closed her eyes, and prayed it would be over fast.

"How're you doing, Gregory?" she asked, as he puffed his way closer.

He held up a hand to indicate he couldn't respond just yet, as all of his energies were going into moving his heft the final twenty feet. Reaching her, he took several gasping breaths and said, "I'm good. You? How's that ankle coming along?"

"Good," she said. "Better every day."

"So . . . ," he said, and when no other words came to him, he rocked on his heels and balled up his fists, holding them a foot or so apart. Stepping forward, he took what she believed was meant to be a golf swing. "I've been looking at your numbers from the past two weeks," he said.

He looked past her, pretending to watch his invisible ball land, then flattened a palm and used it as a visor to shield his eyes from the imaginary sun.

"Ah, there it is," he said. "Right near the, uh, cup . . . thing. With the, um, flag."

He pointed. Markie refused to turn and look. She didn't want to be rude, though, so she smiled and nodded as though she were impressed with his shot.

"So, yeah, anyway," he said, "I've been looking at them, and I just wanted to ask, well . . ."

He put his hand on the side of her arm. Gregory was big on human-resources training, and somewhere he had learned that side-of-the-arm touching was the safest.

"I'm worried about you, is all. You've been my star for the past three months. Your numbers have pushed my team stats into the, you know"—he pointed to the ceiling—"up there. Makes me look good. Makes us all look good. But now . . ." He sighed. "I just want to know

what we can do—what *I* can do—to get you back on track. I mean, can you think of any deliverable I could offer to assist with this derailment? Short of curing your ankle, that is. I can't do that, though, and you've said it'll be a good six weeks until it's better, so we need to come up with, you know, something else."

She expected he thought there might be a poster he could send her for her wall to help her motivation, maybe a close-up of a weight lifter struggling under a loaded barbell, with KEEP PUSHING! written in bold yellow underneath.

"I'm here to help," he said. "And I'm also here to listen." He patted her arm once, then again. "In fact, why don't we take this into my office right now? Huddle around the whiteboard for a full-on brainstorming session. List all the possible obstacles to your productivity, and talk about how we can, you know . . ."

He brought two fists together, one on top of the other, as though gripping a baseball bat, and swung hard. The motion set him off balance, and he struggled to recover. "Bash them out," he finished casually, as though the balance thing were all an intended part of the demonstration. "And get your numbers back up to where we all know they can be. Where we all want them to be. Need them to be."

Markie shook her head vigorously, only somewhat worried that the dramatic gesture might make her seem a bit deranged. She guessed Gregory's managerial cheerleading services didn't extend to dog walking. And she knew what he would suggest if she admitted to the four-legged productivity obstacle in her own home.

"Nothing to discuss," she said. "Just had a few glitches to work out." She lifted her crutches: Exhibit A.

"Are these glitches exacerbated by your work environs?" he asked. "Too many stairs to climb? Narrow spaces to squeeze through? Because you know, if the at-home situation is becoming a barrier to your success, we can swap that out for you." He pointed to the cube prairie,

squinting. "I think six forty-two is free. See? Ninth row from the end there, eighteenth cube down? On the left?

"Could get you plugged in here with no problem. In fact"—he snapped his fingers—"let's go call them down in the loading bay right now, have them hold off on putting the new boxes into your car. Get them sent up here instead. The guys can stock up your new work space while I take you around and introduce you to everyone."

He rubbed his fleshy hands together. "And today is perfect timing, because we're having our weekly team lunch! Nothing fancy, mind you. I just like to have all of my direct and dotted-line reports together in the conference room one lunch hour a week so we can network, you know? Share a meal, share ideas. It's a blast!

"We all bring our own lunches, and I have everyone walk around the room, find someone they don't know very well, and broker a trade. You know, my pickle for your pudding cup, half my bologna for half your turkey and Swiss. Like back in grade school! Great intermingling exercise! Really lets you get to know your coworkers more intimately.

"As we eat, we go around the room and introduce the person we traded with—you sit with whoever you traded with, that's one of the rules—and say a few things about them. Super-short notice for you today, I know. But you could run down and get something from the cafeteria on the thirtieth floor. Or—hey! This is good! You could show up *with no food at all* and see how you do trading conversation for grub! Talk about a good way to get to know people!"

He rubbed his hands again and looked at her expectantly, his wide smile suggesting this was her cue to jump up and shout, "Hooray!"

Markie's throat closed, and she felt a trickle of sweat run down from her hairline, behind her ear. She tasted metal in the back of her mouth, and she feared opening it in case her breakfast, rather than words, came out.

Oblivious, Gregory turned toward his office and motioned for her to follow. "Let's get hold of them down in the loading bay before it's too late!"

She considered faking a cardiac arrest to delay him long enough that the boxes would be loaded by the time he reached his phone. That would take more energy than she had, though, now that all the blood had drained from her head, and she worried that any sudden movement might cause her to faint, so she settled on clearing her throat and squeaking out some words.

"The thing is, Gregory, I didn't factor in the cost of driving downtown, parking, lunches, a work wardrobe, and all of that when I took this job. I don't know if I can swing it financially, you know? The location change? So I think I'm best to just stay where I am."

She took a step backward toward the exit door.

"But your numbers . . ."

"I'll get them up." She took another step back.

"Because the others"—he pointed to the cube farm—"they drive here, too, you know, and park, and . . ."

"Right," she said, shuffling farther backward, "but they took a job that requires that."

There wasn't a great deal of strength in her argument, but she seemed to have flustered Gregory enough by not matching his excitement that he was unable to list for her all the reasons why her resistance was futile, starting with her Global Insurance offer letter, which expressly gave him the right to demand she report to work at headquarters if that's what he decided, in his sole discretion, was best for the team and the company.

"I really think my current work situation provides an environment tailor-made to maximize my performance," she said, hoping it sounded enough like Global Insurance speak. "And . . . uh, efficiency, um, exponents." She took another few small steps backward. "And I really want to get my numbers up. Way up. Higher than they were. For the team. For you. So I think leveraging my, uh . . ." She moved her hand in the air as if the rest of her sentence were obvious—and laced with corporate lingo.

Gregory sighed. "I guess we can give it another try," he said. "Tell you what. I have an all-day meeting next Friday, but let's meet the Friday after that. We'll look at your numbers. If it looks like your performance is being optimized again, then great. If not, well, you remember what the terms of employment are."

He gave her a look that said he might have been momentarily flustered a minute ago, but he had not forgotten who held the power. If he wanted her downtown, in the midst of the insect buzz of the cube prairie, trading pickles for pudding cups, there was nothing she could do about it.

"I'll keep six forty-two open for you," he said. "Just in case."

He turned to locate her potential future cube, then scanned the prairie rows until his eyes rested on his own office door. He smiled. She panicked.

"Unless something comes up closer to me." He pointed to a cube so close to his door that she imagined the person sitting there could smell his breath.

"I'd love to have you right there so I could see you at the start *and end* of my Pep Walks! Maybe take you along with me, even with your, you know . . ." He pointed to her crutches. "Could get you acclimated in no time, plugged in with all your colleagues. Say, maybe we could even set up a little memory game, see if you can learn a new row of names every day!"

He turned to her, beaming with excitement, and Markie hastily rearranged her face so she no longer looked like an audience member at a horror movie.

"But first, I'll give it those two weeks," he said. "Sound good?"

She nodded, told him thanks, and spun toward the exit, forcing herself not to risk reinjuring her ankle by running. When she finally burst through the doors and into the elevator bank, she felt like she had emerged into fresh air and sunshine after two weeks trapped in a root cellar, trying to survive a swarm of locusts.

Chapter Twenty-Three

It was time to get a status report from Jesse about how his Levin repayment plan was going. He had been keeping a tally in his room, and for the first few weeks, he reported his totals to Markie with great pride every Sunday before walking the week's wages up to the pharmacy and handing it to Mr. Levin. But he had gotten out of the reporting habit (though he had never skipped a Sunday's restitution trip to the pharmacy), and she couldn't recall the last figure he'd reported.

With any luck, he was close enough that with a small contribution from her, he could pay Mr. Levin in full that afternoon and retire from Mrs. Saint's employ, effective immediately. That would free him up to spend his afternoons tiring out the dog, allowing Markie to rehabilitate her numbers and avoid choosing between location 642 in the cube prairie and unemployment.

"Close to three hundred," Jesse said, flopping onto the family room floor a few hours later, Angel on top of him.

The corners of her mouth drooped. He wasn't even halfway there.

"What's wrong?" he said, reading her body language. "Did Mr. Levin say something to you? Or to Frédéric, or Mrs. Saint? Does he think I'm too slow?"

He looked so concerned, this boy who was trying so hard to right his wrongs, that she felt guilty for having asked about it. "Nothing's wrong," she lied. "I just . . . my ankle's bothering me."

"You want me to get your pain meds?" he asked. She shook her head no, and he told her to let him know if she changed her mind. "Hey," he said, switching gears, "can you get full-size Hershey bars for Halloween?"

"You mean to hand out? At the door?"

He laughed. "Why do you sound so horrified? You *are* planning to hand out candy, right? We do it every year."

They used to do it every year, but she considered it very much a "Before" activity, and this was "After." The idea of spending an entire evening opening the front door to all their neighbors and their children, most of whom she had managed to avoid meeting, did not fit with her "After" strategy—not nearly as well as turning off the outdoor lights and watching TV in her darkened bedroom.

"Anyway," she said, "I'm on to you with the full-size Hershey bars. Do not bribe that girl with candy to finish her homework." Avoidance, deflection. One didn't stay married to Kyle Bryant for twenty years without learning a few tricks.

"Not as a bribe," he said. "She's planning to go trick-or-treating with Frédéric, because her mom's, I don't know, working or going out or something. I just thought it would be cool if she could get her favorite thing from our place."

"That's nice of you," she said. "Hey, maybe when you've paid back Mr. Levin and you're done working for Mrs. Saint, you and Lola should celebrate the end of tutoring with a Hershey bar party."

"Right," he said, but he didn't say it convincingly, and he hesitated first.

⚜

Not five minutes after Jesse left to take Angel and Lola for their after-noon walk, there was a knock at the back door. Markie, working in the dining room, leaned back in her chair to get a view of the door and spotted the Frenchwoman standing on the other side. Surveying the files spread on the table before her, she sighed. She had less than an hour before the four-legged distraction returned home, and she couldn't afford to waste a moment of it.

"I have a favor," Mrs. Saint said when Markie opened the door. "And considering you, it is a big one. Maybe not so big for Chessie, though. So I am hoping."

"What favor?"

"Frédéric was going to take Lola around for Halloween. Tricking and treating, you know. But I have some appointments at the hospital on Monday. And now they tell me to plan to stay overnight—"

"Oh no!" Markie said. "I hope it's nothing serious!"

Mrs. Saint clucked and tapped her chest with two fingers. "Once you get past sixty, it seems they want you to think everything is serious. But it will all be fine. And I keep telling Frédéric there is no need for him to stay over, too."

"In the hospital?"

"He insists to wait there. It is ridiculous. This I have told him many times. But on some things, he cannot be swayed."

What things? Markie wanted to ask. Surely there couldn't be more than one or two subjects on which Frédéric had the final say between them. "Is he even *allowed* to stay the night?" she asked instead.

"He will stay," Mrs. Saint said, and Markie, knowing it was as much of an answer as she was going to get, didn't push. "So," the old woman continued, "someone needs to take Lola out with her costume. And I thought Chessie."

Markie considered this. Technically, Jesse was supposed to be grounded if he wasn't working, and she wasn't inclined to make an exception. On the other hand, trick-or-treating with a second grader

was hardly a night out. Plus, it was for a good cause. Two good causes: she would make him take Angel along.

"I can ask him," she said. "If he's willing to do it, it's fine with me. Or you can ask, when they get back with the dog."

"He will say yes," Mrs. Saint said. "I know this. He is very good with her. He will want to help."

She gave a brief, tight smile, and Markie couldn't decide if she should be angry or proud. Was the old woman being smug because she believed Jesse would do whatever she asked of him, or was she simply expressing that he was a kind-enough boy that he would want to help Lola?

"He's a good kid," Markie said, deciding to go with the latter interpretation. She eased the door an inch toward closed. "So if that's everything . . ."

"But she will need to stay at your house after, you see," Mrs. Saint said, ignoring the moving door. "This is the favor from *you*. Patty can get her only late. One in the morning. Two, even. When Frédéric takes her, she stays overnight at my house. Which you can. Or if you would rather, her mother can come to gather her when she is finished."

"Finished what?" Markie asked casually, hoping to catch her off guard.

But Mrs. Saint only smiled in a "Nice try" way and said nothing.

Markie felt the familiar sensation of heat in her cheeks. She hadn't liked secrecy when she was married to Kyle, and she didn't like it now. "Can't Patty cancel her plans, just for one night? It's Halloween! What could she possibly have lined up that can't be rescheduled for the sake of her daughter?"

Mrs. Saint flattened her lips into a line. "I couldn't say."

Markie rested her head on the open door and exhaled slowly. She wanted to point out the unreasonableness of the woman refusing to share information about Patty even when she was standing in Markie's

doorway, asking for her help with Patty's daughter. Pointing out the lack of fairness in the situation wouldn't make a difference, though.

"What about Carol?"

"Och, no!" Mrs. Saint said. "Not on Halloween!"

Markie didn't wait for elaboration. She knew it wasn't coming. "Ronda?" she asked. "Bruce?"

Her neighbor smiled patiently, waiting for Markie to reach the obvious conclusion, which she did, that neither of them could handle something like this. A moment passed, and Mrs. Saint continued to smile, and to wait, while Markie worked out in her head a list of reasons why she couldn't agree to what the woman was asking. Letting Jesse take the girl out for an hour or two to collect candy was fine, but having her back to the house until one or two in the morning? That crossed a deep, thick line of intimacy, and while that line might be blurred to the point of erasure on the other side of the fence, it was still as solid as ever on Markie's side.

Markie struggled to think of a version of "I don't want to get involved" that wouldn't make her look like a selfish jerk. She could think of nothing, and Mrs. Saint smiled on, waiting for the answer she wanted, the answer she knew she was going to get. Of course Markie would do it. She had no choice. She was an eight-year-old child's only chance at being able to celebrate Halloween. The Frenchwoman had her, and she knew it.

"Fine," Markie said. "She can come here after. But Patty needs to come get her as early as possible. Lola can start out sleeping in the guest room. I hate to make a little girl get up in the middle of the night on a school night, but she hardly knows me. She's never been in the house, even. And then there's the dog, and I . . ."

Mrs. Saint clapped her hands twice, interrupting Markie's rambling. She had found Lola a trick-or-treat partner and a place to stay until her mother was "finished." The other details didn't matter to her.

"Merci! C'est formidable!"

She turned to leave but swung back around a moment later, a finger in the air. "We will skip homework on Monday and have this instead for Chessie's job. Lola will eat dinner early. Chessie could join her if he likes—"

"He'll eat here," Markie said.

She had been firm about this with Jesse. The odd underbaked cookie or burned cupcake at Mrs. Saint's kitchen table was fine, but she drew the line at his staying to join the others in a bowl of soup or a plate of spaghetti in her formal dining room. In her view, snacks made him nothing more than the neighbor kid who was helping out for a little while. Dinner made him a Defective.

"Ronda will help her into her costume," Mrs. Saint continued. "Chessie will get her by five fifteen. He must have her home by seven fifteen. She will tell you she has no bedtime, but you are to make her go by eight. I have a toothbrush and pajamas for her. I will bring over. Also a timer for her tooth brushing, so she will do it long enough. Otherwise, all that candy . . ." She shuddered.

Markie let an exasperated breath escape. She was the one who had signed on as Lola's keeper, she was the one who would actually be there, and it was her house, yet the bossy old woman was barking out orders as though their roles were reversed!

"I'm sure we'll figure it all out," she said. "I've managed to get my own child through a dozen Halloweens, and he's still with us, as are all his teeth."

"And you will insist on a bath before bed," Mrs. Saint went on. "Her mother does not require it often enough, and—"

"A bath?" Markie laughed, throwing her head back dramatically to emphasize the lunacy of the suggestion. "I've met the child once! And Jesse certainly won't be—"

Mrs. Saint chuckled softly as though Markie were a whining child not to be taken seriously, and Markie was tempted to take the woman out at the knees with a crutch.

"She's been taking baths on her own for years," Mrs. Saint said. "But she will do it if only it is insisted. So you must point her the way and tell her to go."

The hell I will! Markie wanted to scream.

The old woman turned to leave a second time, and again she turned back, her finger aloft.

What now? Markie thought. *An approved list of bedtime stories, in French?*

"But you must listen for the water filling," Mrs. Saint said. "Or she might only sit in the bathroom for ten minutes. Tell her you will be gathering the wet towel after, and that will be the trick. You can also say you will help her comb out her tangles. She will not let you, but it will remind her you will be noticing if her hair is wet."

Markie tried to distract herself from her irritation by taking note of the fact that, clearly, Lola must have spent a certain number of nights at the neighbor's house. Normally, this sort of information caused her to stop everything as she tried (despite countless promises to herself that she would not do this) to piece it into the mysterious puzzle of life on the other side of the fence. But her annoyance drowned out her curiosity—Mrs. Saint could hint that Lola was her secret granddaughter, for all Markie cared, and it still wouldn't smooth the creases she could feel on her forehead or stop her teeth from grinding.

For the third time, the old woman turned for home, and this time Markie wasn't going to be there to hear what she came up with next. She took a big step backward, away from the door, and balancing her weight on her crutches, she used her uninjured leg to push the door shut. The force of her kick almost knocked her backward, and although she recovered her balance, she decided that a fall onto the hardwoods would have been a fair price to pay to hear the satisfying wham! the door made when it closed.

Chapter Twenty-Four

Markie set a bowl of candy in the tiny foyer and turned on the outdoor lights while Jesse went next door to collect Lola. The lights and candy were solely for Lola's benefit, as was the jack-o'-lantern outside the front door. One of Jesse's "jobs" on Sunday was helping Lola carve pumpkins for Mrs. Saint's house, and Ronda had bought enough for them to make one for the bungalow. Once the kids had set off around the corner to trick-or-treat, Markie planned to shut off the lights and hide in her room until a few minutes before their return. She would dump half the candy in the bathroom garbage to make it look like she had given it away.

"We're here!" Jesse called from the side door, and the tone of his voice alerted Markie that she should be prepared when she saw them.

Her jaw dropped anyway. Her son stood in the family room beside a three-foot-tall call girl carrying a plastic pumpkin. Lola wore a bright-pink bikini top that was at least two sizes too small, and a very tight mauve-satin skirt that ended halfway between her knees and hips. Between her bikini top and skirt was a foot of bare stomach, and on her feet were women's-size high heels, the same bright pink as the top.

Her hair was pulled into a high ponytail, and she wore more makeup than Markie had ever had on, complete with bright-pink lipstick, fake eyelashes, purple eye shadow, and long, thick swaths of eyeliner that extended out from the outer corners of her eyes, Aphrodite style. Four different costume jewelry necklaces wrapped around her neck, one of which matched her three-inch-long earrings.

"Well . . . ," Markie said, desperately trying to think of something to say other than, *Oh no you don't! Not on my watch!*

Jesse cleared his throat, and when she met his gaze, he said, "Lola's dressed as a *genie*."

"Ohhhh!" Markie said. "A genie!"

"Like from the show," Lola said shyly. "I watch it with Carol."

"The *I Dream of Jeannie* show?" Markie said. "I didn't know that was still on. I used to love that one!"

"It's only on real late at night," Lola said, in a tone that suggested she didn't expect Markie was the type who would be up late enough to see it.

Markie assessed the child's outfit again. The high ponytail was perfect—she would give her that.

"Ronda wanted to make me a cape," Lola said. "But that's not part of the costume." She looked at Markie plaintively, seeking support from a fellow fan.

"Maybe she was worried you'd be cold," Markie said.

Lola seemed unconvinced—it was a warm night—but moved on, reaching into her pumpkin. "She made me something." Turning to Jesse, she said, "I mean, us."

"You can keep it," he said. "It's *your* 'Best! Night! Ever!'"

He waved his hands in the air as he spoke, clearly imitating something Lola had done earlier. He was smiling, though, not sneering, happy about her excitement, not mocking it. She smiled back as she produced from the pumpkin a small totem of two figures attached together, one holding a paper flashlight, the other clutching a Hershey

bar as tall as the figure itself. She held it out to Markie, who admired it and handed it back. Lola set it carefully back in the pumpkin, pushing it with her finger until she was satisfied with its placement.

"Look at these!" She extended a foot for Markie to admire. "These are Patty's. She said I could use anything I wanted in the whole apartment to make my costume."

"They're beautiful," Markie said. "But can you walk in those for an hour?"

Lola nodded, and Jesse said, "If you consider tripping every few feet to be 'walking,' then yes." He poked the girl gently in her tummy. "I thought I might have to carry her over here. I already warned her that my piggybacking days are over, and no way are we dealing with a scooter tonight."

Angel, who had been weaving in and out between the three of them as they talked, spied Lola's extended leg and attacked it with her tongue. Lola burst into giggles and fell to the floor.

"Not my makeup!" she squealed, pushing the dog's face away. Angel wouldn't be deterred. Turning to the dog, Lola said, "Hey, Angel, can you roll over?" The dog lay down and rolled over, her tongue lolling out the side of her mouth. "Good girl," Lola said, rubbing the furry belly.

"You taught her to roll over?" Markie asked Jesse.

"Patty did," he said. "Yesterday, while we were carving the pumpkins. So what do you think we should do, Mom?" He pointed directly at the back of Lola's head.

Markie nodded conspiratorially. "You know, Lola, I had an idea earlier." She paused to give herself time to make something up. "I have some old sheets upstairs. Some regular-size ones and some from when Jesse was a baby and had a crib."

Lola giggled without taking her eyes off the dog. "Baby Jesse. Baby *girl* Jesse."

"Grandpa Lola," he fired back, and she giggled harder.

Markie looked at her son, who shook his head. "It's just a thing we do. So what was your idea? About the sheets?"

"You two might think it's silly," Markie said, "but I saw it online."

It was a shot in the dark, but it hit—Lola stiffened as she listened to hear more.

"I guess a lot of kids this year are dressing *with their dog*," Markie said. "You know, matching costumes."

Lola's hand came to a stop on Angel's belly.

"And I was thinking about those old sheets. White ones . . ." Markie paused for Jesse to catch up.

"Ghosts?" he said. "As in, cut holes in sheets and be ghosts?"

"Lame?" Markie asked.

"Brilliant!" he said. "Lola! Right? You and Angel could both be ghosts!"

Lola turned to look at him, and it was plain she was thinking about it. She gazed down at her pink high heels, then reached up to touch one of her dangling earrings.

"And," Jesse said, clearly thinking on his feet, "the beauty of it is, you can still be a genie, too! Only, you'd be a genie *under* the ghost. A *secret* genie!"

"A genie ghost," Lola whispered, and her hand moved away from her earring.

"Right, only everyone else would just see the ghost, right?" he said. "And the genie part would be, like, totally covered by the sheet. 'Cause otherwise you won't match Angel."

"Unless she's a genie ghost too!" Lola said.

"That would be so cool," Jesse said. "Except it's . . . uh . . . already getting late, and I don't know how long it'd take to rig her up in both costumes. But it sounds like my mom's got a sheet for her, so I'm thinking we go with pure ghost, right? And you know, if we stopped at Mrs. Saint's first and got those white running shoes of yours, that

would be even better. They'd be harder to see under the sheet than those pink shoes."

"It would look like I'm floating on air!" Lola squealed.

She jumped up and ran to the door, kicking off the high heels before she opened it. "I'll get them now!"

Before Jesse could answer, she was tearing across the patio in her skimpy outfit and bare feet.

"Nice save, Mom," he said.

Ten minutes later, they were ready to go, a resigned Angel wrapped in half of an old crib sheet.

Markie held up her camera. "Lola, can I get a picture of the two ghosts?"

Jesse stepped away, and Markie knew better than to try to coax him to be in the shot. But at the last second, Lola tugged on his sleeve to pull him closer, and to Markie's surprise, he not only consented, but he also agreed to hold Lola's pumpkin so she could pose with her hands in the air.

"No one sees that one but the three of us," he told his mother as he walked out the front door, the two ghosts running ahead of him on the walk.

"I'm pretty sure everyone next door is going to see it if you let Lola have a copy," she warned. "Maybe everyone at her school, too."

He closed his eyes. Clearly, he hadn't considered the full ramifications of smiling for the camera, pumpkin in hand.

"You could always tell her there's only going to be one copy, and it's going to stay in this house."

"Jesseeee!" Lola called from the end of the walk, where she was bouncing on her toes with excitement. "Come onnnn!" She bent to adjust the half crib sheet they had dressed the dog in, then dropped to her knees and hugged Angel around her neck. "Best night ever, Angel!"

His eyes on the girl and the dog, Jesse said, "Nah, it's fine. She can have her own copy."

Markie reached into the candy bowl, then went with her son to the end of the walk, hands behind her back. Bringing them forward, she bent down to Lola. "Here, Miss Secret Genie Ghost. I want to be the first person to put something in your pumpkin. These were Jesse's idea, by the way."

Lola pulled her sheet off to get a better view as Markie dropped three Hershey bars into the orange plastic container. Screeching, Lola threw her arms around Markie's neck, pressing a sticky cheek against her. It felt to Markie as though the child had just glued them together. It wasn't the makeup—she could feel that, too, and it was slippery, not sticky.

Lola's neck and arms and hair had a filmy feel to them, and she had a definite unclean smell about her, although perhaps because she was only eight, it was more sweet than repulsive. She smelled like mushed apples and wet hay, and while it wasn't something Markie would want to bottle and sell, it was far nicer than the preteen body odor that used to settle in the stairwells at Jesse's old school.

Despite the smell of her and the stickiness, Markie held on tight. Hugging Lola reminded her of how it used to be when Jesse was her age, the forceful way he'd throw himself at her, shoot his arms around her, and hold on like he never wanted to let go. No self-consciousness, no concern about whether someone might be watching. It got so much harder as they got bigger. Jesse was skinny, but he had his father's broad shoulders, so Markie had to approach him from a careful angle in order to get her arms right around him, which only made the entire process that much more awkward and unpleasant for him.

"Thank you a big billion billion!" Lola said, pressing her cheek tighter against Markie's.

"Which is not, in fact, the highest number in the world," Jesse said, in a way that made clear he was continuing a conversation they'd had before.

"Is so," Lola said.

She tried to pull away, but she and Markie were stuck fast by whatever was under her makeup. Lola giggled and pulled harder, coming free, and Markie felt a cold, empty space where the child's body had been pressed against her. She told herself she was being ridiculous—she should be relieved to be free of the smell and grime.

Jesse picked up the discarded sheet from the ground and held it out for her, and Lola wriggled into it.

"*Frappez la rue!*" Lola said. "That's 'hit the road' in French," she informed Markie as they turned for the sidewalk.

"Not exactly," Jesse said. "It doesn't—"

"Directly translate," Lola finished for him. "But I still like to say it."

"Just don't—" he started.

"Say it in front of Mrs. Saint," Lola finished. "I know. *Je pas stupid.*"

"*Je* ne suis *pas stupide,*" he corrected, and Markie didn't know whether to feel pride or dismay at his newfound French-language skills.

Lola punched him in the side and whispered something Markie couldn't hear, and the two of them bickered their way down the block as Markie turned back to the house.

Stepping past the carved pumpkin, she thought about the Halloween nights of her childhood—being dragged too fast around their block by an impatient Lydia while her father remained at work, determined not to return home until "the whole ridiculous waste of money and good molars" was over. "There," Lydia would say, "we went all the way around the block. That's more than enough candy for your waistline and for your teeth. And more than enough time for Mommy to have to witness all those mannerless imps grabbing their candy and running, without a pleasant 'Good evening' or even a simple 'Please' and 'Thank you.'"

Markie was allowed to dress in one of four Lydia-approved costumes: nurse, doctor, teacher, or first female president. She was permitted one candy from her pumpkin while they racewalked around the block, one when they got home, and one each dinnertime thereafter

until her pumpkin was empty. With her mother's supervision—the kind that always ended in "Here, why don't I just fix that part. In fact, I'll just finish it for you"—she was given the chance to carve one small pumpkin. More of a gourd, really, the size of a baseball. Clayton didn't like the look of large pumpkins on people's doorsteps once the squirrels got to them.

There were no indoor decorations of any kind, though Markie was allowed to display Halloween-related school art projects on the fridge for the same seven-day time allotment Clayton permitted for all drawings, stories, or other items she brought home. Once the week was up, the "clutter," as he referred to it, went into the garbage. "This is a house, not a nest of pack rats."

Inside the bungalow, Markie switched off the porch light and went to the family room to retrieve her book from the couch. She had an hour of reading time in bed before the kids returned. As she bent to pick up her novel, she saw Patty's pink high heels near the door where Lola had kicked them off, and it occurred to her that she had been luckier than Lola—at least Lydia had taken her around the block each year and helped her with her costume, no matter how uncreative.

Markie set her book down. In the front hall, she flipped the porch light back on, casting the front of the house in a welcoming glow, and racing to the basement as fast as her crutches would allow, she found the box labeled HALLOWEEN. For the next sixty minutes, anytime she had a break from answering the door and handing candy to tiny Dorothys with red shoes, middle-school grim reapers, and the occasional high-school "hobo," she strung pumpkin lights around the kitchen window, set out her collection of ceramic witches and ghosts on the counter, and dangled big plastic spiders from the ceiling, along with the tissue-body ghosts Jesse had made in first grade.

On the fridge, she used her entire magnet collection to post a decade's worth of "scary" drawings he had created each October during his early childhood: green witches with warty noses and hairy chins and

too many googly eyes, graveyards filled with monsters and zombies, the Headless Horseman. As a final touch, she tacked to the guest-room door the construction-paper skeleton with movable joints Jesse had so proudly brought home in third grade, and she set an electric jack-o'-lantern on the table beside the guest bed.

Lola squealed when she walked in the house and saw the decorations. Dropping her pumpkin, she ran into the kitchen, touched each of the ceramic ghosts and witches, studied every single piece of artwork on the fridge, and jumped up to try to touch each dangling ghost and spider. When Markie suggested the girl might want to check out the guest room, Lola yelped and raced up the stairs.

"Wait!" Jesse called after her. "You don't even know where—"

An excited shriek let him know she had found the room just fine.

"Thanks, Mom," he said. "The place looks great." He set one of the dangling spiders spinning. "I'd forgotten about all this stuff."

"She sure seems to be getting a kick out of it," Markie said, lifting her eyes to the ceiling, through which they could hear Lola's continued screeches.

He spun the spider again, then reached out to spin the others, and all the ghosts, before stepping to the fridge. Bending down, he studied each of his old creations carefully, laughing quietly at the witch with her eleven googly eyes.

"Yeah," he said. "She really appreciates it."

Chapter Twenty-Five

When Bruce knocked at eight o'clock the morning after Halloween to tell Markie that Mrs. Saint's house had been broken into the night before, Markie wondered if perhaps she was asleep on her feet and dreaming. Patty hadn't come for Lola until after two, and because the noise woke Angel, who then insisted on going out, Markie hadn't gotten back to bed until close to three.

"Oh my God!" she said, after making Bruce repeat himself twice to make sure she had heard him correctly. "Did they take anything?"

"They sure did," he said.

He nodded, as though he had now given her all the information she needed, and turned his attention to Angel, who was whining in her crate. "You want me to walk her so you can get your work done? I got some things to do now, but I could come for her later."

"No," she said. "Thanks, but you do too much for me as it is, and you won't let me pay you."

He had insisted on changing all the lightbulbs for her after Jesse mentioned the one in the upstairs hallway had gone out and she had almost tripped in the dark. While he was there, he replaced the batteries

in the smoke alarms, and since he "just happened" to have brought extras in various sizes, he changed the ones in the TV remotes, too.

"So what did they take?" she asked. He looked at her blankly, and she said, "From the house."

"Oh, right," he said. "Money, for one. Don't ask me how they knew where to find that. She keeps it in . . . a place that's not so usual, let's just say. They also stole some things from her medicine cabinet. Frédéric says that means it was kids. Because of, you know, drugs. 'Who looks in the bathroom and leaves all the silver in the dining room?' That's what he said. But worst is, they took a little case that was sitting inside the front door. Frédéric was supposed to take it to the hospital for her, but he forgot it."

"What was in it?"

"Family pictures and a few pieces of jewelry from her grandmother. Nothing fancy, no gold or nothing like that. Only worth something to her, which is probably why I found the case beside the garage, lying on its side. There was a couple of her papers inside it still, and I found a photo in the grass a few feet away, but everything else was gone. I don't know if they took it all or tossed it behind the garage once they realized it wasn't worth nothing, or what. Anyway, that's how I knew something was up in the first place—I saw that case. Just happened to be looking in the right direction when I walked up the driveway today.

"And then I went searching around the house, and I found a broken window, and I called Frédéric, and he told me where else to look, and we pieced it together. I'll look again in a minute, and maybe more things will turn up missing. Sure hope not. She's upset enough about the case. I don't want her getting more worked up. Especially with her, you know . . ." He tapped two fingers to his chest, the same way Mrs. Saint had done.

"Is something wrong with her heart?" Markie asked. "She told me it was only old age, and Ronda and Patty both said—"

"Frédéric's not convinced. That's why he made her go in for the tests."

"Frédéric *made* her go?" Markie asked.

But Bruce only looked at her vacantly, so she gave up that line of inquiry and asked, "Why would she have wanted to take that little case to the hospital? I'd be worried something like that would get lost there."

"Oh, she takes it anytime she goes anywhere overnight," he said. "Always has. Not that she goes away much. But when she does, she always has that case."

Markie thought about her ancient neighbor, who was gruff so much of the time yet had also shown quite a bit of sentimentality. Her voice always got softer when she talked about "my Edouard" or watched her Defectives at work, and Markie had seen her eyes glisten more than once in connection with Jesse, a child she had known only since August. She might be cold, even caustic, about a lot of things, but when it came to relationships, Mrs. Saint was quite mushy.

"She must be very upset about losing those family things," Markie said.

"Crushed," Bruce said. "I'm hoping to have time to search for them out behind the garage later. Right now, there's too much else to do."

He looked down, and they stood quietly for a few minutes. It was as though they were having a moment of silence for Mrs. Saint's lost family heirlooms, Markie thought. It seemed crazy and right at the same time.

"I'd better get back," Bruce said finally. "See if Ronda needs any help. Frédéric's going to get refills on all the prescriptions that are missing, but he asked me to move some things around in the cabinet so those shelves aren't standing empty when she gets home. He said she won't want the reminder."

Ten minutes later, Patty was at Markie's door. "I wanted to thank you for taking Lola last night," she said. "She couldn't stop talking about it this morning. About Jesse and you and the costumes and the

decorations, and on and on. It was her 'best night ever'—I must've heard that phrase fifty times."

"No problem," Markie said. "She was no trouble at all. She actually got me and Jesse excited about Halloween, which is something I didn't think would be possible. He was thinking he was too cool for it this year, and I . . . wasn't in the mood."

Patty looked past Markie, at the spiders and ghosts still suspended from the kitchen ceiling, the Halloween artwork on the fridge. "Looks like you were more in the mood for it than I've ever been."

"I only put those things up because of Lola," Markie said.

If it were Mrs. Saint at her door, she would never have admitted to any of this for fear the woman would consider it an opening to suggest she take Lola in again. She didn't feel she had to be as careful around Patty. Maybe it was because Patty didn't seem manipulative or pushy, or maybe it was because she didn't seem all that interested in making arrangements for her daughter.

"Still," Patty said, "I told everyone Lola'd be fine with Carol. Mrs. S didn't have to go to the fuss of finding her a different plan, and she sure didn't need to drag you into it."

"It's totally fine," Markie said.

"How's Angel doing?" Patty asked, nodding toward the crate and the animal inside it, who was trying to squeeze herself out between the bars. "You want me to take her out for a bit so you can get some work done?"

Markie narrowed her eyes. "Did Bruce send you over?"

Patty shrugged. "I was going to thank you anyway. He mentioned the dog was driving you nuts, and it sped up my plan."

"Look," Markie started, preparing to send Patty home with orders to inform Bruce to butt out. But then she recalled how vehemently she had opposed his suggestion that Patty become Angel's regular dog walker. *I can't afford to pay her, and I won't let her do it for free.* Maybe being indebted to someone made Patty's skin crawl, too.

"You know," Markie said, "yes. Thank you. That would be great."

Markie worked for two solid hours in pure, blissful silence, and when Patty returned, Angel walked straight into her crate and fell asleep.

"This is the best gift I've gotten in ages!" Markie whispered, afraid to wake the dog. "But I feel bad. You were gone so long! What about your own job?"

"Mrs. S won't be home till close to dinnertime," Patty said. "I only came over today to keep an eye on Bruce and Ronda. But I left them a list before I took Angel, and I'm pretty sure they'll have gotten it all done. Or most of it." She seemed to consider this. "Some of it. I'll go back now and check."

"I've never seen her so wiped out," Markie said, pointing to the now-snoring dog.

"I'm faster than Jesse," Patty said. "And a *whole lot* faster than him and Lola, even when she's on that scooter. Angel could go all day at their pace. It's the real quick walking that does her in."

"It sure did today," Markie said.

"You know, I could walk her every day."

Markie shook her head. "Absolutely not. Today was great, and thank you. But we're all settled up now. One night with Lola, one long walk for Angel. If you took her another time, it would be too much."

Patty cocked her head. "I didn't offer to take her because I thought I had to repay you for Lola."

"Oh," Markie said, reddening. "I just assumed. I mean, *I* didn't think you needed to repay me, either. It's just that some people are funny about owing others. Like me. I'm funny about that stuff. I can't afford to pay you, and I can't let you do it for nothing, and there's nothing more I can really do for you in exchange, so . . ." She shrugged. "It's a great offer, though, and thanks, but I just can't."

Patty squinted as though Markie had grown antennae. "I don't really get it, but it's cool."

Jesse came home later, looking ashen.

"What?" Markie asked. She thought about Mrs. Saint and her heart condition. He had heard something? "Is it Mrs. Saint?"

"Yeah," he said.

"Oh my God! Did Frédéric call you? What happened? Should we go over there now?"

"What?" Jesse asked. "No. Nobody called me. What are you talking about?"

"Her heart. What are *you* talking about?"

"I saw Bruce when I dropped Lola off, and he told me about last night. He said Frédéric thought some of the things from her case might be behind the garage, but no one's had time to look. So I did, and he was right. I feel terrible. I mean, her most valuable possessions, and they just tossed them? She's, like, eighty years old or whatever! All she's ever done is be nice to people! And then some jerks go and do this to her?" His voice shook, and he swiped a hand across his eyes.

It surprised Markie to see him so upset. Had he become that close to Mrs. Saint? "Anyway," he said, "I've been behind the garage, looking, and . . ."

He brought a hand out from behind his back. She hadn't even noticed he was holding it there. In it, he held a small photograph, old, black-and-white, and creased. He held it up, and together they looked at two baby girls wearing matching dresses, sitting together in an old-fashioned pram. One had her hand on the other's knee. They were twins, Markie guessed, about a year old.

Behind the pram stood two other children, a boy of about fourteen and a girl slightly younger, maybe eleven or twelve. The boy smiled stiffly in a new-looking suit as he looked partly at the camera and partly at something out of the frame. The girl wore a dress with needlework similar to that in the babies' dresses, and she smiled openly, looking directly at the camera, her hand resting on the boy's forearm. Maybe

she was trying to get him to look at the camera instead of whatever else had his attention.

Markie turned the photo over to see if there were names written, or maybe a date or location, but there was nothing. Jesse took the photo back and brought his other hand from around his back and opened it, revealing an ancient-looking ring, flat on the top with an etching on it. She took it from him and held it up to see if she could make out the markings.

"I think it might be an *S*," Jesse said. "For St. Denis, maybe? I don't know."

"It was very good of you to look," Markie said. "Do you want to take these over so she'll see them as soon as she gets home?"

He shook his head. "Frédéric called to say they're coming now, and Bruce and Ronda went into a tailspin, so I came to get you."

"I'm proud of you for finding those things," Markie said.

A few minutes later, they rang the bell at Mrs. Saint's house. "Welcome home!" Markie said when her neighbor answered the door. "How are you? I expected someone else to answer the door. Should you be up and around?"

"Pffft," Mrs. Saint said. "Worry, worry, worry. Why is it we are all supposed to worry so much? Why cannot we enjoy our lives and leave the worry alone? What does it get for you, the worrying?"

"Well, I hope you're feeling better," Markie said. "Should we sit?"

"Enough," Mrs. Saint said. "I have a whole group of people here who want to do nothing but sit me down so they can stare at me and fret about me and ask if I have yet taken this pill or do I need a glass of water."

"Fair enough," Markie said. "Look, I was so sorry to hear about the break-in."

Mrs. Saint looked to the ceiling and pressed lips together. *"Oui."*

"But I have a bit of good news," Markie said. "Actually, it's Jesse's news." She turned to her son and gestured for him to take over.

Jesse handed Mrs. Saint the photograph. "I found this." Mrs. Saint took it from him, and when she realized what it was, she pressed a hand against her heart. She looked at Jesse, and Markie saw tears in the old woman's eyes. "Where?" she asked, her voice a whisper.

"Behind the garage," Jesse said. "In the woods. I found this, too." He handed her the ring.

Mrs. Saint took it and touched a finger to the flat top of the engraving.

"What does it say?" Jesse asked.

"*S*," she said. "For Sabrine. It was my Edouard's mother's ring."

She looked away, not just a few feet off, but far, far away, and Markie wondered if she was thinking of Edouard's mother or Edouard. She could see Mrs. Saint's lips working to press themselves together so they wouldn't quiver. She was trying not to break down in front of Jesse.

Markie stepped closer and pointed to the photo, thinking a change of subject might help. "Is this you? Are you a twin?"

"Och, *non! Ce n'est pas moi.* This is not me. I have no twin. No brothers and sisters at all. Only me."

"Oh, I just assumed, since you kept the photo all these years, that it must be—"

"Relatives," Mrs. Saint said. "Cousins. On my Edouard's side. I hardly even knew them."

She flipped the photo over. *I'll show you how little these people mean to me,* she seemed to be saying. Markie thought the tears she had seen in the woman's eyes when Jesse first produced the picture told a different story. But Mrs. Saint had been released from the hospital only an hour earlier, and she had been robbed the night before. Today was not the day to press her.

"Anyway, I must go," Mrs. Saint said. "Before they all come to check me up."

"Can I walk you to your room?" Jesse asked, and to Markie's surprise, Mrs. Saint agreed.

He stepped to her, and she took his elbow and held out the ring and photograph. "Thank you for finding," she said. "Now, *on y va*. Let us go. Frédéric will be having his own heart troubles if I am not back in my bed very soon."

Markie said goodbye and went home. An hour later, Jesse walked in.

"I thought Lola left," Markie said. "What were you doing over there for so long?"

"Looking for more stuff."

"Did you find anything?"

He held out another photograph. "I'm going back tomorrow, when it's lighter. This was way back, about ten feet from the garage. Must've gotten blown by the wind. I'm thinking there might be more stuff where I found this."

"Why didn't you take it right in the house to her?"

"When I left, she told me she was going to take a nap. And, also, I thought you should see it."

"Why?"

He held it out and she took it. The photo showed twin girls, about seven or eight, wearing matching dresses and birthday hats. They held hands and giggled, and one waved to someone outside the frame.

Markie looked up at her son, then back to the picture. "The one waving," she said as she studied the girls' faces more carefully. "Don't you think she's a dead ringer for—?"

"Read it," he said. "The back."

She flipped the photo over: *Angeline et Simone, 7ème anniversaire.*

Chapter
Twenty-Six

The Frenchwoman was standing in the bungalow again, only a few days after Halloween, trying to convince Markie to keep Lola *every evening* while Patty was "out." Lola hadn't stopped talking about how much fun she'd had at the bungalow, Mrs. Saint said, and for her own part, she couldn't stop thinking about how much better off the girl would be if she spent part of each night in a home that insisted on bathing and teeth brushing. Jesse had even read to the girl before bed! No one did that for her at Patty's apartment.

Markie stood in the middle of the family room, her feet planted wide, her arms crossed in front of her. If there were a mirror nearby, she was certain her reflection would show smoke coming out of her ears. She had told her neighbor twice, and not in a subtle way, what an inconvenience it had been for her and Jesse to be woken in the middle of the night in order to hand Lola back to her mother. How they had been too exhausted to think the next day, let alone complete the work they each had to do.

None of this had registered with Mrs. Saint, evidently, so Markie repeated it for a third time now, adding for clarity that there was no way

she was going to sign on for that kind of interruption on a nightly basis. Mrs. Saint only blinked uncomprehendingly, as though Markie was complaining about nothing. Yet when Markie tossed the issue back to her—"Why doesn't Lola stay with *you* every evening?"—the old woman waved her hands as though it was out of the question.

"Why?" Markie demanded. "Why are you standing there acting like it should be no trouble at all for *me* when *you* won't even take her?"

Her answer was a blank stare.

It didn't surprise Markie, but it aggravated her, and she stomped to the kitchen counter, plucked up the photo that Jesse had found the night before, and marched back to Mrs. Saint, shoving it in her face.

"You are full of requests for things *I* should do to help *your* employees," she said. "And you have no end of questions for me and my son about *our* lives. And yet anytime I ask you the simplest question about anything to do with *your* life, you have no answer!" Mrs. Saint reached for the photo, but Markie hung on to it, and with a dramatic flourish, she turned it over so the handwriting was in the old woman's face, undeniable: *Angeline et Simone, 7ème anniversaire* .

"'Are you a twin?' I asked you last night," Markie said, still holding the photo out of Mrs. Saint's reach. "'Oh, *non*,' you said. 'I'm not a twin. In fact, I never even had siblings! Those twin girls in the pram in the other photo? Edouard's cousins! Not me. Not my twin.' When in fact, it *was* you! You and *Simone*, your *twin sister*! And my guess is that the kids in that other photo were an older brother and sister. So you have *three siblings*, in fact, not 'none!'

"That's two lies from you this week alone! Who knows how many others you've told since we moved in! How many secrets you've kept, all while trying to get at all of mine! And now you're standing here, in *my house*, asking me to look after a child whose mother disappears every night to somewhere *you refuse to name*! You can understand why I'm getting a little tired of this, can't you?"

Before the other woman could answer, Markie said, "Never mind! Don't answer that! I expect you *won't* understand! But understand this: I am *finished* with your secrets and your nonsense! I'm not asking you any more questions about your life. There's no point. But *you* need to be finished, too. Do not ask me anything more about me, and do not ask me to help your employees again!

"Don't ask my son, either. He can work for you until he has paid Mr. Levin. After that, he's done. And when February comes and our half-year lease is up, he and I are leaving. I hear you've been hinting that he should ask me to extend the lease. You somehow know that the landlord would be willing to do that for us, even though my deadline for extending has passed. Of course, I'm sure you won't tell me *how* you know that, so I'm not going to ask that, either."

Trembling, Markie offered the photo at last, and Mrs. Saint took it, staring for a long time at the inscription on the back before finally turning it over to see the two little girls at their birthday. Without waiting for the woman to react or explain, Markie marched to the door, opened it, and motioned with her hand for Mrs. Saint to leave.

"I am sorry," Mrs. Saint said softly, her eyes still on the photograph. "This is something I do not like to speak of. So I lie about it. I . . . pretend she never existed."

"Why?" Markie demanded.

But she didn't step away from the door, and she made another sweeping motion with her hand. Even if she were to get an answer, which she doubted, she preferred to hear it as the woman was on her way out.

Mrs. Saint stepped toward the door, her back to Markie. "Because it is a very painful thing," she said in a small voice. "She is dead."

Markie felt a wave of guilt wash over her. She had been entirely too harsh, especially considering the woman had a heart condition. She was still frustrated by all the secrets, but this was different. Her neighbor

couldn't be the first person to pretend away loved ones because it was easier than facing their absence.

"I'm so sorry," she said. Mrs. Saint had reached the doorway, and Markie reached out to her. "I can imagine why you would pretend she didn't exist."

Mrs. Saint nodded and kept going.

"You don't have to leave," Markie said. "I overreacted. I was annoyed. I still am, about a number of things. But not about that. I'm sorry. I was completely out of line, and I feel terrible about it."

"I should go."

"When did she die?" Markie asked. Mrs. Saint was on the patio now, moving toward the fence, and Markie followed behind her.

"A long, long time ago."

She didn't look back when she said it, and Markie could tell by her tone that that was all she planned to say about her sister. And for once, she didn't think there was anything wrong with that.

When Mrs. Saint reached her side door, she turned. "I have known Frédéric for many years. More than you have been alive, even. We met when we were children. He is . . ." She stared past Markie into the distance. "He is family, for me. This is why he insisted on staying overnight in the hospital. This is why they would allow it."

Markie's mouth fell open. She could think of a thousand questions, but no words.

"I should have told you this before," Mrs. Saint said. "I am sorry I did not. And I should not have asked you about Lola. You are not . . . wanting people in your life. Wanting to be involved in their lives. I have known this. And I should not have pushed about it."

Markie cringed. It made her sound so selfish, so coldhearted. "Well, not *now*," she said. "I might've had a different answer a year ago, but for right now—"

Mrs. Saint held up a hand to stop her. "I am not asking you to explain this. It is your information."

Markie waited, scanning the other woman's face for some indication she was trying to lure Markie into spilling her story by pretending she didn't want to hear it. But Mrs. Saint only looked sad. Maybe she regretted pushing Markie so hard for so long, or maybe she was lamenting her lost childhood with Frédéric, or maybe she was thinking about Simone.

"You said you do not want to always be asked about things anymore," Mrs. Saint said. "And so, I will not."

She nodded, as though that finalized the matter, then turned and disappeared into her house.

Chapter Twenty-Seven

Markie was hobbling outside to put Angel on the tie-out when Ronda called from the screened porch, asking her to wait. When the cook finally reached the fence, Markie saw worry lines on her normally smooth face.

"What is it?" Markie asked.

"Carol's over. I needed to get out of there for a minute." Ronda shuddered as though she had narrowly escaped certain death.

"Oh," Markie said.

No wonder she hadn't seen Frédéric tinkering near the garage. He must be conveniently at one of his meetings/classes/appointments/who-knew-whats.

"Does she come over often? I've heard Lola calling to her a few times, but I've never seen her."

"Oh no," Ronda said. "Just every blue moon or so, when she needs money." She bent her head to watch as the toe of her shoe dug into the garden.

"Mrs. Saint gives her money?"

"Oh, goodness no," Ronda chuckled, shaking her head. "No, she don't, and she never will, and she made that durn clear to Carol first time she asked. Oooh," she laughed again, "that was an awkward day for everyone, let me tell you. No, she gets it from Patty. Usually, she hits her up before Patty goes out at night.

"Plays the Lola card. You know, 'You sure you don't want to lend me money? Well then, I'm not so sure I want to mind the kid. Maybe you'd best stay in tonight.'" Ronda shook her head. "Real nice for Lola to hear that from her own grandma, I'm sure. Anyway, she must've forgot last night, or maybe she had some big financial emergency come up today, after Patty already left to come over."

"And *that's* why Frédéric's never around when Carol comes over!" Markie guessed out loud. "Because he said something to her about borrowing money from her own daughter or about holding it over Lola's head. And Carol got mad."

Ronda looked up, surprised, and Markie blushed at her overexcitement about figuring out the mystery. And for making it so obvious that she had been trying to solve it.

"Well, now, I couldn't say about that," Ronda said, "but it sure sounds like something Frédéric might do. He looks at Patty and Lola like they're his own, in case you never noticed. Looks at all of us that way, really, but especially them.

"And I wouldn't be surprised if he stuck up for Patty in some kind of way like that, about the money or some of the other stuff Carol does. I never seen him do it. But Carol never asks about him, that's for sure. Acts like she don't even know he exists. And I guess it might be because he opened his mouth up and she didn't like it. You make Carol mad, and that's it. She's not one to forgive."

Markie felt foolish at the realization that the "big mystery" about Frédéric and Carol wasn't significant at all. They were simply two people avoiding each other because they'd had words once. Where was the great secrecy in that?

"Not that he asks about her, either, if you want the truth," Ronda said. "And Mrs. Saint is always reminding us not to mention her name or anything about her when he's around. Lola had a picture of Carol once, and Mrs. Saint about had a fit, making her shove it in her backpack before he saw it, telling her never to bring it over again. So maybe he's acting like Carol don't exist, too.

"Only with Frédéric, you know there's more to it than just being mad about some argument they maybe had. It's about those girls"—Ronda smiled—"*his* girls, he calls them. He's always worried about them, and I imagine he worries more because of all the things Carol puts them through, and that's why he don't want nothing to do with her. Not that he's told me any of this. It's just how I've pieced it together." She nodded, satisfied with her own theory. Her gesture reminded Markie of Mrs. Saint.

"With Carol, though," Ronda went on, "it's likely to be pure grudge, through and through. She's one of the tough ones. She's . . ." She gazed at the back of her hands for the right word. "Hard," she settled on. "She's a hard, demanding woman. Patty can't do anything right, if you ask Carol. But then, if you ask just about anyone who knows Carol, they'll tell you *she* hasn't done a lot right in her life herself.

"And she sure ain't doing right by her family these days, always messed up and borrowing money. Or stealing it, if Patty's not around to lend it. So why she's so hard on Patty . . ." She turned her hands over and examined her palms for the rest of her sentence. Not finding it there, evidently, she started a new one. "I've probably made more Carol totems than any other kind. Patty has a drawerful, I think! Not that it's helping."

Markie thought of her own hypercritical mother and considered asking Ronda for a Lydia totem. Then again, she only had to deal with hers on the phone or over Skype. Patty, forced to see Carol every day, was the one most in need of the totems.

"I wonder why Patty doesn't just move out," Markie said. "I assume she makes enough money to get her own place."

"She does," Ronda said. "It's Carol that don't have enough to get by. And since Carol raised Patty on her own, Patty feels like she owes her. Or at least, Carol's told her enough times that she owes her. Plus, there's the fact that Carol's the go-to for minding Lola while Patty's out in the evenings. And you don't move out on Carol and then ask her to look after your kid. That's not how things work with Carol. Like I said, you make her mad, and that's it for you."

Ronda gestured to the house and said, "I should get back in there. I'm burning some muffins, but I don't want to let them go too long or it might make it obvious." Noting Markie's surprise, she winked and said, "Carol'll do some yelling and cursing about my terrible cooking and lay off Patty for a minute. Works every time."

❧

It was the Thursday after Halloween, and Markie was working at the dining room table. She was trying to work, anyway, but mostly she had been staring out the window, trying to keep herself from obsessing about the fact that the gig was likely up for her work-from-home position. She had eight days, including the weekend, to get her numbers up before she was scheduled to meet with Gregory for their mind-mapping session. There was no way for her to get out of it, and at this point, she couldn't see herself coming away from that meeting with good news. Her numbers were still down, thanks to Angel.

She had considered staying up all night to work while the dog was happily cuddling in bed with Jesse. But she had never been able to pull off late nights, even when she was young. It took her days to recover from even a single night of missed sleep, as she had been reminded after Patty's middle-of-the-night Lola pickup. And anyway, she couldn't imagine having to deal with Angel all day when she was tired.

She looked down at her yoga pants and oversize T-shirt and let out a breath. The weight loss she had been so excited about after her short period of dog walking had reversed itself, thanks to her sprained ankle. She might not even be able to squeeze into her lime-green post-baby dress next Friday. And although she had been trying to avoid the mirror in the bathroom, it hadn't escaped her that her gray roots had now grown so long that her hair seemed to belong to two people—the bottom six inches to a young blonde, and the top six to an old brunette.

Not that a slimmer physique, a new wardrobe, and a day at the beauty salon were all that was standing between her and the ability to work in public once more. Emotionally, she still wasn't there. And it wasn't just Gregory and the cube prairie she couldn't face. It was any location, any boss.

Her limited interactions with Mrs. Saint and her employees took more out of Markie than she had. She had taken to buying groceries only on Wednesdays, and only late at night, because that was the shift worked by the least-talkative cashier in the store. The others wanted to chat about the weather or her purchases, innocuous enough in terms of subject matter, but it was torture for Markie, the way they smiled and waited for her to respond. There was no way she would be able to withstand workplace banter in the cube prairie all day long, and the idea of department lunches, with the requisite get-to-know-you pudding-cup trades Gregory was so keen on, made her break into a cold sweat.

Noise from the other side of the window caught her attention. Jesse and Lola were outside on one of their homework breaks. Lola waved her arms above her head and squealed while she ran laps around the yard, Jesse chasing after her, bent forward, his arms hanging limply in front of him, making deranged-creature noises. Angel, who was allowed to lie at their feet under Mrs. Saint's kitchen table while they worked, ran after them, barking.

Markie stood, crossed to the window, and watched as the kids ran in circles. Every few minutes they stopped and pitched forward, hands

on their knees, ribs moving in and out as they caught their breath. No matter how far apart they were when they stopped, Lola always moved closer to Jesse. Markie could see their mouths move as they talked and laughed until finally, one of them would swat the other and they would both take off running again.

A few minutes into their game, the side door opened and Frédéric came out. He said something to Jesse, pointed toward the bungalow, and started for the fence. Markie, always eager to stop any cross-lawn travel when she could, hurried out to meet him.

"I have not yet thanked you for taking Lola the other night," he said, reaching across the fence to take both of her hands in his. "What a wonderful thing you did. Thank you." He bowed stiffly.

"It was more Jesse than me," she said.

Frédéric turned to watch the children, who were now turning in tight circles with their arms straight out, like airplanes. "He is a remarkable young man, to do these things for her," he said. "These childish games of which I am sure he wants no part."

"It's good for him to get the fresh air himself," Markie said, "not to mention the exercise. I think his video game playing has been cut in half since he started spending time with her. Maybe more."

"He has a good mind," Frédéric said. "He is interested in things. Not the same as many his age."

"Listen, I should be the one thanking you, for spending so much time with him," she said. "I can't tell you how thrilled he is to be learning about carpentry from you. The Sundays he's been spending with you have made such a difference. He tells me you've been talking to him about World War Two, as well. He got a terrific grade on his history midterm. Did he tell you? He told me most of his answers came from talking to you. I know he read the chapters, but the written words weren't nearly as interesting as your stories. You made it come alive." Because she couldn't help herself, she added, "You really should have been a professor."

Frédéric smiled. "I enjoy talking about these things with him. There are some who refuse to ever discuss the past. But this does not make it go away." Before Markie could decide if he was talking about Mrs. Saint and Simone or simply making an innocuous remark about people in general, he said, "Angeline tells me she did a very poor job of asking if you could have Lola in the evenings. She feels badly."

"Because I didn't say yes?"

He smiled again. "Certainly, she is sad about your answer. But I believe she feels most badly that her . . . quirks, shall we say, have gotten in the way of what is best for a child."

He turned again to watch Lola and Jesse running in the yard, and so did Markie, and for a few moments they were quiet as they stood together grinning at the two human airplanes and their yapping four-legged wingman.

"Such fun they have," Frédéric said. "Even at such different ages. I have often had the thought that they each would have enjoyed a sibling." Quickly, he turned to Markie and said, "Please. I am not Angeline. I am not asking if you thought of another child or why there is not one. I am only sharing what I have thought about each of them. I hope it is not an offensive thing."

"I know you're not Angeline," Markie said. "I've never lumped the two of you together. You are very different."

"She does mean well," he said. "But she is unfortunately not so able to relate things the way she intends. So tough and bossy! But this is not who she is, in her core."

"Well then, who *is* she, at her core?" Markie asked.

But Frédéric only smiled and let out a quiet laugh and gave Markie a look that said he would sooner face a firing squad than reveal something private about Angeline. It didn't surprise Markie, and just like when Ronda had refused to engage about Mrs. Saint's secretiveness, it didn't annoy her the way it did when it was the old woman herself who avoided the questions. The Defectives weren't the ones prying into

Markie's life while refusing to open up about their own. They were simply being loyal. Markie respected them for that, and in a way, she envied Mrs. Saint for having so many people in her life who were that devoted to watching out for her.

She smiled agreeably at Frédéric and decided to change the subject, but before she could speak again, the side door opened and Patty walked out, calling to Lola that it was time for them to leave. Lola's face sagged, and to Markie's surprise, Frédéric's did the same.

"Two minutes," Patty told Lola, who groaned, then took up running again after Jesse as Patty headed for Frédéric and Markie.

Angel stopped chasing the kids and darted to Patty's side, walking with her. "Hi there, Angel girl!" Patty said, reaching down to touch the dog's head. At the fence, she asked, "What are you two huddled up about?"

Frédéric shifted positions to include her in the discussion, but Patty squatted and took Angel's head between her hands, scratching her behind the ears. "You behaving?" she asked. She planted a kiss on the dog's forehead, then stood. Angel tried to jump up for more attention, but Patty held a flat palm to her. "Down," she said, "and sit." The dog sat. "So?" Patty asked, looking from Frédéric to Markie.

"Only visiting," Frédéric told Patty. "I was going to ask Markie how her job is going." To Markie, he said, "You are enjoying working from home, Jesse tells me."

Markie frowned. "I *was* enjoying it, but I'm afraid I'm not going to be for much longer. I'm not getting enough done at home, so I'm going to be forced to work downtown soon. I've been looking for other work-from-home options, but so far, no luck. I think there's about to be a cubicle at Global Insurance headquarters with my name on it." She pictured the cube prairie and scratched her arms.

"But why is this?" Frédéric asked.

"Because she refuses to accept help," Patty said. "She'd rather drag herself downtown and be miserable in a cube all day than let me take

Angel off her hands for a few hours." She smiled at Markie as if to say she still didn't get it but was still cool with it.

Frédéric looked at Markie for confirmation, and she shrugged.

"You do not like help," he said, and his tone was so matter-of-fact that it caught her off guard. Her parents had said the same five words to her many times, but it was always as an accusation, a judgment.

"Not when I can't pay for it," she said.

He inclined his chin. He understood—or at least, he acknowledged her feelings on the matter. "And do you feel payment for help must always be made in cash?" he asked.

"No," Markie said, "but I . . ." She stopped. She was going to say she couldn't think of a non-cash way to repay Patty, but of course, that was no longer true.

Markie locked eyes with Frédéric, and she could tell from the way he held his neck, stiffly and slightly to the left, that he was listening to the children playing behind him but was determined not to turn around and look at them. To bring her attention to the obvious. To use their laughter against her. That was something Mrs. Saint would do, and he was not, as he had said only moments ago, the same as she was. Mrs. Saint, who let her own quirks—her bossiness, her nosiness, her insistence on barging into other people's lives—get in the way of what was best for Lola.

"You do not like to be so involved with other people," Frédéric said, and again, it was a simple statement, devoid of judgment.

Markie didn't feel the impulse to defend herself to him. She didn't feel the urge to tell him she hadn't always been like this. That she didn't plan to stay like this, alone in her house, hiding from her neighbors, her colleagues, her parents, the rest of the world. Sometimes, even, from her son, and always, always from herself. That it was only something she needed now, until she could stand to look at herself again and could stand to have others look at her.

Frédéric tilted his head to one side and regarded her kindly, then reached for her hand again and held it between his. "It is every bit okay," he said.

He continued to look directly into her eyes, and Markie was certain he was telegraphing to her only kindness, understanding. That he was absolutely not trying to convey the message that *she* was the one who was like Angeline, letting her own quirks get in the way of what was best for Jesse.

He was Frédéric, after all, and he was not the type to send that message.

But she heard it, loud and clear.

"Patty," Markie said, not taking her eyes away from Frédéric's, "I have a proposition for you."

Chapter
Twenty-Eight

They were playing the Anything Game, and it was Lola's turn.

"The category is . . . ," she said, thinking. She looked around the room, and her eyes settled on Angel, who was sleeping on the living room floor. "Animals. And the word starts with *D*."

Jesse looked at Markie and shook his head. "Dinosaur?" he asked.

"Nope!" Lola said, trying not to make her delight too obvious. She took a bite of her sandwich to hide her smile.

"Dingo?" Markie tried.

Normally, an eight-year-old not living in Australia would probably have to ask what a dingo was. But they had been playing this game every night for the past three weeks, and Lola, after gazing around the room for ideas and landing on Angel, had used "category: animal, and letter: *D*" almost every one of those nights. There were surprisingly few animals that began with *D*, so they'd had occasion to discuss dingoes several times.

Other turns of Lola's included, after turning her head to look out the dining room window at the house on the other side of the fence,

"Category: men. Letter: *F*." Sometimes it was letter *B*. Or "Category: women. Letter, *M-R-S-S*." Or "*R*." Or "Category: boys. Letter, *J*."

Lola had shamed them into dinners at the table. At six on the first night she was there, she rose from the family room floor, where she and Jesse had been lying on their stomachs, her coloring and him flipping through a video-game magazine, and announced she was going to set the table.

"For what?" Jesse asked. "And what table? Our homework's all over the card table in here, and the dining room one is covered in my mom's work."

"At Mrs. Saint's, they eat dinner in the dining room," Lola said.

"Yeah, but where do you eat at *your* place?" Jesse said. "'Cause you never eat dinner at Mrs. Saint's. You guys always leave before dinner."

"Carol and I eat on the couch, mostly. But we live in an *apartment*. This is a *house*."

"What does that . . . ?" Jesse started, but by then, Markie had risen from the family room couch, where she had been reading, and walked to the dining room to clear three spots at the table, so she didn't hear the rest.

"Okay, Lola," Markie said, walking back to the family room. "The table's ready for you to set. We only need plates tonight since we're having pizza. Although, we do have . . ." She went to the kitchen, ripped three squares of paper towel from the roll beside the sink, and held them out. "There! Napkins. I think our place mats are in a box in the basement, so . . ." She shrugged, grabbed three plates out of the cupboard, and handed them to the girl.

Lola stared at the plates and paper towels. "At Mrs. Saint's, there's always a knife, fork, and spoon for everyone." Before Jesse could protest again, she told him, "I help Ronda set the table before I leave sometimes. You've even seen me do it." To Markie, she said, "Also a second plate. For the salad."

"Ah," Markie said, opening the fridge and peering in. "Sadly, I'm not sure we have anything that would pass for a salad at the moment."

She dragged out "at the moment" as though the issue was simply that Lola had asked on the wrong day. Jesse coughed from the family room, and although Markie couldn't make it out, she was pretty sure it was one of those "cough—LIAR!—cough" coughs.

"Ronda will have extra!" Lola said, dropping the plates and paper towels on the counter. "She told me I could come over anytime we needed anything."

Markie considered it a personal victory that she managed to stop herself from shrieking, "No!" and clutching her throat. Before she could think of a less dramatic way of expressing her horror at the thought of Mrs. Saint's house supplying the bungalow with food and, indeed, before she could even remind Lola to put shoes on, the girl was out the door and running across the patio.

While she was gone, Jesse groaned about the impending salad. Markie didn't like it any more than he did, but the little girl's life had already been thrown out of whack enough. If eating the kind of dinner she expected, given that Markie and Jesse lived in a house and not an apartment, helped the child regain her bearings somehow, then Markie and her son would suck it up, be prepared to choke down a few greens, and figure out what else to serve that would merit a knife, fork, and spoon.

Markie told Jesse all of this and added that, as he surely recalled, *he* was the reason Lola was there in the first place. It was parenting through guilt, and it had Lydia written all over it. Markie wasn't proud of this. But the boy shut up and headed to the pantry.

"Soup?" he suggested. "We could tick spoons off the list."

"Brilliant," she said. "And the salad will take care of the forks." She turned and reached for a loaf of bread, holding it up to show him. "I'll put some slices on a plate, and we can set the butter dish on the table. Knives."

"Nice," he said.

By the time Lola was back with a container of salad and a jar of homemade dressing, they had the table almost ready. They also had their attitudes adjusted enough that when the three of them sat down at the dining room table, it seemed like it was no big deal at all, Markie and Jesse eating there. Like they had been doing it all along. And they had been ever since, because Markie was not about to shatter an eight-year-old's illusions about what dinnertime in a house was like, and Jesse had been surprisingly pleased to go along with the act.

Markie had been trying to keep food from the other side of the fence from making its way to her side, but it was a losing battle. To prevent Lola from running next door for leftover salad each night, Markie had been buying lettuce, tomatoes, and carrots, and she had picked up three kinds of dressing. But that only meant there was a different angle of attack for her neighbors. Cucumbers showed up one night, so Markie bought two the next day, and soon radishes—cut into flower shapes, no less—came over.

She added some of those to her grocery list, and suddenly, shredded carrots, rather than the regular ones in Markie's crisper, became a must-have. Markie's canned soup dinners were one-upped by homemade broth and stew, and her grilled cheese was sent to the sidelines by Reubens, which Ronda delivered herself. And, of course, any dessert Markie bought—cookies, mini-muffins, ice cream—had a "made from scratch" version, transported over the fence in turns by Ronda, Mrs. Saint, or Bruce. Only Frédéric and Patty appeared to feel that whatever Markie came up with was adequate.

As offended as Markie was, she also felt vindicated, because not one food item had arrived from next door that any of them was actually willing to eat. Lola claimed she liked Ronda's salad dressing, but Jesse and Markie were sure that was only because Ronda's was the only dressing the girl had ever tasted. Jesse talked her into trying one of their store-bought kinds, and after that, although Lola obediently carried

containers of dressing over anytime Ronda made some, Markie had seen her pouring it down the sink, then reaching into the fridge for a bottle from the store.

The kids had taken to spending half an hour after dinner on "kitchen experiments," which basically consisted of their trying to come up with ways to make Ronda's offerings edible. Maple syrup and chocolate sauce had become anchor tenants on Markie's grocery list; there was almost nothing that couldn't be made tolerable by drowning it in some form of liquid sugar.

Almost. One night, Markie heard Lola tell Jesse, "Maybe whipped cream would make the difference. Do you have any of that?"

To which Jesse responded, "I think we need to just give up on this one."

Each night, after the food experiments were over and the three of them had cleaned the kitchen, Jesse spread his homework out on a card table he had carried up from the basement and set up in the family room. For at least an hour, he worked on his homework while Lola, having finished her work sheets before dinner at Mrs. Saint's, sat with him, crayons and coloring books spread before her. Markie had taken to settling nearby on the family-room couch with a book.

Jesse had acted surprised to see his mother follow them into the family room on Lola's first night. "I figured you'd want to hide from the noise," he said, "in the living room or even way up in your room."

"I'm prepared to retreat if you two get carried away," she told him. "But I think it's better for Lola to have me nearby. In case she feels homesick and wants a mom figure around."

"You're not exactly the mom figure she's used to," he said.

"Still," she said.

Each time Lola finished coloring both sides of a page, she ripped it out of the book, carefully printed her name in the top right corner, and set it to the side. Most nights, she ended up with a considerable pile of finished pictures. When she was tired of coloring, she went through an elaborate

process of examining the front and back sides of each finished page to decide which had turned out best. After that, she put herself through a seemingly heartrending task of deciding who would get each one.

Frédéric received the most, and also her best ones; no stray crayon marks outside the lines, no people with green faces or purple arms. The rejects went to everyone else. Mrs. Saint had a number on her fridge, Lola told Markie the first night she presented one to her, and Bruce and Ronda had assured the child that their fridges were covered in her artwork as well. Markie got the hint and clipped the picture to the front of the fridge with a magnet.

"And Frédéric takes all of his to the basement right away," Lola said, beaming. "And he puts them on the walls."

Markie recalled Jesse saying Frédéric had a workshop in the basement and asked Lola if that's where her pictures were hanging.

"Some are," the girl said. "And some are in his room."

"What do you mean, 'his room'?" Jesse said.

Lola's brow furrowed as she regarded Jesse, the World's Stupidest Boy. "His bedroom," she said, leaving off "you idiot" but clearly thinking it.

"Frédéric *lives there*?" Jesse and Markie said at the same time.

"*Mais oui,*" Lola said. "Where else would he live?"

Jesse lifted his hands in a "Where do I begin?" way.

But he stopped himself before he blurted out his list of alternatives, and he angled his chin to one side, considering. Then he let his hands fall to his lap and bent back to his homework. Not, Markie assumed, because he had decided it wasn't worth the effort to school an eight-year-old on the many living-arrangement options available to an adult man. But, because, after reflection, he had reached the same conclusion his mother had come to: Lola was right. Where else would Frédéric live if not at Mrs. Saint's?

"Don't forget Monopoly tonight," Lola said. "Since I got those two math pages done without, you know . . ."

"Whining?" Jesse said, not looking up from his homework.

Lola kicked him under the table. "Monopoly," she said. "You promised."

If she did a good job with her homework after school and then colored quietly while he did his assignments, he let her choose a board game to play for fifteen minutes or so before her bath time. The two of them had traipsed down to the basement at first, choosing a game from one of the packing boxes, bringing it upstairs to play, and returning it to its box downstairs. Markie felt like she was reliving his childhood as they made their way from Sorry! and Connect Four to mancala and Apples to Apples and Clue Junior.

They had moved on to Monopoly a few nights earlier, and Jesse had told Lola that if she could grasp that one, they would pull out Settlers of Cataan next. The prospect of being promoted to such a "big kid game" had thrilled Lola, and she had been attacking Monopoly with a quiet ferocity, determined to earn her prize. They had tired of fetching and replacing one game at a time from the basement, and after about a week, Jesse carried up all three of their boxes of games and puzzles, plonking them down in a corner of the family room. After that, they decided it was a pain to have to dig through the boxes, so they stacked them, open side out, against the wall, and then they restacked the games into neat piles inside for easier viewing and access. It was a far cry from the walnut built-ins in their old house.

"Not bad, right?" Jesse had said one night as he and Markie regarded the makeshift shelving unit after Lola went to bed. "I thought it was going to really suck, but it doesn't. I mean, it's not perfect, but it's, like, good enough." At first she thought he was only remarking on the practicality of what he had done with the games. But he put an arm around her, pulled her close, and tipped his head sideways until it rested on hers, and suddenly she had the feeling he wasn't commenting on the way he had arranged the games.

He was telling her he didn't need walnut built-ins. Or cathedral ceilings. Or his private school. He was telling her he didn't blame her anymore.

Chapter Twenty-Nine

Patty had been getting to the bungalow later and later: one, one thirty, two, two thirty. She was apologetic each time, but Markie had been waving her off, partly because at that hour she was too tired to engage in discussion, and partly because it wasn't like having the entire household woken at two a.m. was appreciably different from having it happen at one thirty. She had yet to figure out how to get Lola downstairs from the guest room and out the door without Angel rousing, barking, and waking Jesse.

"I'm really sorry," Patty said as Markie opened the door at three fifteen one night. Taking a whimpering Lola in her arms, she said, "I really wanted to turn down the . . . overtime. But I can't afford it. Carol's back to her old tricks again."

"Oh, right," Markie said, as though she had any idea what Patty meant or the energy to be curious about it.

She intended to wave good night and shut the door, as she always did, but Patty didn't move from the doorway, and Markie saw Patty's lips part as though she had more to say. Markie was too tired to hear more, but she didn't let on. The woman in her doorway was the sole

reason she was still pulling off her work-from-home position. Patty had been taking Angel for such long walks every morning that the dog snored in her crate for the rest of the day while Markie tore through file after file. Her last file-swap session downtown had gone as well as she could have hoped; instead of accosting her in the hallway and insisting they "interface," Gregory had merely waved from someone's cube and called out, "Nice to see you back on track!"

"Do you want to talk about it?" Markie asked. "About your mom, I mean?"

She leaned on the open door and tried to keep her eyes open. It wasn't exactly active listening, but it was the best she could do.

"Nothing much to discuss," Patty said. "She's an addict."

Her directness woke Markie on the spot. "She spends her Social Security check before she even collects it," Patty said. "And then she takes out loans from the wrong kinds of people and gives my name when they try to collect. Carol's sometimes got herself under control, but she goes through these rough patches now and then, and she's in one now."

Markie tried to think of how to respond. How did Carol sleep at night, she wondered, knowing her daughter was working extra shifts to cover her debts?

"I'm really sorry," she said. *And I will never complain about Lydia again.*

"Anyway," Patty said, "I just wanted you to know I'm not showing up late because I'm inconsiderate. If you want to stop our . . . deal because of this, I'll understand. I feel terrible, getting you all up so late."

"It's fine," Markie said.

A few nights later, Patty arrived close to four a.m. Lola held her arms out, ready for her mother to lift her, but Patty didn't pick her up, and instead, she asked Markie if Lola could stay in the house while Patty slept in her car in the driveway.

"What?" Markie asked. "Why? Are you . . . is there some reason you can't drive?"

"I can drive fine. I just can't get into my apartment. Carol and I got into it about something before I left tonight, and she took my keys and locked me out."

"How did you start the car?"

"Oh, I keep spares hidden. This is one of Carol's favorite tricks. But I forgot to put the extra apartment key back last time I needed to use it."

"Just come in," Markie said. "You can sleep with Lola or on the couch. You're not sleeping in your car."

"I've done it a million times. Lola, too."

"Not on my watch," Markie said, motioning her in. "Couch or Lola's room? Guest room, I mean."

"I'll sleep with her," Patty said. "So if she wakes up and freaks out, I'll be there."

⚜

Far from being upset about waking in the bungalow, Lola skipped into the kitchen in the morning as though she had been starting every day there for years. She said good morning to Markie, who was at the counter with a cup of coffee, and trotted to the card table in the family room to sort through her stack of coloring pages. She held one out to Markie and clutched the others in her fist as she made her way to the door.

"Can you tell Jesse I'll see him next door for school pickup?" she asked, sliding one foot into a shoe.

"You can eat breakfast here if you want, you know," Markie said. "We have cereal and toast. And I think there are frozen waffles."

Lola slid her other shoe on. "Ronda's making oatmeal," she said. "She always makes it for me when it's cold out."

"Oh," Markie said, "is oatmeal your favorite?"

Lola ran back to the counter, leaned close to Markie, and whispered, "Not when Ronda makes it!" Giggling, she raced back to the door to let herself out. "See you after school," she said, tossing Markie a smile and a wave before she disappeared the same way she had arrived, as though she had been doing it forever.

Chapter Thirty

Lydia couldn't comprehend why Markie didn't want to go home for Thanksgiving.

"We *are* home," Markie said, and Lydia laughed as though her daughter had said something ridiculous.

"You always spend Thanksgiving with us. And what about Jesse?"

"He's gotten used to a quiet house," Markie said. "He'll be fine."

"But your father. Have you ever even cooked a turkey?"

"I'm forty-five years old, Mother. Anyway, there's the dog this year, and Jesse has this project he's working on, and . . ."

She looked around the house for more excuses. Water leak, small electrical fire, hole in the roof—any of these would be welcome. If Lydia had called a week earlier, Markie could have milked her sprained ankle and crutches, but a few days before her mother reached out, the doctor had finally declared Markie healed enough to drop the sticks and start putting weight on her leg. She now wore a walking boot and was getting along quite well. And she remained unwilling to lie to her mother. She steered clear of the direct route—telling Lydia she couldn't take a long weekend of passive-aggressive digs from her about the life choices she should have made or lectures from her father on money management and career advancement. Not to mention the McLarens and the Wilsons and the other friends who would parade through the front

door all weekend for her parents' annual Thanksgiving open house. Ice tinkling in glasses, voices getting louder and tongues looser as Clayton kept the drinks flowing and they all went through the predictable comparison of the successes and failures of their children and grandchildren. It had been difficult enough when Markie was on the success list.

Lydia wouldn't appreciate that kind of frankness, but not because it would hurt her feelings to learn Markie didn't like their group of friends. She was Teflon, Markie's mother; insults slid right off her, and before they hit the floor, they morphed into cutting remarks designed to let Markie know that any problem she had with her parents' friends was actually a problem of her own. If she couldn't get along with the McLarens or the Wilsons, well, then, cue the long sigh as Lydia struggled to accept the fact that despite all they had done for her, Markie was simply not the daughter they had hoped for. As for Markie not liking how her parents spoke to her, Lydia wouldn't even hear that part, having long trained her inner ear not to detect any noise approximating criticism directed at her or Clayton.

"But I thought we'd invite Kyle," Lydia said.

"You used to ask me *not* to bring him home for Thanksgiving! Now we're divorced and suddenly you want him there?"

Lydia sniffed. "I just think a nice family holiday would make the two of you see what you've given up."

"We're not getting back together, Mom."

Until recently, she would have added that they were barely speaking. But that was no longer the case, as these days they were interacting quite nicely. Markie didn't think this was the time to tell her mother, though. Lydia would only use it as an opening to push harder for their reconciliation, and Markie was never going to reunite with Kyle, even if the sight of him at the bungalow's side door now made her smile rather than scowl.

A few days after their talk in the coffee shop, and after a number of imploring texts and phone calls from Markie, Kyle had finally agreed

to come over to visit Jesse. By then, she had given some thought to his situation, and she'd had a lightbulb moment when her father mentioned over Skype how handy Kyle was. When he arrived, she greeted him with a welcoming smile and a list of repairs he and Jesse could work on: replace the broken window in the garage, change the filter on the furnace, fix the leaking hot water faucet in the upstairs bathroom. "Frédéric said he'd be happy to lend you his tools," she told him.

While Markie reviewed files on the patio that afternoon, she could hear the sounds of wood being sawed, nails being hammered, and a father and son talking and, from time to time, laughing. When she asked Kyle about it on the phone later, he told her he had never had an easier time relating to his son as he did that day, when their hands were full of tools and their attention was on a broken window frame or a loose pipe. "Sure beats staring at each other in my matchbox of a living room," he said.

He agreed to return the following week, and although he flaked out at the last minute, he made a point to ask for a rain check, something he had never done before. When the new date arrived, he was at the bungalow door at the scheduled time, his own toolbox in hand, with a list of his own. "I noticed a few other things when I was here last," he said.

"Terrific!" Markie said, turning to the basement door to call Jesse.

"Wait," Kyle said. "Before you get him up here." Markie spun around to face him. "I just want to say that I know it's not enough," he said, gesturing to the piece of paper in his hand. She could see his jaw muscle flexing as he struggled, either to find his next words or with the memory of what he had done. Without turning, she called to Jesse.

"He's here?" the boy yelled back, his excitement palpable.

Markie smiled at Kyle and said, "But it's a good start."

"We'll buy the plane tickets," Lydia said now, unwilling to drop the matter. "For Kyle, too."

"I can't let you do that."

"Would you rather drive? It's such a long way."

"I've got to go, Mom."

"What a shame for Jesse to lose his traditions along with his family," Lydia said, in lieu of goodbye.

That night, instead of waking Lola when Patty knocked, Markie let the girl sleep and hurried down to answer the door before Angel woke. "I thought you might want to stay over again, in case Carol took the key, or—"

Patty grinned. "Outsmarted her. Made a few copies and hid them in the car. She can try to keep us out, but it's not going to work."

"Do you really want to go through all that?" Markie asked. "Because you could stay here instead. Lola could sleep the whole night, and you wouldn't have to deal with your mother. Would be a lot easier, right?" She took a step back and gestured for Patty to come inside.

Patty didn't move. "I don't want to put you out just because I've got a difficult mother."

"Believe me, you're not the only one."

"Yeah," Patty said with a laugh, "I'm sure your mom's always getting faded and stealing your money and hiding your keys."

"The details might be different, but the difficulty is pretty much the same." Markie took another step away from the door, clearing the way for Patty to come in.

"Well," Patty said tentatively, still not moving, "it was kind of nice having a shower with actual water pressure that morning I was here. It trickles out at our place, and if the neighbor beats me to it, it's cold by the time I get in."

"Lola and I just put clean towels in the bathroom tonight," Markie said.

"That's good you're putting her to work."

"I didn't intend to. She insisted. She's apparently fascinated by the washer and dryer."

"She's fascinated by a lot of things over here," Patty said. "I'd hate for her to get too comfortable. Count on staying all the time." But she took a step inside, closing the door behind her.

The next morning, Markie was refilling her coffee mug when Patty, back from walking the dog and finished with her shower, came downstairs.

"You want a cup?" Markie asked.

"Mrs. Saint'll have my head for drinking coffee with you over here instead of dragging you to her place," Patty said.

"I won't tell if you don't."

"I'm not really the drag-someone-somewhere type, anyway," Patty said. "I'm more of the live-and-let-live mentality. And you're the drink-your-coffee-alone type, I happen to know. So you do that, and I'll go next door and yuk it up with the others."

"No," Markie said, "really. Stay and have a cup. An entire *group* I'm not keen on, but if it's just one person . . ."

Which wasn't completely true. There wasn't anyone she was eager to have coffee with, even if it were only the two of them. Except for Patty. The conversations they'd had lately—when Patty stayed over, or when she came to get Angel for her walk—had made Markie see that there was something different about her. Patty had an easiness, a certain level of self-acceptance, that most people, in Markie's experience, didn't have, even though plenty pretended they did. Patty wasn't embarrassed or apologetic about her crazy addict of a mother or the conditions under which she was raising her daughter.

And she seemed equally nonjudgmental about other people. She spoke only respectfully about Mrs. Saint, Ronda, Bruce, and Frédéric, despite their peculiarities, and she had never given the impression she thought Markie was odd because of her hermitlike existence or her refusal to accept help from, or socialize with, the people on the other side of the fence. Anyone could say something pithy like "Live and let live," but as far as Markie was concerned, Patty was the only person she

had ever met who actually meant it. It made being around her feel so freeing and uncomplicated that Markie had noticed their visits getting longer and longer only because the clock told her so and not because she found herself feeling anxious and claustrophobic the way she did when conversations with other people started dragging on.

Being around her had even made Markie lighten up on herself a little. Patty didn't look sideways at Markie's faded, tight yoga pants or her messy ponytail or her freezer piled with frozen pizzas, so Markie didn't frown at herself in the mirror as often or gulp with guilt at the contents of her grocery cart. It was such a change from her old life and the censorious gazes of Lydia and the Mothers' Club—looks that had caused Markie to spend years doubting her outfits, her hairstyles, her entire being. It made her cringe to think she had aimed the same stare of condemnation at other women, both at Saint Mark's and in her fancy neighborhood. She wished she had met Patty years ago. She'd have been a happier person with Patty in her life. And a better one.

Chapter Thirty-One

Perspective. A month earlier, the thought of spending an entire day shopping and cooking would have made Markie want to take a long nap. But the day before Thanksgiving, as she unloaded sweet potatoes and onions and flour and cranberries and oranges onto the kitchen counter, she felt positively giddy at the prospect of devoting the rest of her day to making sweet potato casserole, rolls, and cranberry sauce for the next day. Having escaped a weekend of blame and shame at her parents' house, she felt lighter than air and filled with an energy she hadn't experienced in a long time.

To everyone's surprise, she had accepted Mrs. Saint's invitation for Thanksgiving dinner. So had Frédéric—no shock there—along with Ronda and Bruce, which was also nothing new. But Patty's and Lola's presence would be a first. They had resumed spending nights in their own apartment, and things had been okay between Patty and her mother, but recently, Carol had started seeing a man who frightened Lola and made Patty feel she should count her spare change and inventory the contents of the medicine cabinet before she left each day. Carol

insisted on having him over for the holiday, so Markie invited Patty and Lola to stay with her and Jesse for the long weekend.

Markie wasn't a good enough cook to pull off an entire Thanksgiving meal on her own, but after her mother's guilt trip, she couldn't bear to allow Jesse—or Lola, for that matter—to spend the day in the bungalow eating sliced turkey on bagels when they all knew there would be an enormous holiday feast being served on the other side of the fence. So she had agreed to show up on the holiday with a few side dishes and the membership of her house. Even Angel was invited.

Markie was folding the grocery bags when Mrs. Saint knocked at the side door, then let herself in.

"I have brought recipes," the older woman said, producing a thin stack of recipe cards from her coat pocket.

Instead of snapping back that she would follow her own cookbooks, Markie decided to negotiate a bit and trade her compliance for some information. Eyeing the cards the old woman held out but not taking them, Markie said, "Lola tells me Frédéric lives with you."

"Of course he does," Mrs. Saint said, in the same "duh" tone Lola had used when discussing the topic with Jesse.

Mrs. Saint stepped to the kitchen counter and sorted through her cards, searching. "So. For the sweet potato. I do not want marshmallows on top. You Americans are always looking for ways to take a perfectly acceptable vay-gay-tay-ble and turn it into a candy." She curled her lip. "This will not do."

She found the recipe she was after and set it on the counter. "Here. For the casserole. And . . ." She paused while she looked for another card. "Aha! Yes, here." She set another card down. "For the rolls."

Markie scanned the ingredients on the second card. "Yeast" was underlined twice and circled, and she imagined there had been some paperweight-like rolls served next door after Ronda forgot this key ingredient. She pushed the cards toward their owner.

"I find it odd that all this time you've never mentioned he actually lives there. Or where it is that he goes in the afternoons. You want all this information about me and Jesse, yet—"

"Ah," Mrs. Saint said, smiling patiently as though Markie were a child struggling to comprehend the difference between a circle and a square. "But you are not asking about *me*. You are asking about Frédéric."

"Oh, come on! You had no problem telling me things about Ronda and Bruce. And Patty."

Still smiling tolerantly, Mrs. Saint placed a dry, cold palm on the back of Markie's hand, letting it rest there. "*Mais oui*. But there is a difference between the kind of telling that will hurt a person and the kind that will not."

Markie, finally, smiled back. "Yes, that's true."

"But I can tell you this about Frédéric," Mrs. Saint said. "He does not live with me because he is not able to live by his own self or because he cannot afford. He came here for a very good job many years ago, and over this time, he saved much money. And, also, as you have known by now, he is most capable. He lives with me only because he wants me to be safe always. And he trusts this job to no other person."

"Came here for a job?" Markie repeated. "You mean, from Canada? You told me you've known him for many years. Did he grow up there, too? Did you and Edouard move here first? Is that why Frédéric came, so he could be closer to the two of you?"

"About Canada," Mrs. Saint said. "I want to tell you about this, too—"

The side door burst open then, and Patty rushed in, out of breath, Angel running ahead of her.

"And now I must go," Mrs. Saint said. "We will talk of this another time."

"Did you run?" Markie asked Patty when the older woman was gone.

"No," Patty said, still panting. "I carried this."

She pointed to something sitting outside, and before Markie could get to the door, Patty was through it, heaving a wooden bookcase inside. It was small and squat, with only three shelves, but from the way Patty was straining, Markie could tell it was made of solid wood.

"It needs a good wipe-down," Patty said. "But it's a great piece. Better than cardboard, wouldn't you say?" She pointed to the kids' makeshift game shelf in the corner. "I garbage-picked it. Curb retail, I call it. Why spend money when you can spend a little time and energy instead?"

Clearly pleased with herself, she trotted to the kitchen to dampen a paper towel, then returned to the shelves, running the towel over every inch. Before Markie could decide whether she wanted to furnish the bungalow with other people's castoffs, she found herself helping a cheerful Patty push the new unit into place against the wall and transfer the games over. When they were finished, they stood back to admire the scene.

"Much better than cardboard!" Markie said, realizing, to her surprise, how little she actually cared about the origins of the thing.

Together, they carried the empty cardboard boxes back to the basement, and while they were down there, Patty noticed the corner where all of Markie's artwork sat, still boxed up, waiting to be loaded onto the moving truck.

"You mind if I . . . ?" Patty asked, a hand on one of the boxes.

"Go ahead."

"Whoa," Patty said, lifting out a painting. "Mother and girl. Or Madonna, right? That's what they call her? You don't see that too often, do you? Isn't she usually holding a boy?"

Markie smiled. "She's *always* holding a boy. Can you believe that's supposed to be one? The artist got carried away with the curls, I guess, and ended up with a very feminine-looking boy. That's why I got it for such a good price, because it's a reject. I was in this gallery looking for

some things for the nursery after we learned Jesse's gender, and that's the first thing I saw. I bought it anyway, since it was marked down to almost nothing, and I thought, Why not? We might have a girl next. We didn't, obviously, and I never hung that one. I didn't get one for Jesse's nursery, either. I ended up going with a Noah's Ark theme and stopped looking for a proper Madonna. Anyway, the rest"—she swept her hand over all of the boxes marked ARTWORK—"were all hanging in our old house. That one's lived in a box since the day I bought it. Kind of a shame, now that I think of it."

Patty held the painting in both hands, extending her arms so she could admire it. "Reject or not, it's beautiful. I love how the gold in the baby's hair is the same as the gold in the frame. The whole thing is just so . . . hopeful, isn't it? I don't know if that's the word, but it just kind of reaches out and grabs you and makes you stare at it."

Markie nodded. It was what had drawn her to the painting—how joyful it was, not only in its color but in its mood. Since she had first laid eyes on the painting, she had thought of it anytime she heard the word *radiant*. She said the same to Patty.

"Radiant," Patty repeated, still gazing at the painting. "Yeah, that's the word for it. Not reject Madonna. *Radiant Madonna*." She set it gently back in the box and gestured toward the rest of Markie's collection of paintings. "This kind of thing—real art—you don't run across in 'curb retail'! And I'd never spend good money on things like this because Carol'd sell it all out from under me in a flash. Not that she'd appreciate the real value and ask enough for it."

"Oh, none of it's worth anything," Markie said. "It's all just cheap stuff I've collected over the years. I think the Madonna one was ten bucks."

Patty lifted the picture out of the box again, gazed at it for a moment, and then put it back, patting its gold frame. "Well," she said, turning to the next painting, "you've got some real nice things. Valuable or not."

"Do you want to hang *Radiant Madonna* in your room?" Markie asked. She pointed upstairs to the second-floor guest room.

"Oh no, I couldn't—"

"Really. I mean, if it doesn't hang on the wall of a room shared by a mother and daughter, where else is it going to go?"

"Well, that's a fair point."

"I have picture hooks," Markie said. "In that smaller box by your right foot. There, at the top, in that envelope. And there's a little hammer in there, too."

"Organized," Patty said.

"Sometimes," Markie said. "Not lately. Hence all the artwork still in boxes in the basement."

She refrained from adding that Frédéric had been willing to hang it all months ago and she wouldn't let him. And then she thought, *What the hell?* It was Patty she was talking to.

"Actually," she said, "lack of organization isn't the reason it's all still down here. Frédéric was all set to cover the walls the day we moved in. But I didn't feel like . . . I don't know, committing."

"To the bungalow?"

"To anything," Markie said. "Including myself."

"Yeah," Patty said. "I got that feeling from you."

Markie reached a hand up to touch her hair.

"I didn't mean outward stuff," Patty said, making a face as if to say, *Who cares about* that *kind of thing?* "I just meant sometimes you seem . . . not entirely here." Markie bit her lip, and Patty quickly added, "Look, you're not the first person who's wanted to check out of your life for a while, you know. And as far as I can tell, you've picked about the least bad way to do it.

"Believe me. I live with someone who's chosen some pretty dangerous ways to disappear from what she doesn't like. And not just dangerous. Expensive. Not to mention illegal. If the worst you've done is hole up on your own rather than throwing parties on the patio and inviting

the entire neighborhood over, or kept your paintings all boxed up in the basement instead of decorating the place with them . . ."

"That's not the worst I've done."

Patty put a hand on her hip. "Oh, really? So what, then? You get stoned and let your grandbaby crawl out of the apartment? You fight with your dealer and have him push you down the stairs so you end up in the ER? Steal money from your kid? Get arrested?"

"Nothing that bad."

"Then there's no reason for you to stand there looking like you're sorry. There's nothing worth apologizing for. To me, to yourself, or to anyone else." Patty locked eyes with Markie and added, "Including that boy of yours."

Markie had made some assumptions about Patty long before they had ever spoken, the kinds of things one (or at least, one from the Saint Mark's circle) concludes about a woman who wears skintight jeans and low-cut blouses, who smokes a pack a day and lets other people raise her child. One of those assumptions was that when Patty spoke, all that would come out of her mouth was poor grammar and a cigarette-induced rasp, possibly a string of expletives. Nothing, certainly, of real substance.

She had been right about the hoarseness and the grammar. Wrong about the swearing, and so, so wrong about the lack of substance. And she knew, suddenly, with absolute certainty, that Patty knew this. That she knew how she had been judged in Markie's eyes, knew that women like Markie expected nothing of value from her. That she had figured out long ago what the assumptions were behind the looks she got, and what names were being used behind her back.

"God," Markie said, "I've been so—"

But Patty shook her head. "You heard me. Nothing worth apologizing for." She reached into the small box for the packet of picture-hanging nails and the hammer, tucked the *Radiant Madonna* under her

arm, and headed for the basement stairs. "It's not how we got here," she said as she went. "Or even that we *are* here. It's where we go *from* here."

A few minutes later, Markie stood smiling contentedly at the kitchen counter, alternately mixing ingredients for the casserole and wiping tears from her eyes as the tap tap tap of the little hammer sounded from the floor above.

Chapter Thirty-Two

Markie reached for the cooking oil to discover she was out, so she called upstairs to tell Patty she was going to the store. It wasn't until she reached the parking lot that she realized it was midday and she wasn't feeling self-conscious about being out in plain view. She even felt prepared to trade pleasantries with the cashier! She watched her reflection in the front window of the store and swore she could see a bounce in her step, even with the walking boot.

And she didn't look half bad, either, since she had put her hair up into a tidy bun before she left instead of leaving it in her usual haphazard ponytail. The sweatshirt she wore wasn't torn or stained or two sizes two big. Her socks matched. She had even put on earrings. And her grocery list—cooking oil, yeast, and paprika, plus extra toilet paper and toothpaste for her houseguests, a bottle of Lola's favorite bubble bath, and a new box of crayons—made her feel like she had plans, a life. Her usual list made her feel like a shut-in.

For the first time in half a year, she allowed herself to meander through the entire store rather than scurrying into the freezer aisle and out again before anyone noticed her. In the baking aisle, she found the

oil and spices she needed, then added pancake mix to her cart along with ingredients to make muffins and cookies. In the household section, along with the basic toiletries for the upstairs bathroom, she found little soaps for the sink, a matching set of hand towels, and a candle.

She bought a cactus for the kitchen windowsill, too, and two packages of magnetized letters for the fridge. They could serve double duty: spelling practice for Lola and a means to hold up any new coloring pages the girl gifted to Jesse and Markie. In the produce section, she chose a carton of strawberries to go with their pancakes and added some oranges and grapefruits, thinking Lola might find it fun to squeeze them into fresh juice.

Picturing Lola standing on a chair at the kitchen counter making juice brought to mind all the times Markie had begged her mother to let her help in the kitchen. But Lydia didn't want her counters or her child to end up covered in flour, and Clayton didn't like the idea of "greasy little fingers" all over his bread dough. Markie added a child-size rolling pin to her cart, then added a larger one in case Jesse wanted to help, too. He wouldn't want to dress the part, of course, but she found small pink oven mitts and a matching apron for the eight-year-old who would. She estimated her cart total in her head and decided she could afford to splurge on one more small thing, either cookie cutters or autumn-themed muffin cups. Then she pictured Lola's face and decided to buy both.

At home, she met Jesse and Lola, who were on their way back from Mrs. Saint's, and they all walked in together, Markie stooping to set the grocery bags on the floor. Patty jogged into the kitchen to greet them, Angel trailing her.

"Check it out," she said. "I made a few . . . changes."

"Whoa!" Jesse said.

It was an overreaction for a set of garbage-picked shelves, Markie thought, but when she lifted her eyes, she saw he was reacting to something else. Patty had hung a quarter of the art collection in the family

room, and the once-empty walls were now crowded with color and texture as giant oils elbowed their way against small photo prints, and ornate gilt-edged frames cozied up to ones made of rustic wood or black lacquer.

"Wow!" Markie said.

She had always been a minimalist decorator, following the example of her mother in erring on the side of too many large swaths of empty space rather than overcrowding. She had also always complied with Lydia's imperative that one mustn't assault the senses by mixing too many patterns or colors or textures in the same small area. In Markie's old house, just as at Lydia and Clayton's, all of the black-framed pictures occupied one wall, with the brown, wood-framed pieces warranting their own separate section, while the gilt-edged ones took up occupancy far away, to prevent cross-visualization.

"Busy is never a good thing when it comes to decorating," Lydia liked to say. "Simple is always better."

Patty had followed none of Lydia's rules. Her artistic vision was a study in diversity, busyness, and complication.

"What do you think?" Patty asked.

"Whoa," Jesse said again. "It looks as though someone actually, like, *lives* here now." Quickly, he turned to his mother, adding, "I mean . . . I didn't mean . . . I only meant . . ."

Markie laughed. "I get it. And you're right. It does feel like that."

"I love it!" Lola said, moving slowly around the room to examine each piece. "I never saw so many arts in one room in all my life! Where'd you get it all?"

"It's all Markie's," Patty said. "It's been in the basement."

Lola spun to face Markie, her mouth an accusatory *O*. Markie felt pathetic.

"They just moved in, remember," Patty said, and Lola's lips closed into a forgiving smile as she went back to her slow tour of the art.

"I don't remember the shelves," Jesse said.

"Acquired today," Patty said. "By me and Angel."

"From . . . ?" he asked.

"Someone's curb," Patty said.

"Nice," Jesse told her, and Lola echoed him.

"You like it?" Patty asked. "Not everyone wants secondhand stuff."

Markie felt her cheeks flush and wondered if something in her expression had given her away earlier, when Patty had first arrived with the shelves. Or was it that Jesse had come off as a spoiled rich kid? He did that from time to time, and Patty would definitely pick up on it.

"Why not? Way cheaper," Jesse said, saving himself and, Markie hoped, his mother.

"And way more interesting," Patty said, holding up her right hand to show off an old-looking silver ring she wore. "I love old, quirky things."

"Hey!" Jesse crossed the room to her in a single stride, reaching for her finger. "That's the one I found behind Mrs. Saint's garage! She gave it to you? I thought it was in her special suitcase where she keeps all her important things."

"She told me it was her Edouard's mother's," Patty said, holding her hand out, fingers straight, so they could all admire it. "She said she wanted me to have it. It's from '*ta famille*,' she told me, so I should wear it. I'm not really sure what that means"—she turned her hand and admired the ring herself—"but you can bet I thanked her anyway and took it!"

Later, when the kids had raced outside with Angel, Patty showed Markie the ring again. "I wonder why she gave it to me. Maybe she senses she's . . . slipping. She won't say what they told her when she spent the night in the hospital. If Frédéric knows, he's not talking, either."

She stared at her hand, her chin twitching, and Markie was surprised to find herself overcome by emotion as well at the thought of losing the old woman. Four months ago, she would have paid for someone

to swoop in and remove Mrs. Saint from the property next door. Her and all of her "Defectives."

They were quiet for a while, until Markie finally said, "Thanks so much for hanging the art. It makes the room feel so much warmer."

Patty smiled. "Wait'll you see the rest."

She turned toward the archway leading to the living/dining room. Markie couldn't believe it: Patty had hung the rest of the collection, filling the walls of every room and hallway, all in the same crazy mixed-up arrangement she had used in the family room, with professionally matted Matisse reproductions next to art projects Jesse had brought home in kindergarten, framed with Popsicle sticks.

As for the effort of hanging all of the pieces only to have to pack them all back up again in a few months, so what? It wasn't Markie's efforts that had gotten them onto the walls. And although she had already mentally rehearsed her "No, thank you" for when Mrs. Saint offered to send Frédéric and Bruce over in February to pack up the bungalow, she was starting to think, as she followed Patty around and heard her chatter excitedly about why she had put this painting here, that sketch there, that Patty might enjoy packing them all back up again later.

Maybe she would even want to come to the new place and rehang them. As payment, Markie decided, she would give Patty the *Radiant Madonna*. If Carol sold it, so what? At least Patty would enjoy it before then. And maybe she could hang it somewhere in Mrs. Saint's house to keep it safe from her mother.

"I ran out of nails," Patty told Markie once they were back in the kitchen, "so there's some stuff still in a box downstairs. I've seen people prop frames up against the wall instead of hanging them, but I didn't know what you'd think about that."

"What do *you* think about it?" Markie asked.

"I think we should go for it."

"Then let's. But first I need to put all this stuff away."

They hoisted the grocery bags onto the counter, and Markie reached into one and produced the little pink baking mitts. "You think Lola will want to help me bake a few things?"

Patty eyed the mitts and grinned. "I think your eardrums are going to hurt for a long time after she squeals about those. And the chance to help in the kitchen. Can't say she ever gets to do that at my place. I didn't grow up like that."

"Me neither," Markie said.

"But that's not stopping you," Patty said. She thought for a moment before she spoke again. "I feel like I could learn something from you. How to break the cycle. How to not treat her like I was treated so she doesn't go on to raise her kids the same crummy way." She ran a finger over the stitching on one of the oven mitts. "I tell myself it's fine if I'm not with her all the time, not really paying that careful of attention. Carol left me alone more than I do Lola, and I turned out okay.

"But I can't look you in the eyes and say I wasn't lonely when I was a kid. Scared, too, sometimes. I can't tell you I didn't wish for a mom who did things like this, someone who bought me oven mitts and cookie cutters and let me help her roll out dough and mix muffins. I mean, sometimes, I think . . ." Patty's eyelids fluttered closed briefly, then opened. "Maybe this'll sound kind of dramatic. But sometimes I think I didn't really have much of a childhood."

"Not so dramatic," Markie said. "I've had that thought about myself, and I had it a lot easier than you."

Patty smiled gratefully. "I get these . . . twinges. This feeling I should do more than I'm doing to make sure Lola gets to be a kid. I think I could be better. A better mom, I mean. Different from Carol. But anytime I try to think of how, I never seem to come up with anything.

"I'm not one for reading out loud or helping with homework or playing those crazy made-up games she always wants to play. I'll never be that kind of mom." She gestured to the baking supplies. "I wouldn't

have ever thought of something like this. Of asking her to make stuff in the kitchen with me."

Markie held out the baking mitts, apron, and rolling pin. "Why don't you ask her now?"

"Oh no," Patty said, stepping back. "This was your idea. And you paid."

Markie touched a hand to Patty's. "And *you* made this place look, in the words of my son, 'as though someone actually, like, *lives* here.'" She pointed to the sink full of sweet potatoes and the stack of recipe cards Mrs. Saint had left. "I don't have time for it anyway, to be honest. I need to tackle the sides for Thanksgiving dinner or there'll be a tiny Frenchwoman to answer to. Why don't I do that, and you two can bake all this stuff I bought for us to eat this weekend?"

"Oh, about that," Patty said. "Carol told me she'd have what's-his-name out by tomorrow after dinner if me and Lola want to come back to the apartment then."

"Do you?" Markie asked.

"Not really. But it's not up to me. This is your house, and I figured you might—"

Markie thrust the armful of baking gear toward Patty again, interrupting her. "Then you'd better grab your assistant and get to work. Because if we don't get all this food made, we'll have nothing to eat all weekend once we run out of Thanksgiving leftovers."

Chapter Thirty-Three

Frédéric seemed agitated, and at first Markie thought it was because of the extra guests. Maybe he resented the intrusion on the intimate holiday meal he had been used to sharing with Mrs. Saint, Bruce, and Ronda for however many years. But then she realized the moments he seemed most calm were when he was talking to Jesse about the war or looking with Lola at the new coloring pages she had brought over, so she discarded her initial theory and studied him longer.

When he cast three nervous glances at Mrs. Saint in the span of a single minute, she realized it wasn't the four intruders from across the fence who were setting him on edge, but the woman who lived there. They weren't in the middle of a spat, she didn't think; Mrs. Saint had smiled at him like Markie had never seen her do, and she had thanked him warmly for doing little things like putting another log on the fire and calming Ronda down when she thought she had ruined the gravy.

Markie wanted to ask Patty if she noticed it, too, but the young woman was rushing back and forth from the kitchen to the dining room, trying to both set the table and provide moral support to Ronda, all while embroiled in some discussion with Lola, who was attempting

to help with the place settings. The turkey was almost done resting, Ronda had announced, and they were due to sit down soon. Markie didn't want to interfere with the last few minutes of preparation, and they had declined her offers to pitch in, so she stood quietly in a corner of the dining room and observed.

The closer they were to sitting, the more agitated Frédéric became, and when the doorbell rang, most of them were startled—they weren't expecting anyone else—but Frédéric practically jumped out of his skin. Bruce moved toward the door, but the older man held up a hand to stop him.

"Angeline!" he said, his face the picture of dread. "Let us answer, you and me. Alone."

They all loved and respected Frédéric, but after that display, there was no way the rest of them were staying put and missing out on whatever scene was about to play out at the front door. Frédéric, sensing they were all primed to follow, scanned their faces pleadingly, and Markie guessed he was about to beg them not to come. She started to turn back to the kitchen and herd the others with her, but before Frédéric could speak, the doorbell rang again.

Frédéric shrugged. "Maybe the extra people will help, actually," he said to the air above their heads, and turning, he headed for the door, Mrs. Saint by his side.

Everyone scurried after them and stood waiting a few feet behind, their eyes trained on the door, and when Frédéric finally pulled it wide enough to reveal the person on the other side, they sucked in a collective astonished breath. There on the doorstep was an exact replica of Mrs. Saint.

"Simone!" Markie whispered, and from somewhere behind her she heard Jesse's voice whisper the same thing.

"Simone," Frédéric said, bowing low. His voice, like Markie's and her son's, was whisper-quiet.

He stepped backward and extended an arm for her to come inside while he reached for Mrs. Saint with his other hand. Markie didn't have to wonder long whether he was reaching out to comfort her or to keep her at his side, because before Simone took a single step across the threshold, Mrs. Saint turned on her heel and stomped away, through the living room and down a hallway that, Markie guessed, held the bedrooms. Seconds later, a door slammed.

Like spectators at a tennis match, everyone had turned to watch Mrs. Saint march away, and now they all turned back to Simone, who was unbuttoning her coat. When she removed it, along with her gloves and purse, and handed them to a waiting Frédéric, they all took in another collective inhale. It wasn't the fact that she and Mrs. Saint were obviously twins that took their breath away. Wrinkle patterns and hair color (theirs were identical) weren't within a person's control.

It was the fact that everything else about her, all the elements of her appearance that she had power over—clothes, jewelry, shoes, purse, the way she carried herself—were the same as well. The sisters had been apart for who knew how long. Years, Markie guessed. Decades, even. Yet from outward appearances, they might as well have been living in the same house.

"Simone," Frédéric said again, and this time his voice was a little louder.

He handed her things to Bruce, then stood awkwardly, his arms partly extended toward her as though he wasn't sure if he should touch her. She regarded his uncertain arms and took one small step toward him. He closed the distance and they embraced, and the length of their hug confirmed Markie's estimate that it had been decades, indeed, not mere years, since the sisters had seen each other.

When Frédéric finally released her, he was smiling, but Simone planted her feet wide, crossed her arms, and glared at him. His smile faded, and in an instant he was a little boy, standing in front of his mother, waiting to be chastised for breaking a vase. With a speed and

force that resulted in a third collective intake of breath from the group, she slapped him hard across the face.

Frédéric raised a hand to his cheek reflexively, and Markie waited for him to exclaim, "What the hell?" To suggest that maybe Simone had already outstayed her welcome. Instead, amazingly, he nodded.

"You," Simone said. "I am not sure what to call you."

"Frédéric, if you please."

As he said it, Frédéric gave a slight bow, as though he were asking her permission. Or for a favor.

Simone seemed to debate this in her mind, and he shifted uncomfortably, holding his breath. Finally, she gave a short nod and the same slight chin dip Markie had seen her sister perform countless times.

"Frédéric, then."

Frédéric let his breath out in a long, relieved blast and inclined his head, a thank-you.

Chapter
Thirty-Four

Mrs. Saint didn't wait long to return to the group. With apologies to everyone for making them delay their meal, she invented a story about lost reading glasses and her inability to quickly locate them, then summoned everyone impatiently to the table. When they were seated, she introduced her sister without fanfare, as though she had been telling them for weeks that Simone would be joining them that night. Simone began to apologize for her sudden and unexpected entrance, but Mrs. Saint waved her off, saying there was no need to be sorry, there was plenty of food, and now it was time for Frédéric to say grace.

Simone was from New York, she told everyone, as they were passing heaping plates of turkey, mashed potatoes, green beans, rolls, sweet potato casserole, cranberry sauce, and stuffing around the table. She had two boys, and they each had two children, and the busyness of grandparenting had kept her from visiting Angeline. She didn't look at her sister when she said this last bit, and Mrs. Saint busied herself spreading butter on a roll, pretending no disagreement with Simone's explanation for why no one at the table, other than Frédéric, had ever seen her before. But try as they did, the twins could not hide the thick

tension that had settled into the dining room, and not even Lola would believe that it was geographical distance and grandkids that had kept the sisters apart.

They ate fast, everyone refusing seconds and claiming no room even for dessert. They could have it tomorrow, Ronda suggested, and Bruce chimed in that pumpkin pie was always so much better the next day anyway. Frédéric told Ronda and Bruce to leave the kitchen to him, and in fewer than five minutes, the front door was closing behind the two of them as they walked together to the bus stop.

Over Lola's protests, Patty said it was time for them to leave, too, and Markie and Jesse jumped up immediately, saying it wouldn't be right to send their guests home without them. From the moment they all sat down to dinner until the moment Markie and the others were back inside the bungalow, not even thirty minutes had elapsed.

⚜

Markie had every intention of avoiding her elderly neighbor for the rest of the weekend, leaving her to her own secrets. She was as curious as ever about Simone and why Mrs. Saint had denied her existence, but she knew what it was like to have something painful in her past and to want to hide it from others. After seeing Mrs. Saint's face when she saw who was at the door, after watching her bristle at the sound of Simone's voice, Markie had no plans to push in on the matter.

But on Friday morning, Mrs. Saint was at Markie's door, holding out half a pie along with an assortment of other leftovers, all packaged into neatly labeled containers.

"And I brought all the leftover rolls for Lola," she said. "She liked those best."

Markie said thank you and put her hand on the door handle, ready to close it.

"I wanted to explain—" Mrs. Saint began.

"You don't have to. I know what it's like to have something painful—"

The old woman threw her head back as though Markie had said something hilarious, though no laughter came out. "Painful? Och, *non*. *Annoyed*, that is all. She comes after all these years? On a holiday! Who does this?"

"Is she still there?" Markie asked. She took a step backward and beckoned her neighbor in.

Mrs. Saint stepped inside, closing the door behind her, and scanned the family room and kitchen before setting her basket down.

"Oh, the dog's not here," Markie said. "Patty and the kids took her out for a walk."

"*Oui,*" Mrs. Saint said, placing the basket on the floor by her feet, "she is still remaining. I tried to send her home, but her flight is going back tomorrow, and Frédéric tells me it will cost her much to change it. Anyway, she is staying mostly in the kitchen, teaching Ronda to make some things.

"So we do not have to be . . ." She crossed her middle finger over her pointer. "I have been reading in my room, so we have been more like . . ." She separated her fingers into a wide *V*. "Which is better." She cleared her throat. "I know I lied about the picture," she said. "I am sorry for this."

"It's fine," Markie said. "We all have things we don't feel like talking about. And this has been a tough few days for—"

"It is because she stole a boyfriend of mine, you see," Mrs. Saint said. "It was many years ago, and perhaps you think me an old fool to still hang on. But he was very special to me. And not to her. And she has never apologized."

"Why did she slap Frédéric?" Markie asked. "And why did she say she wasn't sure what to call him?"

Mrs. Saint narrowed her eyes. "I was not aware about these things." She considered for a moment and then said, "He has confronted her

sometimes, about her behavior to me. She does not like this. I think this is why the slap. For the name, I suppose . . . maybe she had an intention of calling him something rude."

"Did she say why she came?" Markie asked. "Did she finally apologize?"

"We have not spoken of it," Mrs. Saint said. "But I know she wants my forgiveness. She is not well. And she is not wanting to die with this thing between us."

"Will you forgive her?"

"Forgiveness is not mine to give," Mrs. Saint said. "It belongs to God. And as to whether he will, she will have to wait and see."

"But a lot of people forgive one another."

"I do not believe in it."

"The Catholic Church does, though, doesn't it?"

"I am not the Catholic Church. And I think it is too easy to get forgiveness from a person."

Chapter Thirty-Five

Markie woke in the middle of the night to the wailing of sirens and the flashing of red-and-white lights across the ceiling. She ran to the window that overlooked Mrs. Saint's property, pulled the curtain aside, and gasped. "Oh my God! No!" Flames leaped from one corner of Mrs. Saint's house, and torrents of thick, dark smoke billowed out of every window and all along the roof line.

Two fire trucks were parked along the curb, and another was screaming up behind them. A police car trailed closely behind the last truck, and instead of pulling in behind the others, it made a sweeping arc into the street and stopped, blocking the road to all other traffic. An ambulance sat in the driveway, its back doors thrown open. The lights on all five vehicles continued to flash, and the figures racing over the lawn and between the trucks were alternately illuminated in a red glow and then plunged into darkness, blurry shadows against the night sky.

Three thick shapes with oxygen tanks on their backs worked to pull a hose from a coil in the middle of one of the trucks while another, similarly clad, raced to the fire hydrant on the corner, a long wrench in his hand. Two others, wielding flashlights, jogged from the back of the

ambulance to the front door, one carrying a bag. Down the street, house lights began to turn on, and Markie saw neighbors stumbling out of front doors and toward the blaze, pajama tops pulled up to cover their noses and mouths.

Markie raced down the stairs as fast as her walking boot would allow, ignoring her protesting left ankle, and without stopping to find a shoe for her right foot or pull a sweater over her thin pajamas, she tore out the side door and across the lawn. Behind her, she heard Angel's muffled barking in the basement. The entire bungalow must be awake by now, with the noise and lights and commotion next door. She hoped Patty would think to keep Lola from looking out the window.

Outside, she was overwhelmed by every sense. The acrid smell of smoke choked her as she picked her way over the grass, arms extended for balance as she watched the ground carefully to be sure her walking boot didn't catch on something and send her flying. She didn't dare use a hand to cover her nose and mouth, for fear she would topple sideways.

The sirens had stopped whining, but the staccato lights continued, washing everything around her in a flash of red, then white, then darkness, over and over. Voices shouted from the front lawn, the driveway, and the road, and multiple radios or walkie-talkies crackled and hissed from different directions. A wall of heat pressed against her skin, and her eyes burned with smoke and with the tears that came as panic set in.

All her life she had heard sirens across town, seen fire trucks and ambulances race past her on the highway and through intersections, watched coverage of blazes on the TV news, but never had she been so close to one. And never had she known the victims. What if they hadn't gotten out? What if the firemen didn't know to check downstairs for Frédéric?

She made her way through the gate in the fence and was halfway across Mrs. Saint's lawn, heading for the front of the house, when a white light arced across her. She looked up to see a police officer stepping out of the shadows, a flashlight in his hand.

"Whoa there," he said. "Where'd you come from? Were you inside? Are you related to the homeowner?"

"I'm the neighbor," Markie panted, thrusting a thumb behind her. "Is everyone okay? Did they get them all out? There were three people inside! One in the basement! I need to get to them!"

She tried to move past him, but he put up his hands, motioning for her to stop.

"Sorry, ma'am," he said, "but we can't have anyone on the scene until it's been secured." He pointed toward the fence. "I'll need you to return to your home, please. This is an unsafe environment."

"But I . . . I'm . . . more than just a neighbor! I'm . . ."

She wanted to say, "I'm like a daughter!" or "I'm a close friend!" But she realized the absurdity of both claims. For the entire time she had lived next door, she had tried *not* to be a friend to Mrs. Saint, not to be anything close to a family member.

"Just tell me if they got everyone out!" she said, craning her neck to see around him.

"I'm sorry. I can't give out any information—"

"Well, run around to the front, at least, and make sure they've checked the basement!" she said, shooing him. "And the master bedroom, and the guest room!"

"My orders are to check the perimeter, ma'am, and—"

She pointed to the radio on his belt. "Then call them!"

"They're very capable responders, ma'am. They know how to check a building, and they don't take their time at it. Now, I need to ask you again to leave the premises and return to your home."

"But where will they go once the fire's out?" she asked. "They can't stay in there! They should come to my place. Can you tell them I'm up and waiting for them? They'll need you to walk them with your flashlight. They're elderly, and the ground is uneven."

"Ma'am," he said, waving her toward her house, "please."

"Can you do that? Bring them over?" She took a conciliatory step backward, hoping her obedience would garner this favor from him.

He pushed the air with both hands to get her to continue moving backward, and he didn't answer.

"Can *you* at least come over?" she asked. "When you're finished? To let me know everyone's okay?" She continued backward, still craning her head to try to see around him. "I'll put coffee on," she added.

"Afraid I can't do that, ma'am. You'll have to wait and hear from the family."

"But her only family member was inside the house with her!"

He stopped and took a pen and pad from his breast pocket. "And what's the name of that person?"

"Simone. The woman who lives there is Angeline St. Denis, and her sister is Simone . . . I don't know her last name. But if you'd go over and check to see if they're all out, you could ask yourself, and then you could just wave to me to let me know they're fine." She gave him a last pleading look, but he was busy closing his notebook and didn't notice.

He returned his pad and pen to his pocket, and with an expression that showed he was losing patience and she was pushing her luck, he pointed again to the wooden fence and kept pointing until she turned and retreated.

"I need to check the rest of the perimeter, ma'am," she heard him say behind her. "Please don't come over here again until you've seen all the trucks are gone and the environment has been rendered safe."

He must have lifted his flashlight then, because a lighted pathway appeared from the fence to the bungalow's side door, and it remained until she stepped inside. Peering out the window, she watched him turn and walk toward the garage, checking over his shoulder every few steps to ensure she didn't come back out.

Inside, Jesse and Patty were standing at the kitchen window, trying to figure out where the fire might have started, what rooms it had reached, and whether Mrs. Saint, Simone, and Frédéric had been

injured trying to get out. A frantic Angel, aware that all was not right, raced circles around the kitchen, barking. Lola had come downstairs—whether under her own power or in her mother's arms, Markie wasn't sure—but miraculously, the girl was sleeping through it all, huddled under her blankets on the family room couch.

Jesse wanted to stand on the corner across from Mrs. Saint's and watch with the other neighbors from a better vantage point, but Markie was against it. There was a difference between concern and gawking, she told him. Plus, she didn't know what he might witness. It would be wonderful if he got there in time to watch Mrs. Saint, Simone, and Frédéric all walking out under their own power. But what if he saw something else?

⚜

Two hours later, Bruce appeared at the door. Patty and Markie were on the couch, Lola snuggled beside her mother, and Jesse and Angel lay together on the area rug. Everyone but the still-sleeping Lola jumped up when Bruce knocked. He stepped inside but wouldn't take the spot on the couch Markie offered or the chair Jesse fetched from the dining room. Angel tried to lick Bruce's hands, but he held them high, out of her reach.

It was clear he wasn't in the mood.

"Jesse," Markie said, nodding to the dog.

Jesse grabbed the animal by her collar and pulled her to the middle of the rug, making her lie down. He sat on the floor beside the dog and looked up at Bruce expectantly. Markie and Patty, back on the couch now, did the same.

Bruce shifted from one foot to the other and cleared his throat. He removed his ball cap, something Markie had never seen him do before, and ran a hand over his head. Gripping the cap between the fingers of both hands, he bent his head down, and as he began to speak, he

watched his fingers as they worked to rotate the cap in circles as though it were a rosary, the words he was uttering a prayer.

Frédéric had called him, he said. From the hospital. The older man had been short of breath around eleven the night before, and because Mrs. Saint was already in bed asleep, Simone had insisted on driving him to the ER. The doctors wanted to keep him a few hours for observation, and he told Simone to go home without him, but she insisted on waiting. She was nodding off in a plastic chair when Frédéric's phone, which Simone had offered to hang on to for him, rang: it was the battalion chief from the fire scene, calling in search of Mrs. Saint's next of kin. Frédéric's was the only number she had set on speed dial.

Bruce looked up from his cap, and Markie had time to see his eyes welling up and to feel her chest go cold before he bent his head down again.

"We lost her," he cried, his voice breaking, and when he lifted his eyes from his cap again, they were overflowing.

"What?" Patty cried, leaping to her feet again. "No! That can't be right! It was only a house fire!"

It was a nonsensical thing to say, of course, but Markie, who stood and put her arms around the sobbing Patty and whispered, "It's okay, it's okay," knew what she meant. It had been more horror than they could bear for a night, watching the house burn, seeing the clouds of smoke surround it, the flashing lights and the running shadows and the first responders taking over the property. They had assumed that would be the most terrible part because the alternative, that it could get so much worse, had been too dreadful to consider.

Markie felt Patty sag in her arms, too devastated to hold herself upright. Over Patty's shoulder, Markie watched Bruce as he stood motionless—in shock, no doubt—staring blindly at his cap. What would they do now? To Patty, Bruce, and Ronda, Mrs. Saint was not only employer, mother figure, job coach, and sage, but the fiery ball of energy around which they orbited every day. It was unthinkable that

she wouldn't be there for them anymore. Markie felt a hard lump form in her throat as she imagined Bruce, Patty, and Ronda sitting on their own in their apartments in the morning, drinking coffee and trying to decide how to spend the hours, the days, the weeks, the months that stretched before them.

And as for Frédéric . . . Markie inhaled sharply as a jagged pain lodged in her chest at the thought of him trying to soldier through a single morning, let alone the rest of his life, without his beloved Angeline. She remembered how he had stood in the bungalow's living room on move-in day, gazing like a puppy at Mrs. Saint as he explained so proudly that her accent, one he clearly adored, hadn't been decimated like his. And later, how he had dropped the dog crate and run to her at the fence after seeing how emotional she was about watching Angel and Jesse together.

Mrs. Saint had let him comfort her that day, Markie remembered, and years earlier, she had even let him move into her basement because he wanted to protect her. And he had let her take care of him, too, drinking every drop of the water she forced upon him, "knocking off" for the day at her appointed hour of four. It may not have been the relationship Frédéric wanted, but it didn't seem completely unrequited, at least. Maybe, with more time, he would have won her over entirely. The thought made Markie's eyes sting, and she turned her head and pressed her thumb and forefinger against the bridge of her nose to keep her tears, waiting at the bottom edges of her eyes, from spilling over.

Lola, who had stirred at the sound of her mother's reaction, was moving now, and Markie watched as Jesse took Patty's place on the couch, letting the girl climb onto his lap and curl her body against his waist, her arms tight around him. He smoothed a hand from the top of her head to the middle of her back, then repeated the motion over and over until she drifted back to sleep. He stared vacantly, miserably, ahead, one hand on Lola's sleeping back, his legs stretched out over the dog lying at his feet.

He had seen Mrs. Saint as a grandmother, the way Lola had, and she had treated him like a grandson. The bossiness and snoopiness that had annoyed Markie so much had merely amused Jesse, and Markie was aware that for all the old woman's faults, she had also been wildly generous to him, starting with the furry creature who lay panting on the floor at his feet.

Jesse had begun hinting that maybe their neighbor was right, that they should extend their lease after all. He wasn't ready to leave yet—not Lola, not Frédéric, and not Mrs. Saint.

Markie felt a tear slide down her cheek. She had told herself she couldn't stand the woman's pushiness, but the truth was, she had come to take that pushiness for granted, had come to expect the woman's daily trips across the yard, the insistent rapping at the side door, the baskets of badly baked goods and store-bought replacements and totems. On days they didn't happen, Markie noticed. She had told herself any day without an unannounced visit from the Frenchwoman was a reprieve, but now she wasn't so sure she had meant it. Annoying or not, Mrs. Saint had provided texture to a life that had, because of Markie's apathy, become flat.

Markie had only to look around the small family room to see what the woman had added to her daily existence: walls filled with art and the woman who had hung it all—a woman Markie held on to now, who was returning the embrace. The child, now folded around her son's waist, who had reintroduced the family dinners and holiday decorations and board game nights Markie hadn't realized her son still needed. The dog at Jesse's feet, a royal pain, to be sure, but also responsible for bringing the boy's laughter back, for providing him something to cling to during a time in his life when he most needed it. The man shifting uncomfortably inside her side door, clutching his hat, wishing he knew what to say and completely willing, Markie knew, to do anything in the world for each one of them.

More tears escaped as she watched Bruce twist his cap in his hands, trying to hold himself together, the look on his face one of sheer despondence. This was precisely what Mrs. Saint had worried about, Markie

thought: that something would happen to her and the others would be lost. At the time, Markie had found the subject infuriating, since she was the solution her neighbor had decided upon, and she wanted nothing to do with it. She had batted off an idea about a job-training program, unaware if such a thing actually existed, and tried to change the subject.

Now she wished she had taken the old woman more seriously, for the sake of the people who had come to rely on her to direct their days, supply their meals, provide them with a purpose: Ronda, Bruce, Patty, Frédéric. And for Mrs. Saint's sake, too. Pushy or not, the woman had cared enough to take them all in and worry about their futures, while Markie's only concern had been to spare herself from involvement. More tears tracked down her cheeks as she now saw, too late, that Mrs. Saint had been more good than bad all along, and Markie had simply been too self-involved to recognize it.

Crying openly now, Markie hugged Patty tighter. The feeling of Patty's thin frame against her own soft body made her feel like a giant, but when Patty realized she wasn't the only one weeping, she adjusted her long, sinewy arms and held Markie tighter. Amazingly, Patty's bony embrace, her gravelly smoker's voice as she repeated the same "It's okay, it's okay" that Markie had whispered to her a moment ago, the now-familiar nicotine scent of her, brought more comfort to Markie than she remembered ever feeling in Kyle's big, strong arms.

Bruce's face collapsed at the sight of the tearful women, and he took a half step toward the pair, reaching his arm out, and then he froze.

"It's okay," Markie whispered again, her mouth near Patty's ear but her eyes on Bruce. He stepped back to his original place, and she nodded to him and rubbed Patty's back—the same big, firm circles Patty was making on hers. "Everything's going to be okay."

"Ronda's on her way," Bruce offered, as though the cook's arrival would heal them all, and Markie gave him a grateful smile, letting him believe the news was the relief he intended it to be.

Chapter
Thirty-Six

Ronda had arrived at the bungalow. It was almost noon, and Frédéric had called Bruce to say he and Simone would be there any moment.

"Imagine her allowing someone else to take him to the hospital!" Bruce whispered to Markie in the living room, where she was draping Ronda's jacket over the spindle-leg love seat. That should have triggered something in Frédéric, Bruce said. Something should have fired in his head, warning him. If she wasn't well enough to go with him, she wasn't well enough to be left alone. He would never say as much to Frédéric, of course, he told her. "The guilt's got to be eating him alive already."

She had fallen asleep with a cigarette in her hand. Frédéric had let Bruce know this. She must have gotten up after Frédéric and Simone left. That itself wasn't significant; she had risen in the middle of the night to smoke before. But always—*always*, Bruce repeated emphatically—she had sat in her armchair to smoke it, her ashtray balanced at her elbow. She was aware of the dangers of smoking in bed. The only explanation, he said, was that she had been feeling too sick to sit upright or to think straight.

Markie couldn't imagine how Frédéric must feel. All those years, never leaving her alone for a night, and the one time he does, this? While he was gone with her estranged sister, no less? Not that a trip to the ER was a night on the town, but still. Would he torture himself forever, imagining her last thoughts, thinking about that fact that she was alone, and he and Simone were together?

⚜

They were crowded into the family room. Lola, awake and weeping, was draped over Ronda's legs on the couch, asking questions no one had answers to or energy for. Why didn't she get out of the house? Who called the fire department? Why didn't they get there faster? When would they be able to go back inside? Who would make sure the house got fixed the way she would want?

Jesse and Bruce sat in the wooden chairs they had carried in from the dining room. Markie made preposterous amounts of tea that no one drank and set out cookies no one ate. Patty paced, pausing every minute or so at the couch long enough to stroke Lola's hair or rub Ronda's heaving back and to repeat, without conviction, "It'll be okay. Everything will be fine."

They had managed to get the flames under control before the kitchen was destroyed, Ronda whispered to Markie after she had extricated herself from under Lola and made her way to the kitchen to help with the tea. But what consolation was that? It made her feel guilty, she said. Why would the kitchen be spared?

⚜

Frédéric and Simone arrived, and Markie ordered food. She had run out of patience for dealing with Ronda, who lacked the energy to cook but felt it was her duty to do it, so she kept making listless offers to "rustle

up some things" while whispering to Markie that she hoped there would be no takers.

"Not your responsibility anymore," Markie told her. Stupidly. She had meant for it to be a nice thing, and only after Ronda burst into tears did Markie realize her mistake. What was Ronda to do now, if not cook for Mrs. Saint?

Frédéric stood near the door. Every few minutes he peered out the window, as though maybe the old Frenchwoman would be walking over just then and heading for the bungalow. He refused to sit, take a sip of tea, eat a cookie. He would have refused to breathe, Markie thought, if he weren't too polite to put the others through more trauma.

⚜

Simone was on the couch now, Ronda beside her. Lola lay with her head in Simone's lap, her feet in Ronda's, the cook rubbing the girl's legs while Simone stroked her hair.

"Where will I do my homework?" Lola whispered to Markie when she brought her a glass of water.

"You'll do it here," Markie said.

"But she won't be checking."

"I'll check."

"Thanks," Lola said, but Markie could see in the girl's expression exactly what she was thinking: *It won't be the same.*

⚜

Patty motioned for Markie to follow her to the dining room.

"I'm worried about Ronda and Bruce," she said. She gestured toward Mrs. Saint's house, not visible from the bungalow anymore since Markie had pulled all the blinds. "What do they do, if they don't go there?"

Markie reached for Patty's hand and held it in both of hers. "They come here, I think?"

"What about you, though? And your work? They're not quiet, you know."

"I can work downtown."

"No! Absolutely not! I could keep them in the family room, maybe? You could work in here."

"Frédéric will likely be in there," Markie said. "I think he'll sleep on the couch, so I'm guessing he'll take over the room. And I imagine he'll want to be alone, at least for a while."

"Did you and him already talk about that?" Patty asked. "I didn't hear."

"No. But . . ."

"Right," Patty said. "Where else?"

⚜

Kyle arrived with two grocery bags in his arms. "Jesse told me you've got a houseful of people, and it might be that way for a while," he said. "I thought you could probably use some extra coffee and toilet paper and . . . well, there's a lot of stuff in here. I hope it helps."

"Thanks," she said.

He told her he was happy to help. He knew what Mrs. Saint had meant to her and Jesse. And he offered to take Angel off their hands for a few days if she was getting in the way.

⚜

"I am worried about him," Simone whispered to Markie as they tossed paper plates into the garbage, wrapped the leftover pizza, and rinsed the teacups.

Markie nodded. Frédéric still wouldn't sit. "I think he feels it's disrespectful to her if he relaxes," she whispered back. "I'm concerned he might faint."

"Yes," Simone said. Turning to the family room, she said, "Frédéric, darling. I must insist again that you take a seat. You are worrying Mark—"

"No!" Markie interjected. "Don't tell him that! He has enough on his mind."

But Frédéric had taken the chair beside Bruce. Jesse and Lola were on the floor now, their arms around Angel.

"Sometimes it is good he feels so responsible for everyone else," Simone whispered. "He will not sit for himself, but he does it for you. Anyway, I am going to stay on for some days, I have decided. I can get a hotel room. Perhaps he will want to do the same, though I expect he would be happier here, if you have room for him. He will want to be closer to her." Her voice broke. "To her house, I mean."

"Why don't you stay, too?" Markie said, rubbing Simone's arm. "You can take my room. I'll sleep on the love seat in the living room."

"I could not."

"I think everyone would like it better if you were here with us," Markie said. Simone widened her eyes, and Markie nodded. "It would make them feel more . . . complete, I think. To have all of us together."

"If you are quite sure," Simone said. "In truth, it would be nicer for me, too."

"Listen," Markie said, "I hope this isn't too soon, but while we're alone, I wanted to say how sorry I am that your final hours with your sister weren't better. She told me she doesn't believe in forgiveness, but I'm certain she—"

"Yes," Simone nodded. "You are right. She knew I forgave her. She stopped me every time I tried to say it last night, but I know she knew that is why I came. To tell her that."

Markie's head snapped back. *Simone came to forgive Angeline?* "Wait," she started. "That's not what she—"

But Simone reached for Markie's hand, squeezed it, and continued. "It is a blessing, I feel. Who knows when I might have come, if ever, if Frédéric had not called to tell me about her heart and how it had gotten so much worse. That they were not sure if the new medication would help, and they could not guarantee how long . . ." She let her sentence trail off as she dropped Markie's hand, reached into the cuff of her sweater sleeve for a tissue, and pressed it to her eyes.

Markie turned away, pretending to wipe the counter another time. *Mrs. Saint had a heart condition, and it had gotten much worse? New medication? Things were so dire—"no guarantee"—that he had called her estranged sister?* And meanwhile, Mrs. Saint had merely said, "Oh, it's only old age. The doctors are being dramatic. Frédéric's worrying about nothing."

"I have upset you," Simone said.

Markie turned back to her. "I just . . . I have a lot of questions. I think I've been told a lot of . . . untruths. And I guess it's fine. None of it was ever any of my business, but—"

"Such as?" Simone asked.

"For one," Markie said, "you said you came here to forgive *her*. But she told me you came to ask her to forgive *you*."

Simone sighed as she tucked the tissue back into her sleeve. "This was my sister."

It wasn't really an answer. But then again, Markie decided, it sort of was.

"She also told me she didn't believe in human forgiveness," Markie said. "That it was too easy. She said it's up to God to forgive."

Simone took a deep breath in through her nose and let it out slowly through her mouth. "*La pauvre.* She has been too hard on herself."

Markie wanted to ask what that meant, but Simone was weeping now. She pulled the tissue out of her sleeve again, but it was crumpled

and damp. Frowning, she tucked it back in her sweater. Markie went to the family room to find a box, and Frédéric, noticing, leaped up and raced to the kitchen.

"Simone," he said, and she turned to him and fell against his chest. Their arms went around each other, and they clutched each other, crying, while Markie stood dumbly, holding the tissue box out into space.

Chapter
Thirty-Seven

Late in the day, Frédéric received the all clear from the fire department to go inside Mrs. Saint's house. He blinked, said nothing, and handed the phone to Patty, who jumped into action, taking a seat at Markie's kitchen counter and making notes on the back of one of Lola's coloring pages. Ronda had spoken to Mrs. Saint's insurance company earlier about arranging for a smoke-damage restoration company to come, and now Patty called the insurance agent to put that plan in motion and to make arrangements to meet the agent at the house to discuss further repairs.

Bruce, meanwhile, quietly let himself out of the bungalow, returning later with a small metal box, which he handed to Frédéric, and Simone's two suitcases, which he left outside on the patio to keep the smell of smoke out of the bungalow.

"I wanted to bring you some clothes," he told Frédéric, "but I checked your closet, and the smoke . . ." He shook his head. "Sorry."

Simone's things weren't wearable, either, despite having been zipped inside the larger of her two suitcases. She asked Bruce to set that case in Markie's garage—she would go through it the next morning and

decide if anything was salvageable—while she carried the smaller one to a corner of the patio and looked through it. Markie and Ronda went out to see her, Markie carrying a spare tote bag she thought Simone might want to transfer the contents of the case into and offering, along with Ronda, to help her sort through her things. Simone accepted the bag, but she asked Markie to leave it outside the door and waved them off before they could get close enough to see inside the case.

"I couldn't possibly impose," Simone told Markie, as though helping to sort through a hatbox-size suitcase was a real chore for a woman who was now hosting, indefinitely, four people from Mrs. Saint's house in addition to the two she had already taken in. Ronda and Markie exchanged puzzled looks and went back inside.

By around ten that night, the bungalow's first floor was mostly cleared out. Bruce and Ronda had left together for the bus stop, Jesse and Angel had retired to the basement, and Patty had taken Lola up to bed. Markie carried an armload of sheets and blankets down from the linen closet and delivered one set on the living room love seat before continuing through the archway to the family room to give the others to Frédéric.

When she reached the kitchen, she stopped midstep, her jaw dropping, the linens almost falling to the floor. Frédéric and Simone sat shoulder to shoulder on the couch, her head resting against his, his arm tight around her. From the back, it seemed as though she had walked in on an intimate moment between Frédéric and Mrs. Saint, and for a split second, Markie was elated for the old man to finally have a chance to hold his beloved Angeline closely like this.

The moment passed, though, and her elation turned to dismay. His beloved Angeline was dead. What was he doing, sitting so familiarly with her sister? Why was Simone, a married woman, cuddling like sweethearts with the man who had been living with her twin? Markie felt heat rise to her face with indignation on behalf of her former neighbor.

She forced her body to relax, though, and told herself not to jump to conclusions. Surely this was nothing more than platonic commiseration between two people who had lost a common loved one. There was no reason for her to be upset. But when she cleared her throat and they both jumped up, Simone taking two large steps in one direction, Frédéric in the other, Markie wasn't so sure. Why, if they were innocent, were they acting so guilty?

Frédéric bent quickly to close the lid of his metal box, which, Markie now noticed, sat open on the floor near the couch. Then he reached for the throw blanket, which he tossed over a pile of papers stacked on one of the couch cushions. Markie caught a brief glimpse of the stack before the blanket descended upon it. It appeared to be nothing more than a collection of black-and-white photographs. Why, then, was Frédéric acting like it was a pile of girlie magazines?

"Markie," Simone said. "Let me . . ."

She stepped toward the kitchen, and Markie prepared to hear the older woman say she could explain, it wasn't what it looked like, here, come sit on the couch with us and we'll show you what we were looking at. But Simone wore the same closed-off, unapologetic expression Markie had seen so many times in her twin, and when she reached the kitchen, Simone offered no explanation.

Instead, she held her hands out for the linens and said, "Let me make up the couch for Frédéric. You've done enough for all of us for one day."

If Simone and Frédéric hadn't both suffered such a great loss, if Markie hadn't been too emotionally spent from the day's trauma, too exhausted from having the bungalow filled to capacity all day by Mrs. Saint's beloved Defectives and her estranged sister, if she hadn't been miles past the end of her rope when it came to secrets and lies, she might have told the two older French Canadians where they could stick the linens, along with whatever it was Frédéric was concealing under the blanket. Or, at least, she might

have blown an exasperated breath of air out and turned on her heel to stomp out of the kitchen.

But she could barely stand any longer, or keep her eyes open, or concentrate on how annoyed she was with them. So she handed the sheets and blankets to Simone, told her, "That would be great," wished them both a good night, and stumbled out of the room to the living room, where she collapsed on the love seat and immediately fell asleep.

Chapter
Thirty-Eight

Markie sat, reluctantly, with Frédéric and Simone in the wood-paneled law office of Marvin Schanbaum. It was Sunday afternoon, and Frédéric had received a call from the lawyer that morning, asking him and Simone to come immediately. Markie wondered aloud if it weren't permitted for the two of them to bury their dearest friend and sister before being summoned by her legal counsel, but Frédéric wanted to go, whispering to Markie that it would be good for the others if the meeting happened right away.

When he requested that she be the one to drive them to the lawyer's office, she almost told him to ask Patty instead. She felt an increasing need to marshal and preserve the limited patience she had for Frédéric and Simone and their secret photographs and shared confidences and furtive embraces. But then she took in the noisy, overcrowded bungalow and pictured herself reading, alone, in the quiet of the lawyer's waiting room, and she agreed to take them.

When they asked her to go with them into Mr. Schanbaum's inner office rather than wait in the small lobby, she practically fought them off with her fists. She lost. She didn't know why she was there, she

told them all, as Mr. Schanbaum opened a file on his desk and flipped through it, stopping when he located a thick document, stapled at the top. Last Will and Testament of Angeline St. Denis, Markie made out from the top line on the first page. It made her even more anxious.

"I only came because I didn't want Frédéric or Simone to have to drive," she told Mr. Schanbaum. "Shouldn't I be waiting out there?" She pointed through his office door to the small waiting area. "Surely she would have wanted you to discuss her personal affairs in private."

"In fact, you are one of the individuals mentioned in her personal affairs," he said. "This is why I asked Frédéric to bring you along."

Markie turned, openmouthed, to Frédéric, who was suddenly too fascinated with the floor to acknowledge her. He sat on the other side of Simone, too far away for Markie to nudge with an elbow, so she moved her questioning gaze to Simone.

The older woman shrugged. "Do not ask it to me," she said. "I was hardly the one my sister would have talked to about the contents of her will."

⚜

Mrs. Saint was the owner of the bungalow.

She left it to Markie, free and clear, along with more than enough money to maintain it—and a college fund for Jesse.

Before Markie could get over the shock of her neighbor's staggering generosity, Mr. Schanbaum read further, to the part where Mrs. Saint's house went to Frédéric, along with enough money that he could easily rebuild it and still keep Ronda, Bruce, and Patty employed indefinitely.

And this is where Markie stopped feeling dumbfounded about Mrs. Saint's generosity and started feeling something different, something far more negative, something in the gray, fuzzy spaces between resentment, confusion, and fury.

Because keeping Ronda, Bruce, and Patty on staff, and sufficiently occupied and out of trouble, wasn't something Frédéric could pull off on his own. He was wonderful at helping the others, but he wasn't inclined to direct them—Mrs. Saint had said it herself during one of her visits to Markie's patio. And if ever there were a time when he might have been able to muster the energy to truly lead, it wasn't now. Once upright and vigorous and surefooted, Frédéric now seemed as adrift as the others had always been.

Mrs. Saint had known, of course, that this was what would happen, that grief would knock the vitality out of him. That given his age and the fact that he had lost the love of his life, unrequited or not, his vigor might never return. That in the event he was left to carry on without her, an occasion she had clearly predicted, he would need someone younger and more capable to assist him. Someone to take over where Mrs. Saint had left off.

Someone who knew the Defectives already, who cared about them. Someone who was located conveniently—and permanently, thanks to Mrs. Saint's bequest—on the other side of the low wooden fence.

The bungalow wasn't a gift, Markie now saw—it was a sentence. It wasn't born of Mrs. Saint's generosity but out of her unceasing desire to have things her own way. She wanted her beloved Defectives to stay together. To make that happen, they would need a place to gather, a yard and house that required their constant work and rework. So she had left her house to Frédéric.

They would need money to keep them from needing to find jobs elsewhere. So she had also left him enough cash to pay them.

And they would need a firm, capable leader. So she had arranged to have one installed next door, in exchange for the deed to the bungalow.

Markie almost laughed. She almost asked Mr. Schanbaum to read the part of the will that required her, as a condition of her new home ownership, to attend and supervise the morning meetings on the screened porch. To be sure to ask each of them what their plan was for the day, then offer suggestions for what they should do instead. To make

a point of goading Lola into homework and bathing and getting more exercise. To ensure Frédéric drank an approved quantity of water each day and knocked off work precisely at four.

Surely, too, there must be instructions in the will outlining Markie's care of the bungalow. A list of approved paint colors she would be permitted to use. Instructions for how often she would be required to have the roof replaced. The woman hadn't been able to hand over Lola for a single evening without five minutes' worth of orders about baths and bedtime and teeth brushing. She would never be able to leave a house, forever, without a list one hundred times longer.

The temptation to laugh passed as the full force of the situation hit Markie. All these months, Mrs. Saint had been trying to get her own way, and Markie had resisted. The Frenchwoman had eventually won the vast majority of the battles: the dog, Jesse spending time with Frédéric and tutoring Lola, Markie's artwork making it onto the walls, Markie and Jesse eating more vegetables and fewer frozen meals, Markie getting to know Mrs. Saint's employees.

On only one matter—Markie taking over Mrs. Saint's role as leader of the Defectives—had the old woman not been victorious. But had she been happy with her other successes and left that single point to Markie?

Mais non! Of course not! Instead, the old woman had made the one move she assumed Markie couldn't counter. Because who could say no to a dead woman? Especially a dead woman bearing the precise gifts a person in Markie's financial position would never be able to turn down.

And now Markie saw it all laid out before her clearly, all the timely coincidences and bits of "good luck," or so she had thought. The bungalow that had been empty because of a "bad market," leaving the landlord willing to cut a deal, the mysteriously appearing "free cable" that had not been in the lease and only materialized after Mrs. Saint took such a liking to Jesse and learned that *"le pauvre"* was missing his movie channels.

More secrecy and lies! There was no forgotten lease term offering free cable. There was no bad market. There was only a meddlesome, bossy,

conniving old woman who, knowing her health was deteriorating and her Defectives would have to fend for themselves unless a new leader could be found, had been waiting for just the right person to rope into the job.

Mrs. Saint had been the spider and Markie the fly.

Now Markie didn't want to laugh; she wanted to scream. She wanted to beat her fists against the wooden arms of her chair and yell, "No! Stop right there!" and then lunge across the top of Mr. Schanbaum's desk, grab one of his pens, and strike through the language in the will that mentioned her and the bungalow and Jesse.

Only Frédéric's presence and the way he sat slumped in his chair, despondent over his lost Angeline, kept her silent.

⚜

Once Simone and Frédéric were settled in the car, Markie announced she had left her book in the lawyer's office and needed to run back for it.

"I will accompany you," Frédéric said, as she expected he would.

"No, no. You're all buckled in. You stay with Simone. I'll be back in no time." She shut the door against further protests and made her way back to Mr. Schanbaum.

"I only have a minute," she said, "and I'm sure you have somewhere you want to be. I'd like to set up a time to see you on Tuesday, if you have time available."

"You have . . . concerns," he said. "I sensed this."

"I do. Look, she must have updated it quite recently, because I only met her in August. I'm curious: before she changed it, who was to receive the bungalow and the money?"

He smiled placidly. "It is unfortunately not within my authority to discuss prior drafts of a client's will."

"Tell me this, then," Markie said. "What would happen if I refused to accept what she's left me? What would happen to it, then?"

Mr. Schanbaum's eyes widened. "Are you saying you want to disclaim your bequest?"

"Possibly. But first I want to know what would happen to the bungalow and the money if I did."

He steepled his hands together and closed his eyes momentarily. "In such an event," he said, opening them again, "it would pass through her estate as though you had predeceased her. And since she made it clear that everything else was to go to . . ." He looked at the chair in which Frédéric had been sitting, as though trying to recall the name.

"Frédéric," Markie provided.

"Yes. She made it clear everything was to go him, except for certain bequests delineated specifically, such as the ones to you and to her sister and certain charities. So the bungalow and sum of money set aside for you would go to him."

"In that case," Markie said, "I'd like to talk to you on Tuesday about . . . what did you call it? Disclaiming my bequest? I'd like to talk about that. Not just talk about it. I'd like to do it."

Mr. Schanbaum unsteepled his hands and turned his palms out, facing her. "I suggest we not have such a discussion as early as Tuesday. That is the day after the funeral. I discourage people from making significant proclamations, one way or the other, about these kinds of matters when everything is still so . . . fresh. Give yourself some time to sit with this, to deliberate about it, I urge you. There is no hurry."

"I don't need time. I'd like to come in on Tuesday."

He lowered his hands and opened an appointment book on his desk. "As you wish."

"But you did not find your book!" Simone said when Markie returned empty-handed to the car.

Markie climbed in and patted her purse. "Stupid me. I put it in my purse before he called us in. I forgot until I got back in there. I'm certain he thinks I'm crazy."

Chapter Thirty-Nine

After dinner that night, Jesse suggested a board game in the family room, and while everyone debated what to play, Markie motioned for Simone to follow her into the living room. They sat together on the spindle-legged love seat, Simone with her hands clasped between her knees, and Markie couldn't tell if the other woman was nervous or relieved that it was finally just the two of them, alone.

"I want to ask you some questions," Markie said. "I hope you don't mind. But your sister was . . . evasive about some things. And instead of finding it easier to forget about, now that she's gone, I'm . . . struggling with it."

"You may ask," Simone said. "And I will try to answer. But, of course, I did not know everything about my sister."

"I saw a photo of the two of you when you were seven," Markie said. "It was on your birthday. I asked her about it, and about you, and she told me . . ." She paused, wondering if she should go on. But she was tired of secrets. To get real information, you had to give real information. "She told me you had died," she said. Putting a hand on Simone's knee, she added, "I'm sorry if that's a difficult thing to hear."

Simone nodded, resigned but not crushed by what Markie had said. "This does not surprise me, I must say. We had not spoken in many years. To her, I might have seemed dead, I suppose."

"After Thanksgiving," Markie said, "when I asked her about it, she said you two had had a falling-out over an old boyfriend, and I've been wondering since last night if—"

"Old boyfriend?" Simone said, laughing. "What a story! Angeline and I have never had an eye for the same man! We have each loved one, and one only, and I can tell you it was not the same person. We are too diff—"

Markie cut her off with a long, exasperated breath and stood, then stepped to the window overlooking Mrs. Saint's house. Someone had opened all the blinds, and wincing at the charred remains of the house next door, she crossed the room to the window on the other side of the bungalow.

"I'm so tired of all the misinformation!" she said, keeping her voice low to prevent the others from hearing. "If you had any idea what it's been like to live here beside her. To be constantly intruded upon. Milked for information. Asked for favors. While at the same time . . ."

Markie shook her head, too frustrated to explain further what her neighbor had put her through. "You'd think it would all go away now that she's gone, but there's still as much as before! And I just can't deal with it anymore." She turned from the window to face Simone. "I wasn't going to tell you this until after the funeral, but I'm not accepting her gift. Her . . . bequest. I'm going back to the lawyer on Tuesday and . . . disclaiming it."

Simone took in a sharp breath but said nothing.

"She wanted to saddle me with all of her responsibilities," Markie said, sweeping an arm to encompass the two neighboring properties, "but she didn't trust me enough to be honest with me! She kept so many things from me while she was alive—about you, Frédéric, her health,

and who knows what else. She even lured me into renting this place on pretense and dishonesty!

"And now, this *gift*"—Markie made finger quotes around the word—"of the bungalow. She expected me to stay here when she knew damn well I wanted to leave! She decided to surround me with people when she knew all I want is to be alone! She thought I should have to give up what *I* wanted for my life and take over what *she* wanted for hers!

"To devote my life to"—she angled her head toward the family room—"the people *she* was devoted to. I'm supposed to do all of that for her when she couldn't even bother to tell me the truth! Well, I'm not going to do it! I'm not going to put up with being lied to, tricked, and played!"

Markie's frustration with Mrs. Saint's bequest—and her guilt about her decision to disclaim it—overcame her, and she felt her eyes burn with coming tears. She took a deep breath and spoke more quietly, trying to keep her emotions in check.

"If I'd been trusted, then maybe . . . I don't know. There's more to my wanting to leave than just my relationship with her, I'll admit. I'm not putting it *all* on her. I can't say I'd be jumping at this even if she had been transparent about everything. But I do know the secrets didn't help. Other than to make it easier for me to say no."

Simone rose and went to Markie, touching her arm briefly before moving her hand to Markie's head and stroking her hair. It was such an unexpected gesture that it made the tears welling in Markie's eyes finally spill over and slide down her cheeks.

"I'm sorry," Markie said, sniffing. "She was your sister. I shouldn't have said those things. And you shouldn't have to console me. You lost her, too." She sniffed again and wiped her eyes with her sleeve. "It's been a long day, that's all. A long weekend. I'm not used to having so many people around all the time, and I . . . acted badly."

Simone stroked Markie's head once more, then patted her shoulder. "You will wait one minute, yes?"

Markie nodded, and Simone left the room and went upstairs. Markie heard footfalls on the ceiling overhead as Simone moved around the master bedroom. Moments later, Simone returned holding a stack of photographs.

Nodding to the love seat, she said, "You will sit with me again?"

Markie nodded again and sat next to Simone, who placed the photographs beside her, away from Markie, and shuffled through them.

"Ah!" Simone said. "Here." She held it up: the picture of her and Angeline in their party dresses.

"That's the one," Markie said. She held a hand out, and Simone let her take the picture, which Markie turned over. *Angeline et Simone, 7ème anniversaire.* "I can't believe her little case survived the fire and all the smoke."

"It did not," Simone said. "This is my copy. These others, too. Mine and Frédéric's, actually—he had more than me. Luckily, his things were in that metal box and underground. So we did not lose all of our memories along with our Angeline."

She selected another and laid it on Markie's lap. It was a copy of the first one Jesse had found behind the garage, the infant twins and the two others Markie had thought were their siblings.

"This is the other one I saw," Markie said. "I find it impossible that these could be your parents. They look like children."

Simone took Markie's hand in hers and looked at her meaningfully. "Those are not our parents," she said, speaking slowly and carefully, the way doctors do when they are giving news they don't want to deliver and no one wants to hear. "They are our brother and sister."

Markie slid the picture off her lap and removed her hand from Simone's. "Of course they are! Of course they're your brother and sister! Of course she had *three* siblings when she told me she had none at all! When I shoved the one of your birthday under her nose, she admitted

she had a sister—a *single sister*, that's all! But of course she had another! And a brother as well!"

She shook her head. "I suppose they live across town, and that's where Frédéric disappears to, to report to them on how she is. Or maybe she went to see them herself." She lifted her hands uselessly and let them fall back into her lap.

Simone studied the photo. "Sadly, *non*," she said quietly. "They were taken about a year after our seventh birthday. And they were sent to a camp."

She stared with what Markie interpreted as a message-filled look, but the meaning eluded her.

"I'm not following," Markie said. "They went to camp and never came back?"

"Oui."

"That doesn't make any sense. Was there an investigation? Was this in Quebec?"

"Quebec?" Simone asked, as though it were a word she had never heard before.

Markie looked at the ceiling, then back at Simone. "*Quebec.* Where you grew up?"

She could hear Bruce's voice the day she moved in, saying, "French *Canadian*," could see the way Mrs. Saint had smiled proudly at him. And then, only the day before Thanksgiving, Markie had asked Mrs. Saint if Frédéric had followed her and Edouard here from Quebec, and Mrs. Saint had confirmed it.

Or had she? Markie pressed her eyes closed and tried to remember. "About Canada," Mrs. Saint had said, "I want to tell you about this, too." Then Patty had walked in, and Mrs. Saint said they would discuss it another time, and the time had never come. Well, here it was. Markie opened her eyes and waited for Simone to explain.

"Ah yes," Simone said. "I see what has happened here. What my sister has done. But we did not grow up in Quebec. We are from Germany.

Breslau, to be precise. We left in 1938, right after we turned seven. And then we lived for some time in France. Matias and Lea"—she nodded to the two older children in the photo—"made it partway to France with us, but they were detained before we arrived."

"Did you say 1938?" Markie asked. "How could you have been seven in 1938 when you're only seventy-five years old?"

"We turned *eighty*-five in June," Simone said.

"Of course you did," Markie said. "Of course you are an *entire decade* older than she admitted to."

But Simone appeared not to have heard. Clutching the photo to her chest, she stood and crossed to the window overlooking her sister's ruined house. She leaned forward and rested her forehead against the window, and Markie wondered if it were an effort to be closer to her twin.

Quietly, Simone spoke into the glass. "The camp our brother and sister were taken to was called Drancy. It was a work camp. From there, they were sent to another. Auschwitz-Birkenau. A death camp."

"Oh my God!" Markie said.

She rose, thinking she would rush to Simone, but something in the way the older woman stood, facing her sister's house while she clutched the photo, made it seem like she wanted to be left alone with her siblings, so Markie lowered herself back to the love seat.

"We left Breslau as soon as we could," Simone said, her voice still quiet, as though perhaps she were talking to herself. "On the train. We packed everything we could into a few small packs. But you had to be careful about what you took. You had to make it look like you were going for a day only, a simple, innocent little family outing before you were all to return home again.

"So you could take some clothes, maybe a few photos. If they looked in your bag and saw a family's most valuable possessions—the silver candlesticks, say—they would know you were trying to leave, and you would be sent straight home, your tickets confiscated. The candlesticks, too.

"Of course, this meant we could also not take Matias's dog, Bella." Simone held the photo so Markie could see it. "You see how he looks to the side?"

Markie glanced at the photo and nodded at what she had noticed before, that Matias was looking outside the frame, and his oldest sister was trying to get him to redirect his attention to the photographer.

"He was always looking at Bella—or playing with her or running after her. He got her when we were born, you see, so they had been together a long time. I think our parents felt he would be outnumbered with three sisters. Funny that they got him a female dog in that case, but it did not matter to Matias. He loved the three of us and our parents, we all knew this, but he adored no other being like he adored Bella."

Simone laughed softly, and a furtive smile appeared on her lips for an instant before fading. "To see him have to part with that dog before we left for the station, it was . . ."

A low moan escaped her, and she covered her mouth with a hand. Markie was wiping her own eyes when Simone spoke again. "None of it mattered anyway," she said. "The careful packing we did. Matias giving up Bella. None of it got us what we had hoped. We had not acted soon enough. There were Nazis at every station by then, on every train car it seemed, and Matias and Lea were so healthy and strong. And they were old enough, you see.

"Angeline and I, we were too young, too weak, too useless. Although they would have taken us, too, I think, now that I have read about their . . . interest in twins." Simone held a hand over her mouth briefly, and Markie, having read the horrifying reports of Dr. Mengele's experiments, almost gagged.

"But our mother was sick that day," Simone went on, "and she could only handle one of us. A woman on the train offered to take the other, and she was sitting many rows back, so when the soldiers came through, they did not realize we were a pair. My mother's illness probably saved us.

"If only Matias or Lea had gotten sick as well, if they had caught whatever cold or flu our mother had. I have thought of this so many times. If only they had looked pale, unhealthy. If only they had not dressed so smartly for the train, sat up so straight, so obediently—"

Simone choked on her words then and covered her face with the photograph, and Markie's eyes overflowed as she rushed to the window and put her arms around the older woman.

"I'm sorry," Markie said. "Oh my God, Simone. I am so, so sorry."

They embraced for a time, until Simone withdrew herself from Markie's arms and drew a fingertip under each eye, wiping her tears.

"I am okay," she said. "Thank you. But I am . . . I have made peace about this, as one must, in order to live. If you remain bitter after so many years, you will . . ." She made a circular motion with her hand, the same kind Angeline had made so many times when searching for a word in English. "I can now talk about it without wanting to commit a crime against another person. Many other people. This is progress."

"What a dreadful, dreadful thing for you to have gone through," Markie said. "When you were only children."

Simone looked out the window again, at what was left of her sister's house. "Och," she whispered to the glass. "We were never children."

She stood quietly for some time, and then she gestured to the love seat, and they returned there together, Simone staring at the photograph of the four children, lost in thought, Markie's mind swirling with questions, guesses, wishes. She hoped the twins and their parents had timed it just right, arriving in the south of France while traffic was still allowed out of the ports. That they had managed to get on a ship and sail to Cuba, then to the United States, like so many she had read about.

"They hid us," Simone said. She had been quiet so long that the sound of her voice startled Markie. "There is a town in France, in the Haute-Loire department, in what was the unoccupied region. Le Chambon-sur-Lignon, it is called. It was a town full of Protestants who made it their purpose to hide Jews. Quite an extraordinary thing, *non?*

"Such a risk to them, and still they did this. And not because we were their neighbors, their friends. The people who came to this town, seeking help—people like Angeline and me and our parents—were strangers, from other parts of France or from Germany. Yet without a question, the townspeople said yes, we will help you.

"Many, they smuggled into Switzerland, after making false papers for them. What a chance they took, breaking the laws this way, to help those people escape. Others, they hid until the liberation. Five thousand in all, it is thought, were saved by the brave people of this single town. Mostly children. Imagine! Five thousand! *C'est incroyable!*" Simone clucked in amazement.

"Incredible," Markie whispered. She had never heard of Le Chambon or the rescue efforts there.

"We hid in a barn," Simone continued. "Angeline and me and our parents. It was owned by Monsieur and Madame Aubert. Lucien and Ginette. We were going to stay for a night. My parents had a plan to take us to a children's home the next day. They had heard of this place, and they were going to leave us there, where they felt we would be safe. They would come back for us when they could, and take us home.

"But there were gendarmes all around, and their job was to sniff us out. They got my father when he was filling our water bucket at the well. My mother saw from the entrance of the barn, and she screamed, and so, of course, they got her, too. They searched the barn, and they woke Monsieur and Madame Aubert and their children, and they searched the farmhouse.

"Monsieur pretended with great shock to have had no clue about the 'filthy Jews' who had been squatting in his barn. He stomped and cursed and shook his angry fist at my parents, who were standing at the end of the lane, shivering with fear that the gendarmes would find me and my sister, too.

"My mother had given us a bath that night, only a sponge bath with a bucket and old cloths she found in the barn, but it was very cold out,

and the water was like ice, and we could not warm up. We were so skinny, you see. She was worried about pneumonia, so she asked Madame if she could leave us inside the house by the fire, only for a little while.

"When Madame heard the gendarmes banging on the door, she hurried us upstairs into the bedroom of her children, and she told us to crawl down under the covers, one in her son's bed, the other in her daughter's. The gendarmes came crashing up, looking in closets and everywhere, and they made the children get out of their beds. But they did not flatten the lumpy blankets at the ends of the beds like Madame feared they might, to see if anyone might be hidden there, even though, as Madame told us many times later, she thought it was very obvious there were bodies underneath the bedding.

"For this, I believe, we must have had some lucky star above us, Angeline and I." Simone ran a finger along the outline of the twin girls in the picture and smiled sadly. "They kept us, Madame and Monsieur Aubert. For almost four years! Here they were, with hardly enough to feed their own family's mouths, and yet they took in two more without a hesitation.

"They had heard quite quickly that my parents . . . would not be coming back for us . . ." Simone paused briefly and looked down before going on. "So they knew it would not be only a few months that we would need someplace to stay; it could be years. And they acted as though this were no trouble at all! They would simply eat less. They would share their clothes, their blankets, everything. They would not turn us out—or turn us in.

"When the Germans invaded and things began to look worse for everyone, they decided it would be safest to arrange for their son and daughter to go to America to stay with Monsieur Aubert's cousin, Girard. And because no relatives had come looking for my sister and me, they decided to send us, too. They had enough money for four tickets, and they used theirs on the two of us. They meant to come later, after they could save more.

"They did not make it. He was killed fighting for the Resistance and she must have died shortly after. From what, we never knew." Simone set the picture aside with the others, bent her head, and folded her hands in her lap, as though in prayer. "Lucien and Ginette. I named my first son after him, and after our brother, too: Matias Lucien. If we had had a girl, she would have been Lea Ginette. But we had another boy."

She laughed softly. "My husband was afraid I would insist on giving that name to our second son in any case! But I was not so crazy. I named him Marceau; it was Ginette's maiden name. I think Lea would have approved."

"That's lovely," Markie said. "What Lucien and Ginette did for your family. And how you've carried their names on with your children."

"They used to write us every week," Simone said. "And Cousin Girard would read the letters out loud. He would tell us our life story, too, over and over, from letters Monsieur had written before they sent us over. For Angeline and me, it was our story only from Le Chambon forward, of course. For the others, it was their entire life.

"We begged him to tell us what had happened to Ginette, and why she did not come, but he had no letter about that, of course. So now, here was Cousin Girard, himself struggling to take care of himself and his wife, and now he had *four* children on top of everything. There were some hard years, I can tell you. Edouard went to work as soon as he could, but he was young himself when we—"

"Wait!" Markie said. "*Edouard? The* Edouard? *Angeline's* Edouard?"

"The very one," Simone said. "He was only a little older than us, so he was nine when we came to them, to their barn. He was thirteen when we got to Pittsburgh—that's where Cousin Girard lived. He was fourteen when he left school and got a job to help put food on the table. Later, he was able to put himself through school at night, and he finished high school and then got a college degree."

"Is that what caused the rift?" Markie asked. "Did you and Edouard have an affair? Is the 'old boyfriend' your sister told me about actually

her late husband? I know you said before that there was no fight about a man, but you've told me this much. Couldn't you admit, now—?"

Simone chuckled softly. "My sister and her many stories. I was telling you the truth earlier, I promise you this. There was no affair, no stolen boyfriend. There was only the fact that when we were old enough to really understand our story after Cousin Girard told it—where we came from, what had happened to our parents—Angeline decided to listen one more time and never again.

"From that day, she reimagined her entire history. *Our* history. She was not a refugee—she was Girard's daughter, and so was I. And Girard was not from France—he was from Quebec. We were not Jewish—we were Roman Catholic. We had no dead parents in Europe, and we never had a brother or sister, so Matias and Lea, of course, were also not dead in Europe.

"They simply never existed. Angeline made them . . ." Simone flicked a hand in the air. "Disappear. Poof. And when I argued about this, well, you can guess. I ceased to exist as well."

"What?" Markie said. "But why would she pretend away your entire history, your religion, your own family?"

"Many have done this," Simone said. "There was a thought back then, in some, a fear that it could happen again, and that this time it would spread to the United States. That we would all be rounded up again and sent off, and maybe then we would meet the same fate as our parents, as Matias and Lea.

"It was not entirely popular, but it was not perfectly rare, either. We knew some refugees, friends of Cousin Girard, who suddenly were no longer refugees, but first-generation Americans. Born one week in Kolberg, Germany, and the next in Scranton, Pennsylvania. This is where Angeline got the idea. They convinced her it was the only safe way."

"And at some point, you told her—"

"When we were finished with high school and talking about moving to New York together to find jobs and an apartment, I told her I

intended to tell my real story once we got there. I had gone along with her fairy tale for some years, but when we arrived in our new city to start our new life, I would be taking our family with us, not leaving them in Pittsburgh, where she had hidden them below Cousin Girard's basement without a second thought."

"And that discussion didn't end well," Markie said.

"It ended with me on a train to New York and her staying behind."

"And marrying Edouard?"

Simone nodded. "He was willing to go along with her charade, you see. He loved her so much he would have done anything for her, including allowing her to fabricate an entire story that caused both her family and his to evaporate for all time. Suddenly, they were French Canadian sweethearts who had moved to America for work.

"He was okay with this, or I should say, he was not so very okay with it at all, but he would allow it. He would pretend along with her about it. But at the same time, he knew her real truth. And I believe she needed that, to have someone who would go along with her new future and yet truly understand her past. I would not do this for her. Edouard would."

"And she thought you were coming here now to ask her forgiveness for deciding not to go along with it any longer, all those years ago?" Markie asked.

"No. She thought I was coming to grant *her* forgiveness for betraying our parents. Our brother and sister. Our entire family, for generations. Our culture, our religion, our traditions. She thought I was coming here to forgive her for turning her back on everything we were, everything our parents were so proud for us to be.

"Everything they struggled to protect when they left our most special things, our entire life, behind in Germany and paid their life savings for train tickets to France. When they hid inside a smelly barn, terrified every moment for fear of what would happen if they showed their faces—for fear of what *did* happen.

"For turning her back on all that Edouard's family had done for us. Because surely, if we were not refugees, then Ginette and Lucien could not have been our saviors, could they? They could not have risked their lives, their children's lives, for our sake. Theirs could not have been names worth carrying on through our own children."

"But she didn't let you say it," Markie said. "She didn't want to hear you say it. She thought forgiveness wasn't yours to give. That only God could grant it."

Simone let out a long breath. "I am not sure I would have gone through with it anyway. Even if she had let me."

"You wouldn't have forgiven her?"

"*Non.*"

"Oh . . ." Markie wasn't sure how to respond. Angeline had acted terribly, but if one twin sister wouldn't forgive another when she was dying, wasn't that the end of everything?

"The other night," Simone said, "when we were in the hospital, Frédéric and I, he told me what my sister has done for all of . . ." She waved a hand, indicating the group gathered in the family room, and in that motion, she reminded Markie so much of Mrs. Saint that her chest felt like it might collapse. She had never seen anyone say as much with finger flicks and wrist movements as these two European/Canadian/American Jewish/Catholic twins from Breslau/Le Chambon/Pittsburgh.

"How she took them in," Simone went on, "when they had no place else and no one else." Her eyes shining with tears, her lips forming a quivering smile, Simone reached for Markie's hand and squeezed it hard in her own. "And oh! Markie! You cannot know how it made me feel to hear this! To hear how she has been spending her life!

"Because is this not precisely what Edouard's family did for ours? Is this not a way of honoring our history, our family, as well as anyone could? Is opening her home to people who are not so welcome by the rest of the community not the perfect way of showing her respect for our religion, our heritage, the way our people were treated back then?

"Is this not everything our parents would have wanted for us to become: people who help others in need? Since the two of us lived because of the way other people helped us when we were in need? Is this not the most wonderful way to honor our brother and sister?"

Tears slipped one after the other down Simone's cheeks, but instead of trying to wipe them away, she smiled through them as though they were as welcome to her as the news about what her sister had done.

"I came here to forgive Angeline for not being more like me!" Simone laughed. "Big, important me! Because I have been a pillar of the Jewish community in New York. My husband and I both. We have given money every year to Jewish causes, both here and abroad. So much money! Are we not so special!

"I am sure our money has gone to good use, of course. And the fancy galas we dress up for, those have been for good causes, too. We have flown to Jerusalem many times, to see Yad Vashem, the Holocaust museum. We have given money there, attended ceremonies. So significant are we! But have we taken a single person in off the street? Given them a job in our home, a meal at our table? *Non*, we have not.

"And meanwhile, Angeline! Pretending still to be French Canadian. Pretending still to be Roman Catholic. Pretending still to be ten years younger than she is so no one will think she saw any part of the war. Pretending none of what happened to us, to our family, actually happened. Pretending, even, that our family did not exist. No brothers and sisters for her, only fictional parents in Quebec.

"But so what? She has been helping while she has been pretending. Doing good things for real people. Giving them refuge. Food. Work. Pay. Companionship. I should not have come here to grant my sister forgiveness. I should have come here to ask for hers. I have judged her all these years for refusing to lead a life that is true to who she is, to what our family was. For refusing to honor them. And all this time, she has been honoring them far better than I."

Chapter Forty

Markie and Simone sat for a long time in silence, holding hands, each of them weeping, lost in her own thoughts, until Lola came in. She approached Simone tentatively, and Markie could understand why; more than once, Markie had caught a glimpse of Simone and thought she was seeing Mrs. Saint. Simone seemed to understand, and wiping her eyes, she smiled at the little girl and held still while the child stood before her, scanning her from head to toe.

Finally, Simone said, "It is I, Simone, the sister of a woman who loved you very much. And I would very much enjoy a good-night hug. Could I have one?"

Lola nodded shyly and stepped forward, and Simone pulled her close and wrapped her arms around her.

"I can see why you were so important to her," Simone whispered.

"Bedtime!" Patty called from the bottom of the stairs, and Simone released Lola, who turned to leave, but then she turned quickly back and hugged the older woman fiercely.

Letting go, the little girl pecked Simone on the cheek and said, "I loved her. And I love you!" She kissed Markie next. "And you!" she said, before running out of the room. Seconds later, Markie heard her thunder up the stairs, begging to delay her bedtime until after she had a bath.

Soon after, Bruce and Ronda came in to say goodbye before letting themselves out the side door. Markie offered to drive them, but they insisted they liked the bus. Jesse and Angel disappeared next, Jesse calling good night from the basement door before they clomped downstairs.

Markie heard the kitchen faucet running as Frédéric filled the glass of water he kept beside him during the night. Smiling ruefully, she thought about the day she moved in, when Mrs. Saint was rummaging through the moving boxes, looking for a glass so her "Fraydayrique" could get enough water. Markie thought about how annoyed she had been with the old woman that day. And the day she brought Angel over for "Chessie." And the day she had been so bossy about Lola spending Halloween in the bungalow. And many, many other days.

It all seemed so harmless suddenly, seen in the light that Simone had cast on her sister. Markie had acted badly, she knew now. Had thought wrongly, taking her neighbor's humble kindness and twisting it into something secretive and wicked. The woman had brought Jesse a dog because she thought he needed something to hug, for goodness' sake! She had made sure he had the cable channels he wanted. She had arranged for him to have a job that would keep him away from his sketchy friends. She had provided him with a father figure.

And it wasn't only Jesse she had helped. Before Markie had even made it out of the rental truck, Mrs. Saint had recognized her for the overwhelmed, overextended single mother that she was, and from that point on, she had lent Markie her paid employees to try to make her life easier. Frédéric and Bruce to help them move in. Ronda to provide snacks and ingredients. Bruce to do lawn work and gardening. Patty to help with the dog.

Markie had been incensed at the time. She had acknowledged that when it came to the Defectives, Mrs. Saint was actually trying to help, that the way the older woman had them all assisting one another with their jobs, looking out for one another, had truly been endearing. But

Markie had always felt that when it came to her, the old woman was only trying to meddle. Only now, when it was too late, did she finally realize that Mrs. Saint had helped her as much as she had helped any of the others.

A split second after coming to this realization, Markie gasped. *Oh my God! She helped me as much as she helped any of the others! And she didn't only have the others helping one another, looking out for one another—she had them doing it for me, too!* Markie had been thinking—stewing, really—since their meeting that morning with Mr. Schanbaum, about how Mrs. Saint had tried to trap her into being the new leader of the Defectives. She had assumed her bequest was a bribe to get her to stay on as Mrs. Saint's replacement, the new protector of the group.

Now she saw the truth: the bungalow and money and college fund were nothing more than gifts from a woman who knew Markie lacked financial security and felt Jesse needed a father figure and a community. Mrs. Saint had been as generous with Markie as she had been with Frédéric and the others not because she had seen Markie as the new *keeper* of the Defectives, but because she had seen her as *one of them.*

And she had felt that, Markie now saw, from the very first day. From before the first day, in fact—from the day Markie had filled out the rental application and revealed her plummet from social, marital, professional, and financial grace. Markie had never been a savior, in Mrs. Saint's view. She had always been a Defective.

Markie choked on the thought, and Simone's head snapped up. "You are okay?" she asked, concerned.

"I . . . I . . ." Markie couldn't think of how to explain. She didn't want to admit to Simone what she had just discovered about herself, about how Mrs. Saint had seen her. But she decided to do it anyway, because Simone had told Markie more that night than Angeline ever had, and Markie felt it was only fair.

She felt the heat spread over her cheeks as she waited for Simone's answer. She hardly knew Simone, and after the funeral, she might never see her again. But Markie was the woman who had allowed public humiliation to chase her away from her old town and into a dead-end job: she was not immune from other people's view of her.

Simone put a hand on Markie's and smiled. "Are we not all Defectives?" she said. "And can we not all be saviors?"

Chapter Forty-One

"I would like to show you the rest of these," Simone said, putting a hand on the stack of photos sitting beside her. "I feel it is . . . right . . . that you see them. But I must check with Frédéric first."

"Uh," Markie said, unsure how to respond.

Before she could say more, Simone rose, and a moment later Markie heard murmurs from the family room. It sounded, from the tone and level of their voices, like Simone was trying to talk Frédéric into the idea and he was against it, but soon the voices calmed, and when Simone returned to the living room, Frédéric was behind her. He regarded the photos on the couch, gave Simone a last pleading look, and muttered something in French.

"It is time," Simone said.

He sighed, then nodded, and she moved the photos and patted the small space beside her on the love seat.

"I prefer to stand," he said.

"Very well," she said, and held out the first photo for the three of them to see.

It was Mrs. Saint, radiant and youthful in a white wedding gown, her face tilted up as she smiled adoringly at her equally youthful new husband. Markie leaned closer to Simone to get a better look at the groom, who looked like a decades-younger version of the man standing stiffly, nervously, in the middle of the bungalow's living room.

"What?" she said, and reached for the photo.

Simone let her take it, and Markie heard Frédéric's sharp intake of breath as she flipped the picture over to read the back. EDOUARD ET ANGELINE, JOUR DE MARIAGE, 1953.

"*You* are Edouard!" Markie said, looking up at him with wide eyes as Frédéric's trapped breath escaped in a long stream.

"*Oui.*"

"But why would she say you're dead? Why would you live in the basement? Why wouldn't you tell people you're husband and wife? Why . . ." She stopped herself. There were too many whys to list.

Frédéric shifted uncomfortably, and Simone cleared her throat. "I have told about our beginnings, mine and Angeline's," she told him. "You can now tell the rest."

"I do not think—" he started.

"I do," Simone said. "And I believe she would, too." Frédéric didn't respond to Simone, but he turned back to Markie, and after a deep breath, he said, "I was dead to her. The man she married, who vowed to be true, died, in her mind. I . . . betrayed her. Many, many years ago, I had a brief affair with another woman. It was a terrible thing. It devastated her."

He looked to the corner of the ceiling as though there were a film there, replaying the scene where she discovered his infidelity and fell to her knees, sobbing.

"We were trying to have children, and I destroyed all of that. She told me to leave, to never see her again, and that destroyed *me*. I was a *cochon* to her, but I needed her like I needed air. I fell apart on my own, without her, with the guilt of what I had done. I started to drink more

and more. I had started this before the affair, to be true, but I am making no excuses. Alcohol did not cheat on my wife—I did.

"All I did was work and drink," Frédéric said, and to Markie's surprise, she saw Simone nod as though this part of his story was not new to her. "Until the drinking got too much and I lost my job. I had been a promising engineer with a beautiful wife, maybe children someday soon, and now I was renting a room in a house, passed out most of the day. Going nowhere.

"I stayed away, as she told me. But she heard things, and she came looking for me. She dragged me home and pointed to the basement stairs and told me I could stay as long as I did not drink. I quit right away. Well, with help. This was a condition she set: I had to promise to go to Alcoholics Anonymous meetings every day and to keep no alcohol in the house.

"I did not want to live there without making a contribution, so we agreed I would look after the house, the property. And when she began to bring in people to work for her, I served as the foreman, of a sort. Kept them organized. Kept them on the tasks that she set."

"She went out and found you?" Markie asked. "After everything? And brought you home? She must have still loved you."

Frédéric sighed. "She was careful to tell me it did not matter if she loved me anymore or not. She told me that when my parents allowed her family to hide in our barn, they did not love them, or like them, for that matter—they did not even know them. But they took them in anyway. Angeline told me she must do the same for me or it would be a dishonor to her parents for choosing our barn, for trusting our family with their little girls."

"It was not only that," Simone said. "Of course she still loved you. I do not believe she could have ever stopped. She had every bit as much need for you as you did for her."

Frédéric smiled at his sister-in-law. "Perhaps. I would certainly like to believe that. But perhaps it is simply that she saw someone in need of help and wanted to provide it."

Turning to Markie, he chuckled softly and said, "I was the original Defective, you might say."

"Did she tell you about all this?" Markie asked Simone. "The affair, and . . . all of it?"

"*Non.* We were not talking, her and I. But him and I"—she nodded to her brother-in-law—"we have always kept in touch. Only maybe once per year, and not in any big detail. I did not know about these other people she has taken in, for one. But I knew he was in the basement, and I knew why. He told me this."

Mouth open, Markie looked from Simone to Frédéric. She barely knew Simone, but she was amazed Frédéric would have kept up secret communications with someone without Mrs. Saint's knowledge.

"What is it?" Frédéric asked, before she could turn away or erase the puzzled look from her face.

"I'm just a little surprised," Markie said. "You two have been talking behind her back?"

Frédéric faltered, and Markie wished she could take her question back. He had confessed a major indiscretion. Did she need to point out a minor one?

"I'm sorry—" she began.

Simone cut her off. "I do not believe any of this was behind her back," she said. "I think she knew. I think she expected it."

"She would wonder aloud sometimes," Frédéric said. "And I would posit a guess. 'I suppose she married a wealthy man in New York.' 'I imagine they have had children.' 'I expect it was sons.'" He smiled at Simone. "She always listened intently, you know."

"So it sounds like she did forgive you," Markie said to Simone. "For whatever reason she thought you needed forgiveness. And even though she didn't think forgiveness could be granted by a person . . ."

"She did not think *she* could be forgiven by a person," Simone said. "She thought her sin, her disloyalty to our family, was too great for

that. In her mind, this"—she gestured to Frédéric and the affair he had confessed to—"did not rise nearly to the level of what she had done."

Frédéric agreed. "She blamed herself for my affair and for the drinking," he said. "She said she had driven me to it by forcing me to hide my own past all these years. I told her of course that it was not the least bit true, but she remained convinced. Allowing me to live in the basement was in part her way of trying to make up for the wrong she felt she had done me."

"But I don't understand," Markie said. "If she felt it was wrong, why did she continue the charade? Calling herself French Canadian. A Catholic."

"She was not a simple woman, our Angeline," Frédéric said, his eyes on Simone. "She felt it was the right thing to do for herself. But she knew it came with consequences. Painful ones. To her and also to other people." He gestured to Simone, then himself.

"Why wouldn't she have reached out to Simone years ago, then?" Markie asked him. "Why, if she was doing so much to try to make things up to you, would she not have done the same for her sister?"

"She was not without her faults," Simone said. "But I am not without mine. I did not contact her when I heard that her marriage"—she gestured to Frédéric—"their marriage, had ended. I knew, and I could imagine how devastated she was, and yet I did not call or write. It was a big, terrible moment in her life, and her own sister did not offer solace."

"You were still so angry with her for betraying your family," Markie offered.

"*Non,*" Simone said. "If it were that, maybe I would feel a little justified, but at the time, I was not even thinking about that. I was thinking that a few months earlier I had asked her to come to my son's bris. It was important to me to have her there.

"She is my only family, and he was my first boy, and I was feeling alone and weepy about such a significant event passing with only my husband's family and our friends to see it. I wanted someone from my

life. She did not come. She did not even respond. Later, of course, the same thing happened with my second son. And with both of their bar mitzvahs. I invite. She ignores."

"She was worried people would tell," Frédéric said. "People would see her there and immediately know she was Simone's sister. And word would get back here. Her past would be exposed."

"Would word have gotten all the way back here, though?" Markie asked.

"This is what I told her," Frédéric said. "That I could not imagine the identity of the mother's sister would be a topic of conversation. But Simone speaks truth when she says Angeline was not without her faults. She had a very inflated view of her own importance.

"She assumed if she showed up in New York, all eyes would be on her and all mouths would talk about her. It did not occur to her that these events—the bris for each, the two bar mitzvahs—would remain about the children. She feels every event she attends is about her."

"So," Markie said to Simone, "you were upset with her for a few reasons. I can understand that. She wasn't there for you when you needed her, so when you heard about her marriage, you didn't jump at the chance to be there for her. It's sad it happened, but I don't think you should blame yourself so much."

"She hid her true identity," Simone said. "And she was not a good aunt, a good sister, when it came time to be. But he . . ." She looked up at Frédéric, smiling. "Her dear, beloved Edouard. He understood her. Accepted her decision, even if he didn't agree with it. Stuck by her. While I did not.

"I reached out when I wanted something from her. I did not reach out, ever, to offer her something—my support about her marriage, my understanding about how she had chosen to live her life, my apology for not understanding sooner. She was selfish, but so was I. I was no better a sister than she was."

Simone hung her head, and Markie was filled with sorrow for the two sisters, having spent all of these years apart when they were both in such pain. Before Markie could express it, Simone touched the final two pictures in her lap and looked at Frédéric for permission. He nodded, and Simone handed one of them to Markie.

It was Frédéric—Edouard—as a young man in his midtwenties. He was about Patty's age, Markie guessed, and if the photograph weren't old, if his clothes weren't from a different era, if his hair weren't cropped short, she would have thought the picture was of Patty herself.

"Wha—?" Markie held the picture out to Frédéric, her expression a question.

"Show her the other," he said to Simone.

Simone handed Markie the final picture. It was Frédéric/Edouard at around eight. The spitting image of Lola.

"You had an affair *with Carol?*"

"She was a young waitress at a place near my office," he said, glancing from Markie to Simone, who was leaning forward, listening intently. She had clearly not heard this part of the story before.

"We went all the time for lunch, a group of us. One day I stayed after the others to finish a report. It was a tough time for me at the office. I was working all the time, trying to get a promotion, trying to balance so many projects so I could impress my boss. I had taken on too much and could not admit this.

"She asked if I wanted coffee, and I asked for a scotch instead. She brought one for me and one for herself and sat with me while I finished the report. Her shift was over. I don't know what came over me that day, but I stayed all afternoon, drinking with her. I was two days late with the report, and it was filled with mistakes because I was too busy drinking and flirting to think about my job.

"Or my wife. I offered to drive her home and . . ." He shook his head. "I cannot blame the liquor. I simply was not myself that day. I have no excuse for this. I did not see her again for over a year. I stopped

going to that restaurant immediately. And then one day, I saw her near a shop by my office. I was walking out with some things I had bought, and she was on the sidewalk, pushing a stroller with a baby girl inside. *My* baby girl.

"She let me give her money, but she would not let me see the baby after that day. I begged her, but she was insistent—I was never to go near my child. That was when I lost . . . everything. My mind. My discipline over alcohol. My focus at work. My wife. Angeline could tell something was wrong with me, and she would ask me over and over what it was, what she could do to fix it. When I finally told her, she . . ." He grimaced. "It was terrible. Not a thing I could ever forget."

"But somehow you managed to keep track of the baby," Markie said. "Of Patty."

"*Non,*" Frédéric said. "I did not. Her mother never changed her mind on it."

"Then how . . . ?"

"Angeline. She was working at a food pantry some years ago. Five, I guess it was now. And she saw Patty, with little Lola, waiting in line. And she knew."

"She did? Because I don't think you look all that much alike now. I can see it in these old photos, but I've seen the three of you together . . . how many times in the past few months? And I've never noticed a resemblance."

"Ah yes," Frédéric said, "but Angeline knew me when I was younger."

"So she recognized Patty and brought her home?" Markie asked. "Even though the affair ruined your marriage?"

"Le Chambon," Simone said. Frédéric nodded. "And, also, I believe, out of guilt for her insistence that I go along with her story and never tell anyone my own."

"So she brought you your daughter instead," Markie said. "Because she felt guilty about making you hide your past."

"Oui," Frédéric said. "At least, this is my belief. To this day, we have never discussed the fact that Patty is my daughter, Lola my granddaughter. I think Angeline thought I did not know. She told me about this young woman and her child who she had met, how the woman seemed in trouble. She had a crazy mother, one always involved with drugs."

"She recognized the resemblance, but she didn't think *you* would?" Markie asked.

Frédéric shrugged. "Angeline always felt she knew more and better than everyone else."

Markie tried not to smile, but when Simone burst out laughing, she couldn't help joining, and soon Frédéric was smiling, too.

"More true words were not spoken before, I think," Simone said.

"Does Patty know?" Markie asked.

"I do not believe so," Frédéric said. "I cannot think of why Angeline would tell her. She knew that Carol did not want me near my daughter. I believe if Patty found out who I was and told Carol she had found me, Carol would have forbidden them from ever coming over again.

"I think Angeline believed this as well. I think she kept the truth from Patty to protect me from losing my child again. And to protect Patty and Lola from losing us. We have been the steady hands in their lives."

Markie nodded slowly, and despite herself, despite how exasperated she had been with her secret-keeping, sneaky, pushy neighbor since the day they met, she felt her mouth curving into a smile as she looked up to where Frédéric was standing. It was the same place Mrs. Saint had stood on move-in day, Frédéric to her right and Bruce to her left.

Markie had been annoyed by the old woman already by then; she had pushed into the house while Markie was away, rummaged in Markie's moving boxes for a glass, elicited personal information from Jesse, and made it known she felt it was a mistake they didn't own a dog. Markie had vowed to herself that day that she was not going to let some

irascible old Frenchwoman barge into her house on a regular basis and try to exert influence over her life.

That she would not accept one more offer of help from the pushy old woman, or from any of her employees, and that she didn't plan on helping them, either. That she wasn't going to get involved, because she didn't need any of them, and neither did Jesse. That they were fine, the two of them, keeping to themselves with their frozen dinners in their separate rooms, and that's how things would remain.

Markie smiled wider as she imagined Mrs. Saint in heaven, standing primly in her St. John suit and her pearl earrings and heels, God and her parents and brother and sister at her side as she peered down into the bungalow, raised her fists in the air, and said, "Och! Can you believe this one, thinking she knew better than me?"

Epilogue

"Good morning, Markie!" Frédéric called from the open door of the screened porch as Markie stepped from the bungalow onto the patio.

From a chair on the other side of the screen, the shadowy form of Patty rasped, "Hey, neighbor."

Markie called a greeting back as she made her way across both lawns and up the steps to the porch. She reached up to kiss Frédéric's cheek as she passed through the door. "Lovely day, isn't it? Finally, some warmth!" She tugged at the hood of her sweatshirt. "Don't think I need this after all."

"Indeed," Frédéric said. "I have been admiring the garden. Finally, the beginnings of flowers." He gestured to some newly sprouted growth bordering the fence. "She loved this time of year. All the color, the new life, after months of drab and cold."

Markie squeezed his arm. "I'm not surprised. She was the opposite of dull and lifeless. Hey, did Jesse tell you yesterday? He aced another history test. I really should be paying you for this."

"You are," he said. "My granddaughter is now in the second-highest reading group in her class, thanks to your boy." Jesse had long since paid his debt to the Levins, but he was still walking Lola to and from school, and helping her with her homework. He refused to let Frédéric pay him for either.

"So I heard," Markie said, looking from him to Patty and smiling. "Congratulations."

"Not so fast," Patty said. "She'll be smarter than me soon, and I don't know if I need that."

"Of course, this is not at all true," Frédéric said, taking the chair to Patty's right.

To Patty's left sat Kyle, who, at Frédéric and Markie's urging, had recently taken over Frédéric's roles as overseer of employees and general handyman responsible for both properties. Frédéric was too old for the job, he told Kyle, and he wanted to spend more time with Lola. He was eager to hire someone to replace him, so he was thrilled when Markie told him about Kyle's construction experience. Kyle had resisted at first, worrying aloud that he lacked the work ethic to adequately fill the older man's shoes. He had a long history of letting people down, he said. He didn't want to disappoint his ex-wife and son again, or the people who had become so important to them.

Frédéric gestured to the bungalow and the rebuilt home on the other side of the fence and said, "In these two houses, we believe in second chances." Markie nodded her agreement, and when Kyle asked if there was really enough work to justify a full-time salary, she said, "Actually, I've been thinking it could be a good idea to rebuild the garage and put an apartment on top. Seems like the kind of job that could keep a builder and his teenage helper busy for a long time."

Kyle's daily presence hadn't made Trevorandtheguys disappear, but a few weeks earlier, Jesse had brought Glenn home, a well-mannered boy who, Jesse told his mother later, was on the honor roll and student council and had plans to go to law school. Kyle put the two boys to work for a while and then took them to dinner, and Jesse told Markie after that it was the best afternoon he'd had in a long time. Glenn had come back several times since, enough that although Markie still

cringed when she saw the name *Trevor* light up on Jesse's phone screen, she was feeling hopeful, if not entirely confident, about the path her son would ultimately choose.

Now Markie took the porch seat next to her ex-husband and exchanged good mornings with him and Patty before asking if there had been any word from Carol. Patty's mother had been rushed to the hospital after an overdose weeks earlier, and when Patty and Lola tried to visit, a nurse informed them Carol had requested they not be allowed into her room. They had driven her to the overdose by abandoning her for other people, Carol claimed, and she feared seeing their traitorous faces would push her to OD again.

Lola was crushed, while Patty, who had dealt regularly with her mother's silent treatments, was incensed. She returned on her own the following day to let her mother know she needed to stop her passive-aggressive tantrum immediately, for her granddaughter's sake. But when she arrived, the nurse informed her Carol had had a male visitor in the morning, and she had (against medical advice) walked out with him, refusing to leave a phone number or address. Since then, Carol hadn't answered Patty's calls or come to the door on the many occasions her daughter had gone to her apartment to check on her.

"Still nothing," Patty said.

"She will turn up," Frédéric said. "I believe this."

"I'm sure that's right," Markie said as she produced a jar of jam from the pocket of her sweatshirt and set it on the coffee table. "Thought we could use more. Raspberry this time, like Bruce requested." She checked her watch. "Where are they, anyway?"

"Ronda has burned the tops of the muffins," Frédéric said. "Bruce is helping her cut them off. We will have muffin bottoms and jam today, if this is acceptable."

"Sounds good to me," Kyle said.

"Me too," Markie said. "Listen, Frédéric, Simone called me last night. She couldn't reach you. She wanted to know if they should book hotel rooms—"

"Non!" Frédéric said. "Certainly not! They can stay here, with the girls and me. We insist!" Turning to Patty, he said, "Do we not?"

"Mais oui," Patty said, a hand on his arm. "Of course we do."

ACKNOWLEDGMENTS

This book represents the collective efforts of many people. I am so grateful to:

My agent, Victoria Sanders, for believing in Mrs. Saint and wanting to see her in print as much as I did. And for showing us an original pair of the iconic Harlequin cat-eye glasses invented by her grandmother, Altina Schinasi Miranda. Mrs. Saint wears these glasses on the book jacket. And to Bernadette Baker-Baughman and everyone else at Victoria Sanders & Associates.

My editor, Danielle Marshall, for her enthusiasm and insightful comments. Also, copy editor extraordinaire Jessica Fogleman, who doesn't miss a single thing, the very helpful Gabriella Dumpit, and everyone else on the wonderful Lake Union Team.

My friend and writing guru Benee Knauer, for her wisdom and guidance.

Peter Grose, for his brilliant book *A Good Place to Hide: How One French Community Saved Thousands of Lives in World War II*, for answering my many questions, for introducing me to current and former citizens of Le Chambon, and for allowing me to steal the line "We were never children," originally (and aptly) uttered by Hanne Liebmann, to whom I am also grateful.

Pierre Sauvage, founder of the Chambon Foundation and producer of the documentary *Weapons of the Spirit*, for being instrumental in letting the world know about Le Chambon.

Karen Gray Ruelle and Deborah Durland DeSaix, for their excellent book *Hidden on the Mountain: Stories of Children Sheltered from the Nazis in Le Chambon*.

Assistant Chief Amy Brow of the Ann Arbor Fire Department, for taking time out of her busy schedule to answer my questions about fire department procedures in responding to residential house fires.

My cousin Kate Baker, for reading an early draft and for reviewing and correcting, along with her son Thomas Baker Laprise, all of Mrs. Saint's French.

MaryBeth Bishop, for reading an early version and offering incredibly thorough and on-the-nose suggestions.

Lori Nelson Spielman and Camille Noe Pagan, for their encouragement and friendship.

My children, Jack and Libby, for cheering me on. Also Maddie Timmer and the rest of the Lawson and Timmer families, for their continued generous support.

And, as always, and most of all, to my husband, Dan. Six years and three books later, he still answers the question "Could I run something by you about my book?" with "Absolutely." Every single time.

ABOUT THE AUTHOR

Photo © 2013 Mara Klarman

Julie Lawson Timmer grew up in Stratford, Ontario, Canada, and graduated from McMaster University before earning a law degree from Southern Methodist University in Texas. By turns, she is a writer, lawyer, mom/stepmom, and fledgling yogi. Her first novel, *Five Days Left*, received starred reviews from *Kirkus Reviews* and *Library Journal*; her second novel, *Untethered,* received a starred review from *Library Journal* and was praised by *Kirkus Reviews* as a "thoughtfully written and ultimately uplifting celebration of families that are not bound by blood or by law but by love."

Timmer lives in Ann Arbor, Michigan, with her husband, Dan, their children, and two dogs. Visit her online at www.julielawsontimmer. com, on Facebook at www.facebook.com/JulieLawsonTimmerAuthor, on Twitter @JulieLTimmer, and on Instagram at www.instagram.com/ julielawsontimmer.

90481653R00145